SING UNTO GOD
A NEW SONG

Indiana Studies in Biblical Literature

Herbert Marks and Robert Polzin,
general editors

SING UNTO GOD
A NEW SONG
A Contemporary Reading
of the Psalms

HERBERT J.
LEVINE

INDIANA UNIVERSITY PRESS
BLOOMINGTON & INDIANAPOLIS

The paper used in this publication meets the minimum requirements of
American National Standard for Information Sciences—Permanence of
Paper for Printed Library Materials, ANSI Z39.48-1984.

∞™

Manufactured in the United States of America

Library of Congress Cataloging-in-Publication Data

Levine, Herbert J.
    Sing unto God a new song : a contemporary reading of the Psalms /
Herbert J. Levine
        p.   cm. — (Indiana studies in biblical literature)
    Includes bibliographical references and indexes.
    ISBN 0-253-33341-5 (alk. paper)
    1. Bible. O.T. Psalms—Criticism, interpretation, etc.
I. Title. II. Series.
BS1430.2.L475   1995
223'.206—dc20   94-21826
1 2 3 4 5 00 99 98 97 96 95

This book is dedicated
to my parents, Reevan and Natalie Levine,
who gave me their love of Hebrew and Jewish prayer
as an inheritance;
and to my wife, Ellen Frankel,
who, walking her own pilgrim path,
helped me find my own.

We must not make a false faith by hiding from our thoughts
the causes of doubt, for faith is the highest achievement of
the human intellect, the only gift man can make to God,
and therefore it must be offered in sincerity.
—W. B. Yeats, *Per Amica Silentia Lunae*

> In the deserts of the heart
> Let the healing fountains start.
> In the prison of his days,
> Teach the free man how to praise.
—W. H. Auden, "In Memory of W. B. Yeats"

Rav said: "The world was created only for the sake of David."
(Rashi: "that he might compose many hymns
and praises to God.")
—Babylonian Talmud, *Sanhedrin,* 98b

CONTENTS

PREFACE

When I began studying the Psalms a dozen years ago, I was dissatisfied by the generic focus of twentieth-century Psalms scholarship. Rarely did scholars manifest an interest in the language that made an individual psalm distinctive. All their efforts went toward defining the typical. In the last decade, however, we have seen a number of studies that have offered nuanced readings of individual psalms amid more general discussions of how biblical poetry should be read. The work of Meir Weiss (*The Bible from Within: The Method of Total Interpretation* [1984]), Robert Alter (*The Art of Biblical Poetry* [1985]), and Harold Fisch (*Poetry with a Purpose: Biblical Poetics and Interpretation* [1988]) has made it unnecessary for me to write another literary appreciation of psalmic style from a "New Critical" perspective. Their work has freed me to pursue a number of other approaches to the study of the Psalms, which spring more directly from a contemporary interest in the frameworks of interpretation.

Each chapter of this book offers one or more methodologies for studying the Psalms. I like to think that this diversity arises not from my eclecticism but from the nature of the Psalms themselves. The Psalms are not primarily poems, as some literary scholars would have it, but always prayer-poems, a hybrid of artistic and ritual concerns. Though we moderns encounter them in written form, the prayer-poems describe themselves as speech and song directed to an unseen auditor. The methodologies through which we choose to study them should reflect their hybrid nature. They are dialogic speech acts, shaped by the conventions of human speech and communication, by the phenomenology of religion generally, and by the particular religious symbolism and discourse traditions of the Bible and the ancient Near East. Unlike biblical narratives, the texts offer us a great deal of concrete data about the context in which they were first used. Our methodologies must therefore take into account their ancient ritual setting, the Jerusalem Temple, which is itself illuminated by a more general study of ritual. Since the Psalms have been in continuous use as texts for worship and preaching and as literary models for Jewish and Christian poets, our focus on them is further enriched by drawing on

this liturgical, interpretive, and literary history. To strengthen the method-
ological focus of this study, I have chosen to treat some psalms in several
chapters, using different lenses each time they are presented. It is my
hope that through this intensive analysis, I illuminate not only the chosen
psalms but also the larger hermeneutical issues of how we find meaning in
the texts we interpret.

Chapter 1 surveys the history of Psalms interpretation. Focusing on how
a single psalm has been treated in Jewish and Christian exegesis and in the
supposedly secular domain of early twentieth-century scholarly research, I
show the strengths and limitations of premodern doctrinal approaches as
well as most twentieth-century approaches to Psalms. The chapter goes on
to suggest how the anthropology of ritual can provide a nondoctrinaire
starting point for our inquiry into the significant role of ritual discourse in
human life. Chapter 2 draws on the work of the myth-and-ritual school of
comparative Semiticists, biblical historians, and anthropologists in setting
the Psalms amid the *realia* of Temple worship. My account draws extensively
on Arnold Van Gennep and Victor Turner's concept of liminality as the
organizing principle of ritual action in both the Psalms and the rituals of
animal sacrifice that were carried out in Israel's Temple worship. In linking
the anthropological work that has been done on Leviticus to Psalms, I offer
what I hope are new directions in thinking about sacred song.

Chapter 3 takes a variety of approaches to the speech acts of Psalms,
most notably the linguistic philosophy of J. L. Austin and John Searle, the
religious existentialism of Martin Buber and Franz Rosenzweig, and the
literary discourse theory of Walter Ong, Barbara Herrnstein Smith, and
Mikhail Bakhtin. The chapter first establishes how an understanding of
orality and speech acts helps us ground the poetic speech of Psalms in
natural rather than fictive language. It then uses its dialogical tools to set
 forth the central story in Psalms—the conflict between faith and experience, especially as it is manifest in the give-and-take of the Psalms' competing voices. Chapter 4 examines the representation of deliverance in
Psalms, an idea central to Israelite belief in God. The chapter follows
Mircea Eliade's view of time and space as a culture's most important
markers of the sacred, but unlike other studies inspired by Eliade, my
account focuses not just on sacred time and space but equally on the profane times and spaces in which psalmists do not experience God's deliverance. The chapter thereby underscores the difficulty of the psalmists'
struggle to hold on to a personal relationship with an infinite, transcen-
dental God.

A fundamental insight of chapters 3 and 4 is that the Psalms were created in an environment open to profound theological questioning. Concerns of theodicy are thus never far from the surface in Psalms. This book

builds toward a full consideration of these issues in its final chapter, which looks at how many psalms were written and then later used to respond to Jewish national catastrophe, from the destruction of the First Temple in 587 B.C.E. to the destruction of European Jewry in our century. The chapter looks at how ancient liturgists and midrashists, medieval kabbalists, and modern memoirists, poets, and theologians of the Holocaust have consistently recontextualized the language and concerns of the Psalms. My examples suggest that in posing anew the psalmists' challenges to a supposedly just God, each generation that has responded to ruptures in Jewish national existence has pushed toward a new conception of God's role in history, leading in our time to nonsupernaturalist redefinitions of traditional theological language.[1] It is precisely through such orchestration and reframing of ancient texts and ideas that religious civilizations evolve.

This book's inquiries into how the Psalms work and how they have been construed are intended to help readers appreciate why they continue to have such power in both our religious and our secular culture.[2] The main topics in this book are thus a reprise of the Psalms' gifts: the ceremonial, community-shaping power of ritual, the immediacy of spoken poetic language and the social richness of dialogue, the opening beyond the quotidian provided by the idea of divinity, and finally, the transformations in that idea necessitated by the history of Jewish national existence.

If the Psalms are to speak to us as contemporary readers, then our methodologies for studying them should emerge from and respond to the perplexities of our contemporary situation. If I may be permitted to characterize those whom I imagine reading this book, I would venture to suggest that they are people who look at religions as human creations, yet nevertheless sense in them a power to shape an ideal image of human life that our postmodern, self-conscious culture sorely lacks. Furthermore, the readers whom I imagine are still living through the eclipse of the traditional God cast by the shadow of the Holocaust. Like the authors of Job and Ecclesiastes, they are people for whom the old biblical verities are no longer tenable, yet who find it impossible to live a full life without responding to them, so greatly have they shaped habits of thought and feeling, speaking and imagining. Some of my readers may be willing to take up the challenge Martin Buber laid down in his 1926 essay "The Man of Today and the Jewish Bible," that is, to remain open to the faith of the Bible by struggling with it on their own terms, not knowing which of its sayings or images will enter their consciousness and become renewed in their lives.[3] To take up Buber's challenge, I have required the disciplinary lenses of modernity. Anthropology, the philosophy of language as speech act and dialogue, the phenomenology of religion, the history of biblical interpretation, and post-Holocaust theology have enabled me to approach the language of the Psalms anew. It is my sincere hope that readers of this book will find one or more of these approaches similarly enlivening.

A Note on Translation

Unless otherwise noted, all quotations from the Hebrew Bible are taken from *Tanach: The Holy Scriptures* (Philadelphia: Jewish Publication Society, 1988). With the permission of the publishers, I have consistently altered their translation in one respect. The four-letter name of God is not traditionally pronounced by Jews. The name Adonai, a variant of the word for "Lord," is the standard Jewish substitution. For the JPS rendering of Adonai as "LORD," I have left the Hebrew original, YHWH. That name derives from the verb "to be," which Martin Buber translates as "He who will be present," or "He who is here."[4] Rendering the name in a nongendered idiom, Arthur Green suggests "is–was–will be," the One that is eternal and unchanging, as well as dynamic and evolving.[5] Because YHWH is not just a proper name, as in the translations Jehovah or Yahweh, nor simply an evocation of divine mastery as in Adonai, but most significantly a statement of faith that God (however we mean that term) is, was, and will be present for humanity, I have chosen to let the original Hebrew lend its resonance to my discussion. For the other Hebrew names of God, I have followed the JPS translation.

ACKNOWLEDGMENTS

The seed of this book was planted about twenty years ago, when my then rabbi, Ed Feld, shared with a group of us at Princeton University a literary reading of Psalm 19, which he offered in the name of his friend Michael Fishbane. Readers of my first chapter will see how that occasion has stayed with me. Subsequently, at a National Havurah Summer Institute, Max Ticktin introduced me to the literary study of Psalms. This led me to formulate my own units on Psalms in courses on the Bible in Literature that I taught at Franklin and Marshall College. A grant from the American Council of Learned Societies enabled me to spend a year at Brandeis University, where Nahum Sarna shared with me his bibliography of literary approaches to the Bible. When I returned to my college, Denise Hopkins, then of the Lancaster Theological Seminary, became my regular Psalms study partner. Her excitement in our sessions together helped me to realize that I might have something to say to an audience of biblical scholars. As I began to seek larger cultural frames for my study of the Psalms, Howard Eilberg-Schwartz offered valuable references in anthropology, and later read and commented on a draft of the first two chapters, where that material is prominent. Leonard Gordon and Robert Goldenberg read a draft of the last one, and gave me invaluable advice from their vantage points as specialists in the rabbinic period, and more generally as Jewish historians. Arthur Green also read a portion of my last chapter, and helped me in deciphering some kabbalistic texts. I am grateful for all of their suggestions.

Several chapters had especially long foregrounds. The form taken by chapter 1 came from a lecture I delivered at the Princeton Jewish Center in 1990. Part of chapter 2 was delivered at the Association for Jewish Studies, 1991. Parts of chapters 3 and 4 were presented as papers at the Durham University Conference on Literature and Religion, 1989, and at the Ohio State University Conference on Jewish Geography, 1990. Versions of material included in these two chapters appeared as "The Symbolic *Sukkah* in Psalms," *Prooftexts* 7 (1987), 259–68; "The Dialogic Discourse of Psalms," in *Mappings of the Biblical Terrain: The Bible as Text,* ed. Vincent L.

Tollers and John Maier, *Bucknell Review* 33 (1990), 268–81; and "Divine Timespace and Religious Experience," in *Worlds of Jewish Prayer: A Festschrift in Honor of Rabbi Zalman M. Schachter-Shalomi,* ed. Shohama Harris Wiener and Jonathan Omer-Man (Northvale: Jason Aronson, 1993), 124–35. All have been revised for this book.

I am grateful to Franklin and Marshall College for the sabbaticals during which most of this book was written, which took me to libraries at the University of Florida and the University of Pennsylvania. Librarians at the Shadek-Fackenthal Library of Franklin and Marshall College and at the Reconstructionist Rabbinical College were especially helpful in securing materials through interlibrary loan. Those at the University of Pennsylvania's Center for Judaic Studies and at YIVO were helpful in providing me access to some primary sources.

I am especially grateful for the opportunities I had to teach the Psalms at the National Havurah Summer Institutes, at the Reconstructionist Rabbinical College, and at the Germantown Jewish Center in Philadelphia. These courses were never purely academic; they confirmed for me the importance of making the Psalms live in the lives of those who worship through them. I thank all my students for allowing me to share in their quests for religious meaning, which have so deeply informed my own.

Finally, I want to express my immense debt of gratitude to Ellen Frankel, who has read every draft of this book, and offered her wise and apt professional counsel. It would have been a much poorer book without her.

SING UNTO GOD
A NEW SONG

·I·

FROM TRADITION TO MODERNITY: TOWARD A CONTEMPORARY APPROACH TO THE PSALMS

The Psalms continue to shape the prayer life of Jews and Christians, as they have done for millennia, even though their theological language comes from a social world that no longer exists. There is neither an earthly king in Israel nor a single, centralized dwelling place for God in Jerusalem. Yet the Psalms, which reflect this monarchical, Temple-centered theology, are the gateway to thousands of religious services daily. They provide worshipers outlets for tuneful fervor and quiet solemnity, cries of anguish and shouts of joy. They loom large in mapping the territory of contemporary as well as ancient Jewish and Christian devotional life. Why and how they continue to be applicable in such vastly different social and cultural circumstances will be one of the major concerns of this book.

It almost goes without saying that a great deal of the Psalms' continuing appeal lies in the emotionally satisfying combination of words and music through which they are typically encountered in worship. They have been sung in a simple phrasal chant or set to more complicated melodies in both religious traditions. While a musical analysis lies outside the concerns of this book,[1] we can nevertheless note what some traditional commentators have said about this potent combination. The church fathers who came from the Hellenistic world had never encountered religious singing on a par with psalmody. Augustine, for instance, held psalmody to be a new kind of music invented by David as a mystic way of serving God. Ambrose likened the responsorial chant of psalms, in which men, women, and children all participated, to the power of the ocean. John Chrysostom noted the power of such singing to keep the mind free from the happenings of daily life and produce the feelings of contriteness of heart necessary for turning to God.[2] Similar comments can be found in the rabbinic tradition, though the focus there tends to be on the power of specific texts

1

rather than on the phenomenon of psalmody as a whole. Abraham Ibn Ezra, the noted twelfth-century Spanish commentator on the Bible, begins his commentary on Psalms by speaking first of the power of sound to move us: "There are sounds that delight and sounds that depress; when the meaning of the speech is lofty, it may do great things, even angering one's friend or appeasing one's enemy—all the more so if it is said poetically; and when instrumental music is joined with the poem, then will marvels be beheld." While the epic poetry of European Christians, he says, moves us to think "about war and vengeance," and the lyric poetry of the Muslims about "amours and passion," so the poetry of David, which had originally been set to instrumental music, brings us to the special knowledge that "God alone" is God.[3]

In Judaism, the musicality of the Psalms has been preeminently associated with King David as divinely gifted musician and with the Temples in Jerusalem, where Levites, we are told, stood in the courts and accompanied psalm-singing on harp and timbrel, cymbals and lyre. In deference to those exalted memories, the rabbis who constructed classical Judaism forbade instrumental accompaniment of worship. In the synagogue, then, the Psalms took on a lesser role in prayer than they had had in the Temple. They became a prelude to the rabbinically composed prayers and the Pentateuchal readings. Some scholars have deduced from the rabbinic commentary on Psalms that psalms must have been read alongside the weekly selections from the Pentateuch and the prophets over a three-year period; according to this view, rabbinic homilies were preached from all the major divisions of the Bible.[4] Side by side with their role in congregational prayer, then, the Psalms took on new life as scriptural lessons, a development that also took place within the early centuries of Christianity. In what follows, we will explore these parallel traditions of commentary by focusing on lessons that premodern Jewish and Christian preachers derived from a single psalm.

Psalms Commentary from within the Biblical Traditions

To explore the nature of commentary generated by a community of believers, I have chosen to focus on Psalm 19, in which there is a marked contrast between Jewish and Christian interpretation, both in premodern and in modern times. The psalm first celebrates God's creation and God's law, before its speaker petitions God for forgiveness and guidance. Since I will be dwelling in some detail on episodes in the history of the psalm's interpretation, it is best that we read it in full:

1. For the leader.
   A psalm of David.
2. The heavens declare the glory of God,
   the sky proclaims His handiwork;
3. Day to day makes utterance,
   night to night speaks out.
4. There is no utterance,
   there are no words,
   whose sound goes unheard.
5. Their voice carries throughout the earth,
   their words to the end of the world.
   He placed in them a tent for the sun,
6. who is like a groom coming forth from the chamber,
   like a hero, eager to run his course.
7. His rising-place is at one end of heaven,
   and his circuit reaches the other;
   nothing escapes his heat.

8. The teaching of YHWH is perfect,
   renewing life;
9. the decrees of YHWH are enduring,
   making the simple wise;
   The precepts of YHWH are just,
   rejoicing the heart;
   the instruction of YHWH is lucid,
   restoring strength.
10. The fear of YHWH is pure,
    abiding forever;
    the judgments of YHWH are true,
    righteous altogether,
11. more desirable than gold,
    than much fine gold;
    sweeter than honey,
    than drippings of the comb.
12. Your servant pays them heed;
    in obeying them there is much reward.
13. Who can be aware of errors?
    Clear me of unperceived guilt,
14. and from willful sins keep Your servant;
    let them not dominate me;
    then shall I be blameless
    and clear of grave offense.
15. May the words of my mouth
    and the prayer of my heart
    be acceptable to You,
    YHWH, my rock and my redeemer.

If we stop to eavesdrop on some of the homilies that were preached on this text in the synagogues or rabbinical academies of ancient Palestine or Babylonia, we will encounter no modern debates about authorship. Because so many psalms were attributed to King David by the Bible's editors, he was assumed to have written all the psalms for which no other author was given, with a few notable rivals.[5] There was no question for these ancient preachers of ascertaining distinct literary units or genre boundaries. When the rabbis discussed passages from the Psalms, all of Scripture echoed in their heads, and was fair game to be brought in to make an ingenious connection. Rarely were they interested in a whole psalm, unless it allowed them to teach an interesting lesson. But since an infinite number of lessons could be derived from each phrase, if not from each letter of Holy Writ, preachers often expounded on one phrase at a time.

Our examples are drawn from *Midrash Tehillim*, a collection of rabbinic sermons or classroom interpretations of Psalms, collected and edited in ninth-century Italy, but dating back to the early centuries of the common era. "Midrash" literally means searching out a meaning. Reading midrash is very difficult at times, as it is full of puns, parables, quotations, and allusions. Furthermore, the rabbis do not generally indicate what question their interpretations are trying to answer. When we stop to figure out their questions, however, we can penetrate their seemingly arcane texts.

Here is a midrash that begins by juxtaposing two verses:

> *The heavens declare the glory of God* (v. 2). The prophet Isaiah said: *Sing, O ye heavens, for the Lord hath done it* (Isa. 44:23), and they replied: Indeed, we shall sing the praise of God: *The heavens declare the glory of God.*[6]

The terseness of these comments obviously needs amplification. The preacher wants to explain why in the opening verse of the psalm the heavens in particular are being called on to witness for God. Why not the earth? Why not Israel? The rabbi wants to convince his listeners of the rightness of the text before them. How do we know the heavens declare the glory of God? Because Isaiah told the heavens to sing, and in Psalm 19 they do. The psalm verse "The heavens declare the glory of God" is thus presented in the commentary as if it were the response requested by Isaiah. This answer is possible because, to the mind of the premodern interpreter, all the Hebrew Scriptures constitute one coherent whole.

To further expound the verse, the preacher continues with a parable:

> A parable of a King who had many provinces: the inhabitants of each province used to say, "So-and-so much gold has the king; so-and-so much silver, so-and-so many robes and man-servants and maidservants

has the king." Now in one province was a wise old man, who asked the inhabitants, "Whence do you know this, being so many parasangs removed from the king? In truth, only those of the province in which the king lives can properly declare the wealth and the glory of the king, because they alone know his wealth and his glory." Even so, David said, "The earth and all who are in it cannot declare the glory of God. *The heavens declare the glory of God.*"[7]

What could the preacher mean by saying that "the earth and all who are in it cannot declare the glory of God"? Surely human beings praise God's glory in psalm after psalm. In making this claim, the rabbi emphasizes the theological doctrine of God's transcendence. Only the heavens can declare God's glory properly, because only they experience the unmediated, undiluted fullness of God.

The high value set on transcendence in this midrash represents one pole of rabbinic theology. It leaves out, however, God's immanence, the indwelling aspect of divinity experienced by humankind. The next comment makes us see that this was a deliberate omission, as the anonymous preacher ingeniously balances the score:

And when will the earth and all its inhabitants praise God? When God will exalt the horn of Israel, for *Praise the Lord from the earth* (Ps. 148:7) occurs in the Psalm in which it is also said *He exalteth the horn of His people . . . Israel . . . Praise ye the Lord* (Ps. 148:14).

To understand what is going on in this terse comment, we need to note that the command "Praise the Lord from the earth," from a different psalm, could be said to compete with the assertion from this one, "The heavens declare the glory of God." When an ancient preacher found competing sentences such as these, his task was to reconcile them by showing that both were true, though in different circumstances. The difference in this case lies in the time frame in which each sentence is applicable. "The heavens declare the glory of God" now, but in the future, when God delivers Israel—or, in the biblical phrase, exalts its horn—then God will be praised and, indeed, will truly deserve praise from "the earth and all its inhabitants." The latter phrase reveals the preacher's messianic hope. The Temple has been destroyed, Jerusalem reduced to ruins, and the people of Israel have been dispersed and dispirited. The preaching is intended to bring consolation to the faithful, whether in Israel or in the Diaspora, who seek to return to their rightful place in their own land, and who look forward thereafter to a time of universal peace and freedom from oppression.

This mode of preaching may seem circuitous to us, but to its listeners, schooled in the nuances of rabbinic exegesis on a weekly basis, its basic assumptions would have been articles of faith, namely, that the Bible is God's indisputable word and that its every word finds echo and confirmation everywhere else in it and in the world. Thus, believers can rest assured that what God has promised, God will bring to pass. Otherwise, why would there be a need in one context to say, "The heavens declare the glory of God," and in another, "Praise the Lord from the earth"? Whenever worshipers encounter these verses in prayer, they will understand that even if they are suffering and seem far from redemption, they must not lose hope. After the redemption comes, God will be praised as fully from the earth as from heaven. On that day, God's immanence, as manifested in earthly justice, will be fully revealed and celebrated.

The reader should be clear that this verse-by-verse exegesis brings us into the mind of the rabbis, not into the mind of the psalmist who composed or edited Psalm 19, as modern criticism might attempt to do. Occasionally, however, the rabbis look at a psalm as a whole, by highlighting the psychology of its speaker. One of the few examples of this approach concerns Psalm 19. It helps to read the following passage with the awareness that Rabbi Simeon ben Yoḥai (second century C.E.) takes delight in imagining a heavenly scenario that lies behind the lines of the psalm. The capitalized "Thou" in the dialogue addresses God:

> *Who can discern errors?* (Ps. 19:13). Rabbi Simeon ben Yoḥai taught: How powerful are the righteous, for they know how to win the favor of their Creator; they know just how to praise Him! Behold how David praised His creator. He began to praise Him by making mention of the heavens, saying *The heavens declare the glory of God.* The heavens say: "Is there anything whatever Thou wouldst have of us?" And *The firmament showeth His handiwork.* The firmament says: "Is there anything whatever Thou wouldst have of us?" David, continuing to sing his Psalm, now praised God by making mention of the Torah, as is said *The fear of the Lord is pure, enduring forever* (Ps. 19:10). Then the Holy One, blessed be He, asked David, "What wouldst thou have?" David said: *"Who can discern errors?* I would have that Thou forgive me the errors I have committed!" God replied: "This error is forgiven thee, and that error is forgiven thee," and David continued *Keep back thy servant also from presumptuous sins* (v. 14), that is from deliberate sins. *Then will the mightiest ('etam) have no dominion over me*—that is, the mightiest of iniquities, the word *'etam,* "mightiest," being read like *'etan* in the verse "Mighty (*'etan*) is thy dwelling-place" (Num. 24:21). *And I shall be clear from the great transgression,* that is from my one great transgression.[8]

This interpretation reads the opening movements of the psalm—the praise of God's creation and the praise of God's law—from the point of view of the psalm's ending. Knowing that the psalm ends in David's pleas for forgiveness, Rabbi Simeon analyzes the psychology of one who needs to secure a favor. First that person must become ingratiated with the powerful figure whose help is needed. So David enlists the help of the heavens and the firmament by citing their praise of God. Responding sympathetically to David, they actively anticipate their creator's every need. David then praises the Torah's effect on human beings; it teaches us to feel an enduring awe (a better translation than "fear") before God. After this double-barreled praise, God immediately attends to David's plea. By changing the letter of one of David's words, Rabbi Simeon understands the dialogue between them to conclude in a reference to David's greatest sin, his adultery with Bathsheba and the consequent murder of her husband.[9] Rabbi Simeon is not cynical about David's ability to secure God's forgiveness. On the contrary, that ability demonstrates, he says, the power of the righteous. David may have been a great sinner, but in learning to praise God appropriately, he learns the secret way to God's merciful heart. So that this lesson should be clear to everyone, the editor of the midrash follows Rabbi Simeon's elaborate interpretation with a clear condensation of the matter: "According to R. Levi, David said: Master of the Universe, You God, are great, and I, my sins are great. It is fitting that a great God forgive great sins, as it is said, *For Your name's sake, O Lord, pardon mine iniquity for it is great*" (Ps. 25:11). The moral message cannot be lost on any listener: no matter how grave the sin, one can always approach God for forgiveness and begin a new life.

This sort of sermonizing, using one verse to comment on another without regard to context or literal meaning, is based, we have said, on a belief in the infinite permeability and simultaneity of Scripture. The same tradition is at work in the Christian apostolic writings, where it is used polemically against Jewish self-understanding. Quotations from the Hebrew Bible are brought forward by the New Testament writers to persuade their audiences that the ministry of Jesus and, especially, his death and resurrection as the Christ fulfilled the messianic promises of the Hebrew Bible.[10] This process of interpreting earlier events in light of those that come later is called typology. It too is a version of midrash, a reinterpretation by which the Hebrew Scriptures become the Old (that is, the outmoded) Testament, no longer worthy of belief.[11] The Old Testament provides the shadowy types; the New Testament, their substantial fulfillment.

We see this argumentative process actively at work in the writing and preaching of the apostle Paul. The first great crisis of newly emerging Christianity was the conflict between Jews and non-Jews in the Church. Was the practice of Jewish ritual law, such as circumcision and dietary restrictions, to continue among Jewish and Gentile Christians? How were Gentiles to be admitted to salvation without thereby making God seem to abandon the biblical promises to Israel? Paul had to address these practical and theoretical questions as an apostle to the Gentiles. In Romans, the epistle in which he speaks to a mixed community of Jewish and Gentile Christians, he addresses another significant theoretical question: What was to be made of the overwhelming Jewish refusal to abrogate the Jews' covenant with God and enter into the new covenant with Jesus Christ? And, on the practical level, how were the individual Jews and Gentiles in this particular community to get along? What sort of religion would they practice together?[12]

Paul affirms that Israel has indeed heard the word of God, as recorded in its Bible, but radically misinterpreted it, for Jews believe that a person will be saved merely by practicing righteousness, whereas Christians know that salvation comes to those who believe and profess that Jesus is Lord and has been raised from the dead. Faith comes, Paul says, "from what is heard, and what is heard comes by the preaching of Christ. But I ask, have they not heard? Indeed, they have"; and here he quotes Psalm 19:5, "for 'Their voice has gone out to all the earth / and their words to the ends of the world' " (Rom. 10:17–18).[13] In the psalm, the quoted line, "Their voice has gone out . . . ," refers to the inarticulate but nevertheless profound testimony of the heavens, and of day and night, that the world has been created by God. As a learned Jew, Paul knows the meaning of this verse, but to fit the needs of his preaching, he radically shifts the context for interpreting it. In his text, "their voice" refers not to the heavenly bodies but to Christian preaching, which in such a short time had permeated the Hellenistic world, going out, as it were, "to all the earth." He confirms his point with other, clearer speeches by Moses and Isaiah about Israel's repeated failure to listen to God. Paul's polemic about the failure to listen has, as we have said, two audiences. The Jews in the Church are being asked to learn a new way of interpreting the Scriptures they first learned in a Jewish context, so that they can see the need for a new Christian way of being loyal to God. The Gentiles in the Church, who are being brought into the unfamiliar world of the Hebrew Bible, are learning that the truth of the new gospel is repeatedly anticipated by the very words that the Jews hold in such great reverence. While the Jews' refusal to hear the meaning of their own Scriptures has made it possible for Gentiles to come into God's new covenant, it does not signify that God has rejected Israel. After all, Paul himself is a Jew. Paul claims that his own ministry of saving Gentiles will make the Jews jealous (Rom. 11:14), and one day bring them also to Christ. His reinterpretation of Hebrew Scriptures is the cornerstone of this long-term project of converting the world to Christianity.

One of the most influential Christian preachers, Augustine, Bishop of Hippo (in modern Algeria) during the fourth century c.e., devoted a long course of sermons to the Psalms. Worshipers not only should sing them, he noted, but should know and understand the import of what their mouths utter.[14] For Augustine, as for Paul, the truth of the Hebrew Bible was its allegorical meaning that pointed to Christ. As a mode of interpretation, allegory assumes that the events in a narrative do not just tell the story they purport to tell; rather, there is another meaning that corresponds, sometimes point for point, with the story that is ostensibly being told. Allegorizing allows interpreters to transform that which is displeasing to them in an earlier text, as, for instance, the anthropomorphisms of the Hebrew Bible or the Homeric epics.[15] In Augustine's view, the allegorical method was necessitated by Scripture itself, which had been veiled by God to exercise the speaker. As an outcome of the Fall, human beings had lost direct knowledge of God, while gaining indirect knowledge through signs. Interpreting these signs properly was a matter not of ingenuity but of seeing with the eyes of faith.[16]

In Augustine's allegorical view, Psalms were not simply poems written by that rather flawed human being King David. Rather, they were "a microcosm of the whole Bible—the clear essence of Christianity refracted in the exotic spectrum of a Hebrew poem."[17] As such, they could be seen as a record of Christ's emotions spoken through David. "It is His voice that ought . . . to be perfectly known, and perfectly familiar, to us, in all the Psalms; now chanting joyously, now sorrowing; now rejoicing in hope, now sighing at its actual state, as if it were our own."[18] Psalms could also be seen as descriptions of Christ. In Psalm 19, for instance, Christ, not the sun, is the bridegroom coming forth from his chamber, and his bride is the one Catholic Church, to which Paul had alluded in the phrase "I betrothed you to Christ to present you as a pure bride to her one husband" (II Cor. 11:2). For the opening line, "The heavens declare the glory of God," Augustine offers two interpretations. "The heavens are Saints, raised up from the earth, bearing the Lord." On a more literal level, he concedes that the heavens actually declared God's glory at the birth of Christ, when "a new star, which had never before been seen, appeared."[19] And so he proceeds through his sermon, providing an allegorical interpretation—Christological or church-related—of every verse in the psalm.

In modern interpretation of the psalm, a critical point is the relation between the praise of God as creator and praise of God as law-giver. For Augustine, too, this is a central issue, since any interpretation he gives of the portion of the psalm devoted to Torah—that is, the law Israel received at Sinai—must conform to Christianity's continuing devaluation of the

Jewish conception of law. His translation of 19:8 accordingly reads, "The law of the Lord is undefiled, converting souls." He goes on to explain that "the law of the Lord, therefore, is Himself Who came to fulfill the law, not to destroy it," here alluding to Jesus' words in the sermon on the mount (Matt. 5:17). To interpret the term "undefiled," he cites another New Testament verse describing Christ: "He committed no sin, no guile was found on his lips" (I Pet. 2:22). Reinforcing Paul's antithesis between faith and law, Augustine claims that Christ's law is not one "oppressing souls with the yoke of bondage, but converting them to imitate Him in liberty." His polemic against the Jewish view of Torah continues. What about the statutes of the Lord makes them "right, rejoicing the heart" (19:9)? It is that those statutes reveal "those things which they should do freely with love, not slavishly with fear." What makes "the commandment of the Lord lucid, enlightening the eyes" (19:10)? It has "no veil of carnal observances" attending it, but rather enlightens "the sight of the inner man."[20] Jews observe their law, Augustine claims, in bondage and fear, and with only the outer shell of the person engaged, while Christians experience liberty, love, and innerness in fulfilling their Christian commitments. Psalm 19 is Augustine's ostensible text, but through his allegorical method of interpretation, he transforms the psalm into a proof of Christian doctrine. Through his abilities as an allegorical interpreter, Augustine similarly found Christian doctrine encoded throughout the Hebrew Bible.

A central point I want to make about both Jewish midrashic and Christian allegorical approaches is that neither one travels easily outside of its own faith community. With the rise of Islam in the seventh century c.e., a different form of Jewish exegesis emerged, which eventually influenced Christian interpretation as well. The new methodology, peshat, focused on the contextual meaning of Scripture, drawing on the rational tools of comparative philology and analysis of the historical, literary, and linguistic elements of the text. Peshat served the needs of Jews, Christians, and Moslems living in a pluralistic world. Whether in disputes between rabbinite and Karaite Jews, or between Jews, Christians, and Moslems, the contextual approach enabled its practitioners (from all faiths) to muster the intellectual resources to disprove one another's competing interpretations.[21] Rather than being shaped as sermons, medieval peshat took the form of line-by-line commentary surrounding the text in rabbinic Bibles.

The preeminent rabbinic commentary of Rashi (who lived in Troyes, in twelfth-century France) owes its stature, at least in part, to its seamless blending of peshat and the homiletical mode that came to be known as derash. Though Rashi lived among Christians and occasionally sought to contradict the standard Christian interpretations he knew by reference to the peshat meaning,[22] his primary interest was not in disputation so much as in helping Jews to make sense of the Bible and to relate it to their own lives. To this end, he explained the text in terms of its literary, linguistic, or rhetorical context, but also provided enough homiletical material, much of it from traditional midrashic collections, to satisfy the needs of his co-religionists for moral uplift and support for traditional beliefs. He claimed to be using the midrashic elaborations only when they helped to give a better sense of the literal meaning of a text.[23]

We get the flavor of Rashi's blending of these two modes of commentary by looking at how he handles a crux of interpretation in Psalm 19. Modern interpreters ask why the poet makes no transition between verses 6–7, the description of the sun's centrality in the heavens, and verses 8–12, the hymn glorifying God's instruction to human beings. For Rashi, using an old rabbinic rule of interpretation, the juxtaposition itself provides the answer. Of the phrase "the teaching of YHWH is perfect" (v. 8) he writes, "it too gives light, like the sun, as it is said at the end of the passage, 'enlightening the eyes' " (v. 9).[24] In this contextual interpretation, one kind of light obviously suggests the other. In his next comment, Rashi cites another text to prove that Torah enlightens. Scripture says, he writes, " 'For the commandment is a lamp, / the teaching is a light' " (Prov. 6:23). This confirming prooftext provides Rashi a moral foundation for the juxtaposition of sun and Torah, making the connection seem almost inevitable to his audience. This subtle shift from a contextual to a moral interpretation is carried further in Rashi's next comment, which elaborates on some earlier rabbinic midrashim. Rashi associates the phrase "nothing escapes his [the sun's] heat" (v. 7) with the day of judgment, by way of several prophetic quotations:

> "and the day that is coming shall burn them (the doers of evil) to ashes" (Malachi 3:19); but "the teaching of YHWH is perfect, renewing life" (Ps. 19:8), that is, the paths of life, for it (the teaching) protects its students from that burning, as it is said, "But for you who revere My name a sun of victory shall rise to bring healing" (Mal. 3:20).[25]

Indeed, in this *derash*, nothing escapes the sun's heat, for the wicked are burned by it and the righteous healed by it, as evidenced by the prooftext from the prophet Malachi. Rashi's commentary accomplishes two tasks at once. First, it argues for the unity of the psalm from its total context, by making explicit what rabbinic tradition had long seen as an implicit connection. Second, it interprets the text in a way that bolsters the faith of his readers and turns them back to consider the Bible's prophecies about a future reward and punishment. This latter discussion is, in fact, quite relevant to the psalm, which also claims that in obeying God's teachings "there is much reward" (Ps. 19:12).

While Rashi's commentary is oriented to the needs of ordinary Jews, that of Abraham Ibn Ezra, a poet, grammarian, philosopher, astronomer, and physician who lived in twelfth-century Spain, Italy, and France, is addressed to an intellectual elite, and uses more worldly methods of interpretation. The multitalented Ibn Ezra obviously traveled in very different intellectual circles than did Rashi, who owned vineyards but spent all his intellectual labors within the compass of Jewish tradition. For instance, Ibn Ezra's comments on the imagery of the heavens at the start of Psalm 19 are addressed to students of astrology, who have delved into the revolutions of the heavenly bodies and their impact on human life. In his works on astrology, he sought to reconcile the idea of stellar decrees with a traditional belief in God's providence and human free will. One way he does this is by making an exception of Israel. "Every nation has its own star and constellation," he writes, "but God bestowed His greater favor on Israel by rendering them starless and Himself their adviser."[26]

Psalm 19's juxtaposition of sun and Torah brings to Ibn Ezra's mind those rationalists who seek confirmation in the natural order for the truths of Judaism. He cites an earlier authority, Rabbi Saadiah Gaon of tenth-century Turkey, who claimed that the sun actually spoke the psalm's words, "the teaching of YHWH is perfect." While some might be pleased with this poetic conceit, Ibn Ezra notes that David, the author of the psalm, brings forward a still more faithful witness than the sun, the Torah itself. The Torah renews the soul, he says, insofar as it "removes doubt." This is a remarkable assertion on Ibn Ezra's part, since we know that he himself wrestled with intellectual doubt. In several places in his commentary, using the phrase "the intelligent will understand," he hints that not all of the Torah was written by Moses, thereby putting a hole in the fabric of received rabbinic tradition, which eventually widened into Spinoza's denial that the Bible was divinely revealed.[27] Unlike Spinoza, however, Ibn Ezra relied on practicing the way of life laid down in the Torah and in its rabbinic commentaries. As he says in his comment on Psalm 19:8, the Torah needs no testimony other than that of those who live by it, following its "straight path." In this example, we see Ibn Ezra's commentary skirting the edge of the allowable, as he brings in the discourse of contemporary science for those attracted to it, but also bolsters traditional faith claims, in order to keep his readers safely within the Jewish fold.

Ibn Ezra's blend of practical piety and rationalism is the harbinger of a new era in biblical commentary, which we can note in Christianity as well. The new technology supplied by the printing press encouraged the development of contextual interpretation, for as printed texts of the Bible became more readily available, readers could more easily distinguish the plain meaning of the text from a midrashic or allegorical elaboration. In Reformation Europe, the battle cry of Protestantism was "Back to the sources!" Protestant thinkers, such as Martin Luther and John Calvin, argued that the Scriptures were complete, errorless, and unified. It was the task of scholars to remove erroneous glosses, such as those supplied by Augustine and other fathers of the Church of Rome, and provide instead interpretations that would be authoritative insofar as they reflected the stated word of God.[28] To such ends, Hebrew was studied by Christian humanists, who thereby gained access to Jewish peshat interpretations of the biblical text. The most notable Protestant commentary indebted to such Hebrew knowledge is that of Calvin, which is closer in intellectual spirit to the textually oriented commentary of an Ibn Ezra than to the typological sermonizing of an Augustine. This humanist interest in Hebrew did not, however, indicate a tolerance of Jews; Calvin's Geneva had expelled all of its Jews in 1490.[29]

Calvin maintains that both the Old and New Testaments are complete and necessary revelations of the Word of God, differing only in their chronological position in God's plan of salvation. To be sure, the Old Testament has a greater preoccupation with the visible and the tangible. It promises salvation darkly, while the New Testament reveals salvation through Christ as a present reality, always available in the intangible and spiritual dimension of life. But within these expected doctrinal constraints, Calvin's commentary shows a remarkable openness to what the Jewish revelation might have meant in its own time. Here are some comments of the influential theologian on Psalm 19:

> While the heavens bear witness concerning God, their testimony does not lead men so far as that they thereby learn truly to fear him, and acquire a well-grounded knowledge of him; . . . accordingly, God vouchsafes to those whom he has determined to call to salvation special grace, just as in ancient times . . . he communicated to the children of Abraham alone his Law, thereby to furnish them with a more certain and intimate knowledge of his majesty. . . . The end, therefore, which David has here in view, is to excite the Jews, whom God had bound to himself with a more sacred bond, to yield obedience to him with a more prompt and cheerful affection. Farther, under the term *law*, he not only means the rule of living righteously, or the Ten Commandments, but he also comprehends the covenant by which God had distinguished that people from the rest of the world, and the whole doctrine of Moses, the parts of which he enumerates under the terms *testimonies, statutes,* and other names.[30]

As someone interested in the progressive unfolding of God's word through history, Calvin takes what we might regard as a historical approach to the text, asking what the psalm meant at the time it was written to the community for whom it was written. There is also, to be sure, a not so hidden theological agenda at work here. Just as the Jews' law was the special grace God gave to them, so God similarly shows special grace to the elect group of saints whom God has predestined for salvation, namely, John Calvin and those who have joined his church of "saints." This becomes even clearer in Calvin's comment on verse 13, "Who can discern his errors?" God's grace is not to be found in any doctrine of works, such as the Papists might hold, for no matter how obedient one is to the law, one will always fall short. "As we are personally destitute of the righteousness which the law requires, we are on that account excluded from the hope of the reward which the law has promised; and, in the next place, that we are guilty before God . . . so that we ought, with the bitterest sorrow, to bewail our depravity. . . . This David did."[31] For Calvin, David becomes the exemplar of Calvinism, a religion that focuses on human sinfulness and the impossibility of securing God's favor by any actions that we can perform. While seeming to elucidate the plain sense of Scripture, Calvin, like all commentators before and since, reads his own religious convictions into the biblical text.

Interpreting the Psalms in a Secular World

Both Jews and Christians have certainly continued to practice theologically and doctrinally oriented commentary within their own faith communities. But the Enlightenment began to make possible another approach to Scripture through secular institutions of higher learning, which both Christians and emancipated Jews could attend. In these institutions, faith claims would not be taken for granted but would be subjected to rational critique, as Spinoza had analyzed the ideas of divine revelation and Mosaic authorship of the Pentateuch in his *Tractatus Theologico-Politicus* (1670). In this Enlightenment climate, the Bible began to be studied with the tools of historical and literary criticism.[32] Its supposed unity as the word of God was dissected, and it began to be recast as a human document with many authors, many layers of composition, and many discrete literary forms, each with its own compositional rules and history. Over the course of the nineteenth century, study of the Bible became increasingly the study of ancient Israelite religion. And as archaeologists excavated ancient cities and brought to light data from other Semitic civilizations, an empirically based historical and comparative approach began to be forged. Students trained in these modern scientific methods of biblical study eventually became the professors of Bible at the liberal theological schools of Judaism and Christianity in late nineteenth- and twentieth-century Europe and America, where, alongside the older methods of commentary, the historical scholarly agenda became integral to the training of rabbis and ministers.

A large role in formulating this modern approach to the Hebrew Bible can be accorded to Hermann Gunkel, a professor at the University of Halle in Germany in the early twentieth century. His primary creation, form-criticism, took as its starting point the student's need to know what kind of literature is being studied, to what specific literary category or genre it belongs, and what its characteristic features are. Most important, it aimed to discover the function that the literary genre was designed to serve in the life of the community or of the individual, to learn how it was employed and on what occasions, and thus to situate the literary genre in its precise cultural milieu. This approach focused on the typical and representative characteristics of biblical literature over against the unique, individualized features of a particular text. The biblical world was thought to be ruled by custom and convention; therefore, the most important work for Gunkel and his students, who have dominated twentieth-century scholarship, was describing these conventions and showing how the literature fit into the ritual life of ancient Israel.

Gunkel worked out his methodology most fully in his study of Psalms. David's purported authorship of the Psalms was explained away as a pious fiction to serve the needs of the late biblical community, which sought to link its prayers to the authority of an ancestral figure. Similarly rejected was the idea that the Psalms were the spiritual outpourings of numerous anonymous individuals. Instead, Gunkel and his students showed that behind the Psalms as we have them were a variety of conventional cultic acts. Such and such, they said, were the verbal forms that had originally accompanied a sacrifice of thanksgiving; such and such were the forms used when the community met to petition God. The Psalms themselves were not primarily cultic prayers, Gunkel felt, but later adaptations based on cultic models.

Because the form-critical scholars were primarily interested in the Psalms' origin in the cult, they did not attempt to illuminate individual psalms in detail. Instead, they divided the one hundred and fifty psalms into two large categories: songs of the individual and of the community. The poems of the community, they said, were of two kinds: hymns of praise and laments (for which "supplication" or "petition" is probably a more accurate term). The poems of the individual were likewise of two kinds, thank offerings and laments. In addition, there were songs sung upon entering the temple, royal songs (specifically mentioning the king), and Torah songs. Finally, there were spiritual or eschatological songs supposedly not connected to the cult, and standing closest, Gunkel says in a revealing comment, to the Gospel.[33] That Gunkel held the spiritual to be nonliturgical is extremely significant. This assumption shows the unfortunate antipriestly and anti-Jewish bias in Gunkel's work, which was rife in the German Protestant textual criticism of the Pentateuch, in which he was schooled.[34] Even in this supposedly dispassionate scholarly milieu, it was impossible to escape from the deeply ingrained theological assumptions of his culture.

Gunkel's student, the Norwegian scholar Sigmund Mowinckel, went further in applying the principles of cultic interpretation. He argued that all the Psalms were used in the Temple cult to accompany cultic acts of sacrifice. Any for which Gunkel had not found an original *sitz im leben,* or life situation, were used, he contended, at the annual New Year festival, when God was supposedly enthroned in a ritual drama.[35] Mowinckel's reconstruction of ancient Israelite worship, for all its imaginative leaps and extravagant claims, penetrated to the essence of the Psalms as lived worship in a ritual setting. Along with Gunkel's work in classification, Mowinckel's reconstruction of ancient Israelite worship has generally dominated this century's scholarly consensus about Psalms.[36] Unlike Gunkel, Mowinckel did not separate liturgical from spiritual prayers. Nevertheless, his work is also marred by a curious polemic against ritual. All of the Psalms, he feels, are spiritual when measured against the mechanicalness of sacrificial worship. The work of both scholars, and of many who have followed in their tradition, reflects the continuing antiritualist bias of much Protestant thought, which often polemically separates spirituality from material objects and concrete ritual.

One of the drawbacks of the form-critical method that we have briefly touched on is its commitment to categorizing. The categorizing mind often gets mired in its own categories, creating more and more subcategories to deal with disturbing anomalies. For those psalms that would not fit his classification, Gunkel created the notion of mixed types, which occur, he claimed, when the original setting of their literary types had been forgotten or become unclear. How could it be, for instance, that a psalmist's urgent cry to God, such as "My God, my God, / why have you abandoned me?" (Ps. 22:2), should also contain a thanksgiving refrain, "Because of You I offer praise in the great congregation / I pay my vows in the presence of His worshipers" (v. 26)? Gunkel describes the psalm as a two-part ritual, in which the concluding thanksgiving could be sung only after the speaker had been delivered from calamity.[37] Such a literalist explanation belies the complexity of the underlying human experience.

Surely it is possible to speak words of praise, even in the context of lament, if one's faith commitment is strong enough. After all, even in the midst of feeling abandoned, the speaker addresses God quite personally. He reminds God, "In You our fathers trusted / they trusted and You rescued them" (v. 5). We do not need to imagine a second ritual to explain the shift in the text; the earlier reminder of past trust offers grounds enough. Or, we might posit that a second speaker, perhaps a priest, enters the psalm to speak the more hopeful words of its conclusion and thereby offer consolation to the supplicant.

Psalm 19, the exemplary psalm of this chapter, posed great problems for Gunkel and his followers, as it had done in the previous century for a number of biblical scholars. Scholars could not find either a liturgical or a poetic logic for combining praise of God as creator, praise of Torah, and a petition for forgiveness of sin, so they began to treat the psalm as two independent poems, 19A and 19B, which were combined, they assumed, by a later editor or by the second author (who, it should be noted, perceived enough commonality to link the supposedly disparate parts). From the form-critical perspective, Psalm 19A (vv. 1–7) is identified as a hymn, a song of praise for the creator of nature. Scholars note that the creator is here named El, a generic Semitic and not a specifically Israelite name for the high god of the Canaanite pantheon, and one adopted at a very early stage of Israel's religion. The special prominence of the sun (Heb. *shemesh*) in verses 5–7 further suggests to the student of comparative Semitics a borrowing from Shamash, the sun god of the Babylonians. The Hebrew poet's personification of the sun as a "bridegroom coming out of his chamber," the heavenly tent, calls to mind the warrior Shamash and his bride Ai on the horizon of the heavens. A Babylonian hymn addresses Shamash as the "glory of the heavens" who has granted light "to the face of the land." "All creatures that live, thou dost quicken / . . . O'er the wide earth is thy daily course, / O'er sea and ocean, o'er hills, o'er earth and heaven."[38] And so too the Hebrew poet has the sun rising "at one end of heaven / and his circuit reaches the other" (v. 7). By focusing on the evidence of Babylonian material in the psalm's opening movement, one British scholar says, he "can fully understand why a later psalmist felt impelled to counteract its distasteful pagan atmosphere, as it was to him, by adding a psalm more in accordance with the Hebrew conception of praise."[39]

While most commentators wax rhapsodic about the poetic beauties of 19A, few have a good word for "the Hebrew conception of praise" in 19B. From a form-critical point of view, there is the obvious problem of hybrid types, even within 19B. Why combine a didactic praise of Torah, as from a wisdom psalm, with a plea for forgiveness, as from a lament? And, furthermore, why conclude with a penitential formula when the psalm has dramatized neither guilt nor suffering, as such pleas usually do? From a poetic point of view, the magnificent images and varied rhythms of 19A are generally contrasted with the monotonous litany that begins 19B. Underlying these concerns with form and style, I would suggest, are a number of theological issues relating to the praise of Torah and its sufficiency as a spiritual path. Admittedly, the verse is not impassioned like the visionary scenario that preceded it, but neither is it simply didactic, as form-critics would have it. Rather, it is an inwardly focused meditative chant, one that mentions the unpronounceable and ineffable four-letter name of God six times in as many lines. One would have to share a reverence for this name of God and a life lived in faithfulness to it to find these thoughts personally moving.

A comment by another professor of the Old Testament drives home the conclusion that what passes for educated discourse about such issues as literary form and genre can be driven by the basest prejudice: "Let us face the fact! He is going to talk of religion nourished by a book, rather than on the living words of men of God! Let us admit that in passing from verses 1–6 . . . we have come indoors; the four walls of a room surround us, and we see a face bent over a written roll. And let it be admitted also that the Law of which he tells contains large blocks of ritual prescriptions, such as dietary laws. . . . " This author goes on to note that there are also valuable moral precepts to be found in the Law, which, he insists, still do speak to the "modern Christian."[40] This ideal element in the Law must be what excites the enthusiasm of the psalmist, for "one hardly grows dithyrambic over food-taboos and quarantine regulations."[41] What is most striking about these prejudicial outbursts against priestly Judaism is that they are wholly gratuitous and irrelevant to the interpretation of the psalm being advanced. The scholar from whom I have been quoting is actually disposed to admire the author of 19B. Indeed, he finds that his aspiration to be "blameless" and "clear of great offense" (v. 14) is like that of Jesus, who said, "You . . . must be perfect, as your heavenly Father is perfect" (Matt. 5:48). He therefore disagrees with those scholars from the German Lutheran tradition who see the psalm's concluding plea for forgiveness as somehow too easy, not fully earned. They speak, he writes, of the psalmist's "happy self-satisfaction" (Kittel), or claim that "the consuming hunger after righteousness has never touched" his soul (Schmidt), or argue that he fails to realize that his sin lies subjectively in himself, not in objective deeds, which might be discriminated according to some external hierarchy of badness (Gunkel).[42] These commentators invoke Paul to the effect that the law is an unbearable burden. To them, it is plain that the Torah, which is supposedly *temimah*, pure (the same word is used in Leviticus of the animals that can be brought for sacrifice), does not make this individual feel pure. The psalmist's closing dedication to God, "May the words of my mouth . . . be acceptable," uses the word *rason*, which calls to mind the sacrificial system of Leviticus, where one is commanded to sacrifice *lersono* and *lersonkhem*—so that God may accept one's offerings.[43] A Jewish scholar of the Psalms is willing to aver that "the utterances of the heart in spiritual, prayerful communion with God perform the same function as does sacrifice,"[44] but such connections to salvation by works call forth from the Protestant critics the perennial Christian prejudice that a life of adherence to the Torah's commandments cannot inculcate the faith that would make for a sufficient spiritual path. Under the guise of form-criticism, these Christian scholars repeat the antitheses between the liberty of faith and the servility of works that we encountered earlier in Paul, Augustine, and Calvin.

By pointing out the anti-Judaism that lies within Christianity, I do not mean to imply that all Christian biblical scholarship is tainted by anti-Semitism. I could certainly have chosen psalms that would not have illustrated this Christian bias. I also could have chosen some to illustrate the equally destructive ethnocentrism within Judaism. But the form-critical reading of Psalm 19 confronts us here as an example of how we all, including supposedly dispassionate scholars, bring our worldviews to those objects on which we focus our attention.

Writing from inside the biblical traditions and the perspective of faith, the rabbis and church fathers ask of a biblical text, "What can this teach us about what our group believes?" Writing from the perspective of modernity, historical-critical scholars interrogate the text, asking, "What are its origins?" "Where does it reveal its composite history?" But they too, as we have seen, find evidence for their own beliefs in the answers to such questions. Also writing from the perspective of modernity, literary critics emphasize the role of human creativity, as seen in the shape and nuances of the biblical text. They want to answer the question, "How do the words of this text fit together?" Literary analysis of biblical texts runs the danger of being merely formalist, that is, focused on the beauty or symmetry of the literary forms for their own sake. But when literary critics go beyond formalism to ask how the image patterns and rhetorical strategies they have isolated work together to reveal a distinctive message,[45] then their interpretations can be like a pontoon bridge thrown over the gulf that separates us in time and space from our biblical forebears.

Where historical scholarship assumes the composite nature of biblical texts, literary criticism tends to stress their unity. Beginning with the surface of the text, a literary-minded reader of Psalm 19 might find visual connections between the light of the sun in the heavens, the Torah that enlightens the eyes, and the golden color of the honey to which it is compared. *Nizhar,* the psalmist's word for being warned by the Torah's commandments, can also be translated as "made resplendent by them,"[46] further developing the imagery of light. But while these different kinds of light may indicate that the psalm is not as divided as form-critics claim, they do not draw the psalm into a coherent whole. This collecting and sorting of images is finally little more than a pleasing aesthetic pursuit.

As a starting point for a fuller literary investigation of this psalm, it is worth noting that no Jewish commentary of this or any other century has ever thought to divide this psalm in half. Michael Fishbane has suggested that if we look at the leading ideas of the psalm, we can see that they reveal a complete Jewish theology: God the Creator in verses 1–7; God the Revealer of the Torah in verses 8–11; and God the Redeemer, *go' ali,* the very last word of the psalm, in verses 12–15.[47] No Jewish theology has ever promulgated only one of these roles, without some version of the other two. A close reading might therefore hope to show that the psalm has not two but three complementary parts, which are essential to its vision of God.

It may be helpful to recall here that Rabbi Simeon ben Yoḥai began his investigation of the psalm with the speaker's need to have his prayer accepted: "May the words of my mouth / and the prayer of my heart / be acceptable to You" (v. 15). Fishbane notes that this petition points to two different modes of communication central to prayer: spoken words and unspoken thoughts or meditations. Working backwards from this starting point, he finds the issue of what is spoken and what is unspoken to be central to all three parts of the psalm.[48] His reading does not necessarily answer the concerns of biblical critics by proving that the psalm was indeed composed as a unity. Instead, it shifts our focus away from the psalm's composition to its reception: how we encounter it in prayer.

How do the heavens declare the glory of God? How do day and night express God's presence and greatness? Without utterance, words, or sound. Like the meditations of our hearts, the imagery of Part I points to that which is known and acknowledged without speech. Unlike the heavens, the Torah speaks loudly, clearly, and articulately of God's will for humankind, and especially for Israel. Likewise, the psalmist's words praising Torah in Part II articulate the power of Torah's message in human life. Thus, the heavens and Torah, the unspoken and the spoken, each in their own way echo a dimension of the speaker's spiritual life. In Part III of the psalm, we come to both the words of the speaker's mouth and the unspoken meditations of his heart. We hear that he is painfully aware of himself as a sinner who needs forgiveness for (unconscious?) errors of thought, for willful sins, and finally, for the sort of great transgression that marks one as an irremediable sinner. He speaks of all these sins *and* of what he cannot properly speak about, his *nistarot,* his hidden flaws, hidden even from himself, and known only to God.[49] It is extremely important to the psalmist that he be thoroughly known and accepted by God, just as thoroughly, in fact, as God is known through the inspiring sight of the heavens at sunrise, or through the inward discipline of accepting the law of the Torah. It may be, as the critical scholars posit, that a later editor thought to link these two complementary ways of knowing God, which originally had nothing to do with one another. But it may also be argued that the author of the psalm deliberately summons the heavens and the Torah as witnesses to his personal prayer, because he believes that both his speech and his silence can, like them, become fully articulate and understood. To know God as creator, one need merely look to the heavens, and to know God as revealer, to the Torah. But how to discover God as a personal redeemer?

One can begin, our psalmist might suggest, through the self-revelation of confessional prayer. Confession is the beginning of both honest self-knowledge and knowledge of the self by another. It occurs in the context of dialogue, with the certainty that one is being heard and known, and with the hope that God's hearing and knowledge will bring forgiveness. When the psalmist asks that his words be acceptable, *lerason,* he may be evoking the memory of a penitential sacrificial offering, as the form-critics suggest; he may be intending his words to accompany an actual sacrifice, as Mowinckel and the cultic interpreters might suggest; or he may be pointing, through the language his culture has made available to him, to an essential quality of prayer, sacrifice, and other symbolic communications: the desire to be accepted in all one's imperfection for who one is, constantly striving for perfection but understandably falling short of the mark, and therefore needing a symbolic means of redressing the imbalance between aspiration and deed.

In this last insight, we have passed beyond the boundaries of the approaches thus far surveyed to take up the vocabulary of ritual studies. Though I have partly treated modern approaches to Psalms as straw men, there is a great deal to be learned from all of them: from cultic interpretation, a vivid reenactment of worship in the ancient Temple; from form-criticism, an attention to the relation between that life setting and the development of literary genres; from literary criticism, a commitment to the demonstrable (albeit perhaps subtle) unity of the text, which is how we encounter it in private or public prayer. Since psalms live in performance, we need to go beyond the insights of these disciplines to plumb the phenomenology of worship. In what follows, I step back from lenses that look closely at the text to focus our attention on the broader question of ritual as a mode of organizing our experience of the world. We will not follow New Testament lines and separate out the spiritual wheat from the material chaff. Rather, we will look closely at the materiality of ritual as the ground that nourishes the spiritual growth that is evident in the Psalms.

The Language of Ritual

Since at least the time of the Protestant Reformation, Westerners have lived in a cultural climate prejudiced against ritual. We use "ritualistic" to mean habitual, and "ceremonial" to mean something done just for show. One historian of religion has argued that during the sixteenth and seventeenth centuries, when Reformation theologians launched polemics against Catholicism, ritual came to "be perceived as a matter of surface rather than depth; of outward representation rather than inward transformation."[50] Shakespeare's Henry V, who rules by what his contemporaries think to be a divine right, cries out plaintively in the spirit of this Protestant critique: "O ceremony, show me but thy worth! / . . . Art thou ought else but place, degree, and form, / Creating awe and fear in other men?"[51] If the king himself can take this sort of skeptical view of ceremony, it should be no surprise that his subjects could so far jettison the theory of divine right as to perpetrate the crime of regicide within little more than a generation.

Reformation Protestants did not, of course, invent such a critique of ritual, nor have Protestants been the only ones to be affected by it. It is as old as the Hebrew prophets' attacks on sacrifices offered to God without a corresponding change in moral behavior. It is as recent as the Catholic Church's decision during the 1960s to suspend the obligation to abstain from meat on Fridays. All religious traditions, and, inevitably, students of those traditions, have been affected to some degree by the antiritualism of modern rationalist thought. I have been drawn to anthropology as a disciplinary approach precisely because it does not endorse this antiritualist bias. In the aboriginal cultures with which anthropology typically deals, ritual retains its power to shape both individual identity and society's experience of itself as a whole. This reign of ritual is what Stone Age village-based tribal societies have in common with an Iron Age urban, state-centered monarchical culture such as that of biblical Israel. Increasingly, therefore, anthropology has been drawn upon as a tool for interpreting the Hebrew Bible.[52]

Anthropologists studying rituals in small face-to-face cultures have given us, living in very different societies, a vocabulary for seeing the crucial role that ritual plays in all our lives. We need to understand that the anthropologists' social scientific perspective, however much it has been based on participation and observation, is still that of an outsider to the culture. There are clearly intellectual gains from such a perspective, but there are also losses. Observing a ritual from the outside, we can easily fail to perceive the power it has for those who participate in it. We may speculate about how individual, society, and cosmos are blended in ritual actions and symbols, but we need to remember that these are our categories, not those of the culture we are studying. Ancient Israelites did have words for these ideas, but they did not use them critically, stepping back to create abstractions to understand themselves. The practice of the ritual was their mode of understanding, while ours is the practice of theory.

Nevertheless, there are important things that need to be said about ritual that ritualization itself cannot see. (We can use the term "ritualization" to refer to ritual behavior as a mode of action and power in the world.) Ritualization sees itself, as one recent writer put it, "responding to a place, event, force, problem, or tradition. It tends to see itself as the natural or appropriate thing to do in the circumstances. Ritualization does not see how it actively creates place, force, event, and tradition, how it redefines or generates the circumstances to which it is responding. It does not see how its own actions reorder and reinterpret the circumstances so as to afford the sense of a fit among the main spheres of experience—body, community and cosmos."[53] Applying this insight to biblical Israel, we might say that Mount Zion is not holy until the building of a temple there makes it so, but those responsible for and those participating in that culture's processes of ritualization tell a different story. The Temple, its personnel, and its rituals have been authorized by God from the outset. By claiming that ritual is blind to its own processes of symbolization, I do not mean to suggest that those who performed these rituals did so in bad faith. In their own myths, all religions similarly see themselves and their sacred places as divinely chosen.[54] As soon as religions begin to see themselves as humanly created by specific cultures rather than as institutions mandated by God, or by the primordial ancestors, then the legitimating power of their rituals radically changes, even as their need for ritualization continues to be felt.

Students of rituals all agree that they are means to important social ends, but they disagree about the nature of those ends. Some argue that rituals promote social solidarity, legitimating the powers-that-be in the eyes of the masses, while others argue the converse, that rituals are a means for expressing social conflict, often allowing for the redress of a social imbalance. Still others, focusing on sacrifice, argue that the primary role of ritual is as a mechanism for repressing the violence that would otherwise undermine society. Finally, there are those who suggest that rituals are a collective means of defining reality.[55]

Underlying this last thesis is the assumption that ritual is not distinct from other human activities, but that it shares both in the materiality of life and in the expressive, communicative, and symbolic aspect of human action. The stuff of ritual is acts, gestures, words, music, noises, objects, and physical substances. What we do with this amalgam is akin to what we do with language, namely, to bring what is most important to us into full consciousness, and thereby make these factors "real" in our lives. As a mode of articulation, collective ritual forms in us "a complex permanent attitude," an emotional pattern that governs our individual lives.[56] As metaphor functions within language, so ritual can be a tool for abstract, symbolic thought. Ritual actions can be regarded as figures of speech, in which a gesture stands symbolically for a complex of ideas and emotions. In the figure of metonymy, an associated element of one thing can substitute for that thing or person; thus, a sacrifice can stand for the person offering it.[57] Even more explicitly, ritual words draw upon figures of speech, such as metaphor and symbolism. As a definer of reality, ritualization allows us to compare our life, messy and full of variability, to the order and permanence evoked by ritual, and thereby to gain a sense of how things ought to proceed in our world.[58]

There is an alternative approach to elaborating the analogy between ritual and language. Language is not simply an instrument of symbolic thought. It is also crucially a way of making things happen in the social world. The philosopher of language John Searle points out that there are "a limited number of basic things we do with language: we tell people how things are, we try to get them to do things, we commit ourselves to doing things, we express our feelings and attitudes, and we bring about changes through our utterances."[59] His teacher J. L. Austin termed these the *illocutionary* functions of language, as opposed to the *locutionary,* the simple articulation of sounds in phonemic patterns.[60] Searle's last class of illocutionary acts, those that themselves bring about changes, have been widely called *performative;* that is, they perform actions that could not be done without them. To understand the performative in ritual, a helpful distinction is drawn between two kinds of rituals: those that regulate a preexisting activity, such as eating at the dinner table, and those that actually constitute an activity that is dependent on them, such as blessing, baptizing, circumcising, marrying, or installing a chief or a head of state.[61] In these latter constitutive rituals, the desired outcome does not take place unless the ritual does. And for the ritual to succeed, performative language plays a crucial role. In a civil marriage ceremony, without each member of the couple pronouncing the words "I do," the state's representative cannot declare, "I now pronounce you man and wife." Much analysis has focused on this strictly performative dimension of ritual speech, but we shall have occasion to apply Searle's other categories of illocutionary acts—asserting how things are, directing others to do things, committing ourselves to action, and expressing our feelings and attitudes—to our study of Psalms.

In addition to these linguistic approaches to ritual, many sociologists and anthropologists take a formal approach, trying to ascertain the properties common to rituals in all cultures. Formalists tend to stress the ideal or conventional quality of rituals, their difference from events in ordinary, daily life not surrounded by such a ritual "frame."[62] For something to be considered a ritual, the specific place, time, action performed, and persons performing the action will be crucial to how it is perceived. Something about one or more of these categories must be framed so that it is identified as a special way of acting in a particular culture. Thus, the area in which a ritual takes place is a specially delineated one; the time is set; specially qualified persons are distinguished by their dress, etc. The boundaries of ritual differ from culture to culture, but most groups draw upon these elements: (1) *repetition;* (2) *acting;* (3) *special behavior or stylization;* (4) *order;* (5) *an evocative presentational style;* and (6) *a collective dimension.*[63] Formal analysis tends to stress the fact that rituals are experienced simultaneously through many of our senses and through several modes of performance, such as music, chant, dance, and visual spectacle. These fusing qualities of ritual allow participants to experience an event intensively. Similarly, the repetitiveness of acts and words in ritual ensures that the medium serves the interests of the message. When sent along more than one pathway, the message is sure to be made memorable, as is the vehicle for the message, the ritual occasion itself.[64]

Ritual might be seen as a process of making natural acts, such as swaying or bending or singing, into idealized, conventional ones, which we recognize by virtue of their conventions. But it is also worth reminding ourselves that these cultural conventions are themselves deeply rooted in our human nature. The formal properties of ritual may have such powerful effects on human beings because we have a basic neurobiological need to experience the world through repetitive patterns. Recent research has suggested that the driving stimuli of ritual, such as are produced by the rhythms of chanting, religious procession, or percussion instruments, may lessen the inhibition of the right hemisphere of our brain, allowing it to become temporarily dominant. This creates the possibility for timeless, nonverbal experiences that alleviate stress, create a feeling of well-being in the individual, increase social cohesion, and provide an empirical mode of access to what the society considers sacred.[65] As one anthropologist notes of the Mbuti people in Zaire, "when they have anything important to say it is sung and danced."[66] In such musical speech, the element of nonverbal sound plays a crucial communicative function.

In what follows I will be drawing on conceptual, performative, and formal approaches to ritual, trying to blend insights into form and content whenever possible. To make these ideas less abstract, let me begin with an example close to home. We might say "Good morning" to our family members or housemates every morning, but we probably don't say it in a special place or time, nor in a stylized way that would call attention to itself as a presentation or performance. So we conclude that it is not really ritual behavior. But the phrase "Good night, sweet dreams," might well be construed as a ritual utterance, as it is repeated each night at the same place, at the same time, by the same person, and in the same rhythmic form. The ritual might be filled out by other rhythmic or melodic phrases: "Now I lay me down to sleep; I pray the Lord my soul to keep." "All night, all day, angels watching over me, My Lord." The rhymes, meter, and imagery stylize these utterances and add to the differentness of the occasion. These all intensify our receptiveness to what is transpiring. When we read these words on this page, however much they make us think of a ritual, we recognize that they are not the ritual itself. A ritual is alive only when it is enacted and embodied. Thus, along with these words go repeated gestures and specific bodily postures: a child kneeling by the bedside, an adult bending over to give or a child lying back to receive a kiss, a voice singing in the semidarkness. Ritual is a performance that demands participation, which distinguishes it from theatrical performances. Insofar as ideas about God and God's protecting angels are alive in this ritual, they are so because our own breaths and bodies have given them life.

A single ritual gesture is an embodiment of a whole complex of religious attitudes and prior actions. A telling moment in the biblical Book of Judges occurs when God tells Gideon to test the Israelites who have mustered for a fight. All must drink water from a stream. Those who kneel down to drink, God concludes, have previously knelt down to idols, while those who stretch themselves flat on the ground have been loyal to YHWH, Israel's God (Judg. 7:4–8). The story teaches that our experience of and attitude toward what we consider sacred is stored in the body.

It should be clear from my discussion thus far that we define the boundaries of what is sacred and what is not sacred ritually. For Emil Durkheim, the father of modern sociology, the sacred exemplified the power of society, especially its ability to produce collective representations, such as myths, rituals, and laws, that bind a people in social solidarity, through

their obligation and devotion to those representations.[67] Durkheim therefore argued that a group's religious practices and theology are always a
reflection of the way it conceives itself as a society. For Durkheim and the
many thinkers whom he has influenced, rituals take on different characters depending on the social structure of a given group. In this book, we
will be concerned with the rituals and prayers of biblical Israel at a time
when the institutions of monarchy and priesthood dominated its public
life. Following Durkheim, we will see how ritual reflects Israel's conception
of the individual, the society, and the cosmos. We will see in ritual how
human beings participate in maintaining both their social order and what
they conceive to be a divinely created order. Through ritual, they make
declarations about the impact of that order on their lives, as individuals
and as members of a sanctified group.

Durkheim saw ritual as maintaining what society had agreed upon as
sacred. A contemporary anthropologist working in the tradition of Durkheim has suggested that ritual creates sanctity, which he defines as "the
quality of unquestionableness imputed by a congregation to postulates in
their nature neither verifiable nor falsifiable."[68] Through qualities of
order and invariance, rituals convey certainty to such postulates as the
unity or goodness of God, or God's protection of the faithful, which
cannot be verified by reason alone. In this view, where sanctity is created
by ritual, the performers of the ritual both send and receive its essential
message.[69] Even in directly invoking, addressing, or seeking to affect an
unseen power, they make present their actions to themselves as witnesses
of the ritual.

Not just God, then, but human beings are an equally important audience in worship. We see this in many psalms, but it stands out particularly
in one:

> Now bless YHWH
> all you servants of YHWH
> who stand nightly
> in the house of YHWH.
> Lift your hands toward the sanctuary,
> and bless YHWH.
> May YHWH,
> maker of heaven and earth,
> bless you from Zion. (Ps. 134)

The participants in the scene seem to be a prayer leader (though conceiv-
ably the speaking voice could be plural) and a group of nighttime worshipers. These could be either pilgrims newly arrived at the Temple or a
shift of night guards, who stand nightly before their God. If the latter, it is

possible that the speaker who leads this brief liturgy is himself departing for the night.

The psalm dramatizes a scene of commanding and witnessing. Two of the psalm's three sentences are imperatives. The prayer leader commands those he addresses to perform the ritual gesture of lifting their hands and blessing God. He also witnesses what would have been their immediate response, whether silently or with accompanying words of blessing, such as the congregational response we hear in another psalm: "Blessed is the LORD, God of Israel / From eternity to eternity" (Ps. 106:48). The one who requests and those who perform such a gesture in the Temple know themselves as the community of the faithful, who perform this ritual whenever they are in the Temple at night. Through this action they commit themselves to be servants of YHWH. Witnessed and affirmed by human actors, it also can be witnessed and affirmed, they believe, by God. Just as it is a sign of their loyalty to make their gesture and chant to God, so God can express a reciprocal act of loyalty by blessing them "from Zion," the spot where they stand. The specialness of place, time, action, and performers of the action are all inscribed in this psalm, which bespeaks the way in which ritual creates ritualized agents, who internalize their people's sociology, theology, and cosmology in their own bodily actions.

In their raising their hands to bless God and pronouncing a formula of blessing, what actually happens? If we say that the senders of the message are the primary audience for the message, then we must conclude that this communication is symbolic. It creates solidarity between the priestly elite and the mass of worshipers and reaffirms their sense of what is real and important in the universe, namely, human devotion to God, "the maker of heaven and earth." But if we acknowledge that God is equally a receiver of this gesture and formula of blessing, then the psalm is something more than symbolic expression. It is efficacious. It conveys the human response of devotion to God and thereby secures God's favor. Because those who chant the psalm are in a dialogic relationship to God, they believe that their words make something happen. It has been suggested that in many ancient and traditional cultures, the magical power of words is connected to this performative quality.[70] Many creation myths hypothesize a quintessential performative Word, through which God or the gods named the world into being. Then, as in the Genesis account, humans follow suit by naming things into consciousness. With that sacred and primordial background of words, human culture invests in words the ability to act and produce effects in their own right. These powers of the word are attributed to priests, prophets, and magicians.[71]

Early in this century it was customary to draw a hard and fast distinction between religion and magic. Magic was seen as involving the direct control

by human beings of the forces of nature, while religion was the propitia-
tion of these and higher powers.[72] When a farmer plants crops, fertilizes,
weeds, and harvests them, we regard it as a straightforward technical
activity. When he also performs rites or casts spells to make his crops grow,
we regard these utterances as magical activities. But in the mind of the
performer, these may be regarded as parts of one process. If the prayer for
rain and a good harvest is pronounced by an entire congregation, or if the
congregation fasts in a time of drought, we regard these practices as religious rather than magical, but is there not a parallel juxtaposition of word
and action in both contexts? Do not the magician-farmer and the community with its priests both seek the best possible outcome for human
actions? Does not each want to be in the best possible relation to those
unseen forces that have an impact on human affairs? We can, of course,
distinguish priests from magicians in terms of their respective audiences:
priests perform in collective ceremonies, while magicians ply their arts for
private clients. Even so, it makes far more sense to see in these examples a
continuum of magico-religious practices than to project contemporary
society's dichotomy between effective and symbolic practices onto ancient
or still-existing traditional cultures.

In the discussion of biblical ritual forms that follows, one ritual pattern,
the rite of passage, will be especially important to our analysis. We owe the
concept to the early twentieth-century Belgian anthropologist Arnold Van
Gennep, who showed that all rituals are sacred passages, whether connected
to the individual life cycle, to the natural cycle of the year, or to the community's experience of itself as a distinct people. They all share a basic three-
part structure of separation, transition, and reincorporation. The psalm
quoted above exemplifies this pattern. Depending on how we define the
participants, we can see it marking spatial, temporal, sociological, and metaphysical transitions. If we have here an interaction between a leader and a
group of Temple servants, it may represent a transition between the person
separating from the sacred and those who are entering into it. We imagine
it therefore taking place at the boundary between sacred and profane (or
less sacred) spaces. As a temporal ritual, it may mark a transition between
times of day and service to God. If it is part of the evening service, then it
solicits blessing at the beginning of the night when human apprehensions
of unknown and potentially evil forces start to rise. It also draws on the
hierarchical authority vested in the leader. As part of his separation from
the sacred, he requires a ritual gesture, which will invest the new cohort
with the authority of office. If it is a group of pilgrims being addressed, then
by leading them in an act of worship, he is drawing upon his authority to
bring them into contact with the sacred. This transition is thus a metaphysical one as well. Not only have the initiates made the horizontal transition

into the sacred space and time of their service, but they have also made a vertical transition into proximity with what their culture regards as being of utterly transcendent value, not to be measured by any earthly scale.[73]

This description of one rite of passage emphasizes the middle moment in the structural pattern, the transition between old and new life stages, status roles, territories, times of day or year, and, as we have pointed out, metaphysical planes. Van Gennep associates this moment in many rituals with the crossing of an actual threshold, in Latin, *limen,* hence the adjective "liminal" and the noun "liminality" to characterize this pivotal phase of ritual action. "The door," he writes, "is the boundary between the foreign and domestic worlds in the case of an ordinary dwelling, between the profane and sacred worlds in the case of a temple. Therefore to cross the threshold is to unite oneself with a new world. It is thus an important act in marriage, adoption, ordination, and funeral ceremonies."[74]

In the third quarter of the twentieth century, Victor Turner made liminality the focus of both his anthropological field work and later theorizing. While Turner was studying initiation among the Ndembu people in central Africa, the work of Van Gennep provided him with his analytic starting point. Van Gennep's work emphasized the outward changes of social status accomplished in such rites, but Turner began to focus on the inward, moral and cognitive changes that occurred. Turner came to see ritual liminality—the experience of being physically separated from the ordinary flow of social life and brought into a ritual space charged with vivid symbols, strong emotions, and dramatic actions—as fundamentally transformative and regenerative for the individual. In this initiation process, new adult members of the culture are taught the necessary interrelation of cosmos, society, and individual. The sacred symbols encountered by the initiates, the symbolic actions they perform, the myths they hear recited, the powerful emotions they experience—all reinforce what seem to be inarguable social and cultural truths.[75]

In Turner's later work, visions of social solidarity give way to social conflict. He sees symbolic practices as channels for discovering new insights that challenge the established religious and social orders. Ritual liminality is, in Turner's view, exploratory and antistructural, providing a release from the pragmatic, structural aspects of society: fixed status roles and institutional hierarchies. Such experiences create a new sort of festive, egalitarian community, to which Turner gives the name *communitas.*[76] As a liberation into an alternative way of viewing reality, the special communitas created by ritual can play an important role in what Turner calls "the social drama," the four-phase process he describes as (1) a breach in the established order, (2) a crisis, (3) a redress through ritual, leading to either (4a) a reintegration of the conflicting parties under new terms or

(4b) a schism between them.[77] In his cross-cultural work on pilgrimage, he focused on the new sort of community created among those sharing a liminal experience: a spontaneous, egalitarian fellowship that constantly challenges the prevailing norms of a status-dominated culture.[78]

Van Gennep's and Turner's models for ritual liminality provide the main framework for chapter 2. Unlike the anthropologists, we have no ancient Israelites with whom to conduct our field work. Instead, we will draw on a variety of biblical writings. Priestly writings, especially in the books of Leviticus and Numbers, contain prescriptions for how specific rituals were to be conducted. Occasionally these supply enough detail that we can imagine the sensory and ideological components of rituals as they might have been experienced by participants. The historical books, Samuel, Kings, Ezra, Nehemiah, and Chronicles, contain descriptions, often idealized, of rituals undertaken on behalf of all Israel. These offer glimpses of how ritual helps negotiate moments of great national significance, such as the king's public disobedience of God or the people's assembly to dedicate the Temple. To approach the personal dimension of religious experience, however, we need to look to the Book of Psalms, the verbal and musical experience of both collective and individual worship. It provides our best biblical source for understanding the role ritual played and can play in the lives of individuals and of a people as a whole.

·II·

THE WORLD OF THE PSALMS:
THE PERSPECTIVE OF RITUAL

This chapter tries to reduce the distance between us and the religion of biblical Israel by approaching its rituals as a symbolic language. Ritual practices that might seem to us remote both in time and in sensibility if we approached them literally, can be apprehended when seen symbolically as powerful means of shaping social reality and representing the workings of divinity. Ritual enables us to integrate the whole range of life experiences, because a ritually based community recognizes that all the emotions we experience in life need to be acknowledged and made real through symbolic acts and language.

As we approach the ritual life depicted in the Hebrew Bible, we need to recognize the wide range of sources and time periods represented in the biblical corpus. It has been the task of biblical historians to isolate the various strands of biblical tradition and to anchor them in their respective historical moments, from the period of the Judges (ca. 1200 B.C.E.) to the Maccabean revolt (ca. 165 B.C.E.). Their disciplinary vantage point therefore makes them suspicious of anthropological approaches to the Bible, which look at ritual processes as a single cultural and symbolic system, even though these practices certainly evolved and changed over time.[1] My discussion will draw on the work of biblical historians, without attempting to adjudicate all their controversies. My main purpose is to illuminate the world of the Psalms, many of which reflect a life situation in a temple. It makes sense therefore to anchor the Psalms in the theology of a temple cult, without regard to specific historical period. In that project, our first task is to describe the worldview of the priestly writers of the Bible, who are generally considered responsible for substantial sections of Genesis, Exodus, and Numbers, and all of Leviticus.

In attending to these writings, we will be looking at the practices, symbols, and concepts that mattered most to the priests. The first section of the chapter focuses on the concept of kingship, both divine and human, as it was embodied in the ceremonials and symbolic architecture of the Jerusalem Temple. Drawing upon evidence from the Psalms and a number of other biblical books, we will be describing the central place of the Temple in the religious imagination of Israel. The second section focuses on the two activities for which Temple worship was especially known, sacrifice and psalmody, examined both individually and as a complementary pair. In this section, we will learn a great deal not only from biblical texts, but also from anthropological theory about the relationship between actions and words in ritual. The third section addresses a concern central to the priestly worldview, the danger of impurity, and the concomitant striving for purity and holiness. Here too anthropological theory is an essential part of our inquiry: how societies define their purity rules and how they use rituals and ritual language to orchestrate the transitions from states of impurity back to purity. The final section of the chapter focuses on the nature of the community created by ancient Israelite worship, by highlighting the special experience of pilgrimage worship in the Jerusalem Temple.

The Temple Cult: The Service of the King

Three hundred years after Baruch Spinoza proposed the human authorship of the Pentateuch and one hundred years after the German scholar Julius Wellhausen made famous the hypothesis that there were four pentateuchal documents (J, E, P, D), there is still widespread disagreement about the provenience of these sources. Two theories predominate about P, the priestly school of writers, one associated with Wellhausen, the other with the Israeli scholar Yehezkel Kaufmann. For Kaufmann, P is among the first of the Pentateuchal sources. Its traditions of a wilderness sanctuary or tent provide authentic memories of Israel's early worship. According to Kaufmann, P knows nothing of the centralization of Israel's cultic activities in the Jerusalem Temple, the Deuteronomic reforms (associated with D) carried out by King Josiah (ca. 640–609 B.C.E.), nor does it know of the destruction of the high places of pagan worship, carried out by the reforms of Josiah's grandfather, King Hezekiah (701–689 B.C.E.). Kaufmann therefore dates P to the early centuries of the monarchy.[2] In marked contrast, Wellhausen's P is a pious fraud perpetrated by the priests who returned from the Babylonian exile (ca. 536 B.C.E.). What was valuable in Israelite religion was its prophetic heritage of individual conscience and faith, which the priests obfuscated with their legalism and cultic scrupulousness. For Wellhausen, P's wilderness tabernacle is a reflection of the Second Temple period, when Israel was ruled by priests, serving as deputies of the distant Persian emperors. Those priests, seeing themselves as the only legitimate descendants of the Aaronide priesthood, bolstered their status through the genealogies they inserted in the biblical text.[3] Leviticus ends with dire prophecies of exile if Israel does not uphold God's (priestly) law. For Wellhausen and his followers, the exile marks the beginning of the priestly writings and of their supreme authority within the Israelite community. For those who have followed the basic arguments of Kaufmann, the exile is the terminal date of P. In this view, the priestly traditions were developed and promulgated over a long period (ranging from 300 to 600 years), their influence over Israel's life a more or less continuous process.[4]

This historical debate is not now paralleled in discussions of Psalms because there are no sound criteria external to the book for determining the age of their religious ideas and practices.[5] The language of worship in any culture tends to be conservative, and the Psalms are no exception. The linguistic distance between a poem by Chaucer and one by T. S. Eliot is vast and immediately recognizable, but the linguistic differences between a psalm from the monarchy and one from after the exile are minute, even if they reflect the same span of 600 years.[6] "Terms from ancient Ugaritic literature are here juxtaposed to purely Israelite material. . . . References to an earthly king (as in Ps. 2) indicate the period of the monarchy; but allusions to the Babylonian exile (Ps. 137) and a widespread diaspora (Ps. 106:47) point to the inclusion in the collection of later material as well."[7] And when there are allusions to worship in a temple, we cannot determine which is meant. The sanctuary at Shiloh served by Eli and his sons, the Jerusalem Temple built by Solomon, the temples in the northern kingdom of Israel at Bethel and Dan after the split of the monarchy, the second Jerusalem Temple built by the returning exiles under the leadership of Ezra and Nehemiah, and which lasted (with substantial modifications by Herod) until its destruction by the Romans in 70 c.e.—all are candidates.

Seeking to ascertain what temple and cult meant in ancient Israel, we can proceed, if not historically then textually, by looking closely at texts that reveal a temple cult ideology. From this point of view, it has been suggested that "the book of Psalms and the book of Leviticus should be read in parallel columns."[8] Yet, because of its interest in origins and establishing firm chronologies, the historically oriented disciplines within biblical scholarship have not pursued such parallels very far. There have been other barriers as well. We have already suggested that in much Protestant biblical scholarship there is a virtually Pauline dichotomy between faith and works. The spirituality of the Psalms is thus set against the mere ritualism of sacrifice. Here is a typical comment of this school of thought: "It is . . . understandable that psalm-singing and psalm-writing were felt to be a much more personal and spiritual profession than that of the priest, who had to perform apparently more mechanical ritual functions."⁹ On the part of Jewish scholars as well, polemics have prevented much inquiry into these parallels. In arguing for the utter separation of biblical Israel from its neighboring polytheistic cultures, where the priests used blessings, curses, and hymns theurgically, Kaufmann suggested that sacrificial worship in the Tabernacle and Temple had to have been silent; words were allowed no role in influencing the deity, lest they be considered to have magical power. His conclusion: "biblical psalms have nothing to do with the priesthood and its functions."¹⁰ Others have tried to soften Kaufmann's doctrinaire position, showing that one can accept the idea that sacrifices were performed silently, and still acknowledge that words and music were an integral part of Israelite worship from the earliest times, both in the local sanctuaries and, after centralization, in the Jerusalem Temple.¹¹ Israelite temples were not just places where sacrifice was performed; they were also places of prayer.

One of the greatest students of comparative religion, Mircea Eliade, has paved the way for a comparison of the Psalms and the priestly writings by pointing to the centrality in all religious cultures of the idea of a "sacred center," often a mountain. The earthly temple built on the sacred mountain functions as a microcosm, literally, an image of the entire cosmos. At this single sacred spot, heaven comes down to earth, because this is the navel of the universe, the place from which creation first unfolded, and from which divine energies continue to emanate. At such a sanctuary, religions recapitulate their creation stories in cosmogonic rituals, usually annual events that reenact the events by which their gods established the current order of the universe. Eliade distinguishes ancient Israelite religion from that of its pagan neighbors on the grounds that history replaces cosmogony as the dominant impetus of the Israelite festivals.¹² But the role of creation and cosmogony should not be underestimated, even in supposedly antimythological Israel, as we shall see in some detail below.

In monarchical cultures, there is an obvious pull to envision God or one among the gods as a divine ruler and to correlate celebrations of the divine and earthly king. An annual cosmogonic festival renewing the creation of the world is an important vehicle for celebrating the kingship and glorious primordial deeds of the divine ruler. But in retelling the mythological story of how the forces of creation overcame the forces of chaos, such enthronement festivals also serve to reinstate the divine ruler, whose part is often played by the earthly king, whose own legitimacy is thus renewed. This was the case in Babylon, where, during an annual New Year enthronement festival for the high god Marduk, celebrants read the epic *Enuma elish*, which narrates Marduk's defeat of Tiamat, the sea monster who opposed his creation of the world. In a parade through the city, the current king, however legitimately or illegitimately he had arrived at the throne, played the part of Marduk. All could infer that the civil order maintained by the king was implicated in the order of the cosmos, which was sustained by the ruler of the divine pantheon.[13]

Biblical scholars have been fascinated by the cosmogonic festivals that took place throughout the ancient Near East, including Canaan itself, the land conquered by the people of Israel. Many have argued that Israel, taking over the ritual traditions of the indigenous people, also had its cosmogonic New Year festival, in which YHWH was annually reenthroned, his exploits as divine warrior retold, and the Davidic ruler's covenant with God reaffirmed. The largest body of evidence for such a cosmogonic celebration in ancient Israel comes from the Psalms.[14] A number of psalms, from which I quote below, contain elements of the divine warrior myth:

- the high god emerging from amid a divine council;
- a battle with the primordial sea;
- creation imaged as the victory of divinity over chaos, sometimes named Rahab or Leviathan, sometimes simply the sea;
- the divine king's adoption of the earthly king as his warrior vice-regent on earth and member of the divine council;
- proclamation of the god's covenant with the ruler to the people;
- a procession through the royal capital to enthrone the divine ruler in his sanctuary.

A number of these elements are strikingly borne out by the prose traditions of the monarchy as well. II Samuel 6 depicts David's entry into Jerusalem, dancing ecstatically in a procession of the ark of the covenant. The memory of this moment became the focus of a later liturgy in Psalms.[15]

The psalms in which the divine warrior and enthronement motifs appear show how deeply Israel's monotheism grew in mythological soil:

> Ascribe to YHWH, O divine beings,
> ascribe to YHWH glory and strength.
> Ascribe to YHWH the glory of His name;
> bow down to YHWH, majestic in holiness. (29:1–2)

> Your wonders, YHWH, are praised by the heavens,
> Your faithfulness, too, in the assembly of holy beings.
> For who in the skies can equal YHWH,
> can compare with YHWH among the divine beings,
> a God greatly dreaded in the council of holy beings,
> awesome to all around Him. (89:6–8)

The high god YHWH is called to battle and, as divine warrior, leaves mythological enemies strewn in the sea, much as God drowns Pharaoh and his armies in the historic rescue of Israel from Egypt. The name of the Canaanite sea god, Yam, becomes the Hebrew word for sea, so even as Israel's God enters history, the people's memory of the mythological epics is never totally erased:

> You rule the swelling of the sea;
> when its waves surge, You still them.
> You crushed Rahab, for he was like a corpse;
> with Your powerful arm You scattered Your enemies. (89:10–11)

> It was you who drove back the sea with Your might,
> who smashed the heads of the monsters in the waters;
> it was You who crushed the heads of Leviathan,
> who left him as food for the denizens of the desert. (74:13–14)

> The earth is YHWH's and all that it holds,
> the world and its inhabitants.
> For He founded it upon the ocean,
> set it on the nether-streams. (24:1–2)

In sketching out how this myth might have taken ritual form, we can point to explicitly dramatic elements. In a number of psalms the voices of God and the earthly king take prominent roles, as in a pageant:

> YHWH said to my lord,
> "Sit at my right hand
> while I make your enemies your footstool." (110:1)

> "I have made a covenant with My chosen one;
> I have sworn to My servant David:
> I will establish your offspring forever,
> I will confirm your throne for all generations." (89:4–5)

> ". . . I have installed My king
> on Zion, My holy mountain!"
> Let me tell of the decree:
> YHWH said to me,
> "you are my son,
> I have fathered you this day.
> Ask it of me,
> and I will make the nations your domain;
> your estate, the limits of the earth.
> You can smash them with an iron mace,
> shatter them like potter's ware." (2:6–9)

> "I will set his hand upon the sea,
> his right hand upon the rivers.
> He shall say to me,
> 'You are my father, my God, the rock of my deliverance.'
> I will appoint him firstborn,
> highest of the kings of the earth." (89:26–28)

The king's hand upon the sea and rivers is a metaphoric way of equating his rule with God's. Yet sometimes earthly events shake it. Enemies rise up against the king and are not conquered. The enthronement ritual becomes a vehicle for reminding God to fulfill the unbreakable covenant with Israel's king. The people, led by their priests, take a prominent role in both petitioning and propitiating God:

> YHWH, where is Your steadfast love of old
> which You swore to David in Your faithfulness? (89:50)

> Let us enter His abode,
> bow at His footstool.
> Advance, YHWH, to Your resting-place,
> You and Your mighty ark!
> Your priests are clothed in triumph;
> Your loyal ones sing for joy.
> For the sake of Your servant David
> do not reject Your anointed one. (132:7–10).

Singers and dancers in the procession set the stage for what must have been the climactic moment of the ritual we are adumbrating, the enthronement of God as cosmic king, now and forever.

> O gates, lift up your heads!
> Up high, you everlasting doors,
> so the King of Glory may come in!
> Who is the King of Glory?
> YHWH, mighty and valiant,
> YHWH, valiant in battle. (24:7–8)

> YHWH, enthroned on cherubim, is king,
> peoples tremble, the earth quakes.
> YHWH is great in Zion,
> and exalted above all peoples. (99:1–2)

> YHWH sat enthroned at the Flood;
> YHWH sits enthroned, king forever. (29:10)

This is the ritual foreground of what we might call the Bible's Zion ideology. The king derives his majesty and power through his participation in two parallel hierarchies, one celestial and the other terrestrial. Through the enthronement rituals the people unite around their collective representations of a shared myth. Their union is intensified by the fusion of ritual elements—song, dance, procession, mythological imagery, dramatic speech, and prayer, which involve the people at many levels of participation and spectatorship. Focusing on the relationship between power and pomp, we can choose to see this ritual as hierarchical domination by a monarchical and priestly elite, imposing Yahwism on a populace that is taken in by spectacle. In this vein, we can argue that Yahwism was not the accepted religion of all in biblical Israel. The prophets railed against the people for worshiping "on lofty mountains and on hills or under any luxuriant tree" (Deut. 12:2), where they made offerings to the heathen pantheon, including the Queen of Heaven (Jer. 44:17). We recall the battle atop Mt. Carmel between Elijah and the priests of Baal, the Canaanite version of the divine warrior, each fighting for the allegiance of the people to their g/God (I Kings 18).

Yet, there is more going on than the domination of an unwitting populace in a ritual such as the one we have envisioned. Ceremonies of power do indeed reinforce hierarchy, but the unrestrained enthusiasm and liminal energy that such rituals unleash also create community. Hierarchy cannot continue to exist without negotiated submission or consent.[16] Ceremonies centered on the monarch that stress the legitimacy of the king and the stability of the state (and world) are deeply consensual. If there is conflict between the people and the king over the nature of his rule, the enthronement ceremony can be used, in the model of Turner's social drama, to seek redress. That could explain why in one psalm God's covenant with the Davidic kings is presented as both unconditionally given by God and conditionally dependent on the king's upholding God's decrees (Ps. 132:11–12). In the ritual process, the relationship between God and king is made analogous to that between a father and son. God's adoption of the king extends to the people as well, who know that they are the ultimate beneficiaries of that familial relationship. That is why at the end of one of the ritual psalms we have quoted, after enthroning God, the participants express their hopes for the collectivity of Israel: "May YHWH grant strength to His people; / may YHWH bestow on His people well-being" (29:11).

A sense of well-being flows from the conviction that the God who tamed the seas to establish the firm foundation of the earth is the same one who dwells in Zion. God's cosmic power has been and can continue to be harnessed on behalf of Israel. "May YHWH / maker of heaven and earth / bless you from Zion" (134:3). The explicit connection that this verse draws between creation and Zion brings us squarely to P and the congruence of the priestly and the Zion ideologies. For it is P's account that begins the Bible with the story of creation in six days, climaxing in the seventh-day Sabbath, when "God finished the work" (Gen. 2:2). And it is also P's account that describes Moses' building of the Tabernacle in six actions, each marked off by the phrase "as YHWH had commanded Moses,"[17] followed by the clear echo of the divine cessation from labor in Genesis: "When Moses had finished the work" (Exod. 40:33). The priestly writers could hardly have been more explicit in suggesting that the institution of cultic worship in Israel is a second act of creation, parallel to the first, and in a crucial way completing it.[18] God commands the Israelite people to build a sanctuary so that God might "dwell among them" (Exod. 25:8). We witness God's coming to dwell among the people at the completion of the Tabernacle-building passage: "When Moses had finished the work, the cloud covered the Tent of Meeting and the Presence of YHWH filled the Tabernacle" (Exod. 40: 33–34). Henceforth, priestly worship would mediate between the divine presence and the people.

The institution of the Sabbath plays a central role in this mediating process. The injunction to celebrate it occurs in two different versions: in one, it is a memorial to the exodus from Egypt; in the other, the priestly account, it is a weekly reenactment of God's divine rest from the work of creation.[19] The Israelite Sabbath can thus be seen as a cosmogony. Instead of limiting the re-creation of the cosmic acts of God to an annual festival, with their inevitable mythological trappings, the Israelite priests make it a weekly observance, a human-centered *imitatio dei*. And instead of focusing on action, in which we cannot possibly compete with the heroics of God, the Sabbath focuses human beings on the satisfaction of inaction after action, a far easier model of divinity to imitate. The account of creation without opposition in Genesis 1–2:3, it has recently been argued, deliberately suppresses the mythological traditions of creation by the divine warrior, in which evil has a primordial reality that antedates creation.[20] In the priestly account that begins the Bible, creation responds to a void, not to the presence of evil. The endpoints of God's creative processes are not the defeat of evil beings, who may again threaten revolt and may therefore again need to be subjugated. Instead, the priestly writers offer us the optimistic vision of human beings filling the earth and mastering it.

The divine warrior myth that we have examined in Psalms is but one of several images of creation found in the collection. The psalm that ultimately received the ritual superscription "for the Sabbath day" describes the defeat of God's foes as an inevitable, nonmythological, and totally natural occurrence: "Though the wicked bloom, they are like grass; / though all evildoers blossom, it is only that they may be destroyed forever" (92:8). The psalm concludes with a vision of humanity at its best:

> The righteous bloom like a date-palm;
> they thrive like a cedar in Lebanon;
> planted in the house of YHWH,
> they flourish in the courts of our God.
> In old age they still produce fruit;
> they are full of sap and freshness,
> attesting that YHWH is upright,
> my rock, in whom there is no wrong. (92:13–16)

Not surprisingly, the righteous flourish best when "planted in the house of YHWH." Cultic service, for both priests and psalmists, is the fulfillment of human purpose on earth. That is why a number of psalmists express longings "to live in the house of YHWH / all the days of my life" (Ps. 27:4).[21] "It is the cult that builds and maintains order, transforms chaos into creation, ennobles humanity, and realizes the kingship of the God who has ordained the cult and commanded that it be guarded and practiced. It is through obedience to the directives of the divine master that his good world comes into existence."[22]

Within the world of the cult, the sacred precincts hold pride of place, in both the priestly writings of the Pentateuch and the Psalms. The priestly Tabernacle of Exodus 25–30 is a smaller version of the Jerusalem Temple described in I Kings 5–7 (Figure 1). It has the same articles of furniture, the same configuration of altars—one for burnt offerings in the outer court, one for incense within. The east-west axis of each structure led the worshiper through contiguous courtyards, each framed by a threshold and doorway, each leading to a higher stage of holiness. Holiness was considered by ancient Israel, as by many hierarchical cultures, to be contagious. There were taboos of touch, sight, and access, preventing laypeople from penetrating too far into the sacred precincts, lest the Temple itself, God's dwelling on earth, become tainted with impurity, also considered a contagious force. These taboos concentrated sacred service in the hands of the priests who, after they were anointed with oil, shared in the contagion of holiness.[23] The innermost sanctum was a place of deep darkness, where God's awesome presence could be experienced without any earthly distractions. There, the ark, with its tablets of the Law, rested under the spread wings of angelic beings (*kerubim*), a representation of the heavenly throne. It was penetrable only by the High Priest and only on the holiest day of the year, the Day of Atonement.

This spatial and calendrical structure implies a metaphysic, which we can interpret using Van Gennep's concept of liminality: separation, transition,

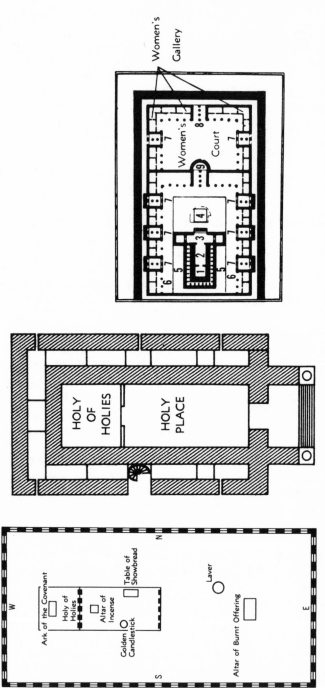

Figure 1. *From left to right:* (a) Plan of the Tabernacle and its courts. Courtesy of the American Schools of Oriental Research. (b) Ground plan and reconstruction of Solomon's temple. From Corswant, *Dictionnaire d'Archéologie biblique* (Neuchâtel: Delachaux and Niestlé, 1956). (c) Ground plan of Herod's temple and courts: (1) holy of holies; (2) holy place; (3) porch; (4) altar of burnt offering; (5) court of priests; (6) court of Israel (men's court); (7) sanctuary gates; (8) Nicanor gate(?) or Gate Beautiful; (9) Nicanor gate. Based on Vincent and Steve, *Jerusalem de l'Ancien Testament* (Paris: J. Gabalda and Cie.). From *The Interpreter's Dictionary of the Bible*, vol. 4, ed. G. A. Buttrick. Copyright renewal 1990 by Abingdon Press. Used with permission.

and reincorporation.[24] The Tabernacle or Temple was a bridge between two worlds, one of ordinary experience and one of transcendent experience. A contemporary scholar has suggested that "the Temple is not a place in this world, but the world in essence, . . . the theology of creation rendered in architecture and glyptic craftsmanship."[25] We can juxtapose this view to a comment by a Jew from the Greek diaspora who observed the Temple service in the first century b.c.e.: "The total effect of the whole arouses awe and emotional excitement, so that one would think he had passed to some other sphere outside the world."[26] I would like to offer the mediating suggestion that the highly symbolic, ritual space of the Temple belongs neither to the visible nor to the invisible world completely, but that with respect to the two it is a liminal zone, partaking of the reality of each. Worshipers entered it from the profane world seeking a channel of communication with the transcendent. The Temple can therefore best be seen as the threshold or margin where these two worlds of consciousness come into contact (Figure 2).

Ritual activity takes place in this liminal zone. Liminality can be understood both temporally and spatially.[27] The times at which worshipers came were set apart from the ordinary times of their lives: Sabbaths and festivals as commanded by God, or at moments of special need or celebration, which they chose to mark through sacrifice and prayer. We know from the Pentateuch that the priests made substantial preparations before entering this sacred zone, including ritual washing.[28] Coming into the precincts of the first Jerusalem Temple from profane time and space, the worshipers also had the opportunity to mark a separation from their daily world by washing in a great bronze laver. Other lavers were available to the priests before they did their sacrificial work.[29] Sacrifice is the climax of all this preparation. It was without doubt a satisfying dramatic spectacle in its own right, providing a sensory focus for participants and spectators. This irreversible act is a pure transformational moment: an animal is separated from its life, and turned into smoke that ascends toward the other world, presumably as an intercessor before God.[30] Likewise, an individual's status before God can be transformed by the act of sacrifice. A transition can be effected from impure to pure, from sin to forgiveness.[31] We shall have much more to say below about the meaning of the sacrificial act. Here, we note that the transition from profane to holy that sacrifice effected was doubtless intensified by the symbolic furnishings and iconography—the seven-branched golden candelabrum, the showbreads placed on gold-covered tables, the brilliant colors and ornate decoration. All these made the Tabernacle or Temple a place set apart as itself an object of contemplation and wonder.[32]

Though the Tabernacle is presented in the Pentateuch as a complement to God's creative work, it did not gain that stature without consider-

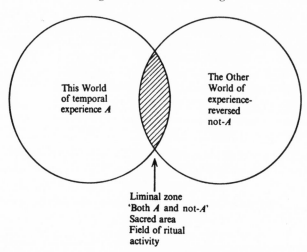

Figure 2. From Edmund Leach, *Culture and Communication: The Logic by Which Symbols Are Connected* (Cambridge: Cambridge University Press, 1976). Reprinted with the permission of Cambridge University Press.

able cost. Before the Tabernacle gets built and begins to serve the religious needs of the people, narratives several times interrupt the priestly description. Each narrative shows how difficult it is to fulfill God's intentions, and how much the people need the mediation of legitimate priests. While Moses atop Mount Sinai hears all God's instructions about building and furnishing the Tabernacle, anointing the priests, and preparing the animal and incense offerings, below in the camp the children of Israel have set God aside to worship a golden calf. As readers of Exodus, we experience the abrupt shift from prescriptive rituals for an ideal order (Exod. 25–31) to narrative rupture of the very order the rituals are designed to achieve (Exod. 32–33). This sense of rupture is concretized by Moses' two acts of destruction: first the tablets, and then the golden calf. After the offenders have been purged, the description of the ritual order resumes. The Tabernacle is built according to plan (Exod. 35–39), and then dedicated in the scene we have already mentioned, when Moses anoints all its parts with oil. After completing his work, Moses moves out and God literally moves in, in the image of a cloud, which henceforth will abide above the Tabernacle (Exod. 40). Underneath this celestial sign, Israel will be able to approach the invisible God. The editors of the Pentateuch chose to follow this narrative with instructions about the people's sacrifices (Lev. 1–7), indicating how the ideal cultic order is to be maintained, but this ritual order is again interrupted by a narrative, the investiture of Aaron and his four sons (Lev. 8–9), culminating yet again in human tragedy, the deaths of two of them (Lev. 10). Like the golden calf narrative before it, this one also shows the tension between the orderly worship that God and the priestly writers desire, and a spontaneous religious outburst. Once more, the text continues with description of rules, this time regarding categories of purity and impurity (Lev. 11–15). These are followed one last time by a piece of narrative. After the death of Aaron's two sons, God instructed the survivors how to prevent the recurrence of such a tragedy. This narrative focus quickly turns, as we have come to expect, into another piece of ritual description: how to celebrate the Day of Atonement and clear the people of its sins (Lev. 16). The priestly writers' primary interest is not in narrative but in ritual.[33] With a securely established ritual system in place, the people can rely on the priests and the Tabernacle to mediate their experience of the liminal zone, with all its attendant dangers.

The cult, then, helps to organize life, minimize its chaos, and tame its dangers. To see how it does so, I would like to look briefly at some details from its rituals of investiture and purgation. Aaron and his sons are installed as the only priestly line entrusted to perform sacrifices for the people. In this initiatory ritual, they are separated from the rest of the camp for seven days. They enter a state of ritual liminality by washing and putting on special garments. They offer special sacrifices of ordination, and then are daubed with blood and oil on their extremities: right ear, right thumb, and right toe. Oil and blood are the life juices of the vegetable and animal realms, living matter reduced to its essential state. At this moment of transition to their new status as the people's ministers before God, they are offered a ritual prophylactic of sacrificial blood and oil. Henceforth they will be protected from the unknown dangers of the liminal zone by the force that creates and sustains life. Their anointing on the right side may signify a desire to strengthen their connection to life-giving sacred power and to protect them from whatever lies in wait on the left side of their bodies, which, universally in traditional societies, symbolizes the profane, demonic, or shadow side of consciousness, often connected to death.[34]

These dangers are immediately dramatized on the eighth day, when Aaron offers the first sacrifice on behalf of the people. First, a fire not lit by human beings "came forth from before the Lord and consumed the burnt offering and the fat parts on the altar. And all the people saw, and shouted, and fell on their faces" (Lev. 9:24). Next, in a parallel but inverted event, two of Aaron's sons, Nadab and Abihu, bring forward their fire pans and offer "alien fire," which God has not commanded. "And fire came forth from the Lord and consumed them" (10:2). Both of these fiery events are also theophanies, revelations of God's presence and awesome power over life and death. Here, the dark side of consciousness is represented in divinity itself.

One anthropologist has suggested that Aaron's two sons are analogous to the carcass of the animal in an ascent offering. They are the part of Aaron that must die, in order for him to become the people's offering to God, the one who opens the channel to the transcendent.[35] The names of the two sons signify their close relation to Aaron; *nadab* is a "gift," or "offering," and *'abi hw'* means "he is my father." They are their father's gift to God, an offering of his first fruits. Their places are taken by two other sons, Eleazar, "God-helper," and Ithamar, "island of palms," a name which reflects the iconic decorations of the First Temple.[36] As this second pair of names suggests, the two surviving sons will become dutiful servants in the Tabernacle. Their succession represents what Max Weber described as the rationalization of charisma, an inevitable consequence of the development of a priesthood.[37]

Aaron's response to God's terrible decree is silence, like Job's after the revelation to him from the whirlwind. Divinity has terrors aplenty for humanity, and so must be approached with circumspection and the utmost care. That is why the narrative continues, "Tell your brother Aaron that he is not to come at will into the Shrine behind the curtain . . . lest he die" (Lev. 16:2). Aaron can penetrate to where his sons had attempted to go only on behalf of the whole people, and then only once a year. He is told not to appear in his regular high priestly attire of golden vestments, but instead all in white linen. He must secure forgiveness for his own sins and his household's and for those of the people. For the priestly sins, a bull is designated, its size indicating the status of the offerer. For the people's sins, two goats are needed, instead of two God-intoxicated sons. One, chosen by lot, is to be offered to YHWH; the other, to be sent off to the wilderness, is for Azazel, which may denote the wilderness itself or the name of a goat-demon believed to be reigning there.[38]

A diagram can help explain these ritual prescriptions in Leviticus 16 (Figure 3). The further into the sanctuary blood is carried, the graver the sin, and the greater the need for expiation. Before risking the danger of these incursions into the innermost space of the Shrine, Aaron is to protect himself by creating a cloud of incense. After that the expiation and purgation can begin. The blood from the bull is sprinkled on the curtain and in front of it. The blood from the goat for YHWH is sprinkled *behind* the curtain, the only time during the year that blood is brought into the Holy of Holies. This blood serves as a ritual detergent that purges the entire sanctuary of the people's accumulated guilt (Lev. 16:16). As he backs out of the Shrine, he is to continue sprinkling blood on the outer

DIAGRAM OF SANCTUARY CONTAMINATION

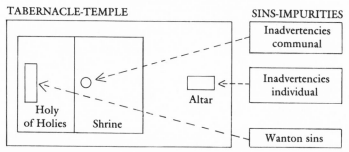

Figure 3. From Jacob Milgrom, *The JPS Torah Commentary: Numbers* (Philadelphia: Jewish Publication Society, 1990). Used by permission.

altar, decontaminating it as well. After this expiation is completed, the second goat, the one for Azazel, is loaded up with the sins of the people by way of Aaron's laying his hand on its head and confessing the people's sins. This goat is then led through the people's midst and set free in the wilderness, though the testimony of the Mishnah indicates that it died from plunging off a precipice.[39] With the people's sins effectively swallowed up by the wilderness, the priest is once again to don his golden vestments. This indicates, according to one interpreter, that while effecting the purgation, Aaron is identified with the profane realm, but once it is complete, he reenters the realm of the holy.[40] He sacrifices the animals as burnt offerings to God, secure in the knowledge that his actions have restored the preexisting equilibrium in the cultic order, which is itself, as we said earlier, a second creation, reminiscent of the ideal order of the universe.

We can understand this ritual in terms of a metaphysical opposition between the world of the Tabernacle, where God dwells, and the uninhabitable wilderness, where only beasts dwell. In between is the camp, a neutral space, which can be made holy by the people's ethical actions and worship of God, or be profaned by their immoral and ritually polluting actions. Under these conditions, the camp loses its holiness and begins to partake of the bestial, uncivilized qualities of the wilderness. We can see this relationship between holy and profane expressed graphically in Figure 4, where ritual is the mediating term. Individuals who impair their own holiness can rid themselves of guilt and pollution by repenting or undergoing ritual purification, and then making an appropriate offering for guilt (ʾašam), or purification (ḥaṭṭat) at the sanctuary.[41] But since not all were likely to do so, and since there were grievous sins, such as adultery and murder, for which there was no ritual redress, a surplus of guilt and

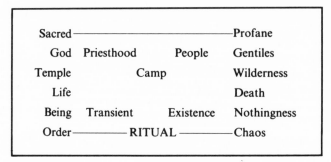

Figure 4. From Douglas Davies, "An Interpretation of Sacrifice in Leviticus," reprinted from *Anthropological Approaches to the Old Testament,* ed. Bernhard Lang, copyright 1985 Fortress Press and SPCK. Used by permission of Augsburg Fortress.

pollution inevitably accumulated in the people's midst. This accumulation was especially dangerous to the sanctuary, presumably because it was thought that God could not be allowed to come into contact with it. If the sanctuary was to continue functioning as ancient Israel's Center for Pollution Control, if it was not to be buried, as it were, under a mountain of sin, then it too had to be purified periodically. The annual Day of Atonement, with its singular aura of great sanctity, provided this outlet. The Day of Atonement enabled the priests to restore the boundaries of holy and profane and to reorder social relations with respect to these ideal categories.[42] Without this equilibrating mechanism, the priests could not continue functioning throughout the year.

Three rituals—the dedication of the sanctuary, the consecration of its priests, and its annual purification—form the narrative and symbolic core of the last chapters of Exodus and all of Leviticus. As we read these rituals as part of an unfolding narrative, we cannot help but realize that the Tabernacle is not just an elaborate setting but, more crucially, a religious ideal. The life of the people unfolds around the *axis mundi* that the Tabernacle defines, a vertical line from earth to heaven that makes it the center of the world, and its priestly custodians the central earthly actors in a cosmic drama of sin and redemption.

Sacrifice and Song

In that drama, there is no act more central than sacrifice. Since the practice of sacrifice is so foreign to our own cultural experience, a good deal needs to be said before we can fully appreciate the central role it played in the religious experience of the biblical world. Different sides of the subject are captured by the English and Hebrew words. Sacrifice, deriving from the Latin words meaning "to make sacred," captures the sense of transformation. Earlier, I spoke of ritual differentiating itself from other forms of action. This is especially true of sacrificial ritual. Something that begins in one category, as ordinary foodstuffs, from animals, grain, or wine, is transformed by an action following special rules in a special place at a special time before or by special people into another category altogether, a holy offering to God. In idiomatic English, to sacrifice is to do without something, often to endure privation for the sake of someone else. In this sense, too, we are transforming something that could have been used in one way by using it in another. The Hebrew *qorban* (pl. *qorbanot*), from the root "to draw near," captures the point of view of the worshiper (as distinct from the priest who offers up the animal to God). He or she begins at a remove, and through performing this ritual action draws near to God, just as he or she draws near by walking through the Temple toward the Holy of Holies.

Why should sacrifice, particularly animal sacrifice, serve this mediating role of establishing communication between the profane and sacred worlds? I find the following classic explanation helpful: The sacrificer has need of being connected to the power that rules over life and death, yet this power is fearful and dangerous to the ordinary person, particularly as it is concentrated in the sacred. The sacrificer cannot approach this power without interposing an intermediary. If he offered himself as the intermediary, he might find "death, not life. The victim takes his place. It alone penetrates into the perilous domain of sacrifice; it dies there, and indeed it is there in order to die. The sacrificer remains protected: the gods take the victim instead of him. *The victim redeems him.* . . . The sacrificer gives up something of himself but he does not give himself. Prudently, he sets himself aside. This is because if he gives, it is partly in order to receive."[43]

This description emphasizes how sacrifice works for the individual, but it also needs to be viewed as part of a whole social system. In ancient Israel, the basic daily sacrifice was performed by the priests on behalf of the whole people. So we need to ask, what are the large social gains of a sacrificial system? As individuals and the collectivity engage daily in acts of abnegation, they thereby reaffirm the importance of the collective forces that require such acts. A priestly elite, a monarchy, a capital city—all are sustained, not just economically but also ideologically, by the observance of the specified ritual. They come to seem the necessary and inevitable context for the all-important communication with the divine. As large numbers of individuals bring sacrifices to validate their vows, their oaths, their marriages, they invest these with the unquestionable authority that society has assigned to sanctity. Sacrifice also allows society to be flexible in readjusting social equilibriums that have been upset by crime or error. Having demonstrated their willingness to perform acts of self-abnegation and contribute their own goods to the general weal, the sacrificers are freed from social stigma and can return to their former status, knowing that this mode of redress is available to all in the society.[44]

Viewed in this dual light as a private and a social act, sacrifice can be seen as both a substitution for the self and a contribution of the self to the structuring principles of society. This tie between sanctity and the social order runs the obvious risk of idolatry, by which the organs of power are themselves turned into objects of sacred worship. In biblical tradition, as we shall see below, prophecy and psalmody self-consciously reorient the sacrificers, for whom social values have become predominant, to the transcendent values of God to which the sacrificial act is meant to connect them. The vertical axis implied in sacrifice thus provides a constant corrective against purely social valuations of its significance.[45]

Sacrifice is not tied just to the social world, but to the natural as well. It follows and reproduces the rhythms of human life and of nature. In ancient Israel, in addition to collective daily offerings, special sacrifices are designated for the Sabbath, connecting human beings to the rhythm of divine creation and rest, and for the new moon and agricultural holidays, connecting human beings to the movements of the moon and the produce of the earth.[46] The sacrificial system required offerings from each sphere of the natural world cultivated by humans: produce of the vine (wine), the tree (olive oil and first fruits), the ground (wheat and barley), in addition to the preeminent sacrifice, produce of livestock (sheep, goats, bulls). This close association of sacrifice with natural cycles and the ecosystem lends a kind of permanence to these culturally created conventions of society. They come to seem as natural as the cycles they celebrate. Perhaps even more important, though, sacrifices point in a seemingly opposite direction: to the provisionality of the food we need to live. Sacrifices are material gifts from those who have received them back to the One who gives. This obligation to return gifts to the giver is balanced by the expectation that other gifts will take the place of what has been given. Whether as gifts of the community or of an individual, sacrifices made in this spirit of exchange undercut the notion of private property.[47] A sacrifice-offering society will be continually aware that its own continuity and achievements depend on gifts received and gifts returned to God through the bounty of the earth.

The ancient Israelite would certainly not have articulated much, if anything, of what we have just said about the social (horizontal) meaning of sacrifice. In his or her mind, sacrifice was a vertical channel to propitiate God, who dwelt in the heavens and ruled the world. For the worshiper, that channeling began when he or she selected an animal without blemish (Lev. 1:3). Before approaching the holy site, the worshiper must consider, then, a binary opposition, blemished/unblemished, and its symbolic implications for his or her own moral condition. Before turning the animal over to the priest to be slaughtered, the worshiper is to lay a hand upon its head, "that it may be acceptable in his behalf, in expiation for him" (Lev. 1:4). This rule demands that, by means of a ritual gesture, the worshiper become symbolically identified with the animal being offered. At the simplest level, the gesture signifies ownership; i.e., this animal is my offering, not that of the person standing near me. Understood magically, it is a transference of essence from the human to the animal, as in the exorcism rites of the Day of Atonement, when the High Priest puts the sins of the people on the head of one of the goats (Lev. 16:21). Understood morally, it signifies the worshiper's understanding that the animal is being killed instead of him or her. Because of specific human failings, the worshiper's life ought to be forfeit to God, but instead he or she is offering up to God an unblemished, perfect specimen, rendering God's best gifts back to God, hoping that the all-sufficient God will forgive the failings of the worshiper. At an existential level, animal sacrifices remind the one who brings them of the shared mortality of animals and human beings. In offering them, individuals submit to their creaturely fate and humbly accept their vulnerability before God. The overlapping of all these meanings makes the sacrificed animal a potent, multivalent symbol.[48] Its creatureliness links it with the human being, while its unblemished perfection links it with the divine. The animal is not the only mediating term in the sacrificial equation. By bringing animals to the priests at a specially designated ritual site, worshipers accept their place in a human hierarchy, in which these ritual specialists and the place they govern serve a necessary mediating role. In handing the animals over to others to be slaughtered, the worshipers may be expressing their ambivalence about taking the lives of the creatures that they have so carefully tended.[49] So they offer them to God, who, after all, is their creator too. The priests thus make possible a multileveled symbolic communication, by means of the sacrificed animal, between the human and divine realms.

The daily sacrifice of yearling lambs was an *'olah*, usually translated as "burnt offering," but more appropriately "ascent offering." In this sacrifice, the animal is turned wholly "into smoke upon the altar"; its materiality is thus transformed into something which can ascend and become a "pleasing odor to YHWH" (Lev. 1:9). At the moment of death, no longer a body, the *qorban* becomes a means of spiritual communication, symbolizing that which seeks to be in contact with the transcendent realm. Its odor is pleasing, not because God likes barbecue, but presumably because

God appreciates the human desire to draw near. When grain was offered by those who could not afford to bring animals, it was combined with frankincense, so that it too could be turned into visible smoke upon the altar as "a pleasing odor to YHWH" (Lev. 2:2). The column of smoke continually ascending from sacrifices is the human counterpart to the divine pillar of cloud by day and of fire by night that hovered over the Tabernacle in the wilderness (Exod. 40:38), a visible sign of human communication with the divine. That a high value was placed upon these smoke signals, we can tell from the arrangement of altars in the Tabernacle and Temple. On the copper outer altar, animals, wine, grain, oil, and incense were sacrificed, but on the golden inner altar, nearer to the Holy of Holies, only incense was offered. The closer the altar to the barely approachable, transcendent realm, the purer its covering, and the more immaterial the substance offered on it. Only on the Day of Atonement was animal blood, the decontaminant of the outer altar, allowed to penetrate the inner sanctum. And on that day the cloud from the incense screened the High Priest from even visual contact with the ark, "lest he die" (Lev. 16:13). For at least one psalmist, incense was as efficacious as animal sacrifice: "Take my prayer as an offering of incense, / my upraised hands as an evening sacrifice" (Ps. 141:2). He may be able to offer prayer only as his personal gift, but he means it to ascend directly to God, as much as incense, or the smoke from a yearling lamb.

As this psalmist makes perfectly clear, two analogous channels of communication with the divine, sacrifice and prayer, were readily available to the ancient Israelite. Though prayer could be offered to God anywhere and at any time, as many biblical narratives attest, it too had its ritual specialists, as much as sacrifice did. Stories are told of Israelites coming to the prophets Elisha and Jeremiah to seek their intercession with God.[50] The prophet was the man of God, communicating the word of the people to God as well as the word of God to the people. Both the evidence of Psalms and a range of historical references to prophecy in the Temple suggest that cultic prophets, whose names are not preserved, may have specialized in this dual role.[51] Temple singers must have been considered among these cultic prophets, since it is recorded that they "prophesied to the accompaniment of lyres, harps, and cymbals" (I Chron. 25:1). Sometimes without music, they delivered God's oracles when "the spirit of YHWH came upon" them (2 Chron. 8:14). The Book of Chronicles proposes a firm division, supposedly rooted in David's time, between two groups from the tribe of Levi, priestly Levites (*kohanim*), who performed sacrificial service for the people, and nonpriestly Levites (*lewiim*), who prayed and sang on their behalf, but most scholars regard this strict division as describing the state of religious affairs several centuries after the exile. Earlier biblical information about the priests suggests that they had a wide range of responsibilities.[52] They are said to have maintained the instruments of divination, the *'urim, tummim,* and *epod,*[53] offered instruction concerning sacred and profane, clean and unclean, ritual and civil law;[54] and played a central role in judgment.[55] The nonpriestly Levites, lacking either landholdings or the support to be gained from sacrificial service, may have come to the Temple to serve in a variety of inferior capacities: as officers, magistrates, gatekeepers, and musicians.[56] It has also been suggested that the lower-status Levites of the Second Temple period may have descended from ancient priestly families, now reduced to subordinate positions.[57]

Most of our information about Jewish worship in the Second Temple comes from the Mishnah, which describes the Levites standing on fifteen semicircular steps between the Hall of the Israelites and the Hall of Women. There they played their instruments and sang psalms to lead the people's worship.[58] In this sense, the Levites occupy a liminal position between the priests and the people, stationed at the threshold of the sacred zone and mediating the people's experience of divine service. Not only are the Psalms liminal in the literal sense, as songs sung to God on the threshold of God's inner sanctum, but the experiences with which many of them deal—whether recovery from sickness, overcoming of guilt and shame through confession, the need for deliverance from an individual or national enemy—can be understood as metaphorically liminal, placing their speakers between two conditions, one that they hope is past and one that they hope will last to the end of their days. Helping the Israelites to negotiate these profound transitions, the psalmists functioned as do contemporary psychotherapists, literally, healers of souls.

Religious poetry, like other media of symbolic communication, is fueled by two basic emotions: gratitude for what we have and longing for what we lack. The more we are buffeted by life, the greater our need to feel secure. Looking for safe passage, we approach God with petitions for help. Or, having been saved from some peril, we express to God our gratitude for the renewed gift of life. Articulating these emotions through the formal medium and conventions of poetry turns a private emotional expression into a symbolic action, which can be repeated by future speakers who find themselves in a similar plight. Moreover, if one relies on a ritual specialist to create poetry in accord with one's feelings, then it is likely that the expression will have the shape of a ritual. When we look at psalms in which individuals overcome alienation, receive promises of future protection, and praise the saving powers of God or laud the community of believers, we need to keep in mind the emotional trajectory made possible by the concrete ritual processes of the society.

In ancient Israel, psalmody provided the artistic medium through which Israel's poet-singers gave shape to the people's feelings when they appeared before God at festival times or at times of special celebration or need. Psalms thus embody the underlying structure of ritual: separation, liminality, and reincorporation. Not all psalms dramatize the full range of the ritual process. Psalms of thanksgiving tend to focus on the feelings of being reincorporated into the community, though often they recall the emotions of earlier stages, when the individual was in need of rescue. This pattern holds true for communal thanksgivings as well, which remember both the peril of battle and the triumphant deliverance at God's hand. In petitions, the speaker generally feels separate from those who are experiencing well-being and longs to be reincorporated in fellowship with them. Such psalms tend to emphasize the experience of being on a threshold between life and death, sickness and health, sinfulness and repentance, vulnerability and triumph. Being on the actual threshold of God's house or inside it at one of the several gateways, or even remembering this experience when absent from it, offered worshipers the opportunity to explore their own emotional thresholds.

Having spoken of both sacrifice and song as the domains of separate ritual specialists, we should remember, of course, as Psalm 141 indicates, that their activities were intimately interrelated. We can think of the priests and psalmists as orchestrating two complementary but radically different modes of ritual performance, one silent and conducted by an elite in the inner area of the Temple, the other articulate and inviting the participation of the populace massed in the outer courts. A contemporary in Second Temple times describes the sacrificial service: "Complete silence prevails, so that one might suppose that not a person was present in the place, though those performing the service amount to some seven hundred, besides the great multitude of persons bringing sacrifices to be offered—but everything is done with reverence and in a manner worthy of the great divinity."[59] Much psalm-singing, by contrast, was performed in an atmosphere of freedom and revelry. The tension built up by prolonged solemnity gave way, especially at the pilgrimage festivals, to ecstatic release and festive celebration. These revelries, as described in the Psalms and in other biblical passages, included playing flutes, drums, lyres, trumpets, and cymbals, as well as dance, processions around the altar, and sacred meals.[60] The music, chants, song, and dance that accompanied psalms served, then, both as entrances to the ritual process in the liminal zone and as exits from it.

Was each considered an equally effective means of communicating with God? As performative actions, sacrifices were certainly stronger than psalms. The British philosopher of language J. L. Austin distinguishes between two kinds of performative statements: those that seek to effect an action (illocutionary) and those that actually cause the desired action to take place (perlocutionary). In this light, psalms can be regarded as illocutionary, sacrifices as perlocutionary.[61] Sacrifices have an immediate effect, it seems, because the priestly worldview made an apparent analogy between the blood of the animal, its living essence, and the blood of the individual that ought to be forfeit to God. Used ritually, the animal's blood effects expiation and purification for the living beings who offer it (cf. Lev. 17:11). By a process of transference, it also carries away (sinful) impurities from the altar and the Shrine.[62] As we saw in our analysis of the Day of Atonement rites, expiatory and purificatory sacrifices, when accompanied by appropriate confession, had the immediate power to realign the created cultic order and restructure the realm of holiness.[63] Psalms had no such immediate expiatory or purgative effect. They are full of requests and entreaties, but the efficacy of these is not immediate; one has to wait for God to respond by acting. In other ways, sacrifice and prayer are parallel. The sacrificial fat burning upon the altar created "a pleasing odor before YHWH" (Lev. 1:9); in Psalms, it falls to the psalmist's prayers and upraised hands to be like "an offering of incense . . . an evening sacrifice" (141:2) in gaining acceptance before YHWH.

The performative power of the sacrificial act, which can be regarded as making it simply mechanical,[64] also points to its centrality in Israelite worship. If the priests forbade words at the moment of sacrifice, it was to enhance the people's sense of its power. I would like to suggest, though, that the very silence in which sacrifice seems to have been performed points to the importance of the Psalms in the religious life of the people. Even when making silent gestures, such as lifting the hands in Psalm 134,[65] the worshipers narrate those gestures to their invisible auditor. The Israelite God is considered invisible, but not deaf. Though the silence of the sacrificial rites must have been awe-inspiring, it left too much of religious life in the hands of a small elite. Though the people may have carried their sacrifices to the priests, they brought their feelings to the cultic prophets or nonpriestly Levites. Through their poetry and music, the people found a necessary and powerful means to express their motives in bringing sacrifices to God in the first place. This is evident in the apocryphal work that describes how sacrifices were followed by trumpet calls and joyous bursts of song from the Levites and prayer on the part of the people.[66] Psalms supply the explicit emotional links to ritual action that are only hinted at, if at all, in the other biblical sources. The Psalms can thus be seen as ritual utterance parallel to the ritual offerings detailed in Leviticus and Numbers, both of them symbolically concretizing for the worshipers their status as vulnerable creatures dependent on God's grace.

The relationship between sacrifice and psalmody can be further explained by analogy to two figures of speech, metonymy and metaphor. The Czech linguist Roman Jakobson has suggested that all linguistic signs involve two axes or modes of arrangement. One he calls *combination, contexture,* or *contiguity,* the other *selection, substitution,* or *similarity.*[67] Jakobson came to associate these, respectively, with metonymy and metaphor.[68] Figures of speech are a basic mode of symbolic thinking. As we build up a picture of a whole out of its various constituent parts (metonymy), or see one thing in terms of another (metaphor), we enlarge our frame for understanding reality. Ritual, being both a symbolic and an efficacious process, translates these figurative mental resources into actions.[69]

Jakobson's typology helps to explain how actions and words complement one another in ritual performance. Metaphor and metonymy are both means of verbal transfer and are thus important in spells that have been transcribed by anthropologists. In Polynesian canoe magic, for instance, the Trobriand Islanders both imitate the building of a canoe, through technical activities, and pronounce magic spells upon it through verbal transfers. They enumerate the parts of the canoe and the human being who is to steer it, using the metonymic technique of building up a realistic picture of the whole from its contiguous parts. In such magical rites, the language can also be metaphoric, departing from the immediate context of physical action to invoke images and comparisons, refer to the past and the future, and relate events that cannot be reproduced in action. Both metaphors and metonyms are accompanied by concrete actions, so that the expressive qualities of language, the sensory qualities of objects, and the instrumental properties of actions can all work together to create the focusing, intensifying, and performative effects of ritual.[70]

We have suggested that in the ritual life of ancient Israel, sacrifice and song exist in a mutually reinforcing context of Temple celebration. In light of the preceding analysis, we should expect to see a synergy of metonymy and metaphor in Israel's worship too. The crucial element in sacrifice is the metonymic substitution of the victim for the sacrificer. Having been drawn from his flocks, it is associated with him by contiguity and context; at the site of sacrifice, its blood works efficaciously on his behalf. In those cases where a confession of guilt was required (Lev. 5:5), a further link was established between the sacrificer and the substitute victim. When an individual brings a voluntary burnt offering, the text specifies that its express purpose is "for acceptance in his behalf before YHWH" (Lev. 1:3). What is true for the individual must also be true for the whole people. Through its obligatory offering, the twice-daily ritual slaughter of yearling lambs (Exod. 29:38–42), the people seeks God's acceptance and special favor. The lamb fulfills this intercessory function presumably because it stands in as a metonymic symbol (i.e., substitute) for a sheep-herding people.

If this metonym works mutely in sacrifice, then it becomes articulated as metaphor in the sacred songs that grew up around the sacrificial service. Metaphors can be considered as strategic predications, means for an individual or group to confirm or change its current status. One anthropologist suggests that metaphors give rise to a syntax of ritual scenes that are designed to put them into effect, and thereby accomplish the goals of the individual or the group. These scenes include concrete metonyms, objects associated with the human beings in the ritual.[71] Thus, in a psalm headed "for the thanksgiving offering," we hear "Acknowledge that YHWH is God; / He made us and we are His, / His people, the flock he tends" (Ps. 100:3). Similarly, in Psalm 23, God is "my shepherd" (v. 1), drawing the speaker, as one of the flock, by "still waters" and along "paths of righteousness" (v. 3), which lead ultimately to the cultic setting of the "house of YHWH" (v. 6). It makes strategic sense to compare oneself to a sheep when eating one in a joyous celebration with family and Temple personnel. In such a situation, when God's "steadfast love" and "faithfulness" are suitably invoked (100:5), comparing oneself to a fattened member of a herd is reassuring, for the ritual presumes that as long as we continue to praise, God will surely continue to provide.

Such metaphoric predications accompany sacrifices of communion, which seek to obtain or maintain closer contact with God. There is another kind of sacrifice, however, undertaken when an individual or a group wants to achieve some degree of separation from the aspect of their deity that is perceived as punishing them.[72] In these very different ritual circumstances, there is no shared festive meal. The sacrifice is undoubtedly a simple ascent offering, meant to communicate a message to God,[73] which we find articulated in psalms of lament. In this context, we find pastoral metaphors of a markedly different character:

> You let them devour us like sheep;
> You disperse us among the nations.
> . . .
> It is for Your sake that we are slain all day long,
> that we are thought of as sheep to be slaughtered. (44:12, 23)

The first type of sheep metaphor underlies this second one. Israel perceives itself as God's flock, a perception no doubt reinforced by its daily practice of sacrificing lambs to God. It is one thing to send up the smoke of burning sheep flesh as a substitute for Israel. It is quite another to have to offer the living flesh of Israel. "They have left Your servants' corpses / as food for the fowl of heaven / and the flesh of Your faithful for the wild beasts" (79:2). The people and their poets need to reconcile this dire fate with Israel's vision of its protected status.[74] They have not abandoned God (44:18–21). Therefore, it must be precisely because they have been loyal to God that they are being murdered by God's enemies ("It is for Your sake that we are being slain," v. 23). The poet therefore goes on to petition the divine shepherd for revenge: "Rouse Yourself, why do You sleep, O my Lord? / Awaken, do not reject us forever" (44:24). A related psalm urges God to pay back their neighbors for the abuse they have flung at God. "Then we, Your people, / the flock You shepherd / shall glorify You forever" (79:13). In this line, we see a transition back to the idea of communion, with its accompanying metaphor of the protected flock.

Israel's sheep metaphor is, as we have seen, bivalent. It expresses a desire to separate from the killing power of God, embodied in Israel's enemies, and it likewise expresses the desire to draw near to the most cherished aspect of God, God's protecting love. It is a common notion in anthropology that the animals surrounding human life play a major role in any traditional culture's self-understanding. Animals are, according to Levi-Strauss, "foundational metaphors."[75] Elaborating that idea, a recent interpreter of the priestly worldview lays out a whole series of analogies between how Israel treats its human members and its domestic animals: the human being and the animal are prohibited from working on the seventh day; each is subject to the death penalty; each can be consecrated to God on the eighth day after birth; each can be disqualified from service to God by a physical blemish; the firstborn of each belongs to God.[76] Following this line of thought, I have tried to suggest that sacrifice is a dramatization of Israel's foundational metaphor. Both the metonym and the metaphor of animal sacrifice converge in the people's experience of itself as innocent lamb, dependent on God's protecting love, or utterly vulnerable to its seeming absence. In the act of sacrifice, the people align themselves with God's power over life and death. Though mute, the sacrificial act is saying, in effect, "We can be like you in killing this sheep, which stands in for us; do not be this kind of God to us."

My account presents sacrifices as effective means of communication, especially when accompanied by psalms that draw out the implications of the conventional act. Without such articulation, it was very possible for the message of sacrifice not to be absorbed by those offering it. Thus, in the Book of Proverbs, a striking point is made about the behavior of a married woman, dressed as a prostitute, who brazenly approaches a young man, lays hold of him, kisses him, and says: "I had to make a sacrifice of well-being; / Today I have fulfilled my vows / Therefore I have come out to you, / Seeking you and have found you" (7:14–15). So much for sacrifice as a means of aligning the worshiper with God! The story shows how easily our social and private selves can become distanced from one another in conventional performances such as ritual, the result being empty formalism and hypocrisy. Notwithstanding this powerful critique, it can be argued that the very idea of a perceptual gap between ritual and moral behavior is itself a function of ritual. Reciting a ritual prohibition against adultery, for instance, "may not prevent a man from committing adultery, but it does establish for him the prohibition of adultery as a rule that he himself has accepted as he enlivened it. Whether or not he abides by the rule he has obligated himself to do so. If he does not he has violated an obligation that *he himself* has avowed."[77] Rituals thus ask us openly to acknowledge our moral identities. If we have not lived up to the ideals articulated in the rituals we perform, then subsequent performance of those rituals will once again make us aware of the gap between our ritual and moral (or, more precisely, immoral) behavior.

We encounter this self-actualizing function of ritual in two psalms that explicitly ask the question, "YHWH, who may stay in Your tent, / who may reside in Your holy mountain?" (15:1; also 24:3). These psalms, which may have functioned as an entrance liturgy to the Temple, go on to enumerate the requirements in full:

> He who lives without blame,
> who does what is right,
> and in his heart acknowledges the truth;
> whose tongue is not given to evil;
> who has never done harm to his fellow,
> or borne reproach for [his acts toward] his neighbor;
> for whom a contemptible man is abhorrent,
> but who honors those who fear YHWH;
> who stands by his oath even to his hurt;
> who has never lent money at interest,
> or accepted a bribe against the innocent;
> the man who acts thus shall never be shaken. (15:2–5)

Those responsible for writing this psalm understood the potential for a gap between ritual propriety and moral impropriety, of the sort described in Proverbs 7. By making this list of virtuous actions itself a part of worship, the ritualizers seek to draw a firm link between the public performance of ritual actions and the private performance of ethical ones. The confessional litany of the psalm seeks to mediate between these two modes of action.[78]

Israel's prophets similarly sought to bring the people to a consciousness of their moral and immoral actions, but in the process they attacked ritual as an insufficient means of communicating with God:

> "What need have I of all your sacrifices?"
> Says the Lord.
> "I am sated with burnt offerings of rams,
> And suet of fatlings,
> And blood of bulls;
> And I have no delight
> In lambs and he-goats.
> That you come to appear before Me—
> Who asked that of you?
> Trample My courts no more;
> Bringing oblations is futile,
> Incense is offensive to Me.
> . . .
> And when you lift up your hands,
> I will turn my eyes away from you;
> Though you pray at length,
> I will not listen.
> Your hands are stained with crime—
> Wash yourselves clean;
> Put your evil doings
> Away from My sight.
> Cease to do evil;
> Learn to do good.
> Devote yourself to justice. . . . ." (Isa. 1:11–17)

God wants no part of ritual actions or utterances that are merely ceremonial. If worship is a matter only of acts and gestures, if it does not symbolize an inner state and a yearning for wholeness and purity, then it is as offensive as any other immoral action, since such worship uses sanctity in the service of a lie. Isaiah did not attack the priesthood and the monarchy that allowed this empty formalism to go forward, because, in his view, it was not the sponsoring institutions but rather every individual who had to validate his or her sacrificial worship through moral behavior. Holding up a mirror to their behavior, he asks each of them the same question implicit in Psalm 15: "Who are you who do these ritual things and what is your business in doing them?"[79] God's image of washing away sin, drawn from everyday life, but also from the ritual practice of the Temple, shows that even in a scathing prophetic critique of ritual, an opening is left for truly sincere ritual performance.

The opening of God's speech, as delivered by Isaiah, plays on the failure of the people to respond to the symbolism of sacrificial worship. If they want to regard the sacrifices literally, that is, as mere animal food for God, then God ironically lets them know that the divine appetite has been sated with burnt offerings, suet, and blood. If the people are so limited as to imagine a God who eats their sacrifices, as pagans might envision their gods' needs, then God urgently needs to let them know what sort of moral God they really have to acknowledge, and what sort of moral life they have to lead for God's sake. This is also the theme of Psalm 50, where the psalmist assumes the voice of God to tell the assembled worshipers that God is not hungry for their sacrifices: "For Mine is every animal of the forest, / the beasts on a thousand mountains / . . . Were I hungry, I would not tell you, / for Mine is the world and all it holds" (50:10, 12). Like the prophet, this psalmist (a cultic prophet?) rebukes the wicked for thinking they can continue their hypocritical recitation of God's laws while falsely assuming that God will not punish them for their deeds. It is obvious enough how they can reform themselves, but those who have a literalist view of sacrificial service need other guidance. To them, the psalmist suggests a link between sacrifice and prayer:

'Call upon Me in time of trouble;
I will rescue you, and you shall honor Me.' (V. 15)

Sacrifice a thank offering to God,
and pay your vows to the Most High. (V. 14)

He who sacrifices a thank offering honors Me,
and to him who improves his way
I will show the salvation of God. (V. 23)

The thank offering, or *todah* (the Hebrew word for both verbal and sacrificial thanks), recognizes God's saving acts in the world. It is the end of a process that often begins when a person in trouble calls upon God for help and pledges an offering if he or she survives.[80] Unlike the *'olah*, the ascent offering discussed above, the *todah* animal is not turned into smoke. Rather, only a token portion is burnt up; the rest is eaten by the worshiper and family and shared with the priests. By partaking of the celebratory thank-offering meal, they all serve as witnesses to God's saving act.[81] In this case, there is no chance that worshipers will make the literalist mistake of assuming that their offerings are God's food. God needs nothing from them beyond their thanks, and, having been saved, they need nothing more from God. Why, according to Psalm 50, does God want to be acknowledged by the *todah,* rather than by any other sacrifice? Precisely because this offering bespeaks the essence of the divine nature as it is encountered through prayer: we call upon God in times of trouble and God hears us and responds.[82]

Purity, Impurity, and Ritual Liminality

That religious ideal of a God who hears and responds to prayer was expressed in a cult that was obsessed with matters such as physical purity and impurity. We need to pay attention therefore to the reality of what constituted purity and impurity in ancient Israel if we are to appreciate the nature of the religious life that evolved there. If sacrifice is seen as the central act in the drama of the Temple, then the rules governing purity and impurity should be seen as defining the essential boundaries of that drama: who could and could not enter to participate in the sacred service of sacrificial worship. The Hebrew Bible will not allow us to make easy and comfortable separations between physical and spiritual life, of the sort that we are used to making in the West. It takes something such as the AIDS epidemic to remind us that our culture can also react to victims of disease as if they were suffering from a moral as well as a physical blight.[83]

The British anthropologist Mary Douglas has given us a framework for understanding why and to what extent different societies develop taboos around issues of impurity.[84] Purity rules emerge, Douglas argues, to protect the social structure where it feels itself endangered. Such rules defend a hierarchical society against challenges to its stability. They isolate a particular class, such as the Israelite priests, and help preserve their power and status. They ensure that marriages take place between parties who will foster the coherence of a specific class or tribe. They defend the social and personal body against unpredictable natural phenomena, which may be perceived as unnatural or demonic in origin. Purity rules defend divinity by protecting the sanctuary where a society's god is thought to dwell. In this connection, it is important to note that Douglas accepts the premise of Emil Durkheim that the theology a society creates is an image of how that society envisions itself.

Writing about ancient Israel, Douglas stresses how much that society felt itself to be at risk as a small monotheist nation in a sea of polytheist neighbors.[85] The great national sin throughout the Hebrew Bible is whoring after foreign gods, some of them brought in by the foreign wives of Judean and Israelite kings, some of them connected to pockets of indigenous peoples remaining in the land after the Israelite conquest. It is quite natural therefore that the sacred texts of the culture concern themselves with boundaries, not only political ones but also social and bodily ones that could be maintained by pollution rules. The priestly legislation of Leviticus sets forth purity rules with numerous applications of the basic dichotomy, pure or impure, clean or unclean. There are purity rules relating to housing, food, sex, marriage, childbirth, bodily emissions, skin diseases, and corpses.[86]

Because impurity was considered contagious, the person who became impure was barred from the central sanctuary until purity could be ritually restored. The priests adopted even more stringent purity rules for themselves to defend the sanctuary against any possibility of pollution.

Why this obsession with protecting the sanctuary? For one thing, a vulnerable sanctuary necessitated an ever-vigilant priesthood. But this sort of class-based explanation will not suffice. Something else more profound lies behind the priestly legislation, a sense of vulnerability not only about the sanctuary, but also about the whole experiment of being God's chosen people in a promised land: "You shall faithfully observe all My laws and My regulations, lest the land to which I bring you to settle in spew you out" (Lev. 20:22). The ten northern tribes were ejected from Samaria in 722 B.C.E., the two southern tribes from Judea in 586 C.E. Whether we take the view that P was composed during the reign of King Hezekiah (post–701 B.C.E.) or just preceding Ezra's return from the Babylonian exile (ca. 458 B.C.E.), it is clear that destruction and exile were very real to the biblical writers. Under these historic circumstances, at whichever date, it was natural that the priests focus their energy on preventing a recurrence of the catastrophe. It has been suggested that what had previously been purity rules just for the priests became more widely shared to encourage a higher standard of purity and holiness in the people as a whole.[87] The priest Ezra, the disseminator (and perhaps editor) of the Torah, found in Judea a tremendous amount of intermarriage, on the part of both those who had stayed and those who had earlier returned from exile with foreign wives. One of his most significant and dramatic acts was to mandate that all men with foreign wives divorce them and expel their children (Ezra 10:3–5). We cannot know the degree to which this plan was carried out, but its prominence in the narrative of Ezra indicates how very threatened was Israel's identity in the early postexilic period. If this was indeed the period in which the Torah took its final form, then it is little wonder that issues of maintaining a distinctive Israelite identity and theology should so thoroughly permeate the Torah traditions.

One of the striking features of priestly legislation in the Torah is the insistence that things belonging in different cognitive categories be kept separate. Just as God divided day from night, water from land, one kind of creature from another, so God's people were to maintain the separateness of all entities in their world, no less than their own national separateness.[88] Thus, Israelites were not to wear clothing made of blended linen and wool. They were neither to plow with an ox and an ass yoked together, nor to mate different kinds of animals together, nor to plant different grains in the same field. Men were to cohabit only with women, not with other men or animals.

According to Douglas, Israelite dietary laws, which separated clean from unclean, created ideal categories for land, air, and sea animals. All animals that did not fit into them were inedible. None of the animals Israelites were allowed to eat, whether from land, air, or sea, could be meat-eating. Furthermore, the edible land animals walked on all fours; edible sea animals swam with fins and tails. Thus, they were not to eat shellfish, which walked in the sea. They were not to eat or even to touch reptiles, which crawled on land, or amphibians, which could live on both land and water.[89] The body itself was the seat of purity or impurity; it too had to fit into established categories. Thus, if a person's skin was all of one color, that person was pure; but if it turned blotchy, the person was impure and was removed from the camp until it became all of one color again. Most important, life and death were to be kept separate. Living beings could be polluted by any physical contact with the dead, or even by a secondary association with death. Thus bodily fluids associated with procreation, menstrual blood and semen, once outside the body, were polluting, since they were evidence of a life that had not been created. The body's waste products, on the other hand, were not considered polluting, since they were not associated with death.[90] The holy was not to be marred through any contact with the profane. Thus, a physical blemish disqualified both a sacrificial animal and a priest from service in the Tabernacle.[91] Though the priestly code contains only regulations, not symbolic interpretations, analyzing them systemically allows us to see that the physical body was certainly regarded, as anthropologists have taught us, as a means of symbolizing the fundamental concerns of the society.

In biblical Hebrew, there is no distinction between ritual and moral pollution; the same word, *tame'*, "unclean" or "impure," applies to both.[92] For instance, an act of intercourse between a married couple renders them *tame'*, unclean, until evening, before they are permitted again to enter the sanctuary. A woman suspected by her husband of adultery is also called *tame'*, but in this case it is a grave accusation, not a description of a transient ritual state. The skin diseases that the Bible calls *sara'at* (usually translated as "leprosy," but probably meaning any scaly skin disease, such as psoriasis) are presented as rendering one *tame'*. One suffering from such a disease needs to be separated from the camp for seven days, until it can be judged whether the condition has been cured. We would likely regard this seven-day period as a quarantine to guard against the potential contagion of a physical illness, and it may well have been. But we can also infer from the story of Miriam, stricken by God with leprosy and excluded from the camp after challenging Moses' authority, that ancient Israelites interpreted the illness as divine punishment, as indeed the later rabbinic tradition did.[93]

The rituals surrounding both the separation and the return of the leper to the camp are given in rich detail. As a manual written by and for priests, Leviticus naturally elaborates on the ritual actions the priests are to perform, but it does not suggest what sorts of prayers a person in these circumstances might have offered. Analyzing one ritual process in some detail will anchor us in the material and symbolic reality of life as experienced by an ancient Israelite. Understanding the ritual intervention of the priest, we will be better able to envision what sort of intervention a sufferer might have sought from the Temple poet-singer as well.

After the priest diagnoses the scale disease and pronounces a person unclean, the individual's physical condition is marked symbolically. "His clothes shall be rent, his hair shall be left bare [or disheveled], and he shall cover over his upper lip; and he shall call out, 'Unclean, Unclean!' " (Lev. 13:45). The rending of the clothes and the uncovering or disheveling of the hair (cf. Lev. 10:6) are signs of mourning. The individual who is pronounced unclean and who must therefore leave the camp while diseased is essentially dead to his or her former self. As Aaron says on seeing Miriam's leprosy, "Let her not be as one dead, who emerges from his mother's womb with half his flesh eaten away" (Num. 12:12). The ritual's actions symbolize and enact this recognition of one's own symbolic death, as does exile to the wilderness outside the camp. In calling out "Unclean, Unclean!" ritual speech communicates this awareness to the community. Muffling the speech by covering the lips may well be a mark of shame.

We have already described the importance of symbolic boundaries in ancient Israel. The camp we have seen as the sphere of divinely created order and holiness, while the wilderness is the sphere of demonic disorder, chaos, and death. Since skin diseases obviously affect the most basic bodily boundary, it is wholly appropriate that the reentry rituals for the leper are especially cognizant of boundaries. The ritual of cleansing and restoring the leper to his former place we can understand as a rite of passage from the realm of death back to the realm of life.[94]

When visible signs of the leper's illness are gone, rituals of cleansing take place in two distinct stages: the first, outside the camp, and the second, in the camp on the eighth day after the purified one returns, but before he or she has returned to his or her own dwelling. To be cleansed, it is not enough for the leper to be cured of disease. The leper requires the ritual intervention of the priest, who orchestrates a vivid symbolic experience on behalf of that person. First the priest inspects the person's skin, and if it has healed, he orders the ingredients needed for the ritual: "two live clean birds, cedar wood, crimson stuff, and hyssop. . . ." The priest orders "one of the birds slaughtered over fresh water in an earthen vessel," and the bird's blood mixed with the other ingredients. The cedar wood and crimson stuff redden the fluid mixture; the hyssop provides a natural brush with which it can be sprinkled. The priest then dips the live bird in the reddened fluid and sets the bird free, as he sprinkles the rest of the mixture seven times on the one whom he is cleansing. After that the one to be cleansed washes his clothes, shaves off all hair on his head and face, then bathes in water. Only then is he considered clean, *tahor* (Lev. 14:2–9).

All of the symbols in this ritual require interpretation from the point of view of the one experiencing it. The reddened fluid is a kind of intensified blood. Sprinkled on the one to be cleansed, it functions metonymically to allow him or her to reexperience the discoloration of the scaly skin disease. Sprinkled on the live bird, it signifies either the remnants or the causes of the disease, which are to be borne away through metonymic transfer. Drawing on Turner's suggestion that ritual symbols condense and unify a number of often polarized meanings, one student of the ritual notes that the blood is appropriately a symbol of both life and death: A bird must be killed in order to acquire new life, but that killing paradoxically marks the restoration of life to the recovered leper.[95] As another ingredient to be mixed in the bowl, the water adds volume to the mixture. It may also suggest the necessary setting for the entire ritual, a brook or river that naturally carries away impurities, reinforcing the whole purpose of the ritual. The phrase "living waters," as used elsewhere in the Bible, carries metaphoric implications that add to the text's symbolic resonance.[96] Both the bird and the "living waters" thus double as medium and symbol of the purificatory process. Such rites are both symbolic communication and effective magic; the actions both describe what has already happened, the curing of the leper from the dread disease, and effectively prevent its recurrence by visibly banishing it.

While the process may seem to be completed for the individual through washing clothes, bathing, shaving, and being declared clean, it was not finished for the community. "He must remain outside his tent seven days," and on that day repeat the washing, bathing, and shaving (14:8–9). Having a shaved head would presumably have made it easier to observe any renewed outbreak of the skin disease. But the shaving is obviously symbolic as well. Since growing one's hair long and leaving it uncovered was a sign of mourning, shaving it off reverses that process. It marks a moment of coming back to life, almost, as it were, as a hairless infant. Since Israelites did not generally shave their beards or sidelocks, encountering a totally shaved man would have signaled to the community that this person was still being set apart as a liminal being, not totally excluded from the camp, yet not returned to his former state.

On the eighth day, the individual is ready to be readmitted to full status. The obvious place for this reincorporation is the sanctuary, where purity and impurity matter most. The cleansed individual brings three lambs as offerings to the sanctuary, one for an ascent offering, one for purification of the sanctuary, and a final one for guilt.[97] He also brings flour and oil for a meal offering and a separate container of oil. As in the ritual of ordination for Aaron and his sons, and just in these two rituals, the blood of one of the offerings is placed on the ridge of the right ear, right thumb, and right big toe, then fixed there with oil. If ancient Israelites regarded disease as demonic in origin, as has been suggested,[98] then protecting the right side with a ritual prophylactic would have signaled to the community that this person could once again be trusted in their midst and in the sanctuary. The remaining oil is poured over the head of the offerer as a final step in the ritual cleansing. By completing all of these steps, the priest makes "expiation for him before YHWH" (14:18), and the already cleansed person is again declared clean.

The ritual process undergone by the leper can be summarized as a movement from alienation to communion. This movement involves separation from the camp and departure in shame, a week's waiting period, exorcism and cleansing by the water's edge, return to the camp with a second waiting period, and finally, at the sanctuary, antidemonic protection and sacrificial offerings to reenter the presence of God and the covenanted community. It is striking how many elements of what Turner describes as liminality are evoked in this extended ritual of separation, transition, and reincorporation. "Liminality," he writes, "is frequently likened to death, to being in the womb, to invisibility, to darkness, to bisexuality, to the wilderness, to an eclipse of the sun or moon." The Israelite leper, in going to the wilderness and in coming back from it, participates in rituals of symbolic mourning and rebirth, and while there is invisible to the community. The behavior of liminal beings, according to Turner, "is normally passive or humble; they must obey their instructors implicitly, and accept arbitrary punishment without complaint," as the leper acquiesces in publicly calling himself "Unclean, Unclean!"[99] As liminality is antistructural, Turner's African initiates have no status indicating rank or property during their initiation period. Likewise, in ancient Israel, purity rules applied regardless of status, as we infer from the story of Miriam, who, in all the pride of her lineage and prophetic status, was nevertheless expelled from the camp when she contracted leprosy.

We can infer a great deal about what might have been the emotions of the Israelite leper: probably shame, perhaps guilt, certainly relief and freedom from anxiety.[100] Over and over again, different psalms telescope similar emotional trajectories into discrete verbal-musical experiences. Because the psalms were intended for use by a variety of speakers in diverse situations, we should not expect a single psalm to correspond closely to the vocabulary of a specific ritual. We can find a close connection, however, between Leviticus 14 and Psalm 91. Both share an interest in banishing demonic forces, and both share the word *nega'*, meaning "plague" or "disease," which is used repeatedly by P to describe a variety of scaly afflictions of skin, clothing, and buildings.[101] I would like to suggest that the two can be seen as a complex ritual of restoration, with the psalm's metaphoric chain of associations complementing the largely metonymic actions of the ritual. Psalm 91 might well have been chanted, among other ritual uses, after purificatory sacrifices were completed. As the former leper is being reincorporated into the community, she needs reassurance that this particular plague will stay far away from her tent.

Psalm 91, then, enacts a ritual to protect God's faithful worshiper. In most translations, the psalm is spoken by two voices, the first an official representative of the cult, the second perhaps a cultic prophet, delivering the word of God in God's own voice. The cultic speaker describes his own relation to God: "I say of YHWH, my refuge and stronghold, / my God in whom I trust" (v. 2).[102] And because he trusts in God, he offers assurances of God's protection, which take up most of the ceremony, until the second, divine speaker authoritatively confirms those promises.

The first line of the psalm seems to refer to the worshiper who has come to dwell in the Tabernacle/Temple. It reads, in my literal translation, "[one who] sits within the hiddenness of *'Elyon* (the Most High); dwells within the shadow of Shaddai."[103] These names for God connote a powerful and majestic supreme being. The theological thrust of this psalm is that this God, whose names might make divinity seem remote, is actually near at hand. In the sanctuary, God offers the worshiper an actual place of *seter*, hiddenness, and *ṣel*, shadow, in which she can have God's attention focused on her and thereby experience feelings of shelter and protection, which are also metonyms for aspects of God.[104]

In the lines that follow, the cultic speaker is essentially a mediator, a human channel for divine blessing. His discourse is founded on establishing a relationship between two pronouns, "you" and "He," the worshiper and God.

> . . . He will save you from the fowler's trap,
> from the destructive plague.
> He will cover you with His pinions;
> you will find refuge under His wings;
> His fidelity is an encircling shield.
> You need not fear the terror by night,
> or the arrow that flies by day,
> the plague that stalks in the darkness,
> or the scourge that ravages at noon.

A thousand may fall at your left side,
ten thousand at your right,
but it shall not reach you.
You will see it with your eyes,
You will witness the punishment of the wicked.
Because you took YHWH—my refuge,
the Most High—as your haven,
no harm will befall you,
no disease touch your tent.
For He will order His angels
to guard you wherever you go.
They will carry you in their hands
lest you hurt your foot on a stone.
You will tread on cubs and vipers;
you will trample lions and asps. (Vv. 3–13)

In this passage, there is a threefold predominance of the second person, indicating how insistently the psalm addresses itself to the individual who has come to God's house. The cultic officiant speaks of a He/God who is personally interested in "you," and will protect the worshiper day and night, at home or abroad. How moving and reassuring that this "He" should become an "I," who speaks directly to the individual at the conclusion of the psalm.

The psalm's metaphoric images of God and the human world are designed to draw the individual along a specific path approved by the culture. Just as the progression of symbolic actions in a ritual shapes the inner experience of the participants, so too the progression of metaphors in a prayer-poem such as this one traces out a symbolic action that has the emotional trajectory of a ritual. As the drama of the verbal ritual unfolds, God and the individual worshiper change their positions relative to each other. At the start, the worshiper is helpless and God is almighty, but by the end, the worshiper is himself envisioned as a powerful force in the world, virtually a divinity, and God has become a close companion, virtually human. One "mission of metaphor in expressive culture," as an anthropologist has theorized, is to convey to the participants a new or enhanced sense of the individual's relation to the whole of existence.[105] A ritual system and its metaphors align one in relationships that are securely linked to the ultimate source of power. One thereby experiences the coherence of the cosmos with respect to one's own actions "and in alignment with the ultimate goals of all action." The result is a redemptive reordering of the cosmos on a personal scale.[106]

Let us look closely at how this transformation of the individual's identity takes place. The human being and God are initially linked by

virtue of their joint presence in the Temple, "in the shadow of
Shaddai" (v. 1). As in other psalms set in the Temple, God is quite naturally associated with the sanctuary and its environs. Like Mount Zion on
which the Temple stands, God is a stronghold or fortress (v. 2). Like the
kerubim represented there, God is a flying being with pinions and wings
(v. 4), extending them over his fledgling, the worshiper. On the battlefield of life, God is "an encircling shield" (v. 4). While God's mighty
attributes are piling up, the human being is implicitly compared to a
helpless bird, a prey to "the fowler's trap" (v. 3). The human being is
never again this small or weak in the psalm. Though a personified
"plague . . . stalks in the darkness," and a "scourge . . . ravages at
noon" (v. 6), and many others, "a thousand" and "ten thousand," will
fall victim to life's antagonists, this one, who is being restored to full
participation in life, walks invulnerably among the dying. Both medieval
commentary and modern scholarship point out that the words used
here for plague and scourge are names of demons, derived from other
Near Eastern religious traditions.[107] Where the ritual for returning the
leper to the camp used blood and oil daubed on ear, thumb, and toe as
antidemonic protection, this psalm offers angels, God's messengers on
earth, as personal guardians to the worshiper. The angels tenderly carry
the worshiper in their hands lest his feet be hurt by a stone (v. 12). As
the image of divinity is humanized in this image, we see a corresponding shift in the power of the human being. He becomes a warrior
endowed with more than human powers. The foot that was so vulnerable as to need protection from mere stones can, in the very next line,
"tread on cubs and vipers," "trample lions and asps" (v. 13). These
hyperboles make the worshiper truly one of the mighty beings on the
planet.

When God appears in the final lines of the psalm, a different sort of
poetic idiom is used. The language is far more conventionally prosaic and
less image-laden. The human being is no longer walking through a surreal
landscape stalked by demonic beings. Rather, he is an ordinary person
who experiences distress and, knowing God's name, calls on God. The
psalm gives us God's reply:

> "Because he is devoted to Me I will deliver him;
> I will keep him safe, for he knows My name.
> When he calls on me, I will answer him;
> I will be with him in distress;
> I will rescue him and make him honored;
> I will let him live to a ripe old age,
> and show him My salvation." (Vv. 14–16)

God's promises to rescue and keep him safe, to "be with him" (v. 15), reflect a straightforward relationship based on mutual acknowledgment. The earlier metaphors have done their transforming work. This individual has attained "the optimum positioning . . . in quality space" characteristic of his culture.[108] God's promise to "let him live to a ripe old age" (v. 16) may be better translated as "I will sate him with long life." Here, as elsewhere in the Bible, the verb to sate, $\acute{s}$-b-$\acute{}$, connotes the satisfaction of eating well. God, who began the prayer-poem as fortress, shield, and winged protector—all rather distant images—is now the one who feeds the individual life, as a parent feeds us food.

There can be no doubt that the individual who came to the sacred threshold feeling alone and needing reassurance is meant to go away feeling secure in God's protecting love. In making that emotional movement possible, the performers who sing/speak to the individual must also reinforce their own perception of God's saving role in the world. Through the ritual, it becomes vivid, dramatic, and concrete. Undoubtedly, such an efficacious ritual performance makes them feel affirmed in their professional role. It is all the more striking, therefore, that they undercut their importance in the ritual process. Through the concluding speech of God, the prayer-poem conveys the paradoxical idea that individuals need no special oracle, no personal intermediary to reach God. As God's voice plainly says, "When he calls on me, I will answer him" (v. 15). God says nothing about his calling on me through "My Levites," or "My priests," or "My prophets," even though cultic performers are clearly responsible for this symbolic representation of God. God's freedom to appear in any site or guise, as one commentator has noted, cannot be constrained by the cult, however much cultic officials might choose to regularize the idea of God's revelation in the sanctuary.[109] Some of our earlier discussion emphasized how public ritual forges an ideological consensus supporting social control by a priestly and monarchical elite. This example shows, however, that ritual also supports a contrary impulse. It can empower an individual as a fully fledged ritual agent, with free and complete access to God. Because ritual encourages this personal appropriation of its gifts, it can cede the power of its professional class at the very moment it is performing most effectively.

We can understand this remarkable capacity of ritual by way of an analogous breakthrough moment in Shakespeare's *The Tempest*. In the last scene of the play, Prospero has announced that he will resign his magical arts. In the Epilogue, he steps forward to break through the dramatic frame that has enabled him to play the role of magician. He now cedes the magical power to us, the audience. It is by our spell, he says, that he remains captive on the bare stage. Only "with the help of your good hands," he says, can you "release me from my bands." Appealing to our mercy that "frees all faults," he urges, "as you from crimes would pardoned be / Let your indulgence set me free."[110] Certainly, this is a courtly manner of soliciting applause and a clever way to bring the dramatic illusion to an end. But Shakespeare, I would venture, is indicating something far deeper in these lines. His dramatic spectacle can succeed only by virtue of our empathetic participation in it. The drama is not staged simply so that we might marvel at the magic of Prospero and his servant Ariel, or laugh at the drunken antics of Stephano and Trinculo. The play is staged because it is about us and for us: our humanness, our capacity for sin and error, but also for mercy, forgiveness, and new beginnings. In his last lines, Shakespeare adroitly sends us from the drama back to our own lives, encouraging us to be aware of the emotions generated in us by the play, even as we bring it to a close. As Prospero and the actors fade away, we are left with the inner work launched by the drama, the pardon of our own crimes, which is yet to come.

Something similar happens in the psalm. The worshiper is in a new relationship to God by virtue of the ceremony that has taken place. It is now up to her to put that relationship into practice by calling on God without the benefit of ritual intermediaries. The social structure that controls priesthood and Temple has provided a mode of access through its mediation of the sacred. In so doing, it has empowered a person who has learned that a highly structured and structuring ritual environment is not the only mode of access available. Following Turner, I suggest that this sort of breakthrough is made possible by the antistructural nature of ritual liminality. One needs to enter the liminal state and be temporarily outside one's fixed identity in order to approach the transcendent being of God. One needs to shed the impurities of one's past life and ritually take on the identity of a newborn, pure person. In that new condition, one plays with alternative possibilities. No longer a weakling in need of protection, through proximity to the divine one is made to entertain the notion of being invulnerable, safer than the mightiest warrior. God's purposes are no longer obscure but luminously clear. Though one's sins may have been "like crimson, / they can turn snow-white" (Isa. 1:18). Liminality allows for the possibility of transformation, not just of the self but in the very structure of society and, in the Durkheimian view, of divinity as well. A hierarchical priestly culture that can imagine immediate access to God whenever and from wherever one calls, is also a culture that can eventually do without a single sacred center, a priestly coterie, and elaborate rules of purity and impurity.[111] It is a culture that can develop a highly inward and portable notion of God.

The Pilgrimage Community

In this chapter, we have looked at a number of the possible rewards—social, emotional, cognitive, and spiritual—of Israelite worship at God's temple in Jerusalem. At pilgrimage time, vast numbers of people converged on Jerusalem to commemorate the historical and agricultural festivals of Pesah, Shavuot, and Sukkot. Many psalms have preserved the religious forms of these pilgrimage experiences for later generations, who lacked this pilgrimage center as their religious focus. We can recapture the impact of these religious experiences by focusing our attention on pilgrimage as a collective threshold experience.[112]

In Psalm 91, we saw the breaking of a preexistent structure and the creation of a new, antistructural possibility, worship without priests or Temple. Victor Turner argues that pilgrimage creates such a breakthrough for the social order on the widest possible scale, "a living model of human brotherhood and sisterhood."[113] During a pilgrimage all kinds of people are mixed together, as we know from Chaucer's *Canterbury Tales.* Highborn and lowborn, scholars and farmers, men, women, and children, all left the constraints of their everyday lives behind to mingle in a festive mood on the road to Jerusalem, as happens today on journeys to pilgrimage centers such as Mecca, Guadelupe, or Lourdes. Turner calls this spontaneous, egalitarian fellowship *communitas:* "Pilgrimages seem to be regarded by self-conscious pilgrims both as occasions on which communitas is experienced and as journeys toward a sacred source of communitas, which is also seen as a source of healing and renewal. In this kind of thinking, too, the health and integrality of the individual is indissoluble from the peace and harmony of the community; solitude and society cease to be antithetical."[114] In such thinking, the pilgrimage center "represents a threshold, a place and moment 'in and out of time,' " where pilgrims will have "direct experience of the sacred, invisible, or supernatural order."[115]

"I rejoiced when they said to me, / 'We are going to the house of YHWH,' " begins Psalm 122, one of a group of pilgrimage songs collected under the title "A song for [of] ascents."[116] The emotionality of the speaker is channeled into the creation of a group energy. The psalm overbrims with love—for the people Israel, for Jerusalem, her capital city, and for her God:

> Pray for the well-being of Jerusalem;
> "May those who love you be at peace.
> May there be well-being within your ramparts,
> peace in your citadels."

> For the sake of my kin and my friends,
> I pray for your well-being;
> for the sake of the house of the LORD our God,
> I seek your good. (Vv. 7–8)

In another of the songs of ascent, the psalmist embraces Jerusalem, people, and God in one verse: "Jerusalem, hills enfold it, / and YHWH enfolds His people / now and forever" (125:2). A loving feeling of unity and brotherhood is also the explicit theme of the very brief Psalm 133:

> How good and how pleasant it is
> that brothers dwell together.
> It is like fine oil on the head
> running down onto the beard,
> the beard of Aaron,
> that comes down over the collar of his robe;
> like the dew of Hermon
> that falls upon the mountains of Zion.
> There YHWH ordained blessing,
> everlasting life.

Ritual's effects are felt both in the physical and in the social body. Human beings, their faces and garments, the social world and the natural world, are all united in the psalmist's feeling of being blessed by God. Such are the sentiments fostered in the pilgrimage community. Pilgrims came "to praise the name of YHWH" (122:4) "with harp and lyre," "with timbrel and dance," "with lute and pipe," with each breath (150:3–6). As Turner notes, "often expressions of communitas are linked with the simple wind and stringed instruments. Perhaps, in addition to their portability, it is their capacity to convey in music the quality of spontaneous human communitas."[117]

Several psalms convey the pilgrimage experience from the point of view of those who cannot participate. In their plaintive tones, we hear what it means to lack the nurturing influence of communitas:

> I long, I yearn for the courts of YHWH;
> my body and soul shout for joy to the living God.
> Even the sparrow has found a home,
> and the swallow a nest for herself
> in which to set her young,
> near Your altar, O YHWH of hosts,
> my king and my God. . . .
> Happy is the man who finds refuge in You,
> whose mind is on the [pilgrim] highways. (84:2–4, 6)

The metaphor of the birds' home points to the speaker's homelessness. He lacks what the pilgrims so easily gain: access to a transforming experience. Even the dry "Valley of Baca," whose name is a homonym for "tears,"[118] appears to them "as a place of springs / as if the early rain had covered it with blessing" (v. 7), so full are they of the consciousness that they will soon appear on the ramparts of Zion (v. 8). The obverse of this image, drought, characterizes the spiritual state of another psalmist who cannot join with the pilgrim crowd.

> Like a hind crying for water,
> my soul cries for You, O God;
> my soul thirsts for God, the living God,
> O when will I come to appear before God!
> My tears have been my food day and night;
> I am ever taunted with "Where is your God?"
> When I think of this, I pour out my soul,
> how I walked with the crowd, moved with them,
> the festive throng, to the house of God,
> with joyous shouts of praise. (42:2–5)

The psalmist goes on to wonder, "Why so downcast, my soul, / why disquieted within me?" (v. 6), but given what we have sketched of the pilgrimage experience, there is little cause to wonder. In a culture on the edge of the desert, water is a natural metaphor for abundance. When one imagines oneself with a killing thirst, when the only symbolic water in one's life is one's tears, when one imagines one's utterance as a pouring forth of the soul, then it is abundantly clear how much that person is defined not by what he or she has, but rather by what he or she lacks. This speaker, we discover later in the psalm, is in exile, ironically in a land dominated by a river, "Jordan," and a snow-capped mountain, "Hermon" (v. 7), making the spiritual drought all the more evident and painful. It is significant that in both these psalms the poet is compared to an animal, as if the state of being cut off from the holy pilgrimage community makes one something less than human. And, as we pointed out above, in the first of these psalms, even the animal finds a place close to God.

While the pilgrimage community is by no means normative, the rest of life nevertheless takes shape in its shadow. As a break in ordinary routine and an opening to the transcendent, the pilgrimage, as Turner has said, is a moment both in and out of time. This is true in yet another way in ancient Israel's pilgrimages. The pilgrimage expands the pilgrims' sense of time by locating their contemporary experience in a historic continuum. When an individual farmer came to offer his first fruits at the early summer pilgrimage holiday, Shavuot, he rehearsed, before the priest and in the presence of God, the history of his forebears:

> My father was a fugitive Aramean. He went down to Egypt with meager numbers and sojourned there; but there he became a great and very populous nation. The Egyptians dealt harshly with us and oppressed us; they imposed heavy labor upon us. We cried to YHWH, the God of our fathers, and YHWH heard our plea and saw our plight, our misery, and our oppression. YHWH freed us from Egypt by a mighty hand, by an outstretched arm and awesome power, and by signs and portents. He brought us to this place and gave us this land, a land flowing with milk and honey. Wherefore I now bring the first fruits of the soil which You, YHWH, have given me. (Deut. 26:5–10)

The first fruits ceremony is clearly about more than fruit. It is structured as an annual rite of social solidarity, reorienting each head of a household to his place in the sacred history of his people. In this rite, history becomes myth, a foundational story organizing the identity of all members of the people. The declaration is not just a description of one's relationship to the past, but a performative utterance, a formal way of entering into that relationship. It begins and ends in the first person, but in between the speaker speaks as part of a continuous "we." That larger history brought him to this land, these fruits, this moment. The ritual that solemnizes this single moment is thus a threshold in time. Stepping across that threshold solidifies the connection between one's own quotidian labors and God's immense labor in bringing the people out of slavery. It is little wonder that the bulk of this identity-forming passage ended up in the annual Passover Seder. When there was no longer a pilgrimage center in Jerusalem in which it could be recited, it became part of a pedagogic ritual binding each new generation to this collective myth of their people's experience.[119]

We have seen that the threshold experiences of ritual provide a context for psalms of both the individual and the community. The rituals and psalms we have examined move through the ritual pattern identified early in this century by Van Gennep: separation, liminality, reincorporation. They commemorate not only the hoped-for events in the cycle of life, such as a birth, a marriage, or the fruit harvest, but also the disruptive and negative elements that make life so hard. The basic ritual pattern moves individuals through and beyond these experiences, by offering them a sense of hope. God will judge; God will deliver; God will hear. This pattern of hope holds true for the historic experience of the nation as well. When Israel went into exile in Babylonia in 587 B.C.E., its experience as a people could easily have terminated, as happened to the ten tribes evacuated from Samaria in northern Israel more than a hundred years earlier. When taunted by their captors, " 'Sing us one of the songs of Zion' " (Ps. 137:3), the new exiles could just as easily have ceased singing and assimilated into the imperial capital of Babylon. Instead, they wrote new psalms that sustained them in their exile. These too disclose the basic ritual pattern, whose roots lie in hope.

One of the most poignant of all the psalms comes out of Israel's national experience of exile and hope. Psalm 126 is short enough to quote in full:

> When YHWH restores the fortunes of Zion
> —we see it as in a dream—
> our mouths shall be filled with laughter,
> our tongues, with songs of joy.
> Then shall they say among the nations,
> "YHWH has done great things for them!"
> YHWH will do great things for us
> and we shall rejoice.
>
> Restore our fortunes, YHWH,
> like watercourses in the Negeb.
> They who sow in tears
> shall reap with songs of joy.
> Though he goes along weeping,
> carrying the seed-bag,
> he shall come back with songs of joy,
> carrying his sheaves.

Tenses of Hebrew verbs are very difficult to render in other languages, because only two aspects of the verb must account for what we divide into past, present, and future. Some translations accordingly place this psalm in the past tense: "When the Lord restored the fortunes of Zion, / we were like those who dream" (RSV, v. 1). ". . . Then they said among the nations / 'The Lord has done great things for them' " (RSV, v. 2). This choice makes sense only until we arrive at the imperative beginning of verse 4: "Restore our fortunes, YHWH."[120] If the Jews have already been restored to their land, why pray now for deliverance? The imperative is the essential moment of the psalm, the voice that makes it not just a poem but a prayer.[121]

While the first stanza is a vision of a hoped-for future, the second stanza is indeed rooted in memory. The singer remembers both the landscape of his homeland and the natural cycle of agrarian life. The two images meld into one another so subtly that we sense here the work of an accomplished poet. The dry streambeds of the Negeb may look barren, but they do become watercourses again after the long-awaited rains. So too the rains provide the turning point in the life of the individual. At the dry season of the year, before planting, the farmer will be anxious, his eyes full of tears, as he "goes along weeping, / carrying the seed-bag." But at harvest time, when he is carrying home his "sheaves," those tears will have turned to "songs of joy" (v. 5). Just as an individual can expect these natural processes to have these transformative emotional results, so too the people can look forward—if only in vision—to a similar transformation in its collective life. This prayer-poem is a plea, but it anticipates being replaced by a song of joy.

In this psalm, the condition of exile is liminal. Israel stands on the threshold between its old and its future existence in its homeland. Lying between two realities, Israel is envisioned as essentially dead, a dry streambed, yet also something full of potentiality, a seed-bag. Now Israel is "among the nations" (v. 2), but it has the potential to be reborn in its own land, as suggested in the images of the second stanza. This duality accords with our sense of ritual liminality as that state most open to the paradoxical nature of existence. In exile, Israel can lament and weep, enter a state of mourning and die. But it can also see images that will join it again to life, whether these be cries for vengeance, as in Psalm 137, or, as here, life-giving water and songs of joy. At this moment, Israel no longer has a sacred center, in which to enact the rituals that expiate the people's guilt and draw them toward salvation. Instead, it has the highly portable institution of psalmody, a vehicle of hope for those standing on the crucial thresholds of life. The psalms of the exile are thus essentially similar to the prophecies of restoration by Second Isaiah (chaps. 40–63), or Ezekiel's celebrated vision of the valley of dry bones (chap. 38). Psalm 126 is prophetic, not only in envisioning the future, but in preserving for later generations ritual's deep structure of hope that allowed for national transformation.

·III·

AN AUDIENCE WITH THE KING: THE PERSPECTIVE OF DIALOGUE

Throughout the Hebrew Bible, God is not an impersonal force, but a person with whom one can speak. Such speeches range from Abraham's and Moses' one-word responses to God's overtures, *hineni,* "Here I am," to psalms of over 175 lines. This personification of God takes even more concrete form, of course, in the incarnational doctrines of Christianity. Even though many since Moses Maimonides have recognized religious language as a projection of human fears and wishes and have therefore turned to a more abstract God-idea, nevertheless the language of Jewish and Christian prayer continues to be shaped by the dynamics of first- and second-person communication, an *I* talking to a *You.* Those who find themselves in a relationship with God inevitably speak *to* their idea of the deity, whether in their own words or in words passed down by tradition, such as those collected in the Book of Psalms. Through the eloquent and urgent voices of those who have been in such a relationship, every succeeding generation learns what it means to enter into dialogue with God.

Since communication with God is modeled on interhuman communication, and since human communication encompasses so many spheres of life, to understand it fully we must necessarily draw on thinkers working in a number of disciplines. Underlying the several approaches I present in this chapter is the recognition that, by its immediacy, spoken language seeks to make things happen in the social world. As a sociolinguistic phenomenon, the Psalms are social acts, triangulating relationships between the individual, the community, and the idea of the transcendent that grounds the community's self-conception and social structure. The methodologies explored here offer various openings into this set of complex social relationships.

The seminal theorists of this chapter are Martin Buber and Mikhail Bakhtin, two of the twentieth century's major dialogic thinkers, whose ideas of dialogue are central to their meditations on the human condition. Buber's friend and colleague Franz Rosenzweig is also enlisted for his valuable comments on the biblical dialogue between God and humanity. In addition to this philosophical orientation to dialogue, I offer a variety of other approaches. Scholars of oral tradition illuminate how the Psalms emerge in the context of speaking and hearing, as opposed to writing and reading, and how this fact affects their qualities as formal prayer-poems. The analysis of speech acts by ordinary-language philosophers sharpens our focus on exactly what courses of action are being specified in Psalms, what requests or commitments are being made, and what it means for individuals to praise, bless, or petition God. Theories about what makes literary language distinctive help us contrast the sincerity of Psalms with the fictiveness of lyric poetry. More dramatic than lyric, they repeatedly tell the story of an innocent individual's struggle for redemptive meaning in a world often seemingly dominated by evil. In this drama, a whole social world and its many contesting voices are evoked. Appreciating the complex inner drama of these communications is the main task this chapter sets for itself.

The World According to Dialogue

Mikhail Bakhtin is primarily associated in this country with literary study, but he worked as well in linguistics, psychology, social theory, and what might be called philosophical anthropology, a broad-based description of human life rooted in an understanding of how we use language. Martin Buber's primary association is with theology and the study of the Bible and Hasidism, but he too applied his philosophical anthropology to the fields of psychology, education, social analysis, and literary criticism. One student of their work has pointed out that there are passages written by each that, if signed with the name of the other, would be virtually indistinguishable from the rest of his writings.[1] Compare, for instance, these two passages:

> The word, the living word inseparably linked with dialogic communion, by its very nature wants to be heard and answered. By its very dialogic nature it presupposes an ultimate dialogic instancing. To receive the word is to be heard. . . . My word remains in the continuing dialogue, where it will be heard, answered, and re-interpreted.[2]

> The importance of the spoken word, I think, is grounded in the fact that it does not want to remain with the speaker. It reaches out toward a hearer, it lays hold of him, it even makes the hearer into a speaker, if perhaps only a soundless one. . . . The word that is spoken is uttered here and heard there, but its spokenness has its place in "the between."[3]

It should be clear from these passages that, as Bakhtin wrote, "dialogic relationships are a much broader phenomenon than mere rejoinders in a dialogue laid out compositionally in a text; they are an almost universal phenomenon, permeating all human speech and all relationships and manifestations of human life."[4] Or, as Buber put it in his memorably epigrammatic style in *I and Thou,* "In the beginning is relation";[5] "Relation is mutual";[6] "all real living is meeting."[7]

It is no accident that these two major thinkers, each of whom chose to make dialogue the center of his life's work, were deeply grounded in their religious traditions: Buber in Judaism, and Bakhtin in Russian Orthodoxy. The biblical religions, as each understood, are fundamentally dialogic, since their Scripture is couched as God's speech to human beings, and humans' speech to God in response. Buber quotes Franz Rosenzweig's teaching in *The Star of Redemption* that through God's address to human beings, we first become established in our capacity to speak.[8] This insight is borne out in a verse from Psalms: "YHWH, open my lips, / and let my mouth declare Your praise" (51:17). A perennial theological question is at issue here: Are our actions determined by God or by human free will? The psalmist expresses the answer in dialogic fashion: I request something from God, and my words are the answer. The action, opening my mouth, may be attributable to God, but what I choose to speak with open mouth is my free human response to the capacity God grants me. This give-and-take at the level of something as basic as our capacity to speak shows how fundamentally a dialogic perspective can inform a view of human life. Bakhtin's trinitarian Christology, as explained by a Russian Orthodox theologian, is similarly rooted in dialogue. Christ, as the incarnation of God's Word, is addressed to human beings. "The Father orients His Word, His Son, to us."[9] Our lives, lived in faith or faithlessness, are our response to this divine word. In Bakhtin's metaphor, our lives represent the text of the interaction with God and the world that each of us authors. The world addresses us, and we must answer from our unique place of existence. None of us has an alibi; we are all answerable.[10]

Human life, then, begins and is sustained in dialogue. Speech, belonging to the entire human community, exists in the realm of what Buber calls "the between." That is not the same as the sum total of the words spoken by two partners in dialogue, but beyond that, the "something *sui generis*" that happens in the relation between them.[11] Bakhtin makes the same claim about human communication, which, he says, is composed of an utterance, a reply, and the relation between the two. Language models this quality of betweenness better than any other human capacity. Even leaving language aside, however, the existence we lead through our senses Bakhtin sees as equally dialogic:

The single adequate form for *verbally expressing* authentic human life is the *open-ended* dialogue. Life by its very nature is dialogic. To live means to participate in dialogue: to ask questions, to heed, to respond, to agree, and so forth. In this dialogue a person participates wholly and throughout his life: with his eyes, lips, hands, soul, spirit, with his whole body and deeds. He invests his entire self in discourse, and the discourse enters into the dialogic fabric of human life, into the world symposium.[12]

Bakhtin and Buber both understood, then, that each of us has a dialogue with the rest of existence. Opposed to the personalist view that "I own meaning" and the deconstructionist view that "no one owns meaning," a dialogic philosophy avers that "we, the human community, own meaning."[13] Selves should not be regarded as closed and self-sufficient, but rather as open partnerships with all that surrounds us. Each self contains the others with whom it has dialogically interacted, both in the past and in the present. The words that each self uses, it has gotten from others. In understanding what we take from others, Bakhtin makes a useful distinction between experience and perception. I can experience myself on my own terms—feel pain, feel happiness, and so forth—but I cannot perceive or understand myself except from some point of view outside myself (though any one external point of view will be necessarily limited). The other's categories—that I'm a good or bad husband and father, a competent or incompetent professional, and so forth—allow me to become an object of my own perception. Meaningful self-perception, then, is generated by our knowledge of each other's multiple perspectives; the more perspectives, the more complete our dialogic knowledge. Bakhtin calls this ideal exchange polyphony or *heteroglossia* (many-voicedness). In this view, my self is not just my own but a constant dialogic interaction.[14]

In this discussion, it is clear that all human perspectives are effectively limited to what is known in the present. Yet, Bakhtin notes, many kinds of discourse are generated by the idea of a "super-addressee" who transcends the present, seeing us from the vantage point of eternity.[15] In Marxist discourse, this role is played by a future version of the state; in literature, by the imagined reader who will understand the author better than his short-sighted contemporaries (Walt Whitman especially comes to mind, with his addresses to the reader "a hundred years hence");[16] and in religious discourse, the generative role of the super-addressee is obvious. As we desire to be fully known and accepted, and recognize that such knowledge and acceptance is only imperfectly achieved by our human interactions at any given moment, prayer is generated as a dialogue with the super-addressee who will understand all and forgive.

Buber's major contribution to twentieth-century discourse is his well-known and fundamental distinction between two ways of being in the world: *I-It* and *I-Thou* relations. Each of them he calls a primary word, and each intimates a way of relating to the world. The primary word *I-It* is rooted in objectivity. We treat everything around us—persons, objects, institutions—as objects to be manipulated, controlled, used. This mode is necessary for the getting and spending of human life. "Without *It* man cannot live. But he who lives with *It* alone is not a man." In the *I-It* mode, we become as objective and mechanistic as that with which we deal. By contrast, the primary word *I-Thou* is rooted in human subjectivity. "When Thou is spoken, there is no thing."[17] The act of becoming fully human is founded on our ability to say *Thou* to whatever and whomever we encounter, to treat the world and all that it contains personally.

According to Buber, the *I-Thou* relation is manifested in three basic relational realms of our life: with nature, with other human beings, and with spiritual beings. All three involve potentially dialogic encounters, if we bring to them the *Thou* rather than the *It*. In our life with nature, our normal relation is beneath the level of speech, but when we address non-human created beings as *Thou,* our words, says Buber, "cling to the threshold of speech." In our life with other human beings, the relation is open and mutual. "We can give and accept the *Thou*." And, finally, in our life with spiritual beings—ideas, artworks, personifications that are the object of religious veneration—our relation does not necessarily use speech but begets it. "We perceive no *Thou,* but nonetheless we are addressed and we answer—forming, thinking, acting. We speak the primary word with our being."[18]

Speech, Buber claims, belongs preeminently to the human realm, but our *I-Thou* relations with both nature and spiritual beings also begin to beget speech. Each of Buber's three worlds of relation, the natural, the interhuman, and the spiritual, is evoked in Psalm 19. Since it is already so familiar to us, we can easily use it to illustrate Buber's philosophy of dialogue. There is a human speaker throughout the psalm, of course, but in the first hymnic section praising God, human words are subordinated to nature's words. How does nature speak words? By conceiving of nature not as an *It* but as a *Thou,* our words cluster, as Buber says metaphorically, around the threshold of speech. "The heavens declare the glory of God, / the sky proclaims His handiwork" (v. 2). Each of the next three verses points to a natural phenomenon that does not speak, yet is heard by humans who stand to these phenomena in an *I-Thou* relation, by virtue of their mutual relation to God. The heavens, the sky, the day, the night—all are creations of God as much as is the human speaker. Just as the speaker hopes the human voice will reach God, so the voice of these natural phenomena "carries throughout the earth / their words to the end of the world" (v. 5). "There is no utterance," whether in nature or in the realm of humanity, "whose sound goes unheard" (v. 4). Nature's unspoken but heard speech testifies all to one end: God is creator.

The second section of the prayer-poem focuses on God's speech, Torah, the teaching that addresses humanity with a more complex meaning than that attributed to nature. God's speech to humans has manifold purposes: it renews life, it makes the simple wise, it rejoices the heart, it lights up the eyes (vv. 8–10). Ultimately, it has as many purposes as there are human beings to interact with it. While the second section of the prayer-poem highlights God's Torah, delivered on Sinai as speech, it also gives us a prime example of how human speech, Buber's second realm of relationality, responds. In Israel's dialogic encounter with God's revelatory word, studying, interpreting, and passing it on, the people encounter that which they cannot encounter elsewhere in human life: perfection, purity, justice, truth (vv. 8–10). The human dialogue with God's teaching translates these ideals into the imperfect social realm that constitutes human life and raises the possibility of transforming that life in God's image.

The primary word *I-Thou* is not actually spoken until the third section of the psalm, though it has been implied from the start. As Rosenzweig notes, "By the very act of asking for the Thou . . . the I addresses and expresses itself as I."[19] In his encounters with the uninterrupted and enduring words of divine creation and the pure, true words of divine revelation, the human speaker becomes markedly aware of the imperfection of human consciousness, marred as it is by guilt from both willful sins and unperceived error. The task for this speaker is to turn speech to holy purposes, to ask to be cleared of guilt and become blameless before God. This dialogic response to God's teaching is manifested as an intention to work at inward transformation and be greeted accordingly with God's acceptance. As we said above, the final moment of the prayer, "May the words of my mouth / and the prayer of my heart / be acceptable to You" (v. 15), links the spoken and the unspoken, words and heart, joining inner intention and outward act. This alignment recapitulates the two earlier movements of the psalm.[20] The unspoken, intentional, yet heard word of divine creation and the spoken, powerfully effective word and deed of divine revelation are each alive in the speaker. Redemption, for this psalmist, lies in bringing the words of creation and revelation to bear on his own human condition from moment to moment, by addressing each as a *Thou*.

For this first-person speaker, the goal of entering into dialogue with God is the discovery, in the words of Rosenzweig, of the "emphatic and underlined" "I," not just "self-understood," because "only self-addressed," but an "I" fully understood and accepted by a partner in dialogue, each of whom inquires into the "Where" of the other.[21] Buber notes of sacrifice and prayer that both are " 'set before the Face,' " and both require "mutual action: they speak the *Thou,* and then they hear."[22] In the mutuality of dialogue, silence is implicit throughout. "Whoever is not silent when another speaks is not in a dialogic situation. He delights in taking refuge in monologue."[23] Some might construe prayer as monologue, but to do so is to miss the response that is given and heard in silence. Expectant silence is the place where human beings and God meet, where they gain knowledge of one another's will. In such silent meeting, the faithful individual does not perceive experience as a lonely event, but rather as an ongoing and continuously unfolding revelation. "There is no utterance / there are no words / whose sound goes unheard" (Ps. 19:4).

Hearing Our Words: Orality and Poetry

Silence surrounds and is essential to dialogue, but it is interrupted and overwhelmed by sound. As an event in time, the sounded word has a palpable here-and-now actuality. Through sound, we take in the totality of our environment at one moment. Sound may be evanescent, but it is also intensely interior and all-encompassing. "The centering action of sound (the field of sound is not spread out before me, but is all around me) affects man's sense of the cosmos. For oral cultures, the cosmos is an ongoing event with man at its center."[24] Oral/aural cultures give great weight to the spoken word as a vehicle of power, in part, no doubt, because the human voice "conveys presence as nothing else does."[25] Visual imagery describing worship speaks of coming *before* God's presence, but the actual sounds of worship put us *in* the presence of power,[26] whether of booming basses or towering sopranos. The Psalms echo with calls for shouts, cries, songs, and instrumental music. There is no question that the world we encounter in Psalms is dominated by an oral/aural perspective.

Biblical civilization has been described variously as an oral culture that learned to accommodate itself to the alphabet, the greatest technological invention of its era, and, conversely, as a culture that was literate from its start.[27] Rather than debating hypothetical origins, we might do well to think of Israelite culture as having complementary centers of orality and literacy at any given point in its history, remembering that oral transmission is primarily popular, and written transmission elitist.[28] The spoken word affords the maximum power and presence of God to an assembled worshiping or studying community, while its preservation through writing

gives the sacred word endurance and stability.[29] One medium intensifies
the dialogic give-and-take; the other codifies it.

Before adopting an alphabet, cultures transmit their traditions orally,
developing forms that facilitate such transmission.[30] Such cultures need
memorable thoughts expressed in rhythmically balanced patterns, shaped
for convenient oral recitation. These might include repetitions, antitheses,
alliterations, assonance, epithets and formulae, standard thematic settings,
and proverbs. The more one can recite, the more one can be said to know.
In traditional oral/aural societies, wise old people are specialists in con-
serving society's knowledge, while writing and print favor new discovery
and speculation. Oral recitation is close to everyday human life, easily
assimilating such details as the porridge in the Goldilocks folktale or the
lists of booty taken in the Trojan War. Its verbal and conceptual style has
been called additive rather than subordinative, aggregative rather than
analytic, redundant and ornate, especially in delivering praise or blame.
An oral style is suited therefore to verbal and intellectual combat: one
proverb or riddle is topped by another. As we shall see later in this chapter,
both the laudatory and the combative qualities in Psalms are a prominent
element of their intensely dialogic style. At the same time that oral communication promotes intellectual struggle, it also unites people in groups,
however contested those may be, while writing and reading isolate individuals in what are clearly more solitary pursuits.[31]

When twentieth-century folklorists encountered Serbo-Croatian bards
capable of extemporizing epic poems thousands of lines long, they real-
ized that Homer's epics could similarly have been composed orally. The
demands of oral composition in the presence of an audience explained
such stock phrases as "rosy-fingered dawn" or "the wine-dark sea," which
conformed to the metrical demands of the Greek hexameter line in which
the epics were sung.[32] In Mesopotamian cultures, the phrases available for
oral delivery were complete versets, organized around fixed word pairs, so
that night would always follow day, silver always accompany gold. The
Psalms also include much formulaic diction, suggesting that at a certain
stage in their development, oral composition may have played a significant
role. Compared to the literature of ancient Ugarit, the use of word pairs in
biblical poetry is quite flexible, leading to the conclusion that writing
modified the orally transmitted cultural legacy well before the Bible
became a written text.[33]

As a written religious culture developed in Israel, oral delivery and
transmission (if we cannot be sure of oral composition) continued to
flourish in prophecy and psalmody. Both genres allude to the fact that
they were spoken or sung before being written down and shared with new
audiences.[34] As memorable speech and song, these oral forms relied

almost exclusively on verse. Recent psycholinguistic studies have shown
that the number of words that can be retained in one's short-term
memory is less than ten. Biblical poetry typically has lines of seven to nine
words in total, while biblical prose sentences tend to be upwards of thirteen words. In biblical poetry, the medial break aids the memory in organizing what it has heard into even shorter, more easily memorable units.[35]
These facts make it quite clear that, however it was composed, biblical
poetry was intended for and is responsive to the ear.

The most striking literary feature of biblical poetry, of course, is its
relentless parallelism, which is obviously allied to its oral/aural quality.
Each verset, or half-line, is always "seconded" by the verset that follows,
the two (or occasionally three) making a complete and memorable poetic
line. "Seconding," a term introduced by James Kugel, describes an
emphatic relationship of "A is so, and what's more, B."[36] Following a
musical analogy, it is helpful to think of this A-B relationship as a constant
modulation of theme and variations. The first verset states a theme, while
its partner varies it slightly, building upon the first. Robert Alter describes
this process as "heightening or intensification," through focusing, speci-
fying, concretizing, and, occasionally, dramatizing.[37] With practice, one
learns to listen for the nuances that make the second verset a meaningful
variation of the first, not just a restatement, as was assumed when "synonymous parallelism" was first identified in the eighteenth century. Almost all
folk poetries have some prominent connection to parallelism, whether it
be phonological, lexical, syntactic, semantic, or metrical.[38] The greater the
number of such linguistic relationships between any two literary units, the
more likely the parallelism will be perceived and remembered.

Any line of Psalms will illustrate how biblical parallelism, or seconding,
works: "YHWH, who may stay in Your tent, / who may reside on Your
holy mountain?" (15:1). In this line, the two parts of which we designate
as 1a and 1b, we note three prominent interconnected instances of parallelism. The first, the interrogative pronoun "who" repeated in each
verset, establishes the framework for a parallel syntactic construction. The
second, the verb "stay" in 1a, is semantically paralleled by the verb
"reside" in 1b, but this is not simply saying the same thing in other
words.[39] The verb "reside," *yiškon,* is an action usually reserved for God,
especially where God's own dwelling place is concerned. So we sense the
line building in intensity; not only does the speaker want to stay in the
Temple, he wants to reside there just as God does. The third term, the
direct object in 1a, the metaphoric "tent," is seconded in 1b by the factual mountain, on which the Temple is built. Here the seconding gives
the impression that Israelite metaphors are built on solid facts.[40] The
nuanced progression from stay to reside and from flimsy tent to solid

mountain suggests the allure of permanence that underlies the entire psalm, which attempts a definition of righteous behavior: "The man who acts thus shall never be shaken" (15:5c).

This is a straightforward instance of what goes on in each and every verse of Psalms: a concentration of verbal associations around a given topic through a verbal style designed to be heard, remembered, and used in a liturgical dialogue with God and the community. Most discussion of such orally based performance focuses on how repetition helps the memory of the performer, especially with lengthy poems such as the Homeric or contemporary Serbo-Croatian epics. Though prophecies and psalms are far shorter, mnemonic techniques would certainly have benefited their performers as well. In worship, however, the central focus is not the experience of the liturgist but that of the congregation. As was clear in our discussion of ritual, oral recitation creates a communal ethos, and repetition, in any form, makes oral recitation more likely to succeed as a mode of communication. A communication that is easy to take in by ear is also one that will be learned by heart, by both its performers and its audience. This is especially so in a case such as the Psalms, where the audience is verbally involved in the performance. Many of the psalms were recited antiphonally (we might prefer to say dialogically), with choruses such as "Praise Yah" (Hallelujah), "Praise YHWH for He is good, / His steadfast love is eternal,"[41] or "Blessed be His glorious kingdom now and forever," a verse that has been found in a Psalms scroll at Qumran, following each line of Psalm 145.[42]

The Psalms share parallelism with all biblical poetry, whether it is gathered in complete books such as Job, Proverbs, or Song of Songs, or scattered through the narratives, such as the Song at the Sea in Exodus or the Song of Deborah in Judges. Unlike Molière's bourgeois gentleman, who thought he was speaking poetry only to discover one day that he had always spoken prose, the psalmists always spoke poetry and knew, by virtue of the parallelistic conventions they were using, that they were doing so. They may well have sung their verse on a pentatonic scale, like that of Gregorian chant, or perhaps spoken it to the accompaniment of a musical instrument, such as a lyre. But it is not music and musicality that distinguishes biblical poetry from prose; it is parallelism. Much biblical prose is also marked, though less insistently, by a tendency toward parallelism, but it would be a mistake to suggest on that account, as one scholar has done, that the very idea of biblical poetry may be a misnomer.[43]

I am helped in sorting out these matters by an account of verbal behavior among the Chanula, a Christianized tribe in the Chiapas Highlands of Mexico. In analyzing their verbal behavior, an observer notes that the community distinguishes three kinds of discourse along a continuum of speech genres: "ordinary speech," "speech for people whose heart is heated," and "pure speech."[44] *Ordinary speech* is unmarked by any formal constraints, while the second and third categories of speech show greater and greater degrees of formalism and fixity. *Speech for people whose heart is heated* is stylistically marked by a degree of verbatim repetition of words and phrases, some reliance on metaphor, and in certain genres, by parallelism in syntax. *Pure speech,* by contrast, relies on a virtual fixity of form and a greater density of parallelism, especially through the proliferation of syntactically parallel lines and metaphoric couplets. In this hierarchy of speech genres, the Chanula convey their sense that certain kinds of speech have great ethical import and therefore require that the speaker's and audience's attention be focused on their formal, aesthetic qualities. The greater the symbolic significance of an interaction, the more condensed and redundant will be the language used to conduct it. Their metaphor of increasing heat to describe this hierarchical progression derives from their cosmology, which centers on the sun, conceived as cosmic progenitor. Heat, like the sun, is divine and primordial; cyclical, like the days and seasons; and capable of expressing divine and human order. The greatest amount of order (heat) is created by the couplet structure of ritual speech, to which the even greater metaphoric heat of musical instruments can be added, thus prolonging the repetition of verbal structures in performance.

I suggest that we can note a similar continuum of orderliness in biblical forms of speech. Narrative description in the Bible is like the ordinary speech of the Chanula. It does not rely on formal syntactic parallelism, though it is occasionally marked by repetitive devices, such as leading words, which Buber and Rosenzweig emphasized in their translation of the Torah into German. I quote an instance of narrative prose from an English translation faithful to the Hebrew word order and rhythms, inspired by the Buber-Rosenzweig version: "Yitzhak grew to love Esav, for [he brought] hunted-game for his mouth, but Rivka loved Yaakov" (Gen. 25:28).[45] This sentence is marked by the repetition of different forms of the verb "to love" in the two main clauses, indicating, it would seem, a contrast between the two parents' ways of loving their two sons. Beyond that lexical connection, the clauses are not syntactically parallel, since the first has an additional dependent element lacking in the second.

The quoted speech of biblical characters is far more marked by repetition and parallelism, and suggests a second, more memorable kind of speech. For instance, when Jacob and Esau are first presented as speakers, each is represented through speech that is more highly patterned than the surrounding narrative prose. Esau's cry "Give me some of that red stuff to gulp down, for I am famished" (25:30) is marked in the Hebrew by the verbatim repetition of the word for red. It reads literally, "let me gulp down that red-red." Jacob's five-word reply similarly draws on repetition, this time the alliteration of the soft, spirant form of *k*. "First sell me your birthright" (v. 31) reads in Hebrew *mikra kayom et bikortika li*, the *k-r* of "sell" repeated in the *k-r* of "birthright," with an additional *k* in the word meaning "first" or "as of today," to make sure the connection is immediately reinforced. The first readers of this written text read these speeches hundreds of years after these words, or something like them, were first spoken. The speeches may have been passed down in memory by oral storytellers, or they may be the creations of latter-day writers. In either case, what we have here is not ordinary speech but, to borrow the metaphor of the Chanula, the speech of people whose hearts have been heated up by the intensity of their passions. The verbatim repetition and alliteration that mark their speeches are literary means of fixing them in the memory of their descendants. Such formal literary devices, it could be argued, are precisely what make these ancestors memorable.

Quoted speech can also approach the formality of highly developed parallelism, drawing on repetitions and variations in the syntactic, semantic, or phonological spheres. For instance, Moses' prayer to heal Miriam of her leprosy, *'El na' refa' na' lah* (Num. 12:13: "O God, pray heal her!"), is virtually divisible into two versets, because the particle of polite address is repeated between the naming of the addressee and the petition. A literal translation might read: "God-pray, / heal-pray her." In the conventions of linguistic notation, we can record this five-word speech as ABCBA, which is not only chiastic in structure but also a virtual palindrome phonologically. In the narrative of Numbers, especially in English translation, it appears as a spontaneous utterance on Moses' part, but when analyzed with the hierarchies of speech genres in mind, it is clearly a rhyming, syntactically parallel, formulaic prayer.

A still greater degree of formality is to be found, of course, in Israel's version of "pure speech," which we find in the Psalms and other biblical poetry. Only a deliberately artful form of speech, acknowledged as such by both performer and audience, could adopt the symmetrical envelope structure of Psalm 8, which begins and ends with the same line, "YHWH, our Lord / How majestic is Your name throughout the earth," and, in between, places the human creature at the very center of its verbal symmetry. As an indication of the form "pure speech" took in ancient Israel, such artful structures remind us that matters of significant ethical value, such as Psalm 8's attempt to determine the human place in the cosmos, deserve and can benefit from aesthetic formality. We should not set the language of the heart in opposition to psalmody; rather, it is embodied and given permanent form in that art.

Speech as Action

Since God is said to listen to personal private prayer, why go to the trouble of composing and using fixed prayers, such as the Psalms? To the democratic Western sensibility, fixed prayer often seems to pose a barrier between the individual and a divine auditor who understands the language of the heart. The Bible, however, finds no discontinuity between fixed and spontaneous prayer. Hannah, for instance, is represented as praying twice: the first time asking for the birth of a son in her own words (I Sam. 1:11), and the second time offering thanks for his birth in the words of a formal prayer-poem, which has all the features of a psalm (I Sam. 2:1–10). Moses likewise prays spontaneously and formally. To deflect God's anger, he prays on behalf of the congregation in conversational prose (cf. Exod. 32:11–13), but he is also represented as praying the full-dress congregational petition, Psalm 90, which is headed "A prayer of Moses, the man of God."

It has been argued that one speaks to God in the Bible as one speaks to other human beings. Just as we bless a loved relative or a friend before a journey or at some other special time in his or her life, so we bless God. Just as we beg favors of those more powerful or wealthier than we, so we petition God for divine favor. Prose prayer is represented in the Bible as emerging spontaneously out of the life circumstances and momentary needs of the pray-er, while psalmic prayer, often coinciding with a visit to a Temple, called for "care, thoughtfulness, and perfection in expression that a commoner could supply only by recourse to a prepared text."[46] Yet both kinds of utterances, it should be stressed, are conventional, obeying certain typical generic constraints. Bakhtin calls such classes of utterance "speech genres." For the dialogic thinker, all utterances have the quality of being directed to someone and anticipating a response. Specific speech genres develop characteristic forms by taking into account the addressee,[47] as, for instance, a petitionary prayer always has God's response in mind. It opens with an address invoking YHWH by name. The heart of the prayer is the petition itself, formulated in the imperative, stating what the pray-er begs God to do. And it is generally concluded by a motive sentence, offering God a persuasive reason to comply. In the Psalms, the motive sentence may be elaborated along further conventional lines, including a confession of trust, an assurance of being heard, or a vow of praise.[48] The primary aim of such prayer rhetoric, whether in poetry or in prose, is to establish what one scholar calls an "identity of interest" between the pray-er and God.[49]

Such prayer is highly personal, directed to an addressee who is presumed to know well the speaker's condition and character. Yet, at the same

time, insofar as all biblical petitions follow a similar pattern, such prayer is
also highly formal and conventional, as if one were putting on a suit of
clothes for a particular occasion. This peculiar blend of the personal and
the formulaic is perhaps the chief stylistic hallmark of the Psalms. They
draw on many stock formulae, but they are never wholly formulaic, as
their speakers build upon a personal relationship to the addressee to
express their passionate feelings.[50] Commenting on what he calls "intimate" or "familiar" speech genres, Bakhtin notes that "intimate speech is
imbued with a deep confidence in the addressee, in his sympathy, in the
sensitivity and goodwill of his responsive understanding. In this atmosphere of profound trust, the speaker reveals his internal depths."[51]
Psalmic speech lives in such an atmosphere of trust, confidence, and intimacy. Because psalms, however, were designed to be used by many worshipers, their emotions are represented in general, rather than in
particular, idiosyncratic terms. They do reveal "internal depths," but these
are contained in the paradigmatic cry itself, rather than in a detailed petition reflecting the speaker's momentary life circumstances, as is generally
the case in biblical prose prayer.

Bakhtin's metaphor of depths calls to mind a familiar psalm, in which
we can see how the characteristic pattern of the petition shapes what it is
possible to say within a given utterance.

> Out of the depths I call to You, YHWH,
> YHWH, listen to my cry;
> let Your ears be attentive
> to my plea for mercy. (Vv. 1–2)

The invocation and petition can hardly be separated; in God's names,
Buber notes, God "is not merely spoken about but also spoken to."[52] To
speak to the God who is present (the root meaning of YHWH) is to know
one's prayer will be heard. God's well-known qualities can therefore be
taken into account:

> If You keep account of sins, YHWH,
> YHWH, who will survive?
> Yours is the power to forgive
> so that You may be held in awe. (Vv. 3–4)

Not only is God's dual capacity to remember sin yet to forgive present in
the speaker's mind. The psalm also builds up a picture of the speaker's
special relationship to God, on account of which s/he is deserving to have
a prayer answered:

> I look to YHWH;
> I look to Him;
> I await His word.
> I am more eager for YHWH
> than watchmen for the morning,
> watchmen for the morning. (Vv. 5–6)

The addressee has been repeatedly invoked, the petition has been tendered, and motives to secure a response have been adumbrated both for the sinner who is eager for forgiveness, and for the merciful One who is known to forgive. All that remains is for the pray-er to contextualize his prayer for the wider ritual community, suggesting that they model their own petitions on his own example:

> O Israel, wait for YHWH;
> for with YHWH is steadfast love
> and great power to redeem.
> It is He who will redeem Israel from all their iniquities. (Vv. 7–8)

This could be interpreted as another reason why God should hear the prayer of this speaker. S/he is a person committed to sharing a personal knowledge of God with the entire community.

The formality of much psalmic speech is modeled, not surprisingly, on speech directed to an earthly king. Having secured an audience with the king, one had best know the forms in which kings were normally addressed, and to which they were most likely to respond.[53] Just as aggrieved citizens ask the king to hear their case and save them, so believers, often the poor and downtrodden, ask God to hear, judge, and save them, perhaps when appeals to the earthly king have gone unheeded, or the channels to reach him were unknown. Similarly, courtiers praise the king for his military victories, and religious poets praise God's past deeds on behalf of the people and request divine aid in current battles. The Psalms are not limited to praise of God, but include many references, as we pointed out in chapter 2, to God's vice-regent on earth, Israel's king. Thus, some psalms express the hope that the king should wipe out his enemies (e.g., 21:9–12), thereby ensuring that his dominion will become universal (72:8) and his name eternal (72:17). These twin themes are also prominently expressed in relation to YHWH's sovereignty and dominion (e.g., Pss. 148–149). We see similar parallels on a semantic level. In a royal marriage hymn, the poet proclaims of his earthly master, "I commemorate your fame for all generations, / so people will praise you forever and ever" (Ps. 45:18), just as the psalmist praises God, his heavenly lord and master: "Every day will I bless You / and praise Your name forever and ever" (145:2).

We all know that speech, whether formal or informal, has consequences in the world, so it matters how things are said. As we have just indicated, a petition to a sovereign will observe certain conventions of praise, just as any speech act will take into consideration the appropriate social and linguistic decorum for its setting. Speech is a game played according to conventional rules understood by the speakers in any given discourse community. For instance, for the illocutionary speech act of petition to be successfully performed, certain conditions must obtain. The speaker must not already have what he asks for. He must be petitioning someone who can grant his request. And he must be sincere in wanting the petition granted. If these conditions of appropriateness are not met, his utterance will not succeed. Similarly, from the other side of the dialogic exchange, it should be noted that if the addressee promises to grant the petition, he must be in a position to do so. Otherwise his promise has no effect as a speech act. Every speech act has its own set of appropriateness conditions. For instance, if a speaker asks a question of another, for it really to be a question (rather than, say, an ironic jibe), he must not know the answer, want to know the answer, or believe that his hearer knows the answer, and he must believe that the hearer was not about to tell the requested information without being asked. All this goes on without our thinking about it most of the time that we speak. We constantly rely on our knowledge of appropriateness conditions, both in producing utterances and in decoding the utterances of others.[54]

Much of the literature on speech acts has focused on utterances that bring about changes simply by virtue of having been spoken. They are often called performatives, though this term can apply more widely to other kinds of speech acts as well. When the king says, "I appoint you prime minister," someone becomes the prime minister at that moment because the king's declaration performs an immediate and universally accepted action. Examples of performative declarations are often drawn from law and ritual, where an extralinguistic institution has special authority to uphold the efficacy of its utterances, and reinforces this authority through the formality of its ritualized proceedings.[55] For instance, the declaration "I pronounce you man and wife," when spoken by a member of the clergy at a wedding, has performative force; the legal status of the man and the woman changes because those words have been uttered in the appropriate context. In an oral culture, ritual words alone are sufficient to effect such a change of status, though in writing cultures, various licenses and contractual documents may need to be added to the utterance for it to have its full performative impact. If an authorized person breaks a bottle of champagne over the bow of an ocean liner, saying, "I christen you the *Queen Elizabeth II*," then he or she has spoken performatively. But if this same person utters this same declaration while pouring champagne over the head of a friend at a cocktail party, then the words are hollow, emptied, as it were, of their performative force. While illocutionary speech acts are often based on widely accepted formulae, such as the above conventions of speech, they need not always be formulaic. If a teacher says to her class, "There will be a test tomorrow," she is doing more than describing reality; she is directing her students to study. But the same sentence expressed by one student to another with a feeling of resentment will not be taken as a directive, but rather as an expressive statement. The appropriateness conditions for these and all other speech acts depend on the speaker and the context of the speech.

Speech-act theorist John Searle has divided all illocutionary acts into five basic kinds: (1) *assertives:* "we tell people how things are"; (2) *directives:* "we try to get them to do things"; (3) *commissives:* "we commit ourselves to doing things"; (4) *expressives:* "we express our feelings and attitudes"; and (5) *declarations:* "we bring about changes through our utterances."[56] J. L. Austin distinguished between *illocutionary force*—that is, an intention to make something happen by the act of speaking, whether or not the utterance actually accomplishes that end—and *perlocutionary effect,* the accomplishment of the speaker's intention.[57] We have already commented on this distinction above, noting that prayer is composed of illocutionary utterances, while the symbolic language of sacrifice in ancient Israel was thought to achieve immediate effects. In an example closer to home, if I say to my daughter, "I advise you not to open the door," my utterance is a directive, but she may easily fail to be directed, taking it rather as an expression of my (perhaps in her mind unfounded) fears for her safety. But if I say, "I forbid you to open the door to anyone under any circumstances," my sentence is more likely to carry its intended illocutionary force as a directive and to have a perlocutionary effect: she will not open the door. Rather than use Austin's somewhat cumbersome terms, we shall use the term "performative" to refer to all illocutionary and perlocutionary utterances, merely distinguishing between performative *force* and performative *effect.*[58]

The notion of performatives is obviously helpful in approaching divine speech, for when God spoke and the world came to be, as Genesis tells the story, God was using language performatively. "Let there be light" is a declaration that manifestly altered reality for all time.[59] Since, in the biblical view, all was created by God's first performative series of speeches, things are inherently related to words, an association preserved by the word *dabar,* meaning both speech and thing. When God

promises protection and long life to a person who has come to the
Temple, as in Psalm 91, God's language performs an action with both
force and effect. The utterance means to be convincing and is, because
it is known to both parties in the dialogue that God has the power to
confer blessing on one who solicits it. The person who has come forward
to receive the blessing therefore goes away feeling that the request has
been fulfilled. If it were pointed out to the devotee that God did not
actually say those words, but that they were pronounced by a Levite representing (or, conceived more dramatically, impersonating) God, it
would not hollow the language of its performative effect. The worshiper
undoubtedly accepts the conventional assumptions of religious discourse
in Israelite culture: God speaks in human language through chosen individuals. Divine speech antedates the writing of such speech in sacred
texts; God speaks to the Israelite people through Moses, before taking
Moses to the mountaintop and turning him into a writer. Israel's covenantal relationship with God is unimaginable without such conventions
for representing the channeling of divine speech.

Human speech addressed to God can also have a pronounced performative dimension. We find a striking instance in Psalm 32, in which an
individual reflects on what it means to be forgiven by God. In order to set
its various speech acts in context, we should first read the whole psalm:

1.   Happy is he whose transgression is forgiven,
      whose sin is covered over.

2.   Happy the man whom YHWH does not hold guilty,
      and in whose spirit there is no deceit.

3.   As long as I said nothing
      my limbs wasted away
      from my anguished roaring all day long.

4.   For night and day
      Your hand lay heavy on me;
      my vigor waned
      as in the summer drought.   *Selah.*

5.   Then I acknowledged my sin to You;
      I did not cover up my guilt;
      I resolved, "I will confess my transgressions to YHWH,"
      and You forgave the guilt of my sin.   *Selah.*

6.   Therefore let every faithful man pray to You
      upon discovering [his sin],
      that the rushing mighty waters
      not overtake him.

7.   You are my shelter,
     You preserve me from distress;
     You surround me with the joyous shouts of deliverance.   *Selah.*

8.   Let me enlighten you
     and show you which way to go;
     let me offer counsel; my eye is on you.

9.   Be not like a senseless horse or mule
     whose movement must be curbed by bit and bridle;
     far be it from you!

10. Many are the torments of the wicked,
     but he who trusts in YHWH
     shall be surrounded with favor.

11. Rejoice in YHWH and exult, O you righteous;
     shout for joy, all upright men!

Because the prayer-poem is retrospective, it loses nothing by beginning with the emotional conclusion of the underlying experience: the happiness of the forgiven person. In the course of the psalm we discover that the introductory lines are not a pious generalization but rather a testimony of personal experience, spoken for the benefit of the assembled congregation. These introductory lines (vv. 1–2), which are in effect the conclusion of the spiritual process that preceded the psalm's composition, are followed by two large units: first, an autobiographical reminiscence in which the speaker tells God the process by which he came to these conclusions (vv. 3–7), and second, an exhortation to the assembled worshipers to follow his path (vv. 8–11). The central autobiographical portion is itself divided into three smaller units, as indicated by the interjection of the word *selah,* which may indicate a stanza break or a musical interlude, in effect, a passage from one mood to the next.

Although the speaker mentions physical symptoms, it is clear that his is not primarily a physical malaise. Looking back on the experience with hindsight, he presents an ironic picture of himself roaring in anguish, like a wounded lion, but while torrents of sound came out of his mouth, he actually communicated nothing of what he needed to communicate. Until he spoke the truth, he was little more than an animal in pain. The speaker suffers constantly, "night and day," with the thought that God's "hand" is punishing him (v. 4). A long decline certainly lies behind the image of his limbs wasting away (v. 3). But his consciousness of being forgiven is immediate. As soon as the speaker verbalizes his need to confess to God, a vast weight is lifted. Uncovering his guilt (v. 5), he discovers that his "sin is covered over" (v. 1). The JPS translation makes this process of uncovering guilt seem entirely internal. The speaker simply had to "resolve" to confess, but the verb *'amarti* could just as easily be translated as "I said aloud." Similarly, the imperfect aspect of the verb, "I will confess," could also be translated as "I hereby confess,"[60] "hereby" being one of Austin's tests for a performative declaration, which serves to indicate that the utterance of the sentence is the instrument making the act (in this case, confession) happen.[61]

For the speaker, his moment of confession is undeniably the threshold to a new awareness of God. In the substitute translation, the thought becomes a speech act with powerful consequences in the world. God responds not merely to the speaker's innermost thoughts, but to the action of one who wants to break through his shame and despair by an intentional act of confession. To acknowledge one's sins with the consciousness that God hears our confession is to speak with performative force. To know that God "forgave the guilt of my sin" is to recognize that one's utterance has had a performative effect. No divine voice boomed out, "You are forgiven." Yet the speaker knows he has been, because the appropriateness conventions that govern his speech act promise such an outcome. Putting a similar thought into theological language, Rosenzweig describes how the act of confession produces in us the awareness that we are loved by God. By saying "I have sinned," he writes, the soul abolishes shame, clearing the way for the acknowledgment "I am a sinner." Throwing away the compulsion of shame, the soul that confesses gives itself up entirely to love. Surrendering itself to the presence of God's love, the soul hears "I forgive" as certainly as if God had spoken in its ear. Confession, then, initiates, indeed produces, the consciousness of atonement. As Rosenzweig makes clear, the certainty of God's love and forgiveness comes to the soul "not from God's mouth, but from its own."[62]

Having been transformed in the process of repentance, the speaker is bursting with his new awareness that there is a clear alternative to wasting away in internal anguish. He is so full of this thought that he wants to communicate it to others, so while he is still speaking to God, he gives a directive, "Therefore let every faithful man pray to You" (v. 6a). In urging others to confess, the psalmist raises the specter of "rushing mighty waters" (v. 6b) always threatening to overtake one.[63] The potential for drowning in guilt, shame, and alienation offers a watery counterpoint to the earlier image of the speaker, paralyzed as in a summer drought. In his stubborn refusal to own up to his sin, he had been both drying up inside and drowning. As a way out of such debilitation, this psalmist, like the speaker in Psalm 91, refers to God as his *seter,* here translated as "You are my shelter," but literally, "You are a hiding (place) to me." The translation "You preserve me from distress" similarly conceals a spatial metaphor: you pull me out of a tight place, *sar.*[64] The psalmist took what was hidden inside him, blocking his development, and uncovered it, offering it to God to be hidden within God's own hidden nature. It is not important that we know anything specific about this man's sin; it has been "covered over" (v. 1) by the process of confession and divine forgiveness.

The psalmist is surrounded, he says, by "joyous shouts of deliverance" (v. 7). This gives us an important clue to the cultic setting of this psalm. Let us say that an individual has just approached God with an offering. He returns to the Court of the Israelites (or the Court of the Levites, if he is one), where there are others gathered at the threshold who are waiting to offer sacrifices. He approaches a cultic prophet or Levite to whom he tells his story of deliverance from guilt, explaining that he wants to make his own passage from guilt to confession and recovery into an example for the community. Perhaps others who are waiting to offer thanksgiving sacrifices may still be harboring secret guilt. Perhaps they do not yet know the benefit of confession or the reality of forgiveness. It is in this spirit that the third and final movement of the psalm originates.

It too centers around a number of speech acts. "Let me enlighten you" and "let me offer counsel" (v. 8) are commissives, in which the speaker commits himself to follow a given course. He carries it out in the directive of the next line, "Be not like a senseless horse or mule / whose movement must be curbed by bit and bridle" (v. 9). His performative urging takes the place of the metaphoric bit and bridle. If his story of personal transformation has not motivated them to come forward and confess their sins, then perhaps his straightforward imperative command can do so. His imperative, of course, is strengthened by a note of ridicule, since these domesticated animals were unclean for both table and altar! At issue here, of course, is the wildness of the two beasts of burden, who, without bit and bridle, were totally ungovernable. Having been wild and ungovernable himself, roaring in his pain like a lion, he urges his fellows to transcend their animal natures and take proper direction from him by affirming their trust in God. Concluding the psalm with a call for rejoicing, he seems to feel that his words have had their intended effect. His use of imperatives defines him as an authority to be respected: "Rejoice in YHWH and exult, O you righteous; / shout for joy, all upright men!" (v. 11). If they respond with an appropriate shout, such as "Hallelujah" or some other formula of praise, then he will have further evidence of his words' performative power. Only the righteous, he knows, can truly shout for joy. These expressive speech acts, these shouts for which he calls, bring us full circle to the happiness affirmed at the opening of the psalm. Only those "in whose spirit there is no deceit" (v. 2) can be truly happy.

To a contemporary audience, the experience reported in this psalm is probably more familiar than it might seem at first glance. A patient comes to a doctor with physical symptoms, which are quite real, though they may be psychosomatic (literally, "of soul and body") in origin. They have lasted a long while, and numerous doctors have thrown up their hands. Finally, the patient is persuaded that only a psychotherapist (literally, "one who attends to the soul") can help. After many sessions the individual admits something to the therapist, never before confessed to another human being. Instantly, the physical pains disappear. Similarly, the relief that people experience in Twelve Step programs designed to help overcome addictions to alcohol, drugs, sex, or overeating stems in no small measure from addicts' taking the step of confessing their addictive behavior to another person and to God, which begins to release them from the paralyzing grip of shame. What we in our society have relegated to the privacy of therapists' offices or the anonymity of Twelve Step meeting rooms happened in a ritual context in ancient Israel. The language of Psalms, with its repertory of speech acts, such as confession, exhortation, and praise, made available to the ordinary individual a vocabulary of inner states and a set of postures to adopt when visiting the ultimate therapist, the One who "heals . . . broken hearts" (Ps. 147:3).

Like the call to worship, with which Psalm 32 concludes, blessings (and curses) were considered to have both performative force and effect. As we know from Esau and Jacob's struggle over the paternal birthright, the words of blessing had a power so efficacious that they could not be retracted once spoken. In the biblical world, human beings could also bless God. "To say 'Blessed be YHWH' is not to call on some higher power to bless the Lord, but to put oneself in a certain posture in relation to the Lord. . . . It is a form of speech which asks for nothing and says nothing about the world."[65] I would put the matter somewhat differently by calling it a form of speech that changes the speaker in relation to the world he or she inhabits.[66] The force of blessing God reattunes one's consciousness to gifts received from God. "Bless YHWH, O my soul / and do not forget all His bounties" (103:2). The psalmist models this opening of the heart at the start of the psalm, and then again after he has enjoined the angels and all God's earthly works to likewise bless God (103:20–22). Blessings from God flow to human beings in myriad ways; human beings return the blessings in language, committing themselves to acknowledge God as the source of blessings they have received:[67] "Blessed is the Lord, God of Israel, to all eternity. / Let all the people say, 'Amen' / Hallelujah" (106:48a-b).

Another speech act that has a pivotal role in Psalms is the question. In everyday conversation, we expect that the questions we ask will be answered by those to whom we address them, just as we expect that our commands will be fulfilled. In Psalms, the questions psalmists pose to God are the hardest sort of questions to answer, the perennial imponderables of religious philosophy: Why do the wicked prosper? Why do the righteous suffer? But they are not presented as philosophical quandaries. The question "How long?" implies the framework of action: How long can I/we abide this injustice? How long can You allow it to prevail? That is why we regularly find the psalmists' questions becoming demands:

> How long, YHWH, will You forever ignore me?
> How long will You hide Your face from me?
> How long will I have cares on my mind,
> grief in my heart all day?
> How long will my enemy have the upper hand?
> Look at me, answer me, YHWH, my God!
> Restore my strength,
> lest I sleep the sleep of death;
> lest my enemy say, "I have overcome him,"
> my foes exult when I totter.
> But I trust in your faithfulness,
> my heart will exult in your deliverance.
> I will sing to YHWH,
> for He has been good to me. (Ps. 13)

In this psalm, questioning God is clearly a prelude to demanding that God act on one's behalf. Each question implies an imperative: Do not ignore me, do not hide Your face from me. Both questions and imperatives are based on the trust expressed in the penultimate verse. If the speaker did not trust that God would answer by acting, then s/he would never have posed questions or made demands. To say aloud, "I trust in Your faithfulness" is to make explicit the speech situation that underlies this and every other psalm.

Imperatives from God to us take the form of commandments to do or to refrain from doing, preeminent among them being the words "You shall love YHWH, your God" (Deut. 6:5). God's "love Me!" is paralleled by ours, which we speak in the dialogic act of prayer.[68] In the imperative mode, which is at the heart of Psalms, we act on our belief in God's responsiveness to our human condition. The sick and depressed speaker of Psalm 38, deserted by his friends, cries out to the One on whom he can rely: "Do not abandon me, YHWH; / my God, be not far from me; hasten to my aid" (vv. 22–23a). The exiled singer of Psalm 126, speaking on behalf of the distressed nation, calls out, "Restore our fortunes, YHWH, / like watercourses in the Negeb" (v. 4). Whether in the mouth of a solitary or a communal speaker, the imperative embodies the essence of dialogic relationship; it is a call that demands an active response. Imperatives in the Psalms can be likened to voice-mail; they always include references to the first-person sender and to the addressee. Regularly, they are coupled with the name of God, the One who, it is supposed, must answer.

The two basic postures of speech in Psalms, petition and praise, both revolve around imperatives conjoined with God's name: "Hear, YHWH, and have mercy on me" (30:11a) is echoed in psalm after petitionary psalm. But this should not be treated merely as an oral formula that helped the composers of psalms fill out their performances. It is the essential moment of prayer, when the human being recognizes a need to be in a personal relationship with God, the Creator of the universe and the Redeemer of Israel. At such a moment, he or she calls out. By contrast, the imperative of praise is not usually addressed to God, but rather to the worshiping congregation. The imperative call by the prayer leaders presumes a community that is willing to speak in one voice, testifying to its love and loyalty to God. "Praise YHWH!" is the community's command to itself as well as its grateful response to God and to one another. It is so central to the experience of Psalms that generations of translators have left it in the original Hebrew: "Hallelujah!"

The Psalms, we can never forget, are performed speech, and as such they show a heightened awareness of their own acts of expression.[69] It should not be surprising, then, that the psalmists keep track of their various speech acts, those made both in the past and in the present, and describe them to God: "I called out to You, YHWH; / to YHWH, I made appeal" (30:9). "I cry aloud to God / I cry to God that He give ear to me" (77:2). ". . . I moan, / I complain, my spirit fails" (v. 4). "Out of the depths I call to You, YHWH" (130:1). "Like a hind crying for water, / my soul cries for You, O God" (42:2). What is true of petitionary speech is also true of acts of praise. "Truly your faithfulness is better than life; / my lips declare your praise. / I bless you all my life; / I lift up my hands, invoking Your name" (63:4–5). "It is good to praise YHWH, / to sing hymns to Your name, O Most High, / To proclaim Your steadfast love at daybreak, / Your faithfulness each night" (92:2–3). "May the words of my mouth / and the prayer of my heart / be acceptable to You, / YHWH, my rock and my redeemer" (19:15). Speech acts performed in the present are envisioned as continuing into an indefinite future. "Every day will I bless You / and praise Your name forever and ever" (145:2). All these named speech acts represent conventions of address, through which the psalmists get and maintain God's attention. A striking number of them are found especially at the beginnings and endings of psalms. Through them, psalmists enter into and exit from their audience with the King of Kings.

The Drama of Psalms

The combination of conventional formality and powerful immediacy that we have noted in Psalms makes them verbal artworks, deserving of careful scrutiny. Typically, we relate to verbal artworks as we would to a highly sophisticated conversational partner, who engages our attention intellectually, emotionally, and sensorily. We do not typically perform speech acts through works of art, because the pleasure and instruction they afford us are ends in themselves. Our relation to the Psalms is rather different. They are not ends in themselves but means to the end of communicating with God. Designed by specialists in religious discourse to be used by all kinds of people, they are, I would suggest, a kind of represented and representative speech. Yet they are unlike other kinds of represented speech, such as the fictive speech that might be created for a character in a play, novel, or narrative poem, the identity of which is always tied to that particular character. Rather than being comparable to such dramatic speech, they are far more like what has been called "natural speech," "the verbal acts of real persons on particular occasions in response to particular sets of circumstances."[70] However conventionalized the Psalms might be, individuals can use these typical speech acts as if they were their own.

The dramatism of lyric poetry offers a closer but still inadequate model of represented speech in the Psalms. Lyric poems can be regarded as scripts for solo performance, to be performed by any reader. The "I" in Shakespeare's sonnets is thus available to be performed by anyone who chooses to identify with the emotional experience and intellectual speculations of that created "I." The French linguist Emile Benveniste makes the relevant point that pronouns always refer to the unique enunciations that contain them, not to some objective position in space and time.[71] Thus, when I speak the lines "Shall I compare thee to a summer's day? / Thou art more temperate and more beautiful," I temporarily become the "I" of the poem and my beloved becomes its addressee. When the poem is treated in this way, its language can have performative force. I can use Shakespeare's words to say "Love me" or "Let's go to bed" and have those words effect actions in my world. It should be noted, however, that this sort of performativeness is not the usual stance we adopt toward works of verbal art, which are literary by virtue of the fact that they are disengaged from just such practical transactions.[72] When my lover and I put aside the poems that we have been reading, we are aware that we must do our best in the everyday language through which we ordinarily express our selfhood.

Even if we conduct much of our courtship through Shakespeare or other lyric poetry, we know that in doing so, we are always quoting.

Like lyric poems, the Psalms are representations of how someone with such and such emotions can and does speak. In this sense, the voices of Psalms are dramatic. The "I" or "we" in Psalms is a pronoun that we inhabit, now and in the future, whenever we use them. The "Thou" of Psalms, however, cannot be filled in, as in lyric poetry, by a whole variety of imagined auditors, but only and always by the super-addressee who is defined in the culture that speaks them as the One who hears them. This suggests the fundamental difference between recitation of a text constructed for aesthetic ends and recitation of one constructed for worship. We can derive great pleasure from aesthetic texts and certainly learn from them, but we do not use them as a primary means of talking to a specific conversational partner. If we did this, we would certainly be considered sociopathic by our partners. But this is precisely how we use psalms when we worship. In talking to God, we consistently use another's words. In doing so, we do not quote psalms; we pray them. And in the Christian and Jewish traditions, psalms offer some of the primary lines of communication to God.

We can see, then, that two different conventions govern the dramatic elements in secular and sacred poetry, based on a contrast between fictiveness and sincerity. When we read lyric poems, we process the information they contain in relation to experiences that we have lived through, so that the meanings we attach to them arise from a process of comparison and contrast. Disjunctions between our own situation and Shakespeare's "I" will inevitably appear, provoked by the texts themselves. When such disjunctions occur, we step back from the "I" of Shakespeare's sonnets and regard them not as our own love discourse, but as the artificial language of the Renaissance sonnet tradition, Shakespeare's fictive creation of a persona interacting with other created personae. Their language is thus hollowed of whatever performative force it might have had, as we provisionally appropriate them as our own. Sacred poetry, however, we presume to be sincere, in both its composition and its later use. Whether that poetry be the Psalms or later Jewish or Christian devotional lyrics, such as those of Yehuda Halevi or George Herbert, its language continues to be performative as long as we use it to address God. The convention that governs the use of such prayer-poems allows for identification between the worshiper's "I" and the representative, archetypal "I" in the written text. If the experience represented seems in some way disjunctive from our own, it may be that we are feeling a different register of religious experience, yet if we are regular psalm-users, we will recognize that the emotion is not completely alien to us but is indeed something we have felt before and are likely to feel again at another time. Once we drop this identification with the speaker, and treat such prayer-poems as just poems and not prayers, we strip them of their performative force and effect. They become merely historical texts, rooted in a remote world, from which we may derive pleasure and instruction about how Israelites used to call out to God, or about how one might still do so, if one were so minded. Harold Fisch has aptly termed the Psalms "covenantal discourse," because they are the verbal means through which the covenant between God and Israel is sustained. As Fisch describes them, the Psalms are essentially different from lyric poems, whose main concern is with self-expression. The Psalms, by contrast, are concerned with establishing a dialogic relationship and, in that relationship, with being heard and answered by a Thou.[73] They give permanent shape to that aspect of our being that wants to be on speaking terms with God.

There is another sense in which we can speak of the Psalms as dramatic. The Psalms contain an implicit narrative that runs through the corpus of one hundred and fifty prayer-poems, connecting them all into a single drama. Traditional exegetes, as far back as the period of the Second Temple, regarded the story in Psalms as reflecting the life experience of David; hence such headings as "When Nathan the prophet came to him after he had consorted with Bathsheba" (51:2).[74] Though we can certainly see many themes of David's life reflected in Psalms, such an interpretive move tends, as we said in another context, to hollow them of their performative force as prayer. We do not in fact pray the Psalms in the person of David.[75] As one student of Psalms has claimed, their story is that of "every just person . . . the story of the reader,"[76] or, as we might prefer to say, the story of the worshiper.

According to this view, the story involves a conflict between the protagonist and an opposing figure, which can be resolved only by the third major character, God. The protagonist can be the psalmist, the just, Israel, or the king; the opposition can be the enemy, enemies, the wicked, or the nations. A fourth character appears in many psalms to witness the struggle among the three major characters. This witness can be community members, the faithful, the just, or the nations. While the specific identity of the characters may vary from psalm to psalm, the underlying story in which they participate is evident in all. Terence Collins, whose analysis I have summarized in this paragraph, recasts Psalm 3 into the constituent elements of this central plot:

> Enemies attack the psalmist.
> The Lord provides protection and assistance.
> The psalmist turns to the Lord in prayer.

> The Lord answers.
> The psalmist feels secure.
> He is not afraid of his enemies.
> The Lord will rise and save him.
> The Lord destroys the wicked enemies.
> The Lord provides deliverance.
> The Lord will bless his people.[77]

These typical Psalm sentences can, in this structuralist view, be conjugated and take different permutations. The sentence "The Lord answers" can become a question ("How long until you answer me?") or an invocation and imperative ("O Lord, answer me"). While these rhetorical moves lend variety to the basic plot, they don't change the story. And if the story is always told in this straightforward way, it would not be very compelling as narrative. Drama needs conflict, preferably what seems at first like irreconcilable conflict, to thrive.

The conflict that fuels the drama of Psalms is one between authority and experience. Israelite religious authority teaches that there are two clearly antithetical paths for the individual to follow, the way of the righteous and the way of the wicked. The first leads to happiness, and the second to ruin. God rewards the righteous and dooms the wicked. When attacked, God will always save the righteous from the hand of the enemy. We hear this voice of authority throughout Israel's scriptures, from the blessings and curses of Leviticus and Deuteronomy to the supposedly well-meaning counsel of Job's friends. But how can this authoritative doctrine be reconciled with an alternative perception of the world, based on the psalmists' own experience, which sees violence, oppression, and evil rampant in a world that a good and just God has created and is supposed to govern? Experience teaches that the righteous path does not necessarily lead to happiness, nor the wicked path to ruin. In fact, the opposite is often the case. Leibnitz coined the term "theodicy" to describe the branch of philosophy that seeks to reconcile the existence of evil with God's governance of the world. In Psalms, theodicy is not treated abstractly but rather experientially. The testimony of Psalms shows a struggle being waged over the identity and integrity of the protagonist. He or she can follow the counsel of the wicked and abandon faith in God, or can call out to God seeking intervention and, knowing God's ability to intervene, can predict a final deliverance and thereby reaffirm and vindicate faith. The endpoint of this drama is rooted in faith. It resolves conflicts in the current moment by referring to an ultimate destiny, an eschatological vision of a world redeemed, justly governed by God, where the conflict between authority and experience will have disappeared:[78]

Let the sea and all within it thunder,
the world and its inhabitants;
let the rivers clap their hands,
the mountains sing joyously together
at the presence of YHWH,
for He is coming to rule the earth;
He will rule the world justly,
and its peoples with equity. (98:7–9)

A vision such as this one brings us back to the definition of sanctity we used above: "the quality of unquestionableness imputed by a congregation to postulates in their nature neither verifiable nor falsifiable."[79] One cannot argue with a vision of the end, yet, because the Psalms are rooted in conflict, they do indeed dramatize arguments with virtually every sacred postulate of Israel's religion. The conflictual drama of Psalms is central to the life of every believer, for all wrestle with recurrent crises in the life of faith. The drama of Psalms affirms doubt, but in the end transforms it. The questioning and petitioning in Psalms—all the urgent imperatives we noted above—ultimately give way to acts of praise, as summed up in the Hebrew name of the book, *Tehillim.*

Aristotle claimed that tragic drama allows us to identify with the characters presented before us on stage. Though the passions of Greek tragic heroes may be larger than life, we bring our own pity and fear to their stories. Witnessing their deaths, we experience a catharsis of negative emotions. We leave the theater purged and perhaps more in touch with our own human limits.[80] In ancient Israel, the closest thing to Greek dramatic form is the Book of Job,[81] but the most immediate witnesses to the spectacle of Job's ruin, his chorus of friends, fail to be moved to pity and fear. Unschooled in dramatic norms, they did not regard Job's tragedy as something broader that had implications for their theology of retributive justice, with its pretensions of fully explaining the human condition. Thus, when his story ends happily, they are unable to understand the divine providence they have been touting all along. Because they do not personalize Job's story as *the* human story, they are denied that vision of the Voice from the Whirlwind that allows Job to place his own suffering within the context of a larger whole.

In considering the dramatic protagonist in the Book of Psalms, it is impossible to fall into the error of Job's friends. We cannot deny the universal implications of the Psalms story, since we each perform it in the first person. Each of us is meant to identify subjectively with the predicament of the "I," rather than to objectify it as if it were someone else's story, someone else's words. Psalms are a kind of proto-drama, generally uninterested in the discovery of objectified dramatic form. Those psalms that bear the traces of the ritual drama of the ancient Near East, a distinct minority in the collection, are generally hymnic tributes rather than full-fledged dramatic enactments.[82] The closest they get to dramatic form is a dialogue between God and the king, the representative self for all Israel. For the Psalms, quite simply, are always voices in dialogue. By taking on the voices of the psalmists as our own, we affirm the existence of a partner who hears us and responds. By praying the Psalms, we remain open to the full range of our humanity. Though we may sink with the psalmists to the depths of despair, we can also rise with them in exaltation.

A Contest of Voices

While Marxist scholars have argued that religion is a form of traditional authority that exercises rigid ideological domination of one group over another,[83] others with a similar political orientation have offered the valuable corrective that all societies with an ordered system of relations require the negotiated consent of their participants. The dominated class neither passively submits to nor freely adopts the ideology of the dominating class, but rather negotiates with it by appropriating its symbols and rituals on its own terms. The symbols are "a common focus of engagement, a negotiated conflict."[84] The discourse of ideology can therefore be seen as "dialogic, not monolithic, defined by opposition even when the antagonistic voices are suppressed into silence."[85] This view of ideological struggle is quite close to that expressed by Bakhtin in his exposition of the way novelistic discourse functions. His views of dialogic discourse will be a central lens for how we view the contest of voices in the Psalms in the remainder of this chapter.

It has been noted that the acceptance of a liturgical order is a fundamental social act. By accepting and performing ritual acts and utterances, one expresses a commitment to the collective mythos of the society and its authority.[86] When the biblical text says, "Let all the people say 'Amen!' " (Ps. 106:48), as one scholar of ritual notes, they are coming together around a Yes, an affirmation of collective will, "even when it is pronounced in a season of death, fear, or disaster."[87] Yet, it must also be acknowledged that in performing collective liturgy, however firm one's assent to it, one is still enmeshed in an order encoded by another. If ritual is to provide a forum for the negotiated consent of the ritualized agents, if it is not to be totalitarian, then it needs to make room for ambiguous private sentiments and individual autonomy, lest these accumulate and blow society apart. Ritual cannot totally fuse an imagined world with a lived-in world. Rather, the world of ritual, as we encounter it in Psalms, remains open to the experience of individuals and thus inevitably becomes involved in ideological struggle. Two central concepts of Bakhtin's are especially helpful in elaborating this notion. Bakhtin sees an inevitable tension between what he calls the "authoritative word" of a culture, its political and religious orthodoxy, and an "internally persuasive discourse," that which is meaningful to the individual on its own and not because of the authority with which it is invested.[88] "The authoritative word demands that we acknowledge it, that we make it our own; it binds us, quite independent of any power it might have to persuade us internally; we encounter it with its authority already fused to it. . . . One must either totally affirm it, or totally reject it."[89]

The psalmists indeed struggle to reconcile what other people say is true with their own sense of what is real. In seeking an internally persuasive discourse, a faith that they can affirm because it is theirs, rather than something that has been taught to them, the psalmists find themselves intimately involved with the words of others, those of both God and the wicked. Their religious tradition has taught them that God saves the people of Israel from its enemies and cares for each and every one of God's faithful. Contrary to these catechistic truths are the pronouncements of the atheists, who deny such claims for a providential God. And, as we shall see, the psalmists take pains to include both sorts of statements within their own discourse. Some men are quoted as saying, " 'There is, then, a reward for the righteous; / indeed God does judge on earth' " (58:12), while others say, " 'How could God know? / Is there knowledge with the Most High?' " (73:11). Through this contest of quotations, of "contentious tongues" (31:21), we witness in the Psalms what Bakhtin calls "the ideological becoming" of human beings, seen in the "process of selectively assimilating the words of others."[90]

The ideological drama of Psalms is sustained by bringing the three major characters of the story vividly before us; the protagonist, the opponent, and God all have speaking parts. In the "I"-drama of Psalms, the psalmists tend to quote the other characters as part of their own discourse. The new Jewish Publication Society version of Psalms, which is conservative in this regard, places quotation marks in no fewer than sixty-six of the one hundred and fifty prayer-poems in the collection.[91] Like other ancient languages, Hebrew had no orthographic means for representing quotation marks, and furthermore, its poets often omitted a verb of speaking to introduce quoted direct speech. Thus, we often experience rapid and potentially confusing shifts in perspective. In chapter 2, we looked at one psalm with such a shifting perspective, and assigned different portions to different speakers/singers, as in a play. That certainly is possible for psalms with well-defined liturgical settings. But most of the psalms in which voices are quoted do not fall into this category. When the quotation is part of the discourse of a single speaker, we need to look at this phenomenon as a contest within a single mind: Whose voice speaks the loudest? To whom should the psalmist listen? God? The wicked? The faithful bystanders? Even the protagonist is further divided among multiple private voices: my past self that trusted in God, my past self that failed to trust.

Quoted voices are not limited to any specific genre of psalms, but are found in them all. Because of its prevalence, we might well point to quoting another's word as one of the stylistic hallmarks of the whole collection of Psalms. In Bakhtin's theory of dialogic discourse, quoting another's word is the essential feature that makes a novel a novel. The narrator creates the voices of fictional characters, who in turn evoke the voices with whom they interact. For example, the narrative statement "He said that I was a fool" includes an indirectly quoted voice, presumably antithetical to the opinion of the one speaking the sentence, yet now a part of his discourse. A question ("Am I or am I not a fool?") or a repudiation ("He is the fool") must inevitably follow. Quoting another's word thus leads to an inner dialogue. As the dialogic principle that underlies prose fiction, quotation allows for the interplay of many voices in all their diversity and stratification, what Bakhtin calls social *heteroglossia*, or many-voicedness. Quotation in effect creates a community of voices that allows for a potentially fruitful mutual interaction between one's own and another's word.

Bakhtin thought that poetry, being a discourse of the first person, lacked this "mutual interaction with alien discourse" that characterized prose fiction,[92] but the evidence of the Psalms does not bear him out. Bakhtin's theory celebrated the novel because its interplay of voices was crucial in his own Marxist-Leninist society, which had cut off the free exchange of ideas. Since poetry tends to be dominated by a "monologic" or single lyric voice, it did not well serve Bakhtin's social ends. He therefore dismissed poetic attempts to bring in multiple voices as merely rhetorical strategies of a controlling mind, which silences other voices even as it may appear to give them freedom to speak. But rhetoric, the art of argumentation, is not alien to the poetry of Psalms, which is a poetry as much of persuasion and dialogue as of self-expression. Hence the equal prominence of first- and second-person pronouns. As the solo voice calls out to You, God, or you, the congregation, it persuasively controls the flow of discourse and could easily shut out alien voices. Instead, they are repeatedly voiced because the psalmists' quarrel with them leads to important internal quarrels over the nature and power of God. Such quarrels provide an ideological fulcrum for the drama of Psalms.

A straightforward example of such quotation, where the various speakers are clearly identified, is Psalm 12. It deals with the troubling issues of theodicy that we have identified as the central story of Psalms. In this as in many other psalms, the righteous are identified as the poor and needy, and, by implication, the wicked are the rich, a characterization made more explicit in other psalms. This polarity reveals one of the important ideological pressure points for this religious culture. The authoritative word promises material rewards for loyalty to God, yet the individual is situated in a stratified economic world, which has no corre-spondence with morality. The situation is intolerable, and demands a response:

> Help, YHWH!
> For the faithful are no more;
> the loyal have vanished from among men.
> Men speak lies to one another;
> their speech is smooth;
> they talk with duplicity.
> May YHWH cut off all flattering lips,
> every tongue that speaks arrogance.
> They say, "By our tongues we shall prevail;
> with lips such as ours, who can be our master!"
>
> "Because of the groans of the plundered poor and needy,
> I will now act," says YHWH.
> "I will give help," He affirms to him.
> The words of YHWH are pure words,
> silver purged in an earthen crucible,
> refined sevenfold.
> You, YHWH, will keep them,
> guarding each from this age evermore.
> On every side the wicked roam
> when baseness is exalted among men.

The world is in crisis because of a breakdown in speech. There is a vast gap between what is in the heart and what is on the tongue, as is indicated in a more literal translation of verse 3b: "with . . . a double heart they speak" (RSV). After the psalmist condemns the wicked on the basis of their false speech, they ironically condemn themselves in their own voices, as they vaunt the very tongue and lips that the psalmist has accused of falsehood. The rank hypocrisy of the wicked is balanced in the psalm by the ultimate truth-speaker, God. While the speech of the wicked is all self-referential boasting, God does not speak of the truly awesome powers of divine speech, but rather of divine action. God's speech is itself a performative action, a promise to the poor and needy. The rhetorical strategy in the first half of the psalm is to present the wicked through the prejudicial view of the psalmist, before summoning them up in their own words, so that we auditors have already formed a clear response to them by the time we hear their words. In the second movement of the psalm, this strategy is reversed, allowing God's words first to speak for themselves, to be followed by the psalmist's praise of their truth. It cannot be accidental that God's words are associated with the refinement of silver, a familiar economic process that forms a standard of value even for the wicked, who are the metaphoric dross (the base metals) purged away by the fiery purity of God's word. If most of "the faithful are no more," and "the loyal have vanished from among men" (v. 2), then at least those who remain can rely on God's incontrovertible words to bolster their faith. If the current lying generation seems to be prevailing, the psalmist assures them that it will not last forever. The last line of the psalm indicates that the task incumbent on the protagonist is to use human speech truthfully: not to flatter the powerful so they are exalted, but to debase them through psalms such as this one.

This psalm offers one of the clearest examples of the contest of dramatized voices in Psalms. It shows us how quoting another's word in the midst of one's own discourse can contribute to the structure of an argument and its persuasive power. Bakhtin noted that each speech genre has its own typical conception of the addressee, which defines it as a genre. The addressee is present in the unfolding of the discourse, for the speaker constructs an argument in anticipation of a particular response. The contest of quotations in Psalms reflects what Bakhtin calls an "internal dramatism."[93] These agonistic prayer-poems are shaped by multiple addressees with conflicting potential responses. The psalmist needs to communicate on several fronts at once: with the wicked, who oppose his belief system, and with God and other believers, who help sustain it. The psalmist cannot afford to have any of them disappear into silence, since their presence in his mind gives shape to the enunciation through which he defines his own existence.

God Speaks

The divine word establishes order, both at the beginning of creation and in the ritual world of the Temple in Jerusalem. While the numinous presence of God certainly can be experienced through silence, the Psalms tend to regard silence as an absence. Their ideal is dialogue. It is no surprise, then, that God's voice is heard in sixteen psalms, comprising several different contexts. In some God recalls past promises made to the Davidic king (2, 89, 110, 132) or the founding events of the nation (68, 81, 95, 105). In others God delivers performative exhortations, judgments, and promises to individuals in distress (12, 35, 91), to the nation and its enemies (46, 50, 75, 90), and to other gods (82). In these psalms in which God is brought forward as a speaker, the human protagonists quarrel with the wicked who deny God's providence, with the nations that oppose Israel, and with God, who seems to have forgotten past promises to judge the wicked (82) and to support the Davidic dynasty (132).

How are we to take such divine speeches? From the point of view of the lay participants in the liturgy, they could be seen as oracles delivered through an individual psalmist, a Levite, or perhaps a recognized cultic prophet.[94] To the devotee who appears on God's threshold, such speeches offer the ultimate promise of religious liminality, a direct encounter with transcendence. From the point of view of the Levitical officials who speak the God-voice, this authoritative word is a channeling of God's ongoing self-revelation to Israel through the legitimate institutions of the Temple cult. The God-voice did not stand apart in any way from the parallelistic poetic idiom used for the rest of their sacred songs. From the point of view of speech-act theory, God's speeches are significant actions in the world of the participants. They have performative force within the ritual, and performative effect in the world that exists beyond the framework of ritual. From a dramatic point of view, a speech by God is significantly positioned within a given psalm. When it is the last word, then we can be sure that it has been arranged to offer incontrovertible and authoritative truth. When God does not get the last word, then it is a signal that we should attend carefully to how the psalmist enters into dialogue with the authoritative word, by framing it with his own.

In describing the role of authoritative discourse in the European novel, Bakhtin comments that because of its absolute nature, "authoritative discourse permits no play with the context framing it, no play with its borders, no gradual and flexible transitions."[95] To remain authoritative and timeless, such a word—whether it be religious, political, or scientific— must not enter into the novelistic dialogue and so must be set apart stylistically from the dialogic interplay of voices. The case is rather different in the drama of the Psalms, where the authoritative word is fused with the sacred context framing it. Thus, at a chosen moment, the human narrator simply begins quoting God in the first person, shifting into third-person descriptions of God's actions and then back into first-person recitations in the voice of God. Here is an example from Psalm 81, which recalls God's providential care for the formative Israelite generation. The reader should attend carefully to the pronouns in the following excerpt:

> He imposed it as a decree upon Joseph
> when he went forth from the land of Egypt;
> I heard a language that I knew not.
> I relieved his shoulder of the burden,
> his hands were freed from the basket. (Vv. 6–7)

> Those who hate YHWH shall cower before Him;
> their doom shall be eternal.
> He fed them the finest wheat,
> I sated you with honey from the rock. (Vv. 16–17)

In these pairs of consecutive lines, a modern reader first is likely to find incoherence, and then may wonder how it is that "He, God" and "I, God" are interchangeable locutions. An ancient listener would presumably have understood that a psalmist's discourse exercised authority precisely because it could blur the line between personal speech and the speech of divinity.[96]

When prophets spoke the word of God, they needed to establish their authority as part of their discourse. As divinely inspired individuals in search of an audience, whether in the marketplace, at the palace, or at the city gates, they begin their discourse with an introductory formula that authorizes their speech, "Thus says the Lord." This phrase demarcates the divine speech that is about to be delivered from the surrounding human context. It gives us a sense of both the divine origins of such speech and its mediation through a chosen (or self-chosen) human being. The psalmists, by contrast, are not only individual speakers but representatives of an institution, the Temple cult, with all its authority and prestige. The context of ritual ensures that God's speech will be treated with the sanctity befitting everything that takes place in the Temple. Therefore, the psalms in which God speaks do not need to set off that speech as a special revelation, signaled, as at Sinai, by thunder and lightning. The psalmists simply present the divine word with the authority of their office fused to it. In Bakhtin's words, "it stands and falls together with that authority."[97]

But God's speech, of course, does go back to Sinai. In the collective memory of Israel, divine speech is lodged in the zone of sacred history in order to be retrieved and applied to the present. Bakhtin explains the process in his terms: "the authoritative word is located in a distanced zone, organically connected with a past that is felt to be hierarchically higher. It is so to speak, the word of the fathers. Its authority was *acknowl-edged* in the past. It is a *prior* discourse. It is therefore not a question of choosing it from among other possible discourses that are its equal."[98]

Psalm 95 is a good example of a psalm in which we can see the continuing power of this prior discourse. The psalm opens with a community procession of praise, led by a choirmaster: "Come let us sing joyously to YHWH" (v. 1a). The people, singing with one voice, are enjoined to bow down, bend the knee, and kneel "before YHWH our maker" (v. 6). A metaphor confirms the subservience of the requested gesture: "for He is our God / and we are the people He tends, the flock in His hands" (v. 7a, b). At this moment, when the choirmaster has the people acknowledging their utter dependence on God, he exhorts them: "O, if you would but heed His charge this day" (v. 7c). He then takes them, without transition, from the present to the remembered past of Israel's early encounters with God. In speaking now, the leader's voice becomes God:

> "Do not be stubborn as at Meribah,
> as on the day of Massah, in the wilderness,
> when your fathers put Me to the test,
> tried Me, though they had seen My deeds.
> Forty years I was provoked by that generation;
> I thought, 'They are a senseless people;
> they would not know My ways.'
> Concerning them I swore in anger,
> 'They shall never come to My resting-place.' " (Vv. 10–11)

Not only does the psalmist now speak as God, but he remembers what God remembers. God made this vow (in slightly different words) in Numbers 14:22–23, after being angered by the ten spies' failure to acknowledge the goodness of the land to which God was bringing them, and after they had demoralized the people. By alluding to the whole series of rebellions in the wilderness, with their familiar consequences, the speaker does not need to make the analogy explicit. The current generation is given to understand that it too can lose God's favor by spurning the covenant. In bringing the authority of sacred history to bear on the present moment, the psalmist plays on the convention that God's word is the strongest and most authoritative in the culture. There can be no stronger speaker than God quoting God. Therefore the prayer leader does not again speak to the crowd in his own voice, which would only diminish the authority he has gained in speaking as God.

This is indeed a rhetorical use of double-voicedness, intended to persuade. The Levite or cultic prophet uses the hieratic divine voice as an extension of his own exhortation to the worshiping crowd. In all the psalms in which the God-voice is given the last word,[99] the psalmist similarly appropriates the performative force of God's speeches and their inherent dramatic quality to bolster his own persuasive powers. The worshiper may or may not believe the psalmist's assurance that God will protect him; it comes to seem unquestionable, however, when promised in

God's own voice. Who can argue with God proclaiming, "All the horns of the wicked I will cut; / but the horns of the righteous shall be lifted up" (75:11)? For all their persuasive power, such speeches nevertheless feel staged. More compelling are the cases in which the divine voice is quoted in order to quarrel with it. Precisely because the conventions of psalmody allowed for the blurring of boundaries between one's own discourse and God's, psalmists could challenge God with God's own words.[100]

In Psalm 90, this challenge revolves around repetition of forms of the verb "to return." "You return man to dust; You decreed, 'Return you mortals!' " (v. 3). The first "return," in the psalmist's language, signals a natural process, while the second is God's call for moral regeneration, familiarly delivered through the prophets,[101] and now quoted back to God by the psalmist. Toward the end of the petitionary poem, the psalmist picks up God's own quoted language to plead, "Turn, Lord! How long? / Show mercy to your servants" (v. 13). The imperative phrases "Return, mortals" and "Turn, Lord" (vv. 3, 13) use plural and singular forms of the same verb. Just as God can ask the people to return in repentance, so the psalmist, as the people's representative, can use God's language to enjoin God to turn back to the people.[102] Natural process need not lead quickly to dust, in this psalmist's word play, if God chooses to respond to their prayer and "prosper the work of our hands" (v. 17).

In a similar vein, but showing a much bolder freedom with the divine voice, is the psalm that most closely resembles a dramatic spectacle. In Psalm 82, God does not speak performatively but rather fictively, in a representation of how God might speak in a divine tribunal if we humans were privileged to overhear it. As commentators have noted, this heavenly council is a mythological motif common to the ancient Near East, appearing elsewhere in the Bible in the prologue to Job, in the story of creation ("Let us make man in our image"; Gen. 1:26), and in the plural name of God, *'Elohim.*[103] The psalm does not, however, depict a purely mythological scene, for God, the chief actor in the psalm, is also its ultimate addressee:

1.   God stands in the divine assembly;
      among the divine beings He pronounces judgment:

2.   "How long will you judge perversely,
      showing favor to the wicked?   *Selah.*

3.   Judge the wretched and the orphan,
      vindicate the lowly and the poor,

4.   rescue the wretched and the needy;
      save them from the hand of the wicked.

5.   (They neither know nor understand,
       they go about in darkness;
       all the foundations of earth totter.)
6.   I had taken you for divine beings,
       Sons of the Most High, all of you;
7.   but you shall die as men do,
       fall like any prince."
8.   Arise, O God, judge the earth,
       for all the nations are your possession.

In this heavenly scenario, God assembles "the divine beings," presumably the inferior gods of other nations, to pronounce judgment upon them for having failed to uphold justice in the world. An alternative translation of v. 1b might read "in the midst of God, He judges." *'Elohim*, the word translated as "divine beings," is precisely the same as that used for God in verse 1a, subtly suggesting the ambiguous subject of the whole psalm. Can God judge God? Can human beings? One view of the poem has the poet interrupting the proceedings at several points: first speaking in an aside (v. 5), then to the defendants (vv. 6–7), and finally to God (v. 8). I have followed the view of most translators that the poet allows God to conduct the entire prosecution (including a dramatic aside in v. 5),[104] and reserves for himself the first and decisive last line.

The psalmist has imaginatively stationed God in a heavenly assembly in order to turn on God from an earthly vantage point at the end of the psalm: "Arise, O God, judge the earth" (v. 8a). The poem begins in the guise of a heavenly court case, but becomes in its sharp final line a plea for God's just government, seemingly absent from the terrestrial order. The justice that God asks of the inferior divine beings in heaven is precisely what the psalmist demands of God on earth. When God challenges the other gods, "How long?" (v. 2), we hear the "how long" of other psalmic laments (e.g., Ps. 90:13). In the inner dialogue of the poem, God's judgment is reheard through the echo of the final judging line, so that the whole poem becomes charged with irony. When God commands the inferior gods to "judge the wretched and the orphan," to "rescue the wretched and the needy" (v. 3b, c), we hear echoes of another sharp biblical genre, the prophetic lawsuit, which is usually couched as God's quarrel with Israel, or with its national enemies, but also, in one memorable instance, as the prophet's quarrel with God:

> You will win, YHWH, if I make claim against You,
> Yet I shall present charges against You:
> Why does the way of the wicked prosper,
> Why are the workers of treachery at ease? (Jer. 12:1)[105]

Jeremiah, like Job, presses on with his suit, even though he does not expect to win, yet simply stating his claim as forcefully as he does indicates how free he feels in his relationship with God. The cultic poet of Psalm 82 is less direct, but if anything more pointed, choosing to challenge God with God's own words. This covert, double-voiced strategy arises from what is certainly a deep internal quarrel. Having taken the authoritative word of the culture as internally persuasive, this psalmist is acutely sensitive to contradictions to that word, embodied in the plight of the lowly poor or the wretched orphan. The dynamism of the prayer-poem derives from the poet's willingness to expose divine injustice as a rift in the fabric of authoritative ideology.

The plea that ends Psalm 82 is, however, a redressive action, an attempt to remedy a breach between human reality and divine rhetoric. Summoning the energy of both divine and human words, the psalmist tries to bring God back into a conversation that God started and human beings feel has been interrupted. This is the reason that the poet speaks God's words of judgment in Psalm 82, words that the people would like to hear God speak and, better still, act upon. With the concluding imperative, "Arise, O God, judge the earth," the poet deconstructs the fictiveness of the discourse that opened the psalm, saying in effect: "My fictionalized words as God have no performative force. But because You listen to human prayer, my direct call can reestablish a relation to You. And I know that Your words are supremely able to perform what they say [cf. Gen. 1]. Since we all know what You *can* say and do, why not do what is right?" Only God's active response to this challenge can make the authoritative faith of the culture internally persuasive again for this psalmist and his community.

The Word of the Wicked

While the word of God is acknowledged as the most potent in the culture, the word of the wicked is perhaps even more central to the ideological formation of the psalmists. "Consciousness awakens to independent ideological life," Bakhtin writes, "precisely in a world of alien discourses surrounding it, and from which it cannot initially separate itself."[106] The words of the wicked awaken the consciousness of many psalmists, because if what the wicked say about the world is true—that there is no God, no deliverance from misfortune, no accountability for one's actions—then the whole of Israel's collective life is a lie. Just as the psalmists attained potency vis-à-vis the authoritative word of God by transmitting it, emulating it, and even subjecting it to ironic reproof, so must they become potent speakers in relation to the word of God's adversaries. The psalmists quote the words of the wicked in poems addressed to God, yet presumably, an omniscient God knows what the wicked say. The psalmists do so in order to challenge God, in the presence of the assembled community, to overturn the words of the wicked.

Yet this process of incorporating an alien discourse inevitably dulls the psalmists' polemical thrust against the wicked. The authoritative word of the culture enters into dialogue with skeptical, alien words that may prove subversive. Raymond Carpentier reminds us that "truly to engage in dialogue would be to question one's own being, through the information that comes from another. It would be to accept the risk that the other might remold us in his image and destroy all that makes us what we are."[107] The psalmists do not want to be in an open dialogue with the wicked. They prefer the security of monologue, of their own self-sufficient vocabulary, but they are in dialogue with the wicked despite themselves. They may hope that "sinners disappear from the earth / and the wicked be no more" (104:35a), but, as Bakhtin reminds us, "in dialogue the destruction of the opponent also destroys that very dialogic sphere where the word lives."[108] Silencing the wicked would be tantamount to silencing the psalmists themselves, who, we should remember, are the ones who quote the atheistic words of the wicked in the Psalms. Whether or not these quoted words represent a shadowy side of their own thoughts, they become part of the psalmists' discourse and enter into dialogue with it. We shall see how this dialogic influence reveals the struggle within the psalmists' faith.

There are twenty-four psalms that quote the wicked, both their direct speech and their thoughts, while numerous others allude to the speech of the wicked without quoting them.[109] While the psalmists' mouths and hearts are occupied in prayer, outside the doors of the Temple is a world whose very foundations are shaken by an alien discourse strikingly opposed to the psalmists' statements of faith. Here is a sampling of jibes directed personally at psalmists, followed by denials directed at the psalmists' God:

> "Aha, just what we wished! . . .
> We have destroyed him!" (35:25)

> "There is no deliverance for him from God." (3:3)

> "When will he die and his name perish?" (41:6)

> "Where is your God?" (42:4, 11)

> "God has forsaken him;
> Chase him and catch him,
> for no one will save him." (71:11)

    ***

"God is not mindful,
He hides His face; He never looks." (10:11)

"There is no God." (14:1)

"Yah does not see it,
The God of Jacob does not pay heed." (94:7)

"By our tongues, we shall prevail;
with lips such as ours, who can be our master?" (12:5)

The Psalms are full of metonymies for speech such as "mouth," "lips," "tongue," "teeth," "throat," and, for unspoken speech, "heart." Hiding something in the heart should keep a person invulnerable,[110] but in their linguistic will to power, the psalmists infiltrate not only the vocal organs but the hidden self-consciousness of their adversaries as well. We know from the formulaic phrase "He says in his heart"[111] that the psalmists represent the speeches of the wicked as inward, and that these can therefore be seen as fictive constructions,[112] and possibly as projections of the psalmists' own thoughts.[113] Similarly, with respect to the outward speech of the wicked, we recognize a thematic consistency in their deliberate negations of Israel's central beliefs. We cannot know exactly what words the psalmists heard some wicked individuals say before inventing these stylized words for them. What we do know is that the wicked and the psalmists both want to prevail with their tongues. But where the wicked insist on the autonomy of human speech, the psalmists make their speech acts contingent on acts of God. The psalms that quote the wicked do not merely ask God to recite authoritative words, as we saw God do in some historically oriented psalms. Instead, to revalidate the sacred history of the past, they demand God's powerful and persuasive acts of salvation and justice.

In their struggle against the influential discourse of the wicked, the psalmists represent their antagonists by quoting their speech and by depicting their deeds. This doubling is apt, since the wicked do not merely speak unjustly, but also perpetrate all manner of evil deeds against the poor and the weak. We can seize on an important link between the representation of the wicked's speech and actions. They are depicted as hunters of the lowly, devising nets that they pull shut when the hapless fall into their power (10:9–10). The same psalm that depicts them as hunters, not surprisingly, wishes that they be "caught in the schemes they devise" (v. 2). Two verses later, this word for schemes is used in apposition to the quoted thought of the wicked, " 'there is no God' " (literal translation v. 4b). These clever links in the psalmist's diction point to the conclusion that the atheistic thoughts of the wicked *are* the net in which they will be caught.

"Let the net they hid catch them" (Ps. 35:8) is the way another psalmist reflects on their fate.

To catch the wicked in the net of their own thoughts is what Bakhtin would describe as conducting experiments and getting "solutions in the language of another's discourse."[114] In order for another's word to be used thus dialogically, according to Bakhtin, that word must first be announced in the speaker's own discourse. Psalm 10, which we have just been considering, opens by announcing the speaker's theme: "Why, YHWH, do you stand aloof, / heedless in times of trouble?" (v. 1). This sense of distance between God and human beings is echoed and extended in the more radical words of the arrogant one who thinks, " 'He does not call to account; there is no God' " (v. 4). The wicked speaker is characterized through further quotation:

> "I shall not be shaken,
> through all time never be in trouble." (V. 6)

> "God is not mindful,
> He hides His face, He never looks." (V. 11)

When the words of the wicked are quoted for a fourth and final time, the words are reaccentuated by the psalmist. "Why should the wicked man scorn God, / thinking You do not call to account?" (v. 13). In the previously quoted speeches, the wicked one spoke of God only in a distant third person; this final quotation, rendered in free indirect discourse, is in the second person, because the psalmist has transposed the words of the wicked into a new context, a direct interrogation of God.

The words of the wicked are alien to the psalmist, and yet, since they are also possible conclusions to be drawn from the psalm's opening lament over the aloofness of God, these alien words exercise a "capacity to further creative life" in the psalmist's ideological consciousness. "The internally persuasive word," Bakhtin writes, "is half ours and half someone else's. It . . . awakens our own independent words, . . . it organizes masses of our words from within, and does not remain in an isolated and static condition. . . . This discourse is able to reveal ever new *ways to mean*."[115] A closed issue for the wicked is an open question for the psalmist. Thus, "He never looks" (v. 11) becomes "You do look!" (v. 14).[116] "He does not call to account" (v. 4), reaccentuated as the interrogative "Why then should the wicked . . . think You do not call to account?" (v. 13), becomes the speaker's entrée for calling God to account, and thereby opening up the very possibility that the wicked have foreclosed. By freely adapting the alien word of the wicked, the psalmist "conducts experiments and gets solutions in the language of another's discourse."[117]

In the remainder of the prayer-poem, the psalmist speaks of God hearing the pleas of the lowly, so "that men who are of the earth tyrannize no more" (v. 18). The economically dominant members of the society have, by their actions and words, alienated themselves from the YHWH ideology, which has here been appropriated by a speaker from the dominated class, or by one who identifies with them, to use against their oppressors. In assuring himself that YHWH identifies with the poor and downtrodden, the speaker reactivates internally persuasive words of faith that had been suspended in the terrifying perception of God's aloofness. But how certain is the psalmist's conviction? Three modern translations offer quite different readings of the closing lines of this psalm. Weiser offers an already completed action: "O Lord, Thou hast heard the desire of the meek."[118] Equally firm, but deferring God's response to the future, is the JPS version, which reads "You will listen to the entreaty of the lowly, O LORD." Dahood uses an imperative to represent the psalmist's urgency: "Hear, O Yahweh, the lament of the poor" (v. 17).[119] Underlying the psalmist's sense of having arrived at an internally persuasive solution, there may yet linger a tone of entreaty, since the justice the psalmist desires has not yet come to pass. However we choose to interpret the ideological closure of the poem, it is undeniable that much has changed between speaker and addressee in these final lines. As a result of the psalm's inner dialogue, the authoritative words of Israel's faith can once again be spoken by the psalmist. The absent God no longer stands aloof, "heedless in times of trouble" (v. 1).

I Am What I Speak

An individual history, says one student of ideology, is a "patchwork of compliance, resistance, misunderstanding," and "personal appropriation" of the controlling discourses that surround us. If we arrive at a point where this process of identity formation has been "redemptive" for us[120]—that is, we feel we have found a satisfying place within the order of society that we acknowledge as our own—then we are likely to offer our individual histories to others as acts of confessional self-disclosure, which will in turn become part of their process of identity-making. Not only do we find out important things about who we are through confessions of loyalty, faith, or sinfulness, but we also make available such knowledge to our discourse communities. An important part of knowing who we are, of course, is knowing who we are not, but this is not always so easy. Consciousness, Bakhtin tells us, cannot initially separate itself from alien discourse. But when it begins to do so, it turns "persuasive discourse into speaking persons," especially when "a struggle against such images has already begun."[121] In a struggle for power, writes Michel Foucault, each side "constitutes for the other a kind of permanent limit, a point of possible reversal."[122] For the psalmists, the wicked define such a permanent limit, beyond which they cannot go and retain their identities. Yet what are they to make of their attraction to this self-defining limit?

We can see the history of a struggle to liberate oneself from a compelling but alien discourse in Psalm 73, a poem that objectifies the wicked, even as it expresses the psalmist's guilty attraction to their image and words. In this psalm the struggle is presented to us as a completed action, told through the hindsight of one who has escaped great peril:

> As for me, my feet had almost strayed,
> My steps were nearly led off course,
> for I envied the profligate,
> I saw the wicked at ease.
> Death has no pangs for them;
> Their body is healthy.
> They have no part in the travail of men;
> They are not afflicted like the rest of mankind. (Vv. 3–5)

Given this idealizing envy, we can imagine the psalmist's susceptibility to their words when they said, " 'How could God know? / Is there knowledge with the Most High?' " (v. 11). "Had I decided to say these things, / I should have been false to the circle of Your disciples" (v. 15). Speeches, as we have said, are acts with consequences. To have said these words would have turned the poet into one of the wicked, cut off from the community of the faithful and from God. To have considered saying them but resisted (until this psalm, that is) reveals the inner struggle into which this psalmist has been led. And it was at this point in the struggle, the psalmist tells us, that "I entered God's sanctuary and reflected on their fate" (v. 17), and a radical shift in perspective ensues. The psalmist sees the wicked and their fate with new eyes:

> You surround them with flattery,
> make them fall through blandishments.
> How suddenly are they ruined,
> wholly swept away by terrors.
> When You are aroused You despise their image,
> as one does a dream after waking, Lord. (Vv. 18–20)

In the next chapter we shall explain this transformation from the point of view of sacred space, but in our dialogic context it can be illuminated by a remark of Bakhtin's. "A conversation with an internally persuasive word that one has begun to resist may continue, but it takes on another character: it is questioned, it is put in a new situation in order to expose its weak sides, to get a feel for its boundaries, to experience it physically as an object."[123] The psalmist reexperiences the existence of the wicked in the context of God's sanctuary to gain a totally new vision of their claims for invulnerability. Earlier in the poem, it was the tangible solidity and physicality of the wicked's bodily ease ("fat shuts out their eyes," v. 7) that made their image and discourse seem incontrovertible to the psalmist. But in the Temple, a different vision of truth emerges. "Nearness to God" defines the "good" (v. 28) that is accessible to the psalmist "forever" (v. 26), while distance from God, as is manifested in the lives of the wicked, limits them to a life that will "perish" (v. 27). They are essentially dead, then, even as they boast of their material pleasures.[124] In this new view, the wicked become as insubstantial as "a dream after waking." Awakened from the common materialistic dream, the poet recants the earlier idealization of the wicked: "I was a dolt, without knowledge; / I was brutish toward You" (v. 22).

In this psalm, we see the poet in dialogue not only with the words of the wicked, but also with the almost-spoken words and thoughts of an earlier self: what he could have said aloud but did not. Insofar as "the ideological becoming of a human being" is, as Bakhtin has said, "the process of selectively assimilating the words of others,"[125] it extends quite naturally to selecting among the words of the various selves that we have been. For a variety of reasons, it can be important to keep open an internal conversation with past selves. In Psalm 32, we saw the psalmist quoting his past performative declaration: "I said aloud, 'I hereby confess my transgressions to YHWH,'[126] / and You forgave the guilt of my sin" (v. 5). Recalling this earlier speech and its immediate efficacy is the psalmist's means of urging those in his worshiping community to similarly confess their sins and accept the guidance of God.[127] One efficacious speech, it is hoped, produces others. Other psalmists who quote themselves do not want to have to reinvent their relationship with God each time they speak. Just as we saw God invoking prior divine discourse, drawing on the divine memory for corroboration of Israel's current sinfulness (cf. Ps. 95), so individuals quote their own prior discourse to corroborate their faithfulness. Having spoken well in the past and been rewarded by a providential act of God, at a time of later distress they do well to remind God of that earlier conversation:

> I said to YHWH: "You are my God;
> give ear, YHWH, to my pleas for mercy.
> O God, my Lord, the strength of my deliverance,
> You protected my head on the day of battle;

> YHWH, do not grant the desires of the wicked;
> do not let their plans succeed,
> else they be exalted." (140:7–9)

Through the act of quotation, the praying self who now speaks establishes continuity with the self who prayed efficaciously in the past. To the prayer which earned deliverance, the speaker now adds the performative force of a curse: "May the heads of those who beset me / be covered with the mischief of their lips; / may coals of fire drop down upon them, / and they be cast into pits, never to rise again" (vv. 10–11).

But what if the psalmists cannot and do not want to establish a continuity with those earlier selves? In such psalms, the dialogic element is quite pronounced. The psalmists recant what they said in the past, because they spoke what they no longer wish to emulate. They mistakenly thought that the self was unshakable (Ps. 30), or unsavable (Ps. 31), or that human beings were not to be trusted (Ps. 116). In the most extended and eloquent of these quotations from a past self, the psalmist admits to having given way to an unjustified flight of fancy:

> I said:
> "O that I had the wings of a dove!
> I would fly away and find rest;
> lo, I would flee far off;
> I would lodge in the wilderness;
> I would soon find me a refuge
> from the sweeping wind,
> from the tempest." (55:7–9)

His thoughts are jumbled throughout the psalm, sometimes accusing God, sometimes an enemy, sometimes a friend. Only at the end of the psalm does a voice offer him a sure point of rest: "Cast your burden on YHWH and He will sustain you; / He will never let the righteous man collapse" (v. 23). He had been wrong when he spoke in the past; there is no refuge apart from God.

At their most dramatic, these recantatory psalms sizzle with the energy of transformation, as can be seen from a brief glance at Psalm 30, which we will look at in more detail in the next chapter. "When I was untroubled, I thought, 'I shall never be shaken' " (v. 7) is a phrase also spoken by the wicked interlocutor of Psalm 10.[128] The rest of the psalm goes on to dramatize the nadir and zenith of the psalmist's experience: the psalmist remembering being on the verge of death, praying not to "descend into the Pit," and afterward, the psalmist redeemed: "You turned my lament into dancing, / You undid my sackcloth and girded me with joy, / that [my] whole being might sing hymns to You endlessly" (vv. 12–13a). The quotation from an earlier self is the hinge on which the experience of transformation turns. If one's words ("I shall never be shaken") can be proven so wrong by the turn of events—from self-assurance to powerlessness, and again, from mourning to dancing—then that transforming experience can teach one to use words properly: "YHWH my God, I will praise You forever" (v. 13b).

In the dialogue with God, then, we open ourselves to an inner dialogue that can assume many forms. We can contrast what we said and thought before to what we are willing to think and say now. We can affirm the continuities in our moral character. Or we can examine the very nature of our self-consciousness. How far do my thoughts extend? Where does my mind leave off and God's mind begin?[129] Such forms of internal dialogue are made known to us, however, only because the psalmist makes them known to God. The psalmists' inadequate words cannot compass divinity, but in uttering them, worshipers affirm that they are not alone in the universe, that they have a Creator, Redeemer, and Companion who listens and responds. As Buber points out, the notion of a dialogue with oneself is possible only as a result of our having opened ourselves up to a *Thou*. The spoken word "does not . . . remain with the speaker. It reaches out toward a hearer, it lays hold of him, it even makes the hearer into a speaker, if only a soundless one. . . . The word that is spoken is uttered here and heard there, but its spokenness has its place in 'the between.' "[130] Because they call out toward that One whom they consider eternal, the Psalms rise off the page and into speech. They are spoken here yet heard there, and it is their very spokenness that makes them a medium for dialogue. Dialogue is more than the sum of the speeches of the two partners. It is the openness created between them in the acts of speaking and listening.

We Are What We Speak

In the first chapter, we talked about the special form of community created by ritual. A multitude gathers at a sacred spot at a sacred time for a sacred purpose. It becomes a community insofar as the diverse individuals in the community are all drawn toward a single goal. One of Buber's metaphors for this process is the circle formed around a central point. "It is not," he says, "the periphery, the community, that comes first, but the radii, the common quality of relation with the Centre. This alone guarantees the authentic existence of the community."[131] For a crowd of people to constitute itself not just as a collectivity but as a community, there must be, in Buber's terms, first "a living mutual relation with a living Centre," and second a "living mutual relation with one another."[132] Elsewhere,

Buber calls this mutuality "a dynamic facing of the others, a flowing from *I* to *Thou*."[133] For "only men who are capable of truly saying *Thou* to one another can truly say *We* with one another." Buber goes on to explain the fragility of such a community. "It is enough to prevent the *We* arising, or being preserved, if a single man is accepted, who is greedy of power and uses others as a means to his own end, or who craves of importance and makes a show of himself."[134] Such a community is virtually unimaginable in human affairs as most of us know them. Yet when a multitude of voices turn to God as the single *Thou* whom they address, and bend their individual wills to God's will, there is no selfish hierarchy or divisiveness in their midst. They are a community based on fellowship and equality before God. For the same reason, Rosenzweig saw congregational hymns, those psalms in which we speak as one voice, as a kind of messianic discourse, a harbinger of the complete redemption to come.[135]

Rosenzweig's analysis of Psalm 115, a psalm whose first and last verses both begin with "we," is so penetrating that it deserves to be discussed alongside any presentation of the psalm. He does not historicize the psalm; on the contrary, he presents it as a glimpse into the world seen from the vantage point of eternity. I prefer, however, to begin in history, before transcending it.

The psalm originates, most scholars would agree, in the experience of the Babylonian exile, where the nations must have taunted Israel, saying, "Where, now, is their God?" (v. 2b). The enemies of Israel, as the quotation of their speech makes clear, are the enemies of God. The people have now returned to their homeland, ready to acknowledge God's role in their redemption. The psalm begins in the negative, as if to emphasize the choice the community is not making. They could congratulate themselves on their triumphant return; instead, they attribute all glory to God:

> Not to us, YHWH, not to us
> but to Your name bring glory
> for the sake of Your love and Your faithfulness.
> Why should the nations say,
> "Where, now, is their God?"
> when our God is in heaven
> and all that He wills He accomplishes. (Vv. 1–3)

The next movement of the psalm continues to develop the opposition between Israel and the nations, as it depicts idols and idolatry:

> Their idols are silver and gold,
> the work of men's hands.
> They have mouths, but cannot speak,

> eyes, but cannot see;
> they have ears, but cannot hear,
> noses, but cannot smell;
> they have hands, but cannot touch,
> feet, but cannot walk;
> they can make no sound in their throats.
> Those who fashion them,
> all who trust in them,
> shall become like them. (Vv. 4–8)

It seems that Israel's being an "us" depends on having a "them," against whose values the community defines itself. Surely this triumphalist ridicule does not bespeak the image of a world redeemed, but rather of one sunk in irreconcilable conflict. We and our God are alive; you and your gods are dead.

But, as Rosenzweig observes, the note of ridicule is replaced by one of hopeful trust. The community calls on itself in a series of three commands, directed first to all of Israel, then to the house of Aaron, and finally to all "you who fear YHWH." Each group in turn is enjoined to "trust in YHWH!" for "He is their help and shield" (vv. 9–11). The medieval Jewish commentator Rashi identifies those "who fear YHWH" (v. 11) as converts, those from among the nations who have thrown in their lot with Israel. Rosenzweig seizes on this identification to deconstruct the us-them divisiveness of the previous lines. In the "we" moment of this psalm, Israel sees itself as open to an infusion from "that messianic, yet-to-be congregation of mankind, of We-all. The triumph of trust anticipates the future fulfillment."[136] The lines that follow are an expression of the trusting attitude the community has assumed. It affirms, in the same three-part order, that God will bless Israel, the House of Aaron, and all "those who fear YHWH / small and great alike" (v. 13). The fulfillment of this trust, Rosenzweig explains, is the growth of the blessing from generation to generation: "May YHWH increase your numbers / yours and your children's also" (v. 14).

The universalism sounded in the psalm's attitude to those who willingly forsake idolatry and embrace the living God is furthered in its several references to God and creation. "For this living growth of the blessing," Rosenzweig notes, "is well established from the very first in the mystery of creation," and as a prooftext he cites "May you be blessed by YHWH, / maker of heaven and earth" (v. 14). The next line goes still further in opening the "we" of Israel to the "we-all" of the human community. "The heavens belong to YHWH, / but the earth He gave over to man" (v. 15). "To the sons of men—not to the congregation of Israel," Rosenzweig comments. In the act of love embodied in this psalm, Israel "knows itself only as sons of men in general, it knows only . . . the neighbor."[137]

Earlier in the psalm, the community distinguished between a world alive to the reality of the living God and a world as dead as the idols it worships. The psalm concludes with another contrast between the living and the dead, but this time without making an invidious distinction among the living:

> The dead cannot praise YHWH,
> nor any who go down into silence.
> But we shall praise YHWH
> now and forever.
> Hallelujah. (Vv. 17–18)

The departed will never join in the hymn of praise to God's redeeming powers. But the hymn of praise never dies. "Death plunges into nought in the face of this triumphal shout of eternity. Life becomes immortal in redemption's eternal hymn of praise."[138] As each new generation sings this or any other congregational hymn, it becomes part of "that We of all voices which . . . drags all future eternity into the present Now of the moment," the moment in which God is praised. In Rosenzweig's view, "the We are eternal"; though the "I" suffers and dies, the "We" lives on.[139]

Rosenzweig's theological interpretation here can be aligned with the speech-act perspective explored at the beginning of this chapter. By understanding, as do the speech-act theorists, that both we and the world are changed by our speaking, Rosenzweig focuses our attention on what it means to speak in the voice of a "we" that we may hitherto have regarded as external to our self-definition. Remembering that Rosenzweig came to Jewish theology from the brink of conversion to Christianity, we can sense the tremendous power this identification with the "we" of Israel held for him. As he succinctly put this matter, "its distress is our distress, its rescue our salvation."[140] In aligning himself with the eternally petitioning, eternally praising people of Israel, Rosenzweig committed himself to a path leading from his limited individual life to what he considered to be eternity, namely, redemption's victory over death. "Death," he writes, "plunges into nought" as we shout out God's praise. Since the overwhelming reality of death was the starting point of his existentialist philosophy, we can understand his attraction to a powerful mode of speaking that, within life itself, enables the individual to transcend the boundaries of his or her finitude. As we shall see in the next chapter, the psalmists reckoned with similar issues in mediating between what they took to be God's perspective on life and their own.

·IV·

FROM HERE TO ETERNITY:
THE PERSPECTIVES OF TIME
AND SPACE

The ancient Greek philosopher Heraclitus remarked that one cannot step twice into the same river, a maxim that beautifully encapsulates the human experience of transience and mutability in the mortal, natural world. For Heraclitus, "everything flows and nothing abides; everything gives way, and nothing remains fixed."[1] As popular songs of all eras remind us, time so conceived waits for no one. Yet in the popular religious songs of ancient Israel, the poets speak of a way to stop time's ineluctable flow and still live. Though ancient Israelites took care to divide up the night into three-hour watches, demarcating one time span from another, they understood that to God a whole era of civilization is but an ephemeral moment. By meditating on God and God's perspective on time, the psalmists could step outside the stream of time as we know it: "For in Your sight a thousand years / are like yesterday that has past / like a watch of the night" (90:4). "Better one day in Your courts than a thousand [anywhere else]; / I would rather stand at the threshold of God's house / than dwell in the tents of the wicked" (Ps. 84:10).

These two verses, with their thousandfold multipliers suggesting the contrast between human and divine time frames, succinctly put the issues of this chapter before us. All of human experience is grounded in irreversible time, endlessly passing away. Yet, religious disciplines the world over grant access to a perspective that encompasses human time but stands outside it too. Humans thirst for this alternate experience of time, which we associate with the sacred and with God. Our passage from Psalm 84 reminds us that this sacred dimension of time, what one scholar has called "filled time,"[2] is often experienced in sacred space, set apart by and for ritual. By ritualizing time and space, religions sacralize the very physical dimensions through which we experience the world.

Ordinary time is continuous and irreversible, leading all created beings toward inevitable death. Sacred time, by its very nature, defies death and

130

transience. It is, according to the influential paradigm of Mircea Eliade, *"reversible."* Sacred time reactualizes in the present "a sacred event that took place in a mythical past, 'in the beginning.' "[3] We have already spoken about the Sabbath as an actualization in human terms, on a weekly basis, of God's primordial inactivity after the activity of creation. All religious festivals can be similarly understood as repetition of acts done under the aegis of divinity. "Religious participation in a festival," continues Eliade, "implies emerging from ordinary temporal duration." The festival offers the participant a chance for "reintegration of the mythical time reactualized by the festival itself. Hence sacred time is indefinitely recoverable, indefinitely repeatable." "Reversibility," "reintegration," "reactualization," "recoverability," "repeatability"—all of these parallel words in Eliade's vocabulary point to what he considers to be the central fact about sacred time. It does not pass away. It existed before, as first instituted by the gods or God, and it will continue to exist into the future, as ensured by the traditions of religious ritual. The problem of irreversible time, which is coterminous with human existence in the world, is resolved by the mediation of religion, whose root meaning, of course, is "to connect again." Through participation in religious ritual, we human beings connect ourselves to the divine perspective on time, an unbroken connection that was ours, according to our myths, before our primordial fall into temporality, discord, and death.

Mythological cultures, as Eliade interprets their cultural practice, live under the sway of archetypal images. In mythological cultures, all human acts reproduce or evoke primordial acts, aboriginally performed by gods, heroes, or ancestors. The locations at which these acts were originally performed retain the sanctity of their primordial antecedents. Theophany, the revelation of the god, thus "reveals an absolute fixed point, a center,"[4] around which, as on a sacred axis, the world turns. At such a sacred center, ancient cultures recapitulated the primordial cosmogonic acts that brought the world into being. In Eliade's view, such mythological recapitulation foreshortens all of time into but two significant moments, which strive to become one: the primordial beginning known through myth, and the ritualized present, which over and over again returns mythological cultures to the beginning of time. For Eliade, a person of a traditional mythological culture is most real—that is, most filled with significance—when imitating and repeating the gestures of a primordial self, thereby ceasing to be an everyday self. Such moments of sacred repetition he views as the essential periods of life, while the rest of life is passed in profane time, attuned to the rhythms of nature, which, like the primordial acts, are also repeated in endless cycles.[5]

Because of this radical foreshortening of history, mythological consciousness as Eliade understands it essentially repudiates history as irreversible flow, our most prominent Western metaphor for time. In Eliade's dichotomous scheme, Judaism profoundly altered the mythological worldview by making ongoing human history—not cyclical nature or ancient myth—the sphere in which God's will becomes manifest. But the more we learn about ancient Israel and its neighboring cultures, the less relevant seems his overstated distinction between the historical and the mythological. The centrality of the seasonal festivals in biblical Israel reveals the cyclical structure of time preserved in the mythological agricultural calendar, in which, supposedly, "nothing new happens in the world"; "everything begins over again"; "no event is irreversible and no transformation is final."[6] The mythological definition of space, focused around a sacred, primordial center, also plays a major role in the Bible and in postbiblical interpretive writings, especially in a repeated analogy between Zion's future and Eden's past.[7] Moreover, as we pointed out in chapter 2, Israel retained, especially in its psalmic worship, memories of a cosmogonic battle between YHWH and certain sea monsters, the outcome of which was the establishment of the world that we know. Certain prophetic passages similarly point to a return to chaos and universal destruction to signify the end of our world and the ushering in of a new Edenic realm.[8]

Even if we grant Eliade's faulty premise that Judaism ended the cycle of archetypal repetition by inventing "history" and passing it on to its progeny, Christianity, Islam, and the secular West, we must note the irony that these supposedly historically based religions, which see history as the arena of God's unfolding will, have kept alive the power of repetition that dominated the mythological worldview they supposedly replaced. The festivals of these three religions lend history a mythological, repetitive dimension by replaying the significance of long-ago historic events, whether these be the exodus from Egypt, the crucifixion of Jesus, or Mohammed's entry into Mecca. Eliade himself recognized this paradox. "In this sense," he writes, "the religious man may be said to be a 'primitive'; he repeats the gestures of another and, through this repetition, lives in an atemporal present."[9] Realizing this should make us wary of distinguishing ourselves religiously from so-called primitives. There are a limited number of responses to the problem of time as ongoing flow. Where secular cultures succumb to time's domination, religious cultures, however different they may be from one another, all attempt to defeat it by periodically changing the character of the time they experience.

For many religious cultures, time can be defeated by invoking an afterlife for the individual or for human history itself—an end-time parallel to the primordial beginning time—as different from time as we know it as Eden is different from life after the fall. In this view of linear human history stretching between two atemporal states, the most distant past in effect becomes the future. At the moment of transition, the present era ends with a great destruction, presaging the beginning of a new era. In such a scheme, human suffering is understood as being determined by the descending trajectory of the cosmic cycle.[10] In ancient Israel, the fullest imagining of this past-become-future is found in the latter part of Isaiah, sometimes called Second or Third Isaiah, a prophet who returned with his people from their Babylonian exile with their painful memories of destruction and displacement at the forefront of their consciousness. To them, the prophet addresses God's consoling words:

> For behold! I am creating
> A new heaven and a new earth;
> The former things shall not be remembered,
> They shall never come to mind,
> Be glad, then, and rejoice forever
> In what I am creating.
> For I shall create Jerusalem as a joy,
> And her people as a delight;
> And I will rejoice in Jerusalem
> and delight in her people.
> Never again shall be heard there
> The sounds of weeping and wailing.
> No more shall there be an infant or graybeard
> Who does not live out his days.
> He who dies at a hundred years
> Shall be reckoned as a youth,
> And he who fails to reach a hundred,
> Shall be reckoned accursed.
> They shall not build for others to dwell in,
> Or plant for others to enjoy.
> For the days of My people shall be
> As long as the days of a tree,
> My chosen ones shall outlive
> The work of their hands.
> They shall not toil to no purpose;
> They shall not bear children for terror,
> But they shall be a people blessed by YHWH,
> And their offspring shall remain with them. (Isa. 65:17–23)

Though Adam's curse of toiling on the land cannot be undone, this vision returns Israel to its antecedents in Genesis, with human age spans once again replicating those of the patriarchal and matriarchal period. As the vision goes on, it becomes clear that as the Israelite experience of history changes, the result will be to re-create the unfallen world of Eden: "The wolf and the lamb shall graze together, / And the lion shall eat straw like the ox, / And the serpent's food shall be earth." This vision applies to the human as well as to the animal kingdom: "In all my sacred mount / Nothing evil or vile shall be done—said YHWH" (Isa. 65:25). This is an end to time and the complexities of history as we know them. This new experience of time without conflict or suffering will be experientially, if not spatially, a new heaven and earth.

This pattern of imagining the future as a recapitulation of the prelapsarian past is clearly traceable to archetypal repetition in mythological thinking. In these borrowings from mythological patterns, it needs to be stressed that Israel's poets and prophets never lost sight of the historical dimension. Though Jerusalem is often compared to Eden, its sanctity was not established by God at the beginning of the world. Rather, God chose it for David and his descendants at a decisive moment in history, which is carefully recorded in the historical books of the Bible. Similarly, the messianic attitude that a new unfallen history will replace the history of suffering and destruction that we now experience differs markedly from the mythological idea of abolishing history by living in an eternal present, renewed through periodic ritual. History will be transformed only once, at a time to be revealed in the future, which is usually seen as dependent on how Israel confronts its historic opportunities of returning to God's ways. When it does so, in some prophetic versions of that future, there will again be a redemption from Egypt, another passing through the sea, more miracles in the wilderness, the creation of a new covenant, and a new Davidic kingdom.[11] This teleological view of history sees Israel and the nations always moving toward a final purpose, in which the one God's reality will one day be acknowledged by all. This prophetic hope points to an *eschaton,* an ultimate unveiling of God's will for humanity at a time yet to be disclosed. In the Psalms, the eschatological faith is expressed in the joyful, anticipatory phrase "[God] is coming to rule the earth; / He will rule the world justly / and its peoples in faithfulness" (96:13; cf. 98:9). This judgment will represent the completion of history, a consummation and universal extension of Israel's own commitment to equity and justice. Israel thus carries its sacred history with it into a time beyond history, fulfilling the destiny for which it was chosen and propelled into history.

In ancient Israelite religion, with its historical focus on the ongoing life of the people, it is not surprising that the idea of a future life for the community is far more developed than that of an afterlife for the individual. Sheol, the mythological home of the dead, often translated as "the grave," is at best a shadowy, indistinct realm, and at worst a place of terrors. There is individual survival there, or at least the illusion of it, as we gather from the story in which Saul uses a conjurer to consult the ghost of the prophet Samuel in his resting place in the underworld. Worshipers address fervent prayers to God to keep them from Sheol, which is personified by psalmists as having a mouth (141:7); as taking individuals away by the hand (49:16); as a deep place of bonds, snares, and ropes (18:6; 116:3), where human forms waste away (49:15). Perhaps most significant from the point of view of the singing psalmists, the grave is envisioned as a place of silence (6:6; 31:18; 115:17). It is a far cry from what later rabbinic Judaism, after its contact with the Hellenist world, made of "the world to come," a place where each person earned a reward commensurate with the life s/he lived.[12]

In these images of death I have just cited, it is clear that all will come to Sheol eventually. At stake is *when* that fate will overtake the individual. The lack of a heaven in Psalms may be difficult to swallow for some contemporary users of the Psalms, whose religious traditions stress the idea of a personal afterlife. Thus, in the most prominent Christian translation of the Bible into English in this century, we find "Thou dost guide me with thy counsel, / and afterward thou wilt receive me in glory" (RSV, 73:24), while the standard Jewish version reads, "You guided me by your counsel / and led me toward honor" (JPS, 73:24). The word translated here as "honor" or "glory," *kabod,* is not an otherworldly term. In fact, it is closely related to the idea of heaviness; the same root names the liver, the densest organ in the body. When Isaiah experiences his initiatory vision in the Temple, he hears the angels say of God, "His presence [*kebodo*] fills the earth" (6:3). *Kabod* is sometimes associated with the earthly side of death (cf. Isa. 14:18), that honor granted to those who "have uprightly fulfilled the task of their life."[13] Sheol terrifies the psalmists precisely because it marks an end to their ability to experience God's presence.

What was most at stake for them, it would seem, was their continuous connection to God. One psalmist memorably expresses the wish for an unseverable bond:

> One thing I ask of YHWH,
> only that do I seek:
> to live in the house of YHWH
> all the days of my life,
> to gaze upon the beauty of YHWH,
> to frequent His temple. (27:4)

We know, however, that such a wish is hyperbolic. Then as now, the demands of life certainly went on outside the Temple; even priests and Levites could serve only a brief, annual rotation. What is more, this very psalmist understands that God is not always available to human perception, that in anger or aloofness, God sometimes appears hidden (v. 9, from the root *s-t-r*).[14] In their great distress, many speakers of psalms want to know whether God will be hidden forever.

The word "forever" can be either comforting or terrifying, depending on the context. It is not surprising therefore that psalmists contextualize the idea through different words. When God's anger, forgetting, or hiddenness seems unending, the psalmists often use the term *neṣaḥ*, from a root meaning "illustrious" or "preeminent," and therefore "enduring."[15] But a second root for hiddenness takes on a far different meaning in the word *ʿolam*, which connotes the idea of the world's eternal age, whose origins are hidden in remote antiquity and whose destiny is equally hidden in remote futurity, known only to God. The positive connotations of everlastingness are signified by the word *ʿolam*, which might best be translated as "for as long as the world lasts," especially when paired with the adverb "until," *ʿad*, or with the related word for perpetuity, *vaʿed*.[16] God's being, God's love, God's glory, God's truth, God's righteousness, God's counsel, God's law, God's reign, God's covenant with Israel, God's messianic king, God's appointed Davidic dynasty, God's city, Jerusalem—all are said in various psalms to last *leʿolam*, forever.[17]

In these phrases, the language of eternity elevates human institutions and grants them the imprimatur of divinity, just as ritual transforms everyday objects into sacred ones. Attributing to human institutions such as a king or a city the divine quality of eternality is another strategy for defeating the corrosive and uncertain effects of time. So when psalmists want the reality of their connection to God to endure as long as it possibly can, they do so with the expression *leʿolam*. It modifies the verbs "to trust," "to bless," "to praise or acknowledge," "to honor," "to rejoice in," "to relate the deeds of," "to observe the commandments of God."[18] The psalmists strengthen their religious commitments by wishing to prolong them for as long as they live. Likewise, priestly speakers promise this same as-long-as-you-live protection to God's devoted servants: "YHWH will guard you from all harm; / He will guard your life. / YHWH will guard your going and coming / now and forever [*ad ʿolam*]" (121:7–8). We can come and go, or sing, praise, and bless, only while we live. One psalmist settles the matter indisputably: "The dead cannot praise YHWH, / nor any who go down into silence / But we shall bless YHWH / now and forever [*ad ʿolam*]" (115:17–18). The contrast between the dead who are cut off in silence and the faithful who go on praising God "from generation to generation" (145:4) is fundamental to the community that worships through the Psalms. Continuing to praise God by proclaiming that it shall bless YHWH forever becomes evidence of the community's commitment to its own everlastingness.

We see then that humans approaching God continually attempt to relate to the eternal time and space of God. To understand how this relation is established, we can remind ourselves that time, unlike space, is not a bounded medium; we experience it as a flow, but we often look at it spatially, as on a clock face or a time line. To some extent, this spatialization halts the flow of irreversible time, which is suggested by the Greek word *chronos*. Through chronology, we demarcate artificial boundaries between past and present, even though we know that these continually interpenetrate in our consciousness.[19] As we go back to examine the past in memory, we discover that time can be reversible. Certain past moments emerge as especially significant in the present; in a religious tradition, these take on the character of revelation, as the divine chooses a specific moment to erupt into human life. This revealed time is often designated by the Greek word *chairos,* the intersection of *chairos* and *chronos* making up sacred history. However much the sacred affects our lives, divine time is also separate from human life, insofar as we are mortal and God exists eternally. Yet we human beings do not want to countenance this difference, so we turn ourselves into immortal souls, or we spatialize God's atemporal existence by erecting a home for God in the world.

Throughout the Bible, God is known to be omnipresent, as Jonah, for instance, discovers when he tries to escape from God at sea. Spatializing the temporality of an omnipresent God is appropriate to convey the belief that God's reality, whether conceived as transcendent or as immanent, is not affected by the dimensions of time and space. God exists, we might say, in *timespace,* a union of human perceptual categories. Both time and space are contained in the key Hebrew word *'olam,* meaning, as we have said, "world" and "age." To seek the qualities of *'olam* for our own limited human perspectives is to break through the artificiality of humanity's spatialized boundaries for time and to be aligned with what we think of as God's unfragmented perspective on reality.

Assuming this distinction between divine timespace and human time and space, we will pursue several interrelated lines of inquiry in this chapter. First, we will explore how the Psalms use the resources of poetic language to present vivid pictures of God's eternal timespace, the cosmos. In this section, we will be focusing on both the incommensurability of divine and human perspectives and the need humans feel to bridge that gap through discourse about God. Then, we will look at communal and individual stories Israelites tell about their experiences of God, especially as divine deliverance is experienced in time and in memory. Next, we will be concerned with how individual Israelites use spatial metaphors to express their relationship to God, especially as this relationship is enacted in and through images representing the Jerusalem Temple, the sacred center to which Eliade's studies have sensitized us. These representations of temporal and spatial images give psalmists ways of talking about God's saving power in a world in which they themselves sometimes perceive God as absent or hidden. Such images help address the perennial problem of evil in a world governed by what all psalmists affirm to be a good and just God. Our chapter will therefore conclude by discussing how images of time and space play a role in presenting and partially resolving issues of theodicy in the Psalms.

Divine Timespace and Human Language

What is God's perspective on creation? The answer to this question cannot be known, yet the psalmists go beyond the evidence of their senses to tell us that God exists before and beyond the created world:

> Before the mountains came into being,
> Before You brought forth the earth and the world,
> From eternity to eternity [*me'olam 'ad 'olam*] You are God. (Ps. 90:2)

Elsewhere, we hear, "from eternity [*me'olam*] You have existed" (93:2). But can we picture that eternal reality? And if we can, can it help us deal with the dilemmas of being human, as we experience them in our time and space? These are the questions this section will address.

The psalmists approach God's eternality by way of the world that they know. The whole created universe, many of them suggest, is alive with the awareness that it has been created by God. "Let the sea and all within it thunder, / the world and its inhabitants; / let the rivers clap their hands, / the mountains sing joyously together / at the presence of YHWH" (98:7–9a). Songs of praise such as this one mirror the cosmos's own activity. We see in nature's praise a connection to the less exultant verses already cited: "The heavens declare the glory of God, / the sky proclaims His handiwork; / Day to day makes utterance, / night to night speaks out" (19:2–3). Here, the image of the heavens, days, and nights speaking out recalls the account of creation in Genesis 1, where God spoke and brought the world into being. Now God's creations themselves, the days and nights through which human beings measure out their existence, speak of God, simply by virtue of the fact that, like humans, they too have been divinely created by a transcendent God. Through praise and interpretation of the world they experience, the psalmists begin to establish a relationship to that which lies beyond their ken.

While the majestic heavens testify to God's existence, they also point, by contrast, to human insignificance:

> When I behold Your heavens, the work of Your fingers,
> the moon and stars that You set in place:
> what is man that You have been mindful of him,
> mortal man that You have taken note of him. (8:4–5)

The human task, accordingly, is to acknowledge the true relation between the incommensurable partners in dialogue: "YHWH, our Lord, how majestic is Your name throughout the earth!" (8:2, 10).

The incommensurability of humans and God can be oppressive to human beings, if it leads us always to focus on our insignificance in the cosmos. In emphasizing the human search for meaning, the Psalms constantly attempt to bridge that gap. The brief, five-verse Psalm 93 is a good example of how conceptualizing God's eternality can allow one to begin to develop means of access to it. Since before the beginning of the common era, this psalm has been specially designated to be recited on the day before the Sabbath,[20] when humans prepare to suspend their everyday experience of time and space. It makes sense in this light to examine in detail the psalm's presentation of the divine timespace.

As human beings, we cannot grasp time as a whole. Since the spatial features within our purview can, however, be grasped as wholes (as, for instance, lines, circles, mountains, lakes, etc.), we spatialize time in order to give it an apprehensible shape. What shape might we give to the temporal omnipresence of God? The psalmist associates it with the physicality of the earth in order to create a symbol of eternal duration:

> YHWH is king,
> He is robed in grandeur;
> YHWH is robed,
> He is girded with strength.
> The world stands firm; it cannot be shaken.
> Your throne stands firm from of old;
> from eternity [*me'olam*] You have existed. (Vv. 1–2)

We note that the two spatial images, earth and throne, are presented temporally. "The world cannot be shaken" calls to mind the picture of an unbroken futurity, while God's heavenly "throne," standing "firm from of old," conjures up dim images of a mythological time before human history. Similarly, the psalm concludes with lines that bring God's enduringness into continuing relationship not only with the world that humans inhabit, but also with the human institution that has the greatest significance for the psalmist, the Temple cult. "Your decrees are indeed enduring; / holiness befits Your house, / YHWH, for all times" (v. 5). "For all times" can be translated more literally as "for length of days." Once again, we see the psalmist spatializing eternal time in order to develop a continuing relation to it.

Between the heavenly image of God's throne and the concluding earthly images of God's "decrees" and "house" comes the sea, the realm of primordial chaos, which God had to tame in making a world for humans to inhabit. We hear its roaring in alliterative phrases that resemble waves. Because of the pronounced aural effects of the poetry, it is worth reading first in Hebrew:

> *Nas'u neharot adonai, nas'u neharot qolam, yis'u neharot dakyam.*
> *Miqqolot mayim rabbim, addirim mišbbere yam, 'addir bammarom adonai.*

> The ocean sounds, YHWH,
> The ocean sounds its thunder,
> The ocean sounds its pounding.
> Above the thunder of the mighty waters,
> more majestic than the breakers of the sea,
> is YHWH, majestic on high. (Vv. 3–4)

Sounds are introduced, fade away, and then immediately sound again. Each of these oceanic verses has three segments, unlike the norm of Hebrew verse's two-part rhythms, thereby intensifying the feeling of the ocean's power, and of God's, which the psalmist claims is far greater. By thus using the imitative dimensions of language, the poet demonstrates the human function of praise: to create a context for imaging God which will bring human beings into relationship with God's eternal power and glory. The phrase *qolot mayim rabbim,* literally "the voice of many waters," calls to mind two of Israel's foundational narratives: the world-founding myth of God destroying a great sea beast in order to establish the earth on a firm foundation,[21] and the nation-founding myth of God stilling the roaring waters of the Red Sea.[22] Thus, the sea, the chief spatial image of the poem, has an added temporal dimension in this phrase that echoes God's own memory of primordial events.

In these several thematic ways, this psalm offers worshipers the universe as God might experience it, an indivisible and enduring unity of earth, sea, and heaven. In this compact and holistic poetic structure, the psalmist provides us images from our own experience for apprehending a dimension of God that lies incomparably beyond our experience. In such a communal hymn, there is no room for the possibility that God's world might be experienced as other than a vast unity of time and space, permeated by divinity. Its analogy between God's heavenly "throne" and human "house" minimizes the incommensurability of God and humans, even as it provides a ritualized structure of access through reference to God's "decrees" that human beings can follow.

Other psalms, however, show that human beings indeed experience the cosmos very differently than does God. The job of such psalms is to make a bridge to God's reality not by minimizing but by acknowledging the differences between divine and human perceptions and time frames: "For in Your sight a thousand years / are like yesterday that has passed, / like a watch of the night" (90:4). Compared to God's sweeping sense of time, our nights and days must seem fleeting and insignificant, endlessly cyclical in their repetitiveness.[23] Obviously, any framework we create to understand God's experience of timespace can be based only on metaphoric comparisons to our own limited perceptions of time. For this psalmist, God clearly exists outside the world of terrestrial time and space—"before the mountains came into being / before You brought forth the earth and the world / from eternity to eternity You are God" (v. 2). Because God is not subject to time and the pressures of generativity, human beings can find in their changeless God a "refuge in every generation" (v. 1). Yet, as the psalm goes on to make clear in many ways, this unchanging, eternal God is intimately involved with the transience of human life. To begin exploring this paradox, the poet punningly juxtaposes God's absolute control of a human lifetime, "You return man to dust," with the one area, morality, that God cedes to human choice: "You decreed, 'Return you mortals!' " (v. 2). Using the same root, *š-w-b,* in both expressions, the poet begins to suggest the dynamic that enables human beings to adjust to their temporal fate. Though we will die, most likely in pain and in suffering, we may yet live well in God's sight, thereby obtaining God's favor for "the work of our hands" (v. 17).

This prayer-poem begins, we might summarize, by setting up two parallel tensions: first, that divine and human time frames are incommensurable, and second, that God decrees our creaturely fate yet inspires us to act morally, by which actions we can transcend that creatureliness in some small measure. The psalm then goes on to develop each of these strands. Where divine timespace is presented as vast, permanent, and essentially beyond human understanding, human time is presented through concrete images as being transient and illusory:

> You engulf men in sleep;
> at daybreak they are like grass that renews itself;
> at daybreak it flourishes anew;
> by dusk it withers and dries up. (Vv. 5–6)

The repetition of "daybreak" gives the momentary illusion that human beings can become self-renewing. But the term of human life is fixed, "seventy years, / or, given the strength, eighty years"; and "the best of them are trouble and sorrow" (vv. 9–10), a far cry from the number "thousand," which is a brief passing interval for God.[24] The psalm is shot through with an awareness of how humans mark time's significance: by mornings and evenings, days and years. "Satisfy us at daybreak with Your steadfast love / that we may sing for joy all our days. / Give us joy for as long as the days You have afflicted us, / for the years we have suffered misfortune" (vv. 14–15). This psalmist wants the most that human beings can request. Having suffered enough, the singer/speaker wants the people's portion of joy to last out the natural term of their lives.

We should be clear that this psalm is a very different type from the previously quoted Psalm 93, the hymn celebrating God's timespace. This is a petitionary psalm, which seeks to turn around what the poet variously calls God's anger, fury, and wrath. The psalm acknowledges that our moral trespasses have occasioned God's displeasure: "You have set our iniquities before You / our hidden sins in the light of Your face" (v. 8). It is our own fault that "we spend our years like a sigh" (v. 9). We can expect divine favor, the psalmist goes on to suggest, only by fulfilling a moral contract: "Teach us to count our days rightly, / that we may obtain a wise heart" (v. 12). That is one of the psalmist's petitions. The other, more urgent one is a cry from the heart that takes the form of two imperatives and a question: "Turn, YHWH! / How long? / Show mercy to Your servants" (v. 13). The question "How long?" can be read as either agonized or fiercely taunting. Whichever nuance we choose, it is clear that it brings back in a different emotional register the opening tension between God's notion of time and ours. The question tellingly interrogates God's perspective on time, by applying to it the standards of human life. It seems to say, "Your experience of time may be different from ours, and we may be but a fleeting shadow in Your universe. And, yes, we have deserved Your anger. But remember that we live for only seventy or eighty years, and what may seem to You a short time of punishment is to us infinitely long. We are Your creatures. We deserve better at Your hands." This single verse, the question and its two surrounding imperatives, brings to a head all the prayer-poem's conflicting perspectives on time and morality. Just as human beings are asked by God to return to God in repentance (v. 3), so God is asked by them to turn divine mercy toward human beings (v. 13). Just as human beings are to behave morally, so their Creator should be bound to a standard of fairness: "Give us joy for as long as You have afflicted us" (v. 15). The poet/singer addressing God on behalf of the Israelite community is not asking for eternal bliss. In the final petition, "O prosper the work of our hands!" (v. 17), the community is expressing its hope for the continuity of this extended human family and its institutions.

Prayer is a dialogue between two radically different partners, one eternal and the other mortal. In most instances of dialogue known to humans, two bodies occupy simultaneous but different spaces.[25] In dialogue with God, not only is the space different, but so is the element of time, as Psalm 90 illustrates so well. The images of both divine and human reality in the psalms that we have just examined are designed to show both participants in the dialogue that human beings understand their limits: the cosmos is eternal; God's time and space are immeasurable; human life is fleeting; only God's law and God's house endure. When psalmists or worshipers using the psalms appreciate that they have been given a rare opportunity to see the world, as it were, through God's eyes, they are full of love and awe for God and the majestic universe in which they find themselves; they sing hymns praising God and cosmic reality. At other times, however, these realities are plainly not enough. The psalmists—and we along with them—want more than we have been given. Our bitter human lot and its limits fill us only with longing. At such times, worshipers need to discharge their anger. They do so in psalms begging God to take another look at the human life span and its suffering. Their perennial question is appropriately concerned with time: "How long, God, how long?"

Deliverance in Time

As Eliade has shown, sacred or mythic time consists of a constant return to primordial events and an anticipation that the future will bring the full restoration of what once was. The poet of Lamentations encapsulates this notion in a single urgent phrase, "Renew our days as of old!" (5:21). Reading the narratives and poems of ancient Israel confirms this view of sacred time. What was important to the culture was what had happened in the past, and what would happen in the future. The present seems to have had significance only as part of an ongoing sacred history of the community. If the people were behaving morally and enjoying prosperity, this was evidence to sacred historians of divine favor, the fulfillment of God's covenant with Israel. Such was a moment for singing hymns to God. But if the people and their monarchs were experiencing misfortune, then it was a sign to those same historians that people and king had deviated from God's laws, deserving divine displeasure. Under these adverse circumstances, Israel's prophets arose, summoning up the past in order to charge their audience to live up to their historic mission as a holy people.

Israel's foundational narratives, from Genesis through Kings, thus tell a
story to be repeated for the benefit of all succeeding generations: God
created the world, chose the seed of Abraham to be a holy people, took
that people from slavery in Egypt, led them as they wandered in the
desert, spurred them to victory as they fought for the land promised them,
and finally appointed David and his descendants to rule over the people
forever. This is history seen, as it were, through God's eyes, a few decisive,
revelatory acts that live on in the memory of God's chosen people, who
were shaped by those acts. Through most of this story, it is no surprise that
God is the leading actor. In the latter part of the history, though, where we
see Israel struggling with self-government, God is less the prime mover
than an interested observer, more like a parent of teenagers or young
adults who intervenes only in their crises. The breakup of the monarchy
and the long slide of Israel's kings into apostasy is such a crisis. The
prophets tell the story of God's terrible intervention through the con-
quering armies of northern empires, first Assyria, then Babylonia, with the
clear implication that God is the ruler not just of Israelite but of world
history. The exile of the people to Babylon and their return to their homeland obviously repeats the most crucial phase of Israel's sacred history, in
which God is once again the prime mover. One historical litany summarizes this movement and describes God, "Who took note of us in our degradation / His steadfast love is eternal" (Ps. 136:23). Because the return
from Babylon so closely recapitulated the exodus story at a time when
Israel's religious leaders were developing its formative texts, the exodus
from Egypt became, for all later generations, the central paradigm of
redemption.[26]

Israel's history of deliverance is represented in several narrative psalms,
such as the one from which I just quoted. Psalms that rehearse the miracles of the exodus, God's providential care for the people in the wilderness, and their triumphs in entering Canaan are obviously important in
the formation of what we might call official Israelite religious consciousness.[27] Like the ritual of the first fruits that we noted in chapter 2, they
provide a means by which members of the community internalize and per-
petuate their sense of belonging. Such ritual recitations of the key
moments of Israelite history, all quintessential moments of deliverance, lie
behind this imaginative conflation of exodus and conquest motifs:

> When Israel went forth from Egypt,
> the house of Jacob from a people of strange speech,
> Judah became his holy one,
> Israel, His dominion.
> The sea saw them and fled,

> Jordan ran backward,
> mountains skipped like rams,
> hills like sheep.
> What alarmed you, O sea, that you fled,
> Jordan, that you ran backward,
> mountains, that you skipped like rams,
> hills, like sheep?
> Tremble, O earth, at the presence of YHWH,
> at the presence of the God of Jacob,
> who turned the rock into a pool of water,
> the flinty rock into a fountain. (Ps. 114)

Forty years separated the crossing of the Sea of Reeds under Moses' leadership from the crossing of the Jordan under Joshua's, yet to the poet singing God's praise, they are as a single moment, linked with another watery miracle, God's opening up a flow from a rock in the desert.[28] When Israel looks at its history from God's foreshortened temporal perspective, such miraculous acts of deliverance are virtually the only ones that matter. They are archetypes recalled in order to connect an unspecified present, which may itself be remarkable or unremarkable, with the sacred history of Israel's past. As narrated here, that past is indeed remarkable for the way in which God's eruptions into history on behalf of Israel took the form of altering the ordinary course of nature. In these archetypes of divine deliverance, historic time unites with mythic time, history's God with nature's God, and Israel's temporal experience is brought into the framework of eternity. Another such moment when nature testified to God's appearance in Israelite history was at Sinai, which the poet may be alluding to in the image of mountains that "skipped like rams."[29] Bringing together the motifs of exodus, Sinai, and conquest in this brief hymn, the poet creates out of the sacred history of Israel a mythologized moment, suspended in time, and capable of being repeated as ritual utterance. Whenever it is sung, it must inevitably remind the singing people that God can again do wonders on behalf of Israel. The earth and, by extension, all its inhabitants should tremble in the presence of YHWH's awesome power.

Given the natural human tendency to keep alive the most significant memories of the past, it is no surprise that the national history of deliverance and redemption takes on special significance in the religious life of individuals. Deliverance is the link between God's time and ours. At moments of deliverance, we know God acting, with great significance for us, in human history. We will now look at three psalms, only one of which directly alludes to the events of the exodus as part of its meditation on deliverance. The other two are psalms of thanksgiving for a deliverance that has already taken place. In them we can see reflections of this mythic pattern transposed to an individual level. Having gone through experiences parallel to the national experience of slavery and liberation, they tell and sing their own sacred stories, each phase of which has significance not only for them as individuals but also for the people as a whole. Their testimony, including remembrances of both past suffering and present joy, is further evidence that God's chosen people has not been forgotten.

Most commentators divide Psalm 77 into two parts: the first, a lament over the speaker's distress; the second, a hopeful hymn celebrating God's glorious deeds in the past. Because there is no apparent transition between the two sections, a variety of solutions have been offered, including the suggestion that a priestly oracle intervened, or that participation in a cultic festival has reenlivened the power of Israel's redemptive past for the speaker.[30] Behind these and other psychological explanations lies the faulty assumption that the real time it takes to recite a psalm must correspond to the inner changes it reports in its speaker. A number of the verbs in the psalm point to a process of repeated meditation, which induces in the meditator a suspension of ordinary temporal perceptions. A psalm based on meditative practice can therefore telescope a lengthy mental process into but a few lines as a guide to those who might one day need to undertake a similar meditation. Furthermore, the many verbal links between the two sections suggest that we have in Psalm 77 one composition, written from the start by someone who knew where it would finish. Didactically, then, it models a movement from despair to hope that is essential to a life lived in faithfulness to YHWH. This model offers future reciters of the psalm a dramatic structure in which to place their own struggle with faith. The disjunction between lament and hymn is thus only apparent. It may seem as if there are separate times for laments and for hymns, but this psalm wants to show that the two are called to mind at once, as believers test and reaffirm their faith in God's powers of deliverance.

Before going further with our analysis, it is best that we hear the first movement of the psalm. The bracketed phrases indicate that the text for this psalm has unfortunately been somewhat garbled in transmission:

2.   I cry aloud to God;
            I cry to God that He may give ear to me.

3.   In my time of distress I turn to the Lord,
            with my hand [uplifted];
            [my eyes] flow all night without respite;
            I will not be comforted.

4.   I call God to mind, I moan,
            I complain, my spirit fails.   *Selah.*

5. You have held my eyelids open;
    I am overwrought, I cannot speak.

This psalm seems indeed to be spoken out of great distress. The standard repertory of complaint is here: in verbal behavior—crying aloud, moaning, complaining to God of one's lot; and nonverbally—arms raised to God in unending prayer (RSV, v. 3),[31] sleeplessness, and failing speech.

In the succeeding lines, the psalmist turns from outward complaint to inner colloquy:

6. My thoughts turn to days of old,
    to years long past.
7. I recall at night my song;[32]
    I commune with myself;
    my spirit inquires,
8. "Will the Lord reject forever
    and never again show favor?
9. Has His faithfulness disappeared forever?
    Will His promise be unfulfilled for all time?
10. Has God forgotten how to pity?
    Has He in anger stifled His compassion?"   *Selah.*
11. And I said, "It is my fault[33]
    that the right hand of the Most High has changed."

Memory recaptures sentences thought or uttered in the past that confirm the psalmist's worst fears: rejection by God and by oneself. In these remembered thoughts, the emotional conventions of lament begin to be modified by those of meditation. In the statement of the complaint, twice we hear the verb "to converse or speak," *'asihah,* and twice "to remember or call to mind," *'ezkerah* (vv. 4, 7), both of which come up again in the hymnic half of the psalm. We also have verbs for inquiring (*darašti,* v. 3), considering (*hišabti,* v. 6), and meditating (*hagiti,* v. 13), and a noun for song or melody (*neginati,* v. 7), suggesting the medium through which all this focused thought attains verbal expression. The diction of the psalm clearly suggests a dramatized speaker as much attuned to mental as to emotional action.

In the mental action of the psalm, memory plays a pivotal role, but in its first movement, memory is expressed with what we might call a poetic stutter. In verse 4, the psalmist simply calls God to mind. There are no memories of God's words or deeds. Then, when his "thoughts turn to days of old [*mi-qedem*] / to years long past [*'olamim*]" (v. 6), these expressions suggest that we can expect to hear of specific events in the remote past. However, what he remembers and quotes in the next verse, his nighttime conversation with God, need not have been any further in the past than the previous night. In the second half of the psalm, we finally encounter the past for which these expressions prepare us. Out of the mythic history of deliverance, the psalmist chooses to narrate one moment, the crossing of the Red Sea, when the people passed once and for all from slavery to freedom. This time when the speaker/singer says, "I recall [*'ezkera*] Your wonders of old [*mi-qedem*]" (v. 12), the poem provides the appropriate context missing when the same words were used in the first movement of the psalm. Struggling to connect with God through memory, the mind turns inevitably, if not immediately, toward God's redemptive acts on behalf of the people, by which, above all else, God is remembered. As one astute reader of the psalm puts it, "The great acts of the tradition are not removed in past time, but recharged with energy they again become a present event. The act of memory forms a bridge which links the psalmist with the God of the forefathers, not because of a Herculean act of self-projection, but because the events of the tradition possess a power which continues to meet Israel in her struggle."[34]

As pivotal as memory in the poem's mental action is an implicit contrast between two visions of the future. The worried question "Will the Lord reject forever [*'olamim*] / and never again show favor?" (v. 8) evokes a miserable future stretching endlessly onward. This is followed, however, by an equally strong evocation of divine favor stretching back to the very foundations of Israel. If we extrapolate from this knowledge, we get an alternative vision of the future, in which this psalmist or anyone speaking this psalm will likewise be saved from distress by the marvelous deeds of God. Before allowing the mind to flood with these liberating collective memories, the psalmist fears that God has ceased to speak (translating literally, *gamar 'omer*, v. 9), but as the presentation of the sea-crossing makes evident, God speaks through actions. The thunder and lightning are not just scenic effects. As at Sinai, they anticipate God's wondrous self-revelation:

16.   By Your arm You redeemed Your people,
       the children of Jacob and Joseph.   *Selah*
17.   The waters saw You, O God,
       the waters saw You and were convulsed;
       the very deep quaked as well.
18.   Clouds streamed water;
       the heavens rumbled;
       Your arrows flew about;
19.   Your thunder rumbled like wheels;
       lightning lit up the world;
       the earth quaked and trembled.

20. Your way was through the sea,
    Your path, through the mighty waters;
    Your tracks could not be seen.
21. You led Your people like a flock
    in the care of Moses and Aaron.

The meditative process on which this composition was based certainly began with an alienated, solitary self. Before the first word of the psalm was written, however, we can surmise that that self had already become a persona, a remembered but no longer existing mask, replaced by a social self at home in the collective world of Israelite history and symbolism. The one who felt God's personal torment by holding his eyelids open (v. 5) has become an exemplary self, whose eyes have been opened to another version of reality. The one who identified only with his own mental anguish is now content to be counted as a member of God's flock.[35] At the opening of the psalm, the speaker's "hand is stretched out without wearying" (RSV, v. 2). Given where the psalm ends up, Israelite listeners could not fail to identify this as an allusion to Moses' stretching out his hands to hold the waters aside as their ancestors crossed the sea. But this speaker, in the first part of the psalm, is deliberately presented as an inadequate Moses. Instead of complaining that God's "right hand" has changed (v. 11), the self exhibited before us is shown to learn, as future generations of Israelites must, how necessary it is to remember that God's "arm" (v. 16) redeemed the Israelite people at the sea.[36] When Moses and Aaron are named in the final words of the psalm, it is obvious that the people's historic leaders have been accepted by the exemplary speaker as personal role models. The didactic burden of the psalm is thus to bring readers to the conviction chosen or arrived at by the speaker. In this way, his personal faith is passed down through the generations.

If an ancient Israelite was to make the sacred history of the nation personally meaningful, then he or she had to develop a personal relationship to its history of deliverance within the context of prayer. This is clearly what happens in Psalm 77. The psalmist is so deeply rooted in the collective story of his people's deliverance from slavery that he can use that national redemption as a paradigm for a personal redemption. As we scrape away layers of personal experience, redemption is revealed, as in a palimpsest, as the experience that underlies all. The links between personal and national themes in this psalm led Rashi to see the whole as a reflection of Israel's exile in Babylonia.[37] The absence of any reference to Israel's being settled in the land of Canaan in Psalm 77 bears out Rashi's suggestion of an exilic origin for this psalm, for in most psalms recalling the exodus from Egypt, entry into the land of Canaan is seen as fulfilling the promise of the original deliverance.[38] Centuries later, the rabbis living after the destruction of the Second Temple stipulated that an Israelite telling the story of the exodus on Passover should "begin with degradation and end with praise."[39] Our analysis of Psalm 77 shows it as a prototype for this structure of the rabbinic Haggadah, in which the fruits of the deliverance from Egypt are not so much present reality as they are a deep structure of memory and hope.

Many more psalms lend themselves to the supposition that the psalmic speaking voice often uses the personal pronoun to represent a collective experience.[40] Psalm 30 speaks of deliverance in the most personal terms, yet its heading, "a song for the dedication of the temple" (v. 1), indicates that at some historical juncture a personal prayer-poem was reinterpreted for use in a collective liturgy. When the Second Temple was dedicated, we know from the Book of Ezra, there was a wide range of divergent emotions that the people expressed. Ezra's description of the event helps us focus on the parallel range of emotions in the psalm:

> When the builders had laid the foundation of the Temple of YHWH, priests in their vestments with trumpets, and Levites, sons of Asaph with cymbals, were stationed to give praise to YHWH, as King David of Israel had ordained. They sang songs extolling and praising YHWH, "For He is good, His steadfast love for Israel is eternal." All the people raised a great shout extolling YHWH because the foundation of the House of YHWH had been laid. Many of the priests and Levites and the chiefs of the clans, the old men who had seen the first house, wept loudly at the sight of the founding of this house. Many others shouted joyously at the top of their voices. The people could not distinguish the shouts of joy from the people's weeping, for the people raised a great shout the sound of which could be heard from afar. (3:10–13)

There are at least five psalms that share the refrain of thanksgiving quoted in Ezra.[41] Two are recountings of Israelite history, devoting a major portion of the narrative to the exodus from Egypt and the journey to the promised land (Pss. 106, 136); two more describe the plight of those redeemed from adversity and perilous battle (Pss. 107, 118); the final one is the psalm specified for the thanksgiving offering, in which the worshipers are urged to "enter His gates with praise, / His courts with acclamation" (100:4). All these psalms share in the hopeful pattern of deliverance that undergirds believers' faith.

Though Psalm 30 lacks this particular refrain and any mention of deliverance from Egyptian slavery, let us assume for the moment that it too might have been used on this day of powerfully conflicting emotions.[42] One might think that the psalm for a community's dedication of its holiest place should be expressed in the plural, as are the narrative hymns I just cited. But if some worshipers are weeping and some are shouting for joy, then the official psalm of dedication needs to make room for quite distinct individuals. An individual whose experience includes both weeping and joy could thus become representative for the group.

In the last chapter, we spoke briefly of the recantatory element in Psalm 30, describing how the psalm pivots on the psalmist's taking back the words of an earlier self. But in memory, the past is never wholly past but remains always partially present, available to be recaptured as we go about our daily lives. In reading the psalm with a focus on temporality, we are aware of how little time the psalmist actually spends in the celebratory present. In the opening verses of the psalm, look how quickly the psalmist goes to memory:

> I extol You, YHWH,
> for You have lifted me up,
> and not let my enemies rejoice over me.
> YHWH, my God,
> I cried out to You,
> and You healed me.
> YHWH, You brought me up from Sheol,
> preserved me from going down into the Pit. (Vv. 2–4)

In these few verses, the psalmist gives us the shape of the whole experience for which thanksgiving is now being offered. The next verses also make this experience seem like a fully completed circle. The others standing in the Temple are asked to confirm the proverbial truth that the speaker has learned so painfully:

> O you faithful of YHWH, sing to Him,
> and praise His holy name.
> For He is angry but a moment,
> and when He is pleased there is life.
> One may lie down weeping at nightfall;
> but at dawn there are shouts of life. (Vv. 5–6)

If life were as simple as this, the psalm would jump from here to verse 12: "You turned my lament into dancing." But memory is not simple. In memory, the speaker recaptures and makes present again earlier selves, in all their complexity and ambivalence. In memory, the individual becomes again one who was untroubled by life, never dreaming that personal security could be undermined, or that God could ever hide the divine countenance:

> When I thought I was untroubled,
> I thought, "I shall never be shaken,"
> for You, YHWH, when You were pleased,
> made [me] firm as a mighty mountain.
> When You hid Your face,
> I was terrified. (Vv. 7–8)

In memory, the speaker reactivates the person who, in confronting death, cried out to God for deliverance, quoting to us a prayer from the edge of Sheol:

> I called to You, YHWH;
> to my Lord I made appeal.
> "What is to be gained from my death,
> from my descent into the Pit?
> Can dust praise You?
> Can it declare Your faithfulness?
> Hear, YHWH, and have mercy on me;
> YHWH, be my help!" (Vv. 9–11)

So much is at stake for the speaker that the ironic taunt to God—"Can dust praise You?"—does not seem out of place in this desperate attempt to save one's own life through prayer.

To bolster my argument that memory reactualizes the past, it is helpful to look at the prayer-poem's verbal forms to see how they make subtle temporal distinctions that would surely have been appreciated by ancient Hebrew speakers. It is often noted that biblical Hebrew does not have past, present, and future tenses as do modern European languages, but rather an aspect system with two kinds of verb forms, perfect and imperfect. Perfect forms of the verb close off an experience, while imperfect ones keep it open and incomplete.[43] When the psalmist tells how he naively used to speak to himself about feeling secure, he chooses a perfect form, *'amarti,* "I said." The perfect form signifies that it is not a speech he ever expected to make again. But what he thought at the time is rendered in the imperfect (" 'I shall never be shaken' "—*bal 'emoṭ leʿolam,* v. 7), as if to suggest his illusion of unending personal security. By contrast, the experience of God's shattering his naive confidence now seems a single definitive event, rendered in the perfect: "When You hid Your face / I was terrified" (v. 8). When it comes to telling us how, at that moment, he called out to God, though the event is long past, he significantly chooses the imperfect forms, *'eqra* and *'eṭḥanan* (v. 9). These signify ongoing actions, perhaps to keep the line of prayer open, perhaps to indicate that the underlying feeling of vulnerability persists. Because this address to God is framed by imperfect verbs and present-tense imperatives (for one can give a command *only* in the present), the entire quoted prayer floats in an indeterminate zone, certainly past, but not quite over and done with.[44] The urgency of its concluding imperatives would be felt even at this occasion of thanksgiving, when God has turned the Israelites' laments into dancing. As a result, a significant element of the remembered distress is always present for whoever recites this psalm.

The main burden of the psalm, however, is thanksgiving. To make a clear transition between the pastness of this plea and the present occasion of celebration, the psalmist chooses a perfect verb. God turned (*hapakta*) events on their head, and this choice of the perfect indicates the psalmist's perception (and, I would add, hope) that this deliverance has the quality of permanence:

> You turned my lament into dancing,
> You undid my sackcloth and girded me with joy,
> that [my] whole being might sing hymns to You endlessly;
> YHWH, my God, I will praise You forever. (Vv. 12–13)

Because deliverance happens only in human time, prayer must keep us attuned to its dynamic flow and surprising reversals. Both lament and dancing need to be reexperienced within the psalm, for as this psalmist recognizes, neither lament nor dancing is wholly true without the other: "One may lie down weeping at nightfall / but at dawn there are shouts of joy" (v. 6). No psalm does more to acknowledge the transience of human emotions and the vicissitudes of life, yet because this psalmist wants to continue feeling close to God, the psalm also seeks to incorporate the divine perspective of eternality into the frame of human action. The psalmist's final words are in the imperfect, representing his ongoing and continuous hope "that my whole being might sing hymns to You endlessly; / YHWH my God, I will praise you forever (*leʿolam*)" (v. 13).

Because lament and dancing are each given a voice in the psalm, they continue to exist in an eternal conversation, in which we participate whenever we recite it. These multiple voices allow each worshiper, or the congregation considered as a whole, to experience potentially conflicting emotions. If we return to our hypothesis that this psalm could have been used historically as a "song for the dedication of the temple," we can see how it would have allowed some worshipers to focus on their preexilic false confidence and failure to heed God's warnings, others to acknowledge the exilic descent into the pit, and still others, most likely the majority, to revel in the joy of deliverance, of renewal and rebirth in the homeland. Similarly, in a contemporary congregation, worshipers bring a wide variety of conflicting life experiences at any moment in their life cycles, and the liturgy must accommodate them all. As a liturgical offering, Psalm 30 gives worshipers language to approach both suffering and joy, past and present emotions.

Though such dual focus is not found in all psalms of thanksgiving, the recitation of past events has been described as an important feature of the genre.[45] Another related psalm of thanksgiving containing this dual focus on past and present is Psalm 116. Since Second Temple times, the group of psalms from 113 to 118, known as Hallel, has been chanted, according to the Mishnah's claims, at Jewish festivals.[46] So while this particular psalm is couched in the first person, its larger ritual context, the sequence of songs celebrating individual and national deliverance, allows us also to see its "I," like that of Psalm 30, as representative.

As poems of the same genre, the two psalms share a great many conventional literary features. Both portray the speaker's suffering as a near-death experience, and both include a prayer spoken to God from death's threshold:

> YHWH, You brought me up from Sheol,
> preserved me from going down into the Pit. (30:4)

> The bonds of death encompassed me;
> the torments of Sheol overtook me. (116:3a)

> I called to You, YHWH;
> . . . "What is to be gained from my death,
> from my descent into the Pit?" (30:9–10)

> I came upon trouble and sorrow
> and I invoked the name of YHWH,
> "YHWH, save my life!" (116:3b-4)

Both prayer-poems describe God's attributes as they have been manifested in the personal experience of the speaker. One's claim that God is "angry but a moment, / and when He is pleased there is life" (30:6) is paralleled by the other's certainty that "the death of His Faithful ones / is grievous in YHWH's sight" (116:15). Each speaker doubles back to the past to discover a momentary betrayal of God, and brings a quotation from an earlier self as evidence of that alienation from God and godliness; egotistically, the one thought, " 'I shall never be shaken' " (30:7), while the other, equally but mistakenly self-sufficient, said rashly, " 'All men are false' " (116:11). Despite, or perhaps because of, these betrayals, each speaker has felt God's touch personally and concretely. God "undid" the sackcloth of the one (30:12) and "the cords that bound" the other (116:16). And, finally, each mentions a ritual means for continually expressing gratitude. One hopes to "sing hymns to You endlessly" (30:13), while the other promises to bring a thank offering to God, paying those vows "in the presence of all His people" (116:17–18).

Like Psalm 30, Psalm 116 cannot help but keep the past alive, even if it mars the celebration of thanksgiving. After an initial verse in which the psalmist defines his open relationship with God ("He turns his ear to me / whenever I call"), he turns immediately back to his brush with death, and the prayer that saved him. He knows God heard his prayer and delivered him from death, yet he remembers how it felt to be "brought low" (v. 6). And remembering brings it vividly back to life. "Be at rest, once again, O my soul, / for YHWH has been good to you" (v. 7). Because the speaker is again experiencing disquiet, he needs to quiet himself, yet he can never become so calm that he feels invulnerable. The person who accepts vulnerability at God's hand cannot afford to see himself as "untroubled," lest he think, "I shall never be shaken" (30:7).

In both of these psalms, the retrieval and reactualization of the past, especially its negative moments, is a crucial element of the psalmist's experience of deliverance. Each psalmist goes back to the past in order to connect it with the very different feelings of the present. "The past only becomes visible to revelation," writes Rosenzweig, "when and as revelation shines into it with the light of the present."[47] The psalmists can look back only because they know what they now know about God. The circuitous form each psalm takes has been described in another context as a "movement back into the past in order to go forward to a fully appropriated present and future . . . a search for a ground . . . that will support time, encompass it, still its movement."[48] This ground, we might say, is deliverance, the moment, whether in the past, present, or future, when God's time and ours intersects. A philosopher commenting on time's supposed irreversibility suggests that even in a secular context we do not ordinarily think of time as irreversible, but rather that each individual, like a psalmist, hopes

> that no one decision has committed him forever and that he still "has time" to make up what he has missed; that, in short, what is once done can at least partly be undone. In such expectation not only the future, but the past also lie before man as an open field of possibilities for transformation. The whole of time must remain open to him in order that he may fulfill his life in it, and in this sense the past also must represent for him a potentiality so that he may then assimilate it into the process of his life. This possibility is not to be thought of as existing only in acts of repentance or forgiving—on the contrary every return to the past by means of memory signifies already in some way a transformation of it.[49]

Celebration, not repentance, is the ostensible purpose of these two psalms. Yet insofar as they revisit the past in order to recognize the decisive moments in their lives, moments of divine intervention in response to prayer, these psalmists in effect repent for their prior obliviousness to God's role in their lives. We spoke earlier of how the collective memory of ritual helps a people overcome time's irreversible flow by allowing it to repeat in historic time acts originating in mythical time. Acts of private memory, as we see in this context, can make time similarly malleable, subject to the reinterpretation of a new perspective on life.

All of us are shaken by life, over and over again. Therefore, deliverance, such as is described in these psalms, cannot be a once-and-done affair. It remains always a memory, always a potentiality, a function of an individual's openness to God. Because the psalms we have looked at in this section manifest this openness, the voices that speak in them come to represent the community of believers' hopes for themselves. Each of the speakers has descended to his own Egypt, whether we construe this as exile, illness, or despair. And each has returned to the land of the living with testimony that the worst can be overcome, that God still brings salvation, just as God did long ago by taking God's chosen people out of Egypt. In this sense, the times of deliverance experienced and reexperienced in these psalms are liminal. They are a doorway from a remote mythic past to some future always yet about to happen. As ritual acts, they bring "the far-away, the long-ago, and the not-yet into the here-and-now."[50]

Deliverance in Space

"Man desires to possess God," Martin Buber writes in *I and Thou;* "he desires a continuity in space and time of possession of God. . . . He longs for extension in time, for duration. . . . He longs for extension in space, for the representation in which the community of the faithful is united with its God. . . . Only when these two arise—the binding up of time in a relational life of salvation and the binding up of space in the community that is made one by its Centre—and only so long as they exist, does there arise and exist, round about the invisible altar, a human cosmos with bounds and form, grasped with the spirit out of the universal stuff of the aeon, a world that is house and home, a dwelling for man in the universe."[51] That home in the universe is what the psalmists seek, a dwelling in time and in space that will channel the sometimes exalting, sometimes terrifying, always overwhelming influx of divine energy into human life. Building such a house and home entails risks. Fixing God in time and space through religious worship focused in and on a sanctuary can easily disturb the pure relationality that is the essence of the *I-Thou* bond, as Buber envisions it. At its worst, such fixing in time and space can become a kind of idolatry of hierarchies: God is here, not there; with us, not with them.[52] On the other hand, without the symbolism of the sacred center and its realization in actual worship, the human thirst for God can easily lack focus and continuity. If a community is constituted by the many lines of relation, temporal and spatial, that join its members together, it is also maintained by its conviction that there is an eternal center where all those extended lines of relation meet.

We have spoken of deliverance as a meeting of God's time and ours, thereby making of human time what Buber calls "a relational life of salvation." God's work in the world and ours in attempting to comprehend it can just as easily take a spatial as a temporal form. There is no time limit on the psalmist's cry, "My soul thirsts for You, / my body yearns for You / as a parched and thirsty land that has no water" (Ps. 63:2bc), in which the desert functions so memorably as an archetype of spiritual drought. Following Eliade's lead, treatments of sacred space in the Bible have focused on the symbolism of the center, especially the portrayal of Zion in Psalms.[53] In describing the divine warrior and enthronement motifs, we have already touched on a number of these psalms.[54] Rather than traversing again that familiar ground, we will examine spatial images in their own right, not so much as expressions of a collective mythology but rather as elaborations of the individual psychology of those who use them to express their spiritual states. A contrast between narrow and wide spaces will help focus our attention on how the psalmists envision both their vulnerability and their liberation. A look into dwellings that offer both concealment and openness will help us approach these same issues from another spatial and emotional angle. Along the way, we will glance at other geographical features, such as rocks and paths, that also can serve as metaphors of spiritual experience.

A noun signifying distress, *ṣar*, is also an adjective describing a narrow or tight place. So the movement from distress to well-being is repeatedly conceived as a movement from a tight to an open space, *merḥab*, a word which in the Bible always has a figurative dimension. My translations from three different psalms may sound unidiomatic, because they stress the root spatial meanings underlying the metaphoric uses of the linked words *ṣar* and *merḥab*.

> Out of the narrow place I called on Yah,
> God answered me in the spacious place of Yah.
>
> *min hammeṣar qarati Yah*
> *'anani bammerḥab Yah* (118:5)

In my tight place I called on YHWH. . . . (18:7)
God brought me out into a wide open space
and rescued me for being pleased with me. (18:20)

baṣṣar li 'eqra YHWH (18:7)
wayoṣieni lammerḥab (18:20)

I will exult and rejoice in your faithfulness
when you see my affliction,
and are mindful of the tightnesses of my soul,
and no longer enclose me in the hand of my enemy,
but stand my feet in a wide open place.

Yada'ta beṣarot napši . . .
he'emadita bammerḥab raglai (31:8–9)

One psalm compresses the figure of speech into just three words: *baṣṣar hirḥabta li* (4:2), "you freed me from my distress," or translating the figure literally, "when I felt tight, you widened things for me." Elsewhere, the desirable spiritual path is similarly portrayed as a wide one.[55]

In each of the psalms I have been quoting, the psalmist represents a sense of threat and insecurity in the image of being surrounded: either by nations swarming like bees (118:10–12), by the bonds of death and Sheol (18:5–6), or by the wicked whispering against his life, "a terror on every side" (31:14). And in each, the threatening surroundings are replaced by the speaker's spatial imaging of God or of being in God's house, with the community gathered there for worship. The authoritative doctrines of the culture assert that loyal and upright believers are safe with God. In two of these three psalms, the speakers testify to that belief without question. The third, however, is an urgent plea for safety, which also includes an expression of thanksgiving for the knowledge that such safety is possible. It is not a talking about but a talking to God about the speaker's plight. By comparing how these emotional movements are correlated with space in Psalms 118, 18, and 31, we will get a sense of how individuals make sacred space central to both their celebration of and their dialogue with God.

Psalm 118, the climax of the Hallel sequence chanted at the pilgrimage festivals, is a psalm of thanksgiving for a great national experience of deliverance, perhaps the return from exile in Babylon. It begins with an antiphonal praise of God, addressed to the assembled congregation, and concludes with instructions to the entering throng about the festival offering. Between these instructions about liturgical performance, the psalm is spoken in the first person as a collective representation of Israel's experience of deliverance. "Out of the narrow place I called upon Yah, / God answered me in the spacious place of Yah" (v. 5). This verse summarizes a complete emotional trajectory for the speaker, which can then be reexperienced by all the worshipers. The narrative of their deliverance is retold in dramatic verses built around repeated forms of a spatial verb, "to surround," and repeated namings of God.

> All nations have beset me;
> by the name of YHWH I will surely cut them down.
> They beset me, they surround me;
> by the name of YHWH I will surely cut them down.
> They have beset me like bees;
> they shall be extinguished like burning thorns;
> by the name of YHWH I will surely cut them down. (Vv. 10–12)

As the psalm is chanted, the rhythmic and lexical repetitions create the excitement of being on an imagined battlefield, beset and surrounded, but finally victorious in God's name. This incantatory passage is followed by another, quoting the triumphant shouts from the field of battle, "The right hand of YHWH is triumphant! / The right hand of YHWH is exalted! / The right hand of YHWH is triumphant!" The speaker, clearly now representing the nation, feels as one resurrected: "I shall not die but live / and proclaim the works of YHWH" (v. 17).

The psalm goes on to turn the space of the Temple into an arena for a victory parade:

> Open the gates of victory for me
> that I may enter them and praise YHWH.
> This is the gateway to YHWH—
> the victorious shall enter through it. (Vv. 19–20)

Whether translated as the gates of victory or righteousness makes little difference, since Israel feels self-righteous in being victorious. Symbolic meaning inheres not only in the liminal gateway but in the very building blocks themselves, which take their place in an allegorical drama: "The stone that the builders rejected has become the chief cornerstone" (v. 22). Those who denigrated Israel when it was brought low are thus dismissed, while Israel itself is entreated to exult and rejoice in "the day that YHWH has made" (v. 24). As they enter the Temple gates and are blessed by the Temple's officiants, the worshipers move from human time and space, where battles can be won or lost, to a sacred timespace, where cosmic order reigns. Creation itself is evoked in the phrase "God YHWH has given us light" (v. 27). The psalm concludes by focusing on the actual space where the sacrificial ceremony is being enacted in the here and now of the psalm. The "festal offering" is bound "to the horns of the altar with cords" (v. 27); God's praise is re-sounded, and the people acknowledge, as at the start of the psalm, the eternality of divine love.

In the triad of psalms whose movements we are analyzing, all of which share a similar pattern of moving from constriction to liberation, two share the image of the *sukkah* as covered space. In the narrative books of the Bible, the *sukkah* is a small covered hut used during harvests, and during the harvest pilgrimage festival of Sukkot, on which Israelites were specially commanded to be joyous as they commemorated the Israelites' forty years of wandering in the desert. In these huts, Israelites were vulnerable to the elements yet protected from them. While living in them (or in some other portable dwelling), they were also protected by God during their desert wanderings, their most vulnerable period as a people. These joint associations make the *sukkah* a powerful liminal image.[56] It is a dwelling, yet not a regular dwelling. One dwells in it between two settled periods, whether these are construed historically, as being between Egypt and Canaan, or agriculturally, between the growing and rainy seasons. The harvest is the time when the fate of the people is hanging in the balance: will there be enough food for the coming year? It is no wonder, then, that the liminal *sukkah* found its place in psalms representing deliverance as a transition from feelings of vulnerability to protection.

This transition is nowhere more evident than in Psalm 18, which, like Psalm 118, is full of military images. A scribal comment in verse 1 links this psalm to episodes in the life of David, but we need not confine ourselves to those associations to interpret the prayer-poem's imagery. The most striking image is a revelation to the speaker's eye of the divine presence, reminiscent of the people's experience at Sinai:

> Then the earth rocked and quaked;
> the foundations of the mountains shook,
> rocked by His indignation;
> smoke went up from His nostrils,
> from His mouth came devouring fire;
> live coals blazed forth from Him.
> He bent the sky and came down,
> thick clouds beneath His feet.
> He mounted a cherub and flew,
> gliding on the wings of the wind.
> He made darkness His screen;
> dark thunderheads, dense clouds of the sky
> were His pavilion round about Him.
> Out of the brilliance before Him,
> hail and fiery coals pierced His clouds.

Then YHWH thundered from heaven,
the Most High gave forth his voice—
hail and fiery coals.
He let fly his shafts and scattered them;
He discharged lightning and routed them. (Vv. 8–12)

On earth, a massive quake; in the heavens, the flaming sky-God riding upon a cherub, swooping on the wings of the wind, making a celestial pavilion, a personal *sukkah,* amid the dark, thick, watery clouds. The drama of lightning bolts and hailstones is matched by the far-reaching effects of the theophany: "The ocean bed was exposed; / the foundations of the world were laid bare" (v. 16). Is this a new creation or an uncreation? The speaker gets a personal answer to this question, when the God he has seen plucks him out of "the mighty waters" (v. 17), saves him from his enemies, and sets him down, as quoted above, in "a wide open space" (v. 20). Subsequently, he is able to overcome his enemies' spatial advantage. With God at his side, he can "rush a barrier, . . . scale a wall" (v. 30). The final spatial image has him standing "firm on the heights" (v. 34), an image of military invincibility. In this encounter with divinity, God's names and attributes are also solidly spatial. Three times God is called *ṣuri,* "my Rock" (vv. 3, 32, 47), as well as "my Fortress" (v. 3). The speaker and God mirror one another as warriors who prove themselves worthy on the field of celestial and terrestrial battle.

The escape from peril in these two military psalms makes their feelings of liberation unambiguous. There is no deliverance more real than that experienced on the field of battle. The speaker of Psalm 31, however, feeling oppressed at the start of the psalm, must work toward a liberation yet to come. As one who has trusted (vv. 7, 15) and taken refuge (vv. 2, 20) in God, the psalmist repeatedly demands to be saved (vv. 3, 16, 17), couching his requests in the formulaic language characteristic of the Psalms.[57] Putting himself in God's hands, he asks for public acknowledgment of divine favor (vv. 8, 17, 22), the special love shown to those who keep the covenant. Instead, the wicked shamelessly conspire against him, whispering and lying arrogantly (vv. 14, 19). He is even shunned in public by mere acquaintances (v. 12). In this mood, he wishes that his shame be visited upon the wicked, and that they "be silenced in the grave" to which he feels he has been consigned (v. 18).

Spatial imagery is a primary means through which this psalmist expresses distress. "Bring me out of this net which they [the wicked] have hidden for me" (v. 5). The psalmist is trapped in a besieged city, *be'ir maṣor* (v. 22), feeling caught in extremely narrow straits, *ṣarot napši* (v. 8) and *ṣar*

li (v. 10). Like the victor in Psalm 18, he appeals to God as *ṣur maʿoz* (v. 3),
a rock of strength. These alliterative word plays between *ṣar, maṣor,* and *ṣur*
are a powerful linguistic means for the psalmist to connect up his plight
with his plea. This speaker looks forward to being free from such distress,
when, no longer confined by his enemies, his feet will stand "in a wide
open place" (v. 9). Open places can turn threatening, however, as the
speaker reports being surrounded by the whispering of the wicked on
every side (v. 14). Disgraced and shunned by neighbors, he is reduced to
seeing himself as "a lost vessel" (v. 13). Like other distressed speakers
whom we have encountered, this one also feels responsible for his own
suffering. But apart from a brief confession, the theme of his "iniquity"
(v. 11) is not developed at any length.

Shame, however, is fully pictured: "I am the particular butt of my neighbors, / a horror to my friends; / those who see me on the street avoid me"
(v. 12).[58] Because shame is a social stigma, it can be removed only in the
presence of those who accept the speaker on his own terms. The speaker
therefore seeks to restore his personal honor by reconstituting his community. We learn from the closing exhortation that the speaker has come to
the Temple to be with the community of God's faithful (vv. 24–25).
Together with them, he can, in effect, shun those who have been shun-
ning him. For moral support, the psalmist petitions that all God's devoted
ones be hidden, from the root *s-t-r,* within the divine presence, treasured
in God's *sukkah* (v. 21). My literal translation stresses the spatial dimension
of the plea:

> Conceal them in the covert of Your face/presence,
> (*tastirem beseter paneka*)
> against scheming men;
> hide them as a treasure in a covered shelter
> (*tisppenem besukkah*)
> from contentious tongues. (V. 21)

In the two previous chapters, we noted several uses of *seter* to signify
shelter and protection for a favored human being. The word can also
signify hiddenness, and when God's presence seems hidden from
human beings, it invariably has negative connotations.[59] Here, the movement is in the opposite direction. The psalmist asks that the faithful be
hidden within *seter paneka,* God's hidden presence. Through parallelism,
the poet compares *seter paneka* to a *sukkah,* an actual shelter in which a
human being can hide, or as the verb literally puts it, be treasured. This
linkage explains why this is the only positive use of the expression in the
Bible. God's *sukkah* is a liminal doorway that transforms vulnerability

into protection. God may at times seem hidden, but one can be concealed even with the hidden God.

After envisioning this movement toward God, the speaker is relieved of his negative emotions and gratefully expresses his newfound assurance that God will indeed judge the arrogant ones who have plagued him (v. 24). This ultimate justice is part and parcel of God's covenant love, which can open up the self-enclosed person, even within a besieged city (v. 22). He was wrong when he thought, " 'I am thrust out of Your sight' " (v. 23). Feeling now protected and at one with the community of believers, the psalmist turns his petition into praise for God's delivering power. After praise comes exhortation, a movement we have encountered in other psalms. The speaker wants his experience to serve as a model for others. Other worshipers will find the deliverance they seek if they too preserve strength, courage, and patience in waiting for YHWH (v. 25).

The Divine and Human *Sukkah*

This terrestrial image of God's *sukkah* functions very differently from the celestial *sukkah* envisioned in Psalm 18. In that psalm, God was manifest to the speaker in a spectacular spatial image. The clouds formed a screen and a pavilion, *sukkah,* enabling God to ride through the heavens, throwing down thunder and lightning as his weapons. In Psalm 31, the speaker needs God to become manifest, and so uses a spatial image that has come to be associated with God and the Temple to bring God's sheltering presence down to earth for him. The spatial imagery of this prayer-poem can be understood, then, as a tool in the psalmist's dialogue with God. To appreciate the range of God's associations with the *sukkah,* it is useful to take a brief excursus away from the Book of Psalms.

In the narrative books of the Hebrew Bible, as we have said, *sukkah* always refers to a small hut, or booth. In addition to harvest and fall festival time, such huts were also used during military campaigns, and at least once on a celebrated prophetic mission.[60] Stemming from a root meaning "to cover," the word *sukkah* describes the hut's function as a small covered place. But in the poetic books of the Hebrew Bible, each use of the covering *sukkah* is figurative. Studying these metaphors and metonymies discloses a great deal about the biblical literary imagination: its conventionality, its creativity, and its bivalent approach to words, and through words to the world.

A metaphoric *sukkah* can have political and economic implications. In the final verses of Amos, after a bitter denunciation of the sins of the northern kingdom of Israel, the prophet consoles his audience with the promise that God will rebuild the fallen *sukkah* of David. The prophet follows with imagery of a fortified house; God will "mend its breaches," "set up its ruins anew," and "build it firm as in the days of old" (9:11). The contrast between the two house images is deliberate. The makeshift, temporary *sukkah* is not an appropriate image for a flourishing royal house, but it is an apt one for the breached kingdom to which Amos preaches. Similarly, in Job, the human *sukkah* is an image of something soon to be gone. The house of the wicked "is like a bird's nest, / Like the booth [*sukkah*] a watchman makes." He goes to bed in the evening with his wealth intact, only to discover in the morning that, like the night watchman's *sukkah*, it is gone (27:18–19).

Isaiah plays on related connotations of the forlorn *sukkah*. The land of Judah has been laid waste, its cities burned down, its produce consumed by occupying strangers. Against this dismal background, the prophet compares "Fair Zion," the feminine personification of Jerusalem, to a "booth [*sukkah*] in a vineyard," "a hut in a cucumber field," and "a besieged city" (1:8). All three similes emphasize the solitariness of a dwelling place in the midst of surroundings not normally inhabited. Once fair, Zion has become powerless and abandoned. The concluding image of the section intensifies these negative associations: "Had not YHWH of Hosts left us some survivors / We should be like Sodom, another Gomorrah" (1:9).

A second metaphoric use of *sukkah* in Isaiah and Job utterly transforms the negativity of the image. The booth is envisioned as a celestial pavilion, like the one we encountered in Psalm 18. Toward the end of Job, Elihu's speech anticipates the divine Voice from the Whirlwind. He points to God's incommensurable power over the elements: "Can one indeed contemplate the expanse of clouds, / The thunderings from His pavilion [*sukkato*]? / Behold, He spreads His lightning over it; / It fills the bed of the sea" (36:29–30). The *sukkah* is the celestial home of God. Isaiah juxtaposes God's celestial and earthly homes in this consoling vision of the sacred center:

> YHWH will create over the whole shrine and meeting-place of Mount Zion cloud by day and smoke with a glow of flaming fire by night. Indeed, over all the glory shall hang a canopy, which shall serve as a pavilion [*sukkah*] for shade from heat by day and for shelter and protection [*maḥseh* and *mistor*] against drenching rain. (4:5–6)

The vision of God's glory invoked here, recalling the cloud that hovers over the Tent of Meeting in the wilderness,[61] indicates that God ultimately chooses where God will dwell. Mount Zion can be seen as a solitary booth when God has departed from it, or as a permanent celestial abode when God chooses to favor it with his cloud. Covered by God's *sukkah*, Zion, now desolate, can again become resplendent.

As a human habitation, the *sukkah* is invariably weak: transient, solitary, or already fallen. As a divine habitation, it reflects God's glory and power, whether located on Mount Zion, a metonymy for the Temple in Jerusalem, or in the skies above. The agricultural *sukkah* offers little shelter from the elements, but God's *sukkah,* the place covered by the divine presence, offers enduring protection for the people of Israel. This repertory is expanded by the biblical poets' representation of the *sukkah* as an animal habitation, the lair of a hidden power. The Voice from the Whirlwind addresses Job as follows: "Can you hunt the prey for the lion, / Or satisfy the appetite of the young lions, / when they crouch in their dens [*me'onot*] / or lie in ambush in their covert [*bassukkah*]?" (RSV 38:39–40). The lions' lair is called *sukkah* by way of a metonymy: any covered place can be represented by any other one. The image of the lions' covert becomes metaphoric when it is applied to either the human or the divine realms. The lions' *sukkah* (Ps. 10:9) and *mistarim* (Ps. 17:1 2) are associated with the wicked who lie in ambush for the helpless poor. God also dwells occasionally in a leonine den, as in Psalm 76:3, where the psalmist pairs *me'onoto* and *sukko.* In this instance, God makes war like a powerful lion "on the mountains of prey" (v. 5). For the lion, for the wicked, and for God, the covering of the *sukkah* allows a hidden power to burst forth from a secret space into public view.

The imagery of hiddenness is theologically significant, since God's power is not always manifest to human beings. For instance, as we saw above in Psalm 31, the speaker seeks to enter God's *sukkah* because he feels exposed and unprotected. A recent study of the hiding of God's face (*hester panim*) in the Hebrew Bible argues that the motif of a hidden God is not to be understood simply as a perception of God's anger, nor as a failure on the part of the individual worshiper to understand or perceive God's presence in the world, but rather as central to the Israelite experience of faith. The study points to the language of hiddenness in the Psalms, where the faithful poets communicate their knowledge of God's presence alongside their knowledge of God's absence.[62] This rich ambivalence is especially characteristic of the psalms of supplication, those poems in which an individual complains to God of his or her bitter lot and seeks redress of grievances during the course of the prayer-poem itself. This genre has been characterized as providing for "both the articulation of the experience and a means of coping with the experience."[63] Often, like Psalm 31, petitionary psalms end with an expression of thanksgiving for having come through an ordeal.

We can analyze the *sukkah* image in Psalms under this twin rubric: because of its dual qualities of openness and concealment, the image articulates the paradox of God's hidden presence and therefore helps the speakers cope with their experience of both God's hiddenness and God's presence. In coming to terms with the role of such imagery in developing a personal relationship to God, it helps to distinguish between psalms of "orientation," "disorientation," and "reorientation."[64] We might say that in the midst of their disorientation, psalmists reorient themselves to believe in the power of a saving God by envisioning themselves hiding within God's presence, in the image of a concealing, sheltering *sukkah.* The metaphor allows psalmists to express conflicting, even paradoxical, emotions. They sorely feel their vulnerability in a world where God's justice often seems to be hidden, so they focus on their need to feel specially sheltered, in fact, treasured, by a sheltering God, whose special intimacy is available to them through worship in God's sanctuary. The physical space of the *sukkah* lends itself to expressing this theological and emotional duality. Its walls conceal its occupants from those outside who are arrayed against them, but its roof, open either to the sky or to the golden rafters of the Temple, allows a special access for the divine presence.

The *sukkah* that is such a compelling metaphor may well be a literal description of what worshipers saw in the First Temple, if the ancient Tabernacle was reerected within the Holy of Holies, as some hypothesize. Within that large *sukkah*-like structure, there may also have been a *sukkah* around the ark itself, as is suggested by God's instruction to Moses: *wesakkota* (Exod. 40:3).[65] Theological metaphors linking divine concealment and presence would have arisen altogether naturally in such an architectural setting.

We noted above that architecture can give rise to recurring poetic conventions, as when gates and courtyards come to stand for the Temple as a whole. And in this chapter, we have noted poetic conventions for depicting two *sukkah* images, the transitory human one and the resplendent celestial one. The sacred poet-singers of Israel also had a set of poetic conventions for representing a third *sukkah,* the divine tent, which, whether or not it actually existed within the Temple, functions within the prayer-poetry as a metonym for God's house, the sacred center of the culture. We have already looked in some detail at Psalm 31. Its partner in depicting this Temple-based *sukkah* is Psalm 27. Not only do the psalms express the twin themes of concealment and presence in the divine *sukkah,* but they do so in virtually the same words, arranged in what has been called a "formulaic system."[66]

At the start of Psalm 27, the seeming confidence of the opening, "Whom should I fear?" (v. 1), is immediately countered by the vivid evocation of evildoers, tormentors, and foes. The vulnerable speaker seems to be out in the open with these threatening enemies. Can they be the only ones who are liable to "stumble and fall" (v. 2)? This threatening open space is further concretized in the image of the hypothetical army encamped against the speaker:

> Should an army besiege me,
> my heart would have no fear;
> should war beset me,
> still would I be confident. (V. 3)

The psalmist avoids this space by imagining its opposite, the house of God, which offers both openness and protection.

> One thing I ask of YHWH,
> only that do I seek:
> to live in the house of YHWH
> all the days of my life,
> to gaze upon the beauty of YHWH,
> to frequent His temple.
> He will shelter me in His pavilion [*besukko*]
> on an evil day,
> grant me the protection of His tent [*oholo*],
> raise me high upon a rock [*besur*].
> Now is my head high
> over my enemies roundabout;
> I sacrifice in His tent with shouts of joy,
> singing and chanting a hymn to YHWH. (Vv. 4–6)

In the triplet of verse 5, the three spaces imagined—pavilion, tent, and rock—all may be epithets for the Temple: its inner holy space and its immovable foundation.[67] We can also understand them as a spatial and emotional sequence. Because the poet is comforted by envisioning himself in the intimate space of God's pavilion/tent, he is then able to imagine himself high on a rock, exposed once more, but this time triumphantly invulnerable. This is certainly a climactic image of divine protection: openness without vulnerability.

At this point, the mood of the psalm shifts dramatically, as most commentators have noted, many suggesting that our text is a fusion of two very different psalms:[68]

> Hear, YHWH, when I cry aloud;
> have mercy on me, answer me.
> In Your behalf my heart says:
> "Seek My face!"
> YHWH, I seek Your face.
> Do not hide Your face from me;
> do not thrust aside Your servant in anger;
> You have ever been my help.
> Do not forsake me, do not abandon me,
> O God, my deliverer. (Vv. 7–9)

Critics who divide up the psalm fail to note that an exalted feeling of security can easily produce the most profound insecurity. If two emotions happen sequentially, that does not mean that the earlier emotion dies away completely; as we pointed out above, vulnerability often lingers in psalms expressing gratitude for deliverance. The opening question of the psalm, "Whom should I fear?" indicates that fear remains very much on the speaker's mind.

Having entered into the concealment of God's tent, *seter 'oholo,* the psalmist remembers the opposite feeling of God's hiding his face, *hester panim:* "do not conceal Your face/presence from me" (*'al taster paneka,* v. 9).[69] The expression of both security and vulnerability through the root *s-t-r* indicates the necessary interrelatedness of these emotions and the pivotal, unifying role played by *s-t-r* in the psalm.[70] Each emotion must be played out in full. In the extremity of crying out against God's *hester panim,* the psalmist imagines himself abandoned by both father and mother, though God, he is sure, will take him in (v. 10). Being taken in by God calls to mind the psalmist's earlier representation of wanting to be taken into God's pavilion/tent.

In the second half of the prayer-poem, spatial images again help the psalmist address himself to God. He urges God, "Show me Your way, YHWH, / and lead me on a level path / because of my watchful foes" (v. 11). Paths are obviously spatialized images for temporal existence. The paths of the righteous and of sinners, the psalmists repeatedly aver, lead to very different ends.[71] The image of the "level path" in this psalm defends the psalmist against the way of the wicked, both literally and metaphorically. On such a path, he will be able to see and avoid the foes who may actually lie in wait. But the word for "level" or "straight," *mišor,* also means "just," and naturally connotes right action.[72] We get a sense, therefore, that the psalmist is seeking a middle path for himself, neither secluded in God's tent nor exposed on the field of battle, but leading safely through the world of human choices. If only the speaker can wisely learn to follow this path, and not be distracted by the "false witnesses and unjust accusers" who keep appearing against him (v. 12)! "Had I not the assurance / that I would enjoy the goodness of the Lord / in the land of the living . . . " (v. 13). The syntax breaks off here, perhaps to indicate how easily he might be turned aside from the "level path" were it not for his belief in divine providence.

Turning to the bystanders in the last verse, the psalmist turns his poem into a model of how others might also overcome fear. In urging strength, courage, and patience in waiting for YHWH, he echoes, in almost the same words, the concluding advice of Psalm 31. Both psalmists have imaged their emotional progress spatially. One's vulnerability was felt (or acutely imagined) in a tight place, a besieged city (31:22); the other's, in a wide open space, with an army encamped against him (27:3). However different their circumstances, both look to the divine *sukkah* and to the worshiping community gathered there to sustain them in the pain of their solitude and alienation. The *sukkah* in these psalms thus functions as a figure of inversion: God's perceived hiddenness is turned by the poets into a secret space where believers can encounter God, singly or collectively. *Seter,* we remember, is bivalent, depending on who is being hidden from whom. When a faithful psalmist desires the *seter* of God's sheltering presence, he can choose among God's tent (27:5), wings (61:5), shadow (91:1), shield (119:114), and, only when it is joined with *sukkah,* God's face or presence (31:21). Through these personal images of God, God's hiddenness turns into the psalmist's place of concealment, God's seeming absence into manifest presence. Within the shadows of the divine *sukkah,* the psalmists hold in tension the twin faces of an invisible God.

The *sukkah* is obviously not the only image through which biblical poets could express their desire to be sheltered in God's presence. The shadow of God's wings, an image often used by the psalmists, offers both shelter and concealment and suggests an equally intimate experience. But the *sukkah* is more centrally connected to human life: it offers a dream of intimacy with God, dreamt from within the simplest, most basic human habitation, the agricultural hut.[73] The transformation of that hut into the divine *sukkah* is not just a dream of ultimate solitude, however rewarding and necessary such a place of private meditation and prayer might be. It is also centrally connected to the political and liturgical life of the people. To the divine *sukkah,* Israel brings its complaints about the seeming injustices of God's reign as well as its songs of praise for God's gracious gifts.[74] Under the ambivalent sign of that poetic image, the individual poet and the congregation are united in their faithfulness to the hidden presence of their Lord.

Time and Space in Theodicy

In a number of the psalms we have examined, the continuing predominance of the wicked troubles the psalmist's worldview. In Psalms, more so than in Job, there is a pronounced attempt to reconcile the goodness and sovereignty of God with the existence of evil. In the last chapter, we focused on dialogue as a dramatic means of treating issues of theodicy. In the remainder of this chapter, we will look at several ways the psalmists use images of time and space to wrestle with the troubling persistence of evil in God's world.

Continuing to look, then, at the image of the *sukkah,* we find that the formulaic system which links the divine *sukkah* with roots for hiddenness is shared by a psalm in which an earthly *sukkah* is occupied by the wicked. Psalm 10 begins by announcing God's perceived disappearance from the world. The taunting question "Why, YHWH, do you stand aloof [*ta'alim*], / heedless in times of trouble?" (v. 1) describes God's inaction by hinting at God's disappearance. The root of *ta'alim* is the same as that for *'olam,* the word for eternity that has been so central to our explorations in this chapter. As a result of God's seeming disappearance (which may well seem endless), a space is opened up in which evil can flourish. A wicked one lies in hidden places (from the root *s-t-r*), on the lookout (from the root *ṣ-p-n*) for the innocent and helpless, like a lion in its *sukkah* (vv. 8–9). Given the cluster of the same three roots we noted in Psalms 27 and 31, we are struck precisely by the absence of the divine *sukkah* from this psalm:

> He lurks in outlying places;
> from a covert [*bammistarim*] he slays the innocent;
> his eyes spy out [*yisponu*] the hapless.
> He waits in a covert [*bammistar*] like a lion
> in his lair [*besukkah*];
> waits to seize the lowly;
> he seizes the lowly as he pulls his net shut;
> he stoops, he crouches
> and the hapless fall prey to his might. (Vv. 8–10)

Since God's seeming absence from the world is the psalm's theological and emotional starting point, it must be more than coincidence that our psalmist chose to characterize the godless wicked with the same roots that characterize God's capacity to shelter his dear ones.

Inverting an established metaphor for God's own turf, the poet betrays his anger at the state of affairs he finds in the world.[75] In effect, he challenges God with his characterization of the wicked, seemingly invulnerable in their covert. In a related characterization in Psalm 17:12, the wicked hide like young lions in secret places (*bemistarim*). So the psalmist asks to be similarly hidden (*tastireni*) in the shadow of God's wings (v. 8), for he knows that God's treasure (*sepuneka*) awaits him there (v. 14). These roots align this psalm too with the motif of the divine *sukkah,* while substituting God's wings as the protecting image. Rather than sheltering his dear ones, God has left them vulnerable to their predators. The poet cannot renounce his complaint until God reappears to condemn the wicked and provide justice for the oppressed.

The wicked one can freely commit his outrages because he believes that there is no God, and that even if there were, the great El would not look into his affairs. "He thinks, 'God is not mindful, / He hides his face [*histir panaw*], / he never looks' " (v. 11). The play on the root *s-t-r*, with both the wicked and God in hiding, points again to a tension at the heart of the prayer-poem. Rather than continuing to question God's disappearance, the poet challenges God to reappear by using the wicked as a mouthpiece for expressing his own doubts.[76] To vindicate divine justice, the psalmist urges God (not the Canaanite name, El, used by the wicked, but the specifically Israelite, YHWH) to rise up (v. 12) and save the lowly and downtrodden (vv. 17–18). The final movement of the psalm is an exhortation to fill up the world with the divine presence so noticeably absent in its first half. It specifies no habitation for God, nor does it need to, since at the day of reckoning, God's power will be everywhere manifest.

Similar issues are treated in Psalm 73, which lays out the psalmist's questions about why the wicked prosper. In this psalm, the wicked are not hidden away in concealed dens. Proudly, they display their wrongdoing:

> . . . pride adorns their necks
> lawlessness enwraps them as a mantle.
> Fat shuts out their eyes;
> their fancies are extravagant.
> They scoff and plan evil;
> from their eminence they plan wrongdoing.
> They set their mouths against heaven,
> and their tongues range over the earth.
> So they pound His people again and again,
> until they are drained of their very last tear.
> Then they say, "How could God know?
> Is there knowledge with the Most High?" (Vv. 6–11)

Tempted by the prosperity of the wicked, the speaker says he had almost left the path of righteousness to join them, almost, in fact, decided to join in their atheistic words, as we noted above.[77] Because the psalmist is a believer, he applies himself to understand how God could allow them to thrive, "but it seemed a hopeless task / till I entered God's sanctuary and reflected on their fate" (v. 17). The meditative process yields a flash of insight, in which he sees "How suddenly are they ruined, wholly swept away by terrors" (v. 19). The psalm makes no attempt to explain this religious experience; it takes for granted that being in the space of the sanctuary allowed the speaker this insight or vision. Students of ritual understand that an idea of place is enacted with each ritual occasion. Thus, for the speaker and his audience, the connection between place and doctrinal understanding must be so self-evident that it need not be expressed.[78]

It is helpful to remember that ancient Israelites had a specific spatial orientation in walking into the sanctuary. They were coming to what they thought of as the center of the world, designed to be a representation of the cosmos itself. On their way in from the southeast, at least during First Temple times, they would have passed a three-dimensional image of the cosmos as tamed by God, the huge brazen sea, supported by twelve oxen, in teams of three facing in each direction. In whichever direction one looked, and during all twelve months, one could perceive the cosmic order.[79] Many psalms were written and performed ritually just to instill and maintain this profound sense of order among Israelite believers.

One such composition offers a marvelous panorama of the timespace of the created universe. Psalm 104 begins with a picture of the heavens as God's dwelling, then looks to the permanent foundations of the earth. It then recalls a primordial past in which, to establish this earth as our permanent dwelling, God had to tame the ungovernable sea. The next twenty verses portray the earth that we know, cataloguing its waters, plant life, geological features, and its creatures in their various habitats. Human beings are here too, working on land and sea ("man then goes out to his work / to his labor until the evening," v. 23), but occupying less than two verses in the scene. This is the universe as seen from God's point of view, a psalmic version of what the Voice from the Whirlwind makes Job see. The catalogue of creation climaxes in an acknowledgment of all creatures' utter dependence on God:

> All of them look to You
> to give them their food when it is due.
> Give it to them, they gather it up;
> open Your hand, they are well-satisfied;
> hide Your face, they are terrified;
> take away their breath, they perish
> and turn again into dust;
> send back Your breath, they are created,
> and You renew the face of the earth. (Vv. 27–30)

This psalm shows the world to exist by virtue of God's cosmic battle with the elements and by virtue of God's continuing provision for all living beings. Creation was not completed once and for all but is renewed, according to this psalmist, on a daily basis. In its final movement, the psalmist therefore turns to the one area of God's governance about which unanswered questions remain, the role of the wicked in the scheme of salvation. If creation can be daily renewed, then surely God can complete the work begun at the start of time when chaos was banished and the land emerged as the home of life. God's ultimate work is yet to come: "May sinners disappear from the earth, / and the wicked be no more. / Bless YHWH, O my soul. Praise Yah!" (v. 35).

Israelite religious narratives present the universe as having a consummate order, both at its creation and at a moment of eschatological hope, like the future portrayed at the end of Psalm 104. The community tells its foundational stories—God's creation of the world, the exodus and wandering in the wilderness, the entry to the land, the founding of the Davidic kingdom—to ritually bind the generations of Israelite worshipers one to another. The community celebrates its sacred spaces—the universe as the arena of God's creative activity and Zion as God's earthly dwelling place—in order to complete a vertical axis between heaven and earth, ritually binding Israelites to the chosen place where they worship their universal God. In an environment such as God's temple, where this order is not only an intellectual postulate but also a felt reality, sustained by a full ritual calendar, one's doubts and misgivings are set to rest.

We are now in a better position to appreciate the previously quoted Psalm 73. Fears of the ultimate triumph of the wicked, which plague the psalmist and many other would-be believers, vanish when he enters the sanctuary and momentarily assumes God's perspective on timespace. "You despise their image," he says to God, "as one does a dream after waking" (v. 20). The human experience of the wicked is a dream, easily banished when juxtaposed with God's view of them. "Those who keep far from You perish / You annihilate all who are untrue to You" (v. 27). The visionary experience in the Temple is not a dream but a glimpse of divine reality. It allows the psalmist to put a different value on human life. "Having You," he addresses God, "I want no one on earth. / My body and mind fail; / but God is the stay of my mind, my portion forever" (vv. 25–26). Does the psalmist believe that, unlike the wicked, he will not perish? Has his meditation conquered time once and for all? His answer is simple: "As for me, nearness to God is good" (v. 28a). This practical wisdom is the fruit of living in a ritualized universe of spiritual discipline. The ritualized world of the Temple is structured to grant believers the practical knowledge that they can be constantly near to God through patient meditative mindfulness.[80] The psalmist enters the liminal zone in one mindset and leaves with another, having broken through the old frame of his existence to gain a new clarity about reality.[81] The shift from human to divine temporal perspective, from profane to sacred ground, allows this psalmist to make his peace with the world in which he lives for as long as he can remain connected to God.

Seeing, Bakhtin wrote, requires "outsideness." To perceive oneself and human existence as a whole requires wider temporal and spatial categories than any one individual can come to.[82] That is why in the interest of truth, the personal needs to be viewed side by side with the collective, and the human with the divine. Any one individual's story of deliverance will have far more lasting impact if it is aligned with a national story of deliverance, as we saw in Psalm 77. Similarly, any individual expression, whether of thanksgiving, trust, or supplication, can be complemented by the broader social unit, as we have seen in the many psalms that involve the congregation in the speaker's discourse. Asking the community to affirm one's experiences and learn from them is a proven way of coming to that external view of oneself that transcends pure subjectivity. Adopting as one's own the view of sacred space accepted by the community turns the individual spaces of one's life and one's psychological experience into windows onto a larger canvas. Adopting as one's own the view of time and space associated with divinity allows one to widen that canvas to the greatest extent possible, so that the entire world of temporal suffering and injustice can be viewed as but a moment of eternal reality, a truth that human beings can welcome, the better to endure their reality.

One of the most extraordinary meditations in the Book of Psalms stresses the necessary outsideness of all true vision. For all the intellectual gains to be made from seeing oneself and one's world from the outside, it can also trap one in static fixity, which the self cannot abide for long. The author of Psalm 139 attempts to identify with God's seeing of him, which Bakhtin calls "surplus seeing," that which another sees about us that we ourselves cannot see:

> YHWH, You have examined me and know me.
> When I sit down or stand up You know it;
> You discern my thoughts from afar.
> You observe my walking and reclining,
> and are familiar with all my ways.
> There is not a word on my tongue
> but that You, YHWH, know it well. (Vv. 1–4)

No matter how much we want our loved ones to know us, which one of us would not find it uncomfortable to be so thoroughly known as these verses imply? The psalmist's discomfort surfaces in the next verse, with the verb "to hedge," *ṣartani,* from the root we examined earlier, meaning literally "You've made it narrow for me": "You hedge me before and behind; / You lay Your hand upon me. / It is beyond my knowledge; / it is a mystery; I cannot fathom it" (vv. 5–6). Four times in these first six lines, the root for "knowledge" sounds and re-sounds. Like the Book of Job, this psalm is a meditation on the limits of human knowledge, attempting to assess that self-consciousness which was gained from our first eating of the Edenic tree.

God is everywhere, but, like Jonah, this psalmist wants an avenue of escape from the feeling of being in a universe that affords no private space:

> Where can I escape from Your spirit?
> Where can I flee from Your presence?
> If I ascend to heaven, You are there;
> If I descend to Sheol, You are there too.
> If I take wing with the dawn
> to come to rest on the western horizon,
> even there Your hand will be guiding me,
> Your right hand be holding me fast. (Vv. 8–10)

Earlier in the chapter, we spoke of the intellectual coherence to be gained from assuming the point of view of God's omnipresence, but here we see how the very idea puts the psalmist at risk. This human being wants autonomy above all else, and in the succeeding lines discovers that it is no more available in time than in space:

> If I say, "Surely darkness will conceal me,
> night will provide me with cover,"
> darkness is not dark for You;
> night is as light as day;
> darkness and light are the same. (Vv. 11–12)

No space or time is hidden from God, not the speaker's innermost thoughts, not even the dark, secret places where he says he was formed, neither his "mother's womb" (v. 13) nor "the recesses of the earth" (v. 15)—in effect, the cosmic womb.

This is not a Temple-centered meditation, in which the psalmist can imagine an escape into God's sheltering, mystifying presence. For this psalmist, the only space that matters is the inward space of consciousness, and this preoccupation leads to a breakthrough similar to that which we just saw in Psalm 73, the realization that there is no inwardness, no time or space, apart from God. God's thoughts, the praying poet concludes, "exceed the grains of sand; / I end—but am still with You" (v. 18). A transcendent perspective on terrestrial time and space, that is, a secure point of vision outside the self, has enabled the psalmist to know and accept human mortality. The phrase "I end—but am still with You" brilliantly combines that affirmation of accepted mortality with its converse, an intimation of infinitude that comes from being allied with God's immanent presence within the human being.

Since the movement of the psalm has been toward ever greater understanding of God's relationship to human beings, it makes sense that before the prayer-poem can come to a point of resolution, it must take up theodicy, the greatest challenge to human understanding throughout the Psalms. For four verses, the psalmist develops the complaint theme "O God if you would only slay the wicked!" (v. 19). Central to the presentation of this complaint is the psalmist's belief, vividly dramatized earlier in the psalm, that human consciousness is totally knowable by God. "O YHWH, You know I hate those who hate You" (v. 21a). The unstated subtext of this line is clear. "If God knows how much I, the faithful and upright psalmist, hate the wicked, then how can God not act to defeat the wicked?" One might have expected such egocentrism to disappear along with the psalmist's earlier recognition of human limits. But it is precisely because human limits come together in this psalm with divine immanence ("I end—but am still with You") that this very finite psalmist can call on the infinite and eternal God to become manifest in the workings of the world as a creator of what humans will perceive as justice.

In this psalm in which verbs of knowing play such an important role, one's consciousness is all one has to offer up to God. To conclude the discourse, the psalmist offers God the opportunity for one final interrogation: "Examine me, O God, and know my mind" (v. 23). This is obviously a reprise of the opening line, "O YHWH, You have examined me and know me" (v. 1), but with a significant difference. Where before the psalmist resented the oppressive burden of such knowing, here the imperative to God is offered with an acceptance of human vulnerability before God. "See if I have vexatious ways," the psalmist writes, "and guide me in ways everlasting" (v. 24). *Derek ʿolam,* as this psalmist certainly knows, is not a path human beings can literally walk in this lifetime. What the psalmist holds out by means of this figurative expression is the hope of walking in partnership with God toward ends within this lifetime, such as justice and righteous living, that God has taught are endless. Through imaging God as a guide on the human being's path of *derek ʿolam,* this psalm brings together the perspectives of human time and eternity better than any other in the Psalter. The terror of the omnipresent, transcendent God, dwelling in light and darkness, in heaven and Sheol, is in the end mitigated by the comfort of the immanent God, walking together with the human being "in ways everlasting."

·V·

THROUGH THE VALLEY OF THE SHADOW OF DEATH AND BEYOND: THE PSALMS AND JEWISH NATIONAL CATASTROPHE

Envisioning a "walk through a valley of deepest darkness," one psalmist testifies, "I fear no harm, for You are with me" (23:4). But at other moments, other psalmists confronting fearful evil understandably lack this supreme confidence in God's protection. As they question God about the rationale for evil in the world, they enter into dialogue with the voices of the wicked, so that, through those challenging voices, they can better challenge God to act justly. As they pray in the midst of their suffering, often experiencing God as remote, aloof, or hidden, they develop temporal and spatial images to turn such divine hiddenness into divine presence. In this final chapter, these issues of theodicy take a darker turn, as we confront from the collective perspective of Jewish history those psalms that articulate the irremediable pain of the people Israel in the face of its catastrophic suffering. We will examine how some psalms articulated a theological response to national catastrophe in their own time, and also how later generations of Jewish liturgists, poets, and theologians reaccentuated and reframed such psalms as part of an extended dialogue with them, in response to the catastrophes of later periods in Jewish history, including our own post-Holocaust moment. This chapter, then, uses psalms to limn a selective essay in historical theology.

Rather than attempting a survey of this long dialogical history, I have chosen to focus on what are widely acknowledged as the most significant moments of rupture in Judaism, during each of which psalms have been framed and reframed to respond to national catastrophe. These moments of rupture are the destruction of the two Jerusalem Temples in 587 B.C.E. and 70 C.E., the expulsion of the Jews from Spain in 1492, and the destruc-

177

tion of European Jewry between 1933 and 1945. By identifying these as breaking points, I mean to suggest that after them Judaism could not continue business as usual, but in each case evolved (and, in response to the Holocaust, continues to evolve) new theological paradigms.

Theologian Arthur Cohen has taken the position that the Holocaust is not just one among these catastrophes, but rather should be regarded as a category unto itself. He identifies the Holocaust of our era as a *tremendum,* an event of unparalleled immensity in its revelation of human malignity, and because of this a caesura, that is, a total break in the old forms of Judaism, since all prior theological paradigms are exposed by it as inadequate. Previous catastrophes do not become caesurae, he claims, for in response to them, "the tradition took up the frayed ends of time and knotted them. . . . A mythos of incorporation and consolation emerged with which to supply a nexus and continuity, where previously only despairing caesura had been palpable."[1] Concerning these earlier ruptures, I would suggest that by focusing, as Cohen does, on the compensatory strength of Jewish mythmaking, we can easily overlook the tensions— and real breaks—evident in earlier reformulations of Jewish theology under the pressure of national catastrophe. As we shall see in considerable detail below, each Jewish generation responding to overwhelming catastrophe has, in part, recast its understanding of God's power and role in history, and incorporated that understanding in new literary and liturgical forms.

Cohen emphasizes post-Holocaust rupture and despair in order to mark the gravity of the theological task facing the current generation of Jews and Christians.[2] He urges us, in the wake of the Jewish people's catastrophic experience in our century, not "to rush to prayer and midrash without first formulating the questions appropriately designated as theological," and, in that process, to "make certain that it is still the ancient God whom we seek."[3] There are already signs, however, of a new consolatory myth emerging in certain sectors of the Jewish people, so it is probably too soon to accept Cohen's historical assessment that the Holocaust represents a unique rupture within Jewish historical consciousness. Cohen's theologizing, we should remember, comes in the context of widespread disbelief, such as that notably expressed by Richard Rubenstein, who wrote, "When I say we live in the time of the death of God, I mean that the thread uniting God and man, heaven and earth, has been broken. We stand in a cold, silent, unfeeling cosmos, unaided by any purposeful power beyond our own resources. After Auschwitz, what else can a Jew say about God?"[4] But as another contemporary theologian has pointed out, disbelief is not "new in the history of Jewish spiritual struggle"; each generation has had its "radical theology."[5] The psalmists also theologized in the face of those who claimed to be living by their own strength, unaided by any higher power, and judged, if at all, only by human standards. It would be a mistake therefore to assume, with either Rubenstein or Cohen, that this generation's questions or its answers are wholly new.

That must be our conclusion, if we look from the prayers and midrash written by earlier generations to contemporary expressions that formulate theological questions after catastrophe. Our key texts will be psalms written in the wake of catastrophe, at least one datable to the Babylonian exile; liturgies from the Second Temple period; midrash from after the destruction of the Second Temple; kabbalist liturgies from the century after the expulsion from Spain; and, finally, memoirs, poems, and theologies written during and in response to the Holocaust. In examining these texts, this chapter will show how definitions of "the ancient God" have indeed changed for each Jewish generation that has faced catastrophic destruction and chosen to keep the tradition alive. It will also show the continuities among the questions and answers offered by the Jewish people, as one generation's text responds to another's to create the intergenerational dialogue that makes up a religious tradition.

The Shock of Catastrophe

The destruction of the Jerusalem Temple in 587 B.C.E. threatened the collapse of Israelite religious life as it had been known and practiced for centuries. Was the violence perpetrated against the sanctuary and the citizens of Jerusalem and Judea truly a punishment from God, as the prophet Jeremiah foretold? With the collapse of the symbolic sacred center, could the holiness and separateness of God's people be maintained? And what of God's eternal covenant with the descendants of Abraham, and the more recent ones with the priestly house of Aaron and the royal house of David? Would God continue to abide in the people's midst, with no sanctuary in which to dwell? Could the people Israel sustain its covenantal life on foreign soil?

These are the mighty questions with which Jeremiah's contemporaries had to engage. But before they could begin to approach the reconstruction of Israelite religion and the creation of a post-Temple Judaism, they had to mourn their great loss. The biblical response to catastrophe offers a window on how a nation comes to terms with its vulnerability in the face of its own possible death. The destruction of the Temple and Jerusalem, the exile of Judea's religious and political leaders, the radical break in religious ritual and expectations evoked in the survivors feelings similar to those of an individual being diagnosed with a terminal illness. The individual may deny what is happening, become angry, bargain with God, become depressed, or ultimately accept the fate that cannot be altered.[6] In ancient Israel's postcatastrophe literature, comprising the Book of Lamentations, the latter chapters of Jeremiah, and Psalms 74, 79, and 137, all these stages of grief are manifest. These emotive responses do not form a single orderly progression, but rather are mixed together differently according to the temperament and experience of each author who filters the experience of the people.

We cannot say exactly when Psalms 74 and 79 were composed. They could be responses to Nebuchadnezzar's destruction of the First Temple in 587 B.C.E., or to Antiochus IV's desecration of the Second Temple in 168 B.C.E., amid the religious persecutions that prompted the Maccabean revolt. As laments of the community, they are filled with stereotypical phrases that could be reused whenever the situation called for them; thus, Psalm 79:6, "Pour out Your fury upon the nations that do not know You," is repeated almost verbatim in Jeremiah 10:25. Not only do the psalms share similar phrasing, but their structures are similar: the first movement of each is a description of the calamity, the second movement a plea to God. Though similar in many ways, the two psalms offer rather different interpretations of the catastrophe. One asserts the innocence of Israel, while the other sees evidence of Israel's guilt and punishment, the justified result of God's anger, which can be mitigated, however, through repentant prayer.

One literary strategy that both psalms adopt is to make metaphors out of the facts of the destruction, lending a realism to the poetry, however remote it may be in its origins from an actual eyewitness account. Thus, we hear how

> Your foes roar inside Your meeting-place;
> they take their signs for true signs.
> It is like men wielding axes
> against a gnarled tree;
> with hatchet and pike
> they hacked away at its carved work. (74:4–6)
>
> They have left Your servants' corpses
> as food for the fowl of heaven,
> and the flesh of Your faithful for the wild beasts.
> Their blood was shed like water around Jerusalem,
> with none to bury them. (79:2–3)

The bodies have not even been buried, nor will they be, for "as food for the fowl of heaven," they have become literally carrion. The image of

blood "shed like water," though virtually a cliché in our culture, is especially powerful in this context of the defiled Temple, for there water had
been used on a daily basis to cleanse the altar of any remaining blood.
Now, blood itself is the water that flows through the streets, defiling, not
cleansing, whatever it touches.[7] The sanctuary, which had served to
remove the people's defilement through the purgative power of spilled
animal blood, is no more. Gone also is the people's self-esteem as guardians of God's holy seat. While the enemies "take their signs for true signs"
(74:4b), "no signs appear for us; / there is no longer any prophet; / no
one among us knows for how long" (74:9). The enemies who mock
Israel's monotheist pretensions cannot be given the last word; the self-pity
of the victims gives way to their empowering anger: "How long, O YHWH,
will You be angry forever, / will Your indignation blaze like fire?" (79:5).
"Why do You hold back Your hand, Your right hand? / Draw it out of Your
bosom!" (74:11).

Confronting the gruesome reality, mourning, and protesting the loss
are indeed necessary and inevitable responses to catastrophe. But preeminent for the psalmists is the need to arouse God's compassion for "the
flock that You tend" (74:1), "the flock You shepherd" (79:13). To this
end, both psalms present the attack on the Temple as equally an attack on
God's own name and reputation: "Till when, O God, will the foe blaspheme, / will the enemy forever revile Your name?" (74:10).[8] "Why
should the nations say, 'Where is their God?' / Before our eyes let it be
known among the nations / That You avenge the spilled blood of Your
servants" (79:10). At least for the sake of the divine reputation, if not for
the sake of Israel's merit, God should be motivated to pour out divine fury
"upon the kingdoms that do not invoke Your name" (79:6). If God
avenges, then the people will know that YHWH is a faithful and forgiving
God, loyal to the covenant with Israel.

But what if Israel is being oppressed for a reason? Psalm 79, having
already acknowledged Israel's "former iniquities" (v. 8a) as well as "our
sin" (v. 9b) of the current generation, needs a persuasive strategy to conclude its plea. The final verse of the psalm takes the form of a bargain, like
the one the patriarch Jacob offered to God before he set out on his
journey away from Canaan.[9] If God avenges "our neighbors sevenfold,"
"Then we, Your people, / the flock You shepherd / shall glorify You forever; / for all time we shall tell Your praises" (v. 13). In a world rent by
catastrophic violence, the popular metaphor of the sheep and shepherd
represents the psalmist's wish to restore the *status quo ante,* the comfortable relationship with God once known, perhaps taken for granted, and
now desperately longed for. At the end of this psalm, pastoralism offers a
calming influence to counterbalance the horrendous animal image with

which the psalm opens, God's faithful become "flesh . . . for the wild beasts" (v. 2).[10] No longer to be attacked as defenseless sheep, God's flock are to be defended, now and for always. It is worth recalling what we noted in chapter 2, that conceiving of the people as satisfied members of God's flock once bolstered the sacrificial system, whose abrupt end this psalm implicitly laments. With the Temple in ruins, with the people still reeling from the blow, praise can be glimpsed only as a possibility for the future.

Psalm 74 is on surer ground as a persuasive speech, because it sees Israel as blameless. The psalmist's strategy is to remind God of who God has been "from of old." First, God established Israel as God's own community by redeeming it [from Egypt] (v. 2); second, God won battles against far more awesome enemies, Leviathan and other primordial "monsters in the waters" (v. 13), before establishing the earth as we know it; and third, God's long-standing commitment is to "the downtrodden, . . . the poor and needy" (v. 21), whose cries are being drowned out, it would seem, by "the shouts of Your foes, the din of Your adversaries that ascends all the time" (v. 23). The implication of the psalm's logic is all too clear: how can God, being who God is and has been "from of old," not act on behalf of oppressed Israel?

A third communal lament belongs with the pair we have been considering. Psalm 44 is the cry of a nation that has been resoundingly defeated in battle, and exiled from its land. The psalmist, speaking on behalf of Israel, attempts to arouse God to intercede once more for the nation, as in Psalm 74, by recalling God's deeds for Israel in the past. By being credited with all Israel's prior military victories, especially its conquest of the land, God can be blamed for the undoing of those earlier victories in the present moment. For it is clear to the psalmist that God has abdicated the role of divine warrior:

> . . . You have rejected and disgraced us;
> You do not go with our armies.
> You make us retreat before our foe;
> Our enemies plunder us at will.
> You let them devour us like sheep;
> You disperse us among the nations.
> You sell Your people for no fortune,
> You set no high price on them.
> You make us the butt of our neighbors,
> the scorn and derision of those around us.
> You make us a byword among the nations,
> a laughingstock among the peoples.
> I am always aware of my disgrace;
> I am wholly covered with shame

at the sound of taunting revilers,
in the presence of the vengeful foe. (Ps. 44:10–16)

In making God the agent of Israel's disgrace, the psalmist sees the people as wholly innocent: "we have not forgotten You, / or been false to Your covenant" (v. 18). Therefore, the only possible explanation for this catastrophe is that "it is for Your sake that we are slain all day long, / that we are regarded as sheep to be slaughtered" (v. 23).

Few other verses in Psalms have been as important as this one in the history of Jewish response to catastrophe. It adumbrates a theory of martyrdom that has been drawn on since biblical times to explain the inexplicable, and justify the unjustifiable. If Israel cannot understand why it is being persecuted, despite its loyalty to God through adherence to the covenant, then it can always fall back on the idea that "it is for Your sake that we are slain." Yet it is crucial to note that in its original context, the ideas of submission and willing martyrdom are by no means acceptable to the psalmist. Israel is downtrodden; a mere remnant lies "prostrate in the dust" (v. 26). On behalf of this suffering people, God must be summoned from stupor: "Rouse Yourself; why do You sleep, O YHWH? / Awaken, do not reject us forever! / Why do You hide Your face, ignoring our affliction and distress?" (vv. 24–25).

The idea of divine hiddenness (*hester panim*) has arisen in several earlier contexts in this study, all of them psychological. We have seen individual psalmists terrified lest God's seeming unavailability in their moments of personal distress become a permanent estrangement.[11] We have also seen them creatively turn hiddenness into a metaphor for divine presence.[12] In the collective context we are examining here, divine hiddenness is perceived in terms not of individual psychology, but rather of historical catastrophe. Whereas individuals may transform their relationship to God's hiddenness by reconceiving the way in which God offers shelter, the people suffering from historical calamity cannot easily accept as a source of comfort the God who allows them to be slaughtered. The idea of being sacrificed for God's sake, at the risk of destroying the historical continuity of the people, is utterly baffling to the psalmist. "All this has come upon us / yet we have not forgotten You, / or been false to Your covenant" (v. 18). At times of defeat such as this, there were other Israelite voices ready to dispute the psalmist's protestations of innocence. The Deuteronomist, for instance, speaking in the voice of God, predicts that when the people break the covenant, "My anger will flare up against them, and I will abandon them and hide My countenance from them. They shall be ready prey; and many evils and troubles shall befall them" (Deut. 31:17). Similar passages could be quoted from Isaiah, Jeremiah, and Ezekiel.[13]

The self-proclaiming hidden God who speaks through the Deuteronomist and the prophets also promises to redeem the people and restore them to their land. To the psalmist, however, there is no promise implicit in the present degradation.[14] Sure that the people has been completely loyal to God, the psalmist finds God's hiddenness an intolerable betrayal of trust. That is why the psalm begins and ends by considering God's role in history. "We have heard, O God, / our fathers have told us / the deeds You performed in their time / in days of old" (v. 2). Salvation history, the deeds of exodus and conquest, belongs to *qedem,* the remote past, while the present seems utterly cut off from God's deeds. "Arise," they say, "and help us, / redeem us, as befits Your faithfulness" (v. 27). Only if God becomes present to the people through a dramatic act of redemption will they again take comfort in their divine shepherd, as had their fathers "in days of old" (v. 2).

In the generation after the destruction, the issue of God's role in history was kept alive for the exilic community in Babylonia on several fronts: by the prophet Ezekiel, by those circles responsible for the reformulation of Israel's ancient traditions as Torah, and by psalmists chronicling the bitterness and humiliation of exile. The well-known Psalm 137, "By the waters of Babylon," gives as its anecdotal origin a dialogue between captors and captives that evokes powerful, poignant memories of home. It is no accident that the psalm goes on to enjoin memory on human and divine auditors alike, for the psalm is preeminently a song of the Levitical guilds entrusted with the nation's ritual memory, their task made more momentous because that memory is threatened as never before. Though the opening of the psalm refers to the exile as a completed event, it is not primarily a retrospective of the exile but rather an embodiment of its tensions, reflecting tremendous anxiety about the continued future of God's people.

Those who had destroyed Jerusalem want to be amused by hearing a song of Zion, yet for the Levites to play lyres from the Temple and sing songs made sacred through long use there would, in their view, desecrate God's holy name "on alien soil" (v. 4). The question, "How can we sing a song of YHWH? . . ." is followed by the celebrated verses 5–6, "If I forget you, O Jerusalem. . . ." Are these to be regarded as the thoughts that went through the singers' minds on refusing to sing for their captors? Or is it the song that they indeed sang, though without reference to YHWH, to satisfy their tormentors without sacrificing their own dignity? Or can we regard these lines as composed for recitation at a solemn gathering of the people, when their captors were not present at all? Whether as internal monologue or ideological instrument, the power of these lines is enhanced by the fact that they take the ritual form of a curse, a speech act that makes its utterance a matter of ultimate consequence:

> If I forget you, O Jerusalem,
> let my right hand wither;
> let my tongue stick to my palate
> if I cease to think of you,
> if I do not keep Jerusalem in memory
> even at my happiest hour. (Vv. 5–6)

The fulfillment of the curse, we should note, would destroy the possibility of speech and action; playing and singing, the very activities being performed at the moment of the song, would become impossible. All meaningful action and communication are thus made dependent on one quintessential attitude: keeping the memory of Jerusalem alive. In these lines, we see how ritualizing memory, rather than chronicling history, responds to the exigencies of exile, promising to keep memory alive for future generations.[15] Given this ritualizing power, it is little wonder that generations of Jews have chosen to recite this psalm on the anniversary of the destruction of the Jerusalem Temple.[16]

After answering the question of what Israel needs to remember in order to continue as a people, the psalm goes on to tell God what to remember, on Israel's behalf. "Remember, O YHWH, against the Edomites / the day of Jerusalem's fall; / how they cried, 'Strip her, strip her / to her very foundations!' " (v. 7). Psalm 74, a much longer psalm, had solicited God's remembrance three times: "Remember the community You made" (v. 2); "remember the enemy" and the "base men [who] blaspheme YHWH" (vv. 18, 22). Throughout the Bible, God's remembering is a prelude to God's acting. In this psalm, Israel is so eager to see its revenge fantasy carried out that it does not wait for God to devise a strategy. It is confident that praiseworthy human beings will arise to repay Babylon (and perhaps Edom too):

> Fair Babylon, you predator,
> a blessing on him who repays you in kind
> what you have inflicted on us;
> a blessing on him who seizes your babies
> and dashes them against the rocks! (Vv. 8–9)

Christian commentators have tended to be horrified by the bloodthirstiness of Israel's wish.[17] Seen in the context of the other psalms we have been considering, it is a verbal counterpart to the all-too-real bloodshed in the streets of Jerusalem at the time of the destruction. It is also a counterpart to the derision Israel endured from the destroyers of Jerusalem, who tauntingly asked them for songs of Zion. Israel had no physical means to exact its desired revenge for such psychic violence; its only weapon was words.

The singers record their experiences in Babylon for the sake of Israel's posterity. Even if they are not privileged to see their enemies requited, the continued recitation of the psalm ensures that some future generation will remember and applaud, if not perpetrate, the desired act.[18] In the Temple, singers had blessed the people with abundance for themselves and for their children. "May you share the prosperity of Jerusalem / all the days of your life, / and live to see your children's children" (128:5).[19] As a counterpart to the curse levied on Israel's own failure to remember its past, the continuation of the psalm takes the form of a blessing. If Babylon is the eternal enemy of Israel, then those who cut off its posterity are ensuring the future survival of Israel's remaining sons and daughters. In the name of justice and national continuity, then, vengeance is required. Only in this way can the Levitical singers, coping with the pain of exile, imagine the fulfillment of their ancient mission to channel divine blessing to the broken remnant of God's people.

Grief, anger, bargaining, denial—we have seen them all play a part in the psalms responding to catastrophe. Psalm 137 is no less angry than the others, but it has displaced anger against God onto anger against the enemy. The problematic issue of God's role in past history has been, in effect, bracketed by the psalm. There is no question that this is a more supportable burden for Jewish memory, allowing survivors to accept the tragic reality of their losses without sinking under feelings of betrayal by their divine protector. Ritualizing anger against the enemy has the obvious effect of strengthening the bonds of group identity among the survivors and their descendants. It also enshrines the memory of the persecutors long after they have exited from the stage of world history. This is in keeping with the paradoxical injunction in the Torah to "blot out the memory of Amalek from under heaven. Do not forget!" (Deut. 25:19).[20] From such texts we learn that the memory of oppression and victimization can become a seemingly permanent feature of a people's identity.

All the themes explored in this brief introduction will recur again in the latter part of this chapter, in relation to the Holocaust. Twentieth-century survivors of catastrophe have returned to these texts, to their protests, pleas of innocence, expressions of anger, and bargainings with God, to find their own ways to continue in the midst of cataclysm and in the aftermath of immense and prolonged suffering.

Liturgy, Midrash, and the Problem of Evil

In the history of religions, orthodoxies are upset by catastrophe, but then tend to reassert themselves in new forms in periods of normalcy. The orthodoxy of Second Temple–period Judaism was similar to that of the First, namely, that God organizes the world according to notions of retributive justice, rewarding or punishing each person according to his or her just deserts. Yet the Book of Job was written during this period to challenge this orthodoxy with a contrary view. If human beings look for retributive justice from God, rather than from each other, they are looking in the wrong place. The concluding chapters of Job, Martin Buber has written, reveal that God distributes justice as creator of the universe, bestowing upon each creature what belongs to it. And what belongs to human beings is relatedness with their creator, the recognition that even in the midst of manifestly unjust suffering, God will be available to the sufferer.[21]

Though Job is a universal figure in ancient Near Eastern wisdom literature, in the Bible, according to Buber, he becomes an objective correlative of the nation's catastrophic suffering at the time of the Babylonian exile. Even though the majority of biblical scholars disagree with Buber's nationalizing of Job, who is not identified as an Israelite, and date the book several centuries later, let us for the moment assume Buber's view and identify Job with the generation that witnessed the destruction of the Temple, the exile to Babylon, and the seeming end of national life in Israel. That, however, is only one of Job's two lives. The text makes clear that he lived on for one hundred and forty years after he lost his children, content to see "four generations of sons and grandsons" (42:16).[22] If Job's innocent tragedy makes him the archetypal figure of Jewish catastrophe, then his long, virtually posthumous existence as progenitor of new generations makes him also the archetypal Jewish survivor, who witnessed not only the people's restoration to Judea, but also the rebuilding and dedication of the Temple and promulgation of the Torah, with its Deuteronomic law of retributive justice, so similar to the rejected doctrine of Job's false comforters. We might well wonder how Job would have regarded this Torah and the worship conducted under its auspices in the rebuilt Temple. Moreover, we need to ask how Job might have reacted to the opening chapter of the book that bears his name had it circulated during his second lifetime, revealing a God who gambled away the lives of his children in a bet with Satan, the opposing angel. In the words of T. S. Eliot, "after such knowledge, what forgiveness?"[23] Could he possibly still have participated in the ongoing ritual life of Israel?

Buber asked a similar question of our post-Holocaust generation: "Dare we recommend to the survivors of Oswiecim [Auschwitz], the Job of the gas chambers: 'Call to Him, for He is kind, for His mercy endures forever'?"[24] Adapting Buber's question to this phase of our inquiry, we can legitimately wonder what psalms could have been sung by Job, the surviving postcatastrophe Jew, who had encountered the dark knowledge that just reward and punishment belong to the realm of folktale, not of divine or human reality.

Issues of theodicy were indeed on the public liturgical agenda in the Second Temple period. Attending to them helps us see that there was a place within established Jewish worship even for Job, the survivor of catastrophe. The Mishnah records that the Levites in the Second Temple sang a psalm for each day of the week.[25] While Rabbi Akiba explained the practice through an ahistorical juxtaposition with Genesis 1,[26] a few subsequent commentators, including Rashi, have suggested that the frequent allusion to evil in these psalms is connected to the prolonged Jewish sufferings under the empires of Persia, Greece, and Rome.[27] It has been justly argued that in order to understand the choice of these psalms as a liturgical practice, we must view them as a deliberately arranged sequence concerning God's governance of the world and relations with Israel. If we take seriously the correspondence of these psalms to particular days of the week, then we find that the worshiper begins and ends the week in harmony, appropriate to the first day of creation and to the Sabbath, but in the middle of the sequence s/he experiences a world of evil, injustice, and suffering. The sequence thus raises to the level of public ritual the liturgists' doubts and hopes about the justice of God.[28]

The first of the sequence, Psalm 24, is intended to accompany a procession of worshipers into the Temple. After invoking the earth founded "on the nether-streams" (v. 2), with its suggestion of divine order imposed upon primordial chaos, the psalm focuses on the scene being enacted in the Temple, where worshipers gather to witness the entrance of God, who is portrayed in their poetic tribute as the divine warrior returning to earth through the massive gates of the Temple.[29] Being present for this glorious liturgical entrance is the privilege of the one who can "ascend the mountain of YHWH," the person with "clean hands and a pure heart / . . . who has not taken a false oath . . . / or sworn deceitfully" (vv. 3–4). The psalm thus upholds an ideal of purity in deeds and in thought—through a process of self-examination—that underlies the exalted drama of Temple worship. The language reminds worshipers that they are also capable of the converse: dirty hands, impure hearts, falsehood, and deceit. Assigning this psalm to the first day of the week, the ancient liturgists chose to convey the message that worshipers enter into the week, as into the Temple, in pursuit of holiness and harmony. On this day, the presence of evil is the fault of the individual's failure to live up to God's laws. The consequences of such evil fall appropriately on that individual, who thereby fails to secure "a blessing from YHWH, / a just reward from God, his deliverer" (v. 5).

On the second day, in Psalm 48, we leave behind the perfection of creation and Temple and the doctrine of individual responsibility and reward. Here we enter the complexities of history; we hear how the holy city of Jerusalem has been attacked by foreign kings, and disaster only narrowly averted. Evil has grown in scope, threatening not just the individual's status before God but the safety of the nation itself. While evil may threaten, in this psalm it is still easily overthrown; as in a folk legend, all's well that ends well. We hear how the antagonists were miraculously turned back, for by "the mere sight" of God's city, "they were stunned, . . . terrified, . . . panicked, / . . . seized with a trembling / like a woman in the throes of labor" (vv. 6–7). A second simile for their destruction, "as the Tarshish fleet was wrecked in an easterly gale" (v. 8), may compare this episode to another well-known event.[30] With the enemy siege aborted, the psalm invites the pilgrim worshipers to circle the city free from the dread of attack, and to count its towers, note its ramparts, and take home to hand down through the ages stories of the "fair-crested" city of God, "joy of all the earth" (v. 3a), where God "made Himself known as a haven" (v. 4). The circle of holiness has moved outward from the Temple to Jerusalem; its saga will extend "evermore" (v. 15).

On the third day, not only Jerusalem is threatened; in Psalm 82, the whole of the earth has been given over to inferiors who govern with no concern for justice.[31] Because of them "all the foundations of the earth totter" (v. 5c), undoing God's work of creation that the worshiper celebrated on the first day of the cycle. "Care for the poor, the widow, and the orphan," God instructs these "sons of the Most High" (v. 6); but the efficacy of this instruction is in doubt, for God goes on to portray these beings as other psalms portray fools: "They neither know nor understand, / they go about in darkness" (v. 5).[32] God's judgment on them is like the divine punishment meted out in the Garden of Eden: they will die as human beings do. There are not, then, two opposing divine powers in the world, one good and one evil, as some might aver, for those beings who seem to have power, whether angels, pagan gods, or human rulers, ultimately have none. The only real power belongs to the one supreme God. But God, the judge of all the earth, is effectively hidden from humankind. God can be imagined, as in this trial in heaven, and God can be reached, the psalmist still believes, through prayer. Thus, the psalm's climactic cry, "Arise, O God, judge the earth" (v. 8), puts both God and prayer to the test. Will the divine judge continue to allow injustice to rule, or will this ironic prayer succeed in bringing justice where more straightforward pleas have not succeeded before?

On the fourth day of the weekly cycle, the evil of injustice is no longer cloaked in heavenly allegory. In the psalmist's present, the innocent Jewish people are being mightily afflicted by their enemies:

> They crush Your people, O YHWH,
> they afflict Your very own;
> they kill the widow and the stranger;
> they murder the fatherless,
> thinking "YHWH does not see it,
> the God of Jacob does not pay heed." (Ps. 94:5–7)

Only a just God can avenge Israel's losses; thus the cry "God of retribution, appear!" (v. 1b). There is more at stake here than the characteristic desire for vengeance that we have noted in postcatastrophe psalms. The paramount issue in the psalm is the nature of justice in the world, and God's relationship to that justice. "Rise up, judge of the earth, / give the arrogant their deserts!" (v. 2). The psalmist finds it impossible to believe that "He who implants the ear" does "not hear," that "He who forms the eye" does "not see," that "He who disciplines nations" does "not punish" (vv. 9–10).

More than any of the other psalms in the weekly cycle, Psalm 94 reveals the incredible tension under which Israelite belief struggled in response to the troubling issues of theodicy. The rhythm of the psalm is to alternate incredulous questioning of God with pious assurances of divine justice. The latter are posed both as general statements of doctrine and as personal declarations of faith. Happiness and tranquility may come from knowing that "a pit" will "be dug for the wicked," but amid these comforting thoughts, the psalmist returns to his provocative questions: "Who will take my part against evil men? / Who will stand up for me against wrongdoers?" (v. 16). "Shall the seat of injustice be Your partner, / that frames mischief by statute?" (v. 20). Like Job, the psalmist finds it intolerable that flagrant injustice can persist so long without a response from God. The psalmist and the people desperately need protection against the life-threatening actions of evildoers. Confident that God is "my help" (v. 17), "my haven," "My sheltering rock" (v. 22), the psalmist ends with the repeated conviction that "YHWH our God will annihilate them" (v. 23). And if God does not? The psalm remains as part of the weekly cycle, keeping alive the tension between Israel's historic faith in retributive justice and its doubts arising from unrequited evil, in the midst of which it constantly lives.

In the psalm for the fifth day of the week, Israel, rather than God, is challenged and seen as responsible for its own fate. In Psalm 81, Israel is reminded of its backsliding and enjoined to listen once more for the divine voice that came forth from Sinai: "I YHWH am your God / who brought you out of the land of Egypt" (v. 11).[33] The central section of this psalm is structured around the theme of listening versus not listening.

God "heard a language that I knew not" (v. 6c), Israel's strange slave language in Egypt. Then, at Sinai, "the secret place of thunder" (v. 8b), Israel reciprocated, hearing God and accepting the commandments.[34] Finally, at "Meribah" (v. 8c), a name which means "rebellion," the people effectively stopped listening, attacking God for bringing them to die without water in the wilderness. Though the complaint at Meribah is narrated in the Pentateuch before the theophany at Sinai, the psalmist places it after, so that it might stand for Israel's rebellious relationship to God throughout the forty years in the wilderness.[35] Returning to the present, the psalmist implores the people with the voice of God, " 'Israel, if you would but listen to Me!' " (v. 9). This focus on listening suggests that Israel's redemption in the present moment once again depends on its hearing the revelatory command "You shall have no foreign god" (v. 10a). "If only My people would listen to Me / if Israel would follow in My paths, / then would I subdue their enemies at once, / strike their foes again and again" (vv. 14–15). Confronted with the authority of God's own voice, Israel must abandon its sense of itself as innocent victim. Instead of lamenting its fate, or protesting against God, the people is enjoined to sing and celebrate festivals, making God hear praises arising from "song," "timbrel, "melodious lyre and harp" (v. 3). The open mouths of Israel's singers will in turn be filled by God (v. 11c), returning them both to the intimacy of the relationship in the desert, when God "fed them the finest wheat / I sated you with honey from the rock" (v. 17).[36] These metaphors of food as reward for Israel's responsiveness to God bring the psalm sequence back to the notion with which it began: divine blessing as reward for moral behavior.

The image of divine nurturance of Israel leads appropriately to the psalm designated for the sixth day of the week, the day on which Israel prepares for its Sabbath. In Psalm 93, we see God sustaining not just Israel but the entire cosmos. In chapter 4, we spoke of how this psalm allows us to see the world from the harmonious perspective of creation, making it especially appropriate for the eve of the Sabbath, when God's completion of creation is celebrated anew each week. Though "mighty waters" (v. 4) recall the primordial chaos that once threatened the stability of the earth, the world as we know it "stands firm; / it cannot be shaken." Its foundation is YHWH, "robed in grandeur / . . . girded with strength" (v. 1). The human microcosm is similarly protected by divine "decrees" coming forth from God's house in Jerusalem, promising to endure for eternity (v. 5). This final image focuses worshipers on what happens in the Temple itself, as was also the case in the opening psalm of the sequence. Alone among the seven psalms, this one makes no mention of evil. It seems that the arrangers of this sequence chose a psalm that would effectively clear psychic space for the Sabbath, temporarily removing from consciousness the conflicts entertained during the rest of the week.

The only one of the seven psalms to have retained mention of its liturgical role in the Masoretic text is Psalm 92, "A psalm. A song; for the Sabbath day" (v. 1).[37] Even though there is no explicit mention of the Sabbath in the body of the psalm, it has been shown that its thematic concerns suit the ideological matrix of the holy day.[38] We can therefore assume that this psalm was chosen for the conclusion of the weekly psalm cycle because it offers a resolution to the issues of evil raised earlier in the sequence. The psalm sets out to explicate God's "works" and "designs" (v. 6), focusing on the problematic issue of how evil fits into the divine plan.

Where other psalms in the cycle present the seeming triumph of the wicked as a matter of urgency that requires God's immediate attention, Psalm 92 takes the long view: "Though the wicked sprout like grass, / though all evildoers blossom, / it is only that they may be destroyed forever" (v. 8). The destruction of evil will occur in God's time frame, if not in ours. The ignorant may not understand the delay of this promised destruction, but the wisely righteous, who meditate on God's works, know that there is both judge and justice, and that their faith will ultimately be rewarded. Just as the wicked are compared to vegetation, so too are the righteous. In a counterbalancing image, they are likened to sturdy and fragrant date palms and cedars, natural images that were included in the decoration of the Temple, in whose courts the righteous are metaphorically said to be "planted" (vv. 13–14).[39] Naturalizing wickedness and righteousness through the metaphors of grass and trees makes it possible to claim that human behavior is as much subject to God's will as is the life of nature.

Looking at the psalm structurally, we see that the fate of the wicked is effectively sandwiched between the praise of psalmody that begins it and the praise of the life of the righteous in the Temple that concludes it. We conclude that entering the Temple on the Sabbath, singing and playing within its sacred precincts, brings the worshiper into harmony with the order and purpose of creation as does no other human activity. The psalm thus makes the Sabbath the day of true vision, on which all the contradictions of everyday existence are resolved.

The Mishnah comments that Psalm 92 is a hymn "for the future that is to come, a day that will be wholly Sabbath and eternal rest."[40] Thus, if the wicked are not defeated today, the weekly return to the Sabbath psalm provides grounds for the eschatological hope that one day they will be. While this hope provides a fitting climax to the week's sequence of worship, it by no means obviates the radical challenges to God's justice included earlier in the liturgical week. By allowing the psalms' different perspectives to coexist, the liturgical order makes theological ambivalence a permanent feature of Israel's worship. As Israelite worshipers experienced the sequence each week, their faith would have been poised between two sets of contradictions: first, that Israel both is and is not what it sometimes claims to be, an innocent victim of history; and second, that God both is and is not yet what God always claims to be, the Redeemer of Israel. The endpoint of the sequence, and the fulcrum that allows these contradictions to be expressed, is the hope that God one day will be all that God can be: just, loving, and powerful.

The liturgy's ability to manage these contradictions was abruptly halted by the destruction of the Second Temple in 70 c.e. Within two generations, this catastrophe was followed by the unsuccessful revolt of Bar Kochba in 135 c.e., and the Hadrianic persecutions of those who studied and taught Torah. Not content with simply destroying Jerusalem, the victorious Romans made the whole province of Judea a wasteland and exiled the majority of its Jews. In the face of these catastrophic events, how were Israel's new spiritual leaders to help the people make sense of their fate and their relationship to God? Old prayers had to be modified and new liturgies created to express Israel's hopes for the rebuilding of the Temple, the flourishing of the Davidic line,[41] the ingathering of the exiles to Jerusalem, and the return of God's presence to Zion, all of which became part of the daily Amidah, the central statutory prayer. Only on the additional service for the festivals, when memories of the lost pilgrimage center would have been especially acute, did a note of collective self-blame enter the rabbinic liturgy. The version preserved in the Siddur comes from the Babylonian community: "on account of our sins we were exiled from our land, and . . . are unable . . . to fulfill our obligations in thy chosen house."[42]

As this prayer indicates, one strain of rabbinic thought continued the old prophetic tradition of seeing Israel's suffering as punishment for its sins, though with an important shift of focus. Rather than blaming the nation as a whole, the rabbis told stories about the moral failures of particular individuals and communities that caused the chain of events leading to the destruction. And rather than identifying terrible sins, such as murder, adultery, and idolatry, the rabbis listed a variety of ritual, moral, and social offenses, suggesting their difficulty in coming to a vision of Israel's collective sin.[43] In reinterpreting biblical texts, the rabbis also disagreed widely about the causes of the destruction. At least some of them took the occasion of the annual reading of Lamentations to represent a radically altered way of perceiving God's role in history. Consistent with our focus here, midrashic comments on two of the postcatastrophe psalms we have already analyzed will show how the rabbis marked a sense of rupture in Israel's relationship to its divine partner, even as they continued in dialogue with God and with the ancient texts that they revered as God's word.

In commenting on Psalm 79, which begins, "O God, heathens have entered Your domain / defiled Your holy temple," the midrashists created a dialogue between Asaph, the musician named in the psalm's superscription, and God. Asaph wants to resolve a contradiction: how could it be written in the Torah that "any outsider who encroaches" upon the Tabernacle "shall be put to death" (Num. 1:51), yet the "uncircumcised ones" emerged unscathed? God allows that they came in with divine permission, indeed by divine command, and goes on to quote an appropriate prooftext.[44] Proceeding in a boastful vein, God interrogates Asaph: " 'What did the heathen do?' " and quotes back to him the psalm, "They turned Jerusalem into ruins" (v. 1c). God continues, " 'But I shall set it up anew,' " and quotes another prooftext from Isaiah.[45] In this imagined dialogue, Asaph is not willing to simply accept the divine promise to restore Jerusalem, as if it absolved God of all responsibility. "Asaph asked God: 'Master of the universe, the heaps [ruins] Thou wilt renew, but Thy children who were slain, what of them?' "[46] Here the dialogue breaks off. God is not given a chance for a last word, because there is no possible rejoinder to Asaph's query. While God is thought powerful enough to destroy a city, and powerful enough to rebuild it, God is powerless, in the view of this midrashist, where it really matters most, namely, to restore the lives of those who were murdered.

If the first part of the text berates God, the second part elevates God's victims. Questioning whether the psalm's phrase "Your faithful" (v. 2) appropriately denotes the slain, the commentator points out their lack of faithfulness in marriage, citing a prophetic rebuke against the generation that was destroyed.[47] This view may be that of a straw man, however, for it is immediately countered by the speaker's justifying Asaph's choice of phrase. "Asaph meant . . . that once judgment was executed upon them, they became saints."[48] No matter how unfaithful they might have been in life, their deaths make them into religious martyrs. Those who would support the prophetic view that Israel was punished for its sins now have to contend with the sainthood of its victims.

Another midrash on a verse from this psalm couches a complaint against God as an adjudication of who is to blame for Israel's suffering. From the sentence "their blood was shed like water around Jerusalem / with none to bury them" (v. 3), the commentator derives that "the heathen did not permit even the bones to be buried." To come to terms with this inhuman behavior, the interpretation takes the form of a parabolic comparison between a human being and God. The parable first plays out the scenario in human terms: "When a mortal owes one hundred minas to his friend, and his friend says, 'Give me money,' and he answers, 'I have no money,' what is there for his friend to do? He must go along!" Human friends clearly set a standard of decency and reasonableness. The midrashist goes on from this baseline to depict the outrageousness of God's behavior in a similar circumstance:

> Not so the Holy One, blessed be He. He makes the soul pay. When the soul goes forth, He makes the body pay, as is said *He will consume both soul and body* (Isa. 10:18). When there is neither soul nor body, He makes the bones pay, as is said *At that time, saith the Lord, they shall bring out the bones of the kings of Judah . . . and the bones of the inhabitants of Jerusalem out of their graves* (Jer. 8:1).[49] Nay, to pay even more, for the heathen taunt us, as is said *We are become a taunt to our neighbors, a scorn and derision to them that are round about us* (Ps. 79:4). Nay, still more to pay, for the heathen say that they offend not in what they do to us, as is said *All that found them have devoured them; and their adversaries said: "We offend not because they have sinned against the Lord"* (Jer. 50:7).

This parable falls into the biblical genre of the *rib*, the complaint against God.[50] From Abraham to Job, the Bible gives human beings in covenant with God the right, and perhaps even the obligation, to hold God to account. The comparative framework of the parable emphasizes "how unjustly God has acted even in terms of human norms, and it is precisely God's shameless violations of these norms that gives the complaint its credibility."[51] As in other complaint parables, our midrashist is at pains to imply that if Israel's enemies do not act like human beings, it can only be because they are directed by an inhumane God. Out-shylocking Shylock, God not only takes the soul and the body and the bones of his creditors, but adds insult to injury by allowing Israel's destroyers to justify their inhumane acts in God's name. God, the prophets, Israel's enemies—all blame the victim. In destroying the Second Temple and stripping the land of its people, God, Israel's former "friend," had betrayed the people, without stating any cause for the betrayal. No wonder the maker of the parable does not allow God the opportunity to respond to the complaint, lest any hint of apologetics enter his discussion.

That righteous indignation dominates the midrashim on Psalm 79 is no surprise, since that psalm is itself so full of pained anger. The elegiac opening of Psalm 137, "By the rivers of Babylon / there we sat, / sat and wept / as we thought of Zion" (v. 1), elicits a different response. "What is meant by the word *gam*, 'also,' in the sentence *Also, we wept?* [JPS: "sat and wept"]. That the children of Israel, by their weeping, caused the Holy

One, blessed be He, also to weep with them."[52] We find several similar comments in the rabbinic commentary on Lamentations. A number of its narratives lead to the conclusion that God must be the speaker of Lamentations, who, in mourning for the destroyed city and its dead, also bewails God's own loneliness without the Jewish people as partner. In one especially poignant self-revealing moment, God is quoted as saying, "Woe to the King Who succeeded in his youth, but failed in His old age."[53]

A radically new view of God is present here. If God can be represented as weeping over what happened to Israel, indeed over what God *made* happen to Israel, then the angry, all-powerful God of retribution has been dethroned.[54] In exile, it would seem, it is not God that has power over Israel, but Israel that has power over God. In the mutuality of their weeping, God and Israel are put on a par, though their tears are quite different. Israel's tears are tears of grief, not tears of repentance, which might indicate their submission to God's view of them as sinful. Israel is doing what human beings do when they suffer irretrievable loss. God's tears, on the other hand, reflect a change in God's self-sufficiency. In weeping, God experiences loneliness and remorse, and learns humility. In making God weep and admit to powerlessness, the midrashists radically recast the central Israelite concept of chosenness. For in reenvisioning a God who learns compassion through tears, it is not God but Israel who now does the choosing. Israel chooses a God with whom it can continue to identify, namely, a God who identifies with its pain. This and other similar midrashim speak for those who refused to take into their long exile the God who had so cruelly expelled them from their land.

This disempowering of God represents but one strain of midrashic thinking; the commentaries also keep alive through many prooftexts the view that Israel deserved its fate as the people specially chosen and disciplined by a powerful God. Among the comments on Psalm 137, we find a description of those whose sense of guilt impelled them to enter into perpetual mourning:

> After the Temple was destroyed, the number of ascetics increased in Israel; they ate no meat and drank no wine. R. Joshua met with them and said: "My children, why do you not eat meat, and why do you not drink wine?" They replied: "How can we eat meat, seeing that it would have been offered daily as a sacrifice upon the altar which no longer stands? How can we drink wine, seeing that it would have been poured daily as a libation upon the altar which no longer stands?" Thereupon R. Joshua answered: "According to you, then, we ought not eat figs or grapes because the first fruits of these would have been brought as an offering; and we ought not eat bread because two loaves of it would have been brought as an offering, and on every Sabbath show bread would

have been brought; and we ought not drink water because libations of it would have been poured as offerings on the Feast of Tabernacles." The ascetics were silent, and R. Joshua went on: "To mourn not at all is impossible. To mourn too much is also impossible." Thus it was the opinion of R. Joshua that a prohibition ought not be imposed unless the majority of the community is capable of enduring it.[55]

While Rabbi Joshua prevails in this exemplary story, the ascetics' argument was adopted with respect to many religious practices to aid the people in remembering what they had lost. Thus, Jews would not worship with instrumental music to signify a difference from what had gone on in the Temple. Adopting the spirit of the verse "If I do not keep Jerusalem in my memory / even at my happiest hour" (Ps. 137:5), the destroyed Temple was to be recalled explicitly in Sabbath and festival liturgy and, more obliquely, in such rituals as the breaking of a glass at a wedding.[56] Rather than mourning constantly, Jewish tradition chose periodic commemoration. Since both Temples were thought to have been destroyed on the same day, the ninth of Ab was set aside for annually remembering the two destructions, marked by the somber chanting of Lamentations and the recitation of Psalms 79 and 137.[57]

History also complemented ritual in keeping alive the memory of these momentous destructions, for during its long exile and subjugation to both Christian and Islamic rulers, the Jewish people suffered numerous persecutions and expulsions. The two complementary strands of midrashic theology that we have explored were therefore constantly brought to bear in interpreting the meaning of Jewish suffering. Jews could feel themselves chastened by a just, though perhaps inscrutable, God, or consoled by a compassionate, humbled God accompanying them in their exile, weeping with them at every new blow that they suffered. The first view preserves a sense of God's justice by blaming evil entirely on human beings, while the second brackets the question of justice by reenvisioning divine power. While neither view of God satisfactorily explains innocent human suffering, both were tolerated because messianism kept alive the promise of return to the homeland and inauguration of a utopian era in world history, founded on justice, prosperity, and universal worship of Israel's God.[58]

Messianism, Mysticism, and the Utopian Use of Scripture

The German sociologist Karl Mannheim defines a utopian state of mind as one "incongruous with the state of reality within which it occurs." It is oriented toward "objects which do not exist in the actual situation."[59] The

Jewish orientation toward the coming of the Messiah is utopian in this sense, not in the narrower colloquial sense of being an unrealizable idea. Utopian ideas grant the oppressed the power to resist the prevailing order as but a temporary aberration en route to a more permanent consummation of their hopes. Quite naturally, then, we would expect to see Jews during their long two-thousand-year exile reflect this utopianism in their interpretation and liturgical use of Scripture, especially during intense periods of Jewish suffering.

A psalm traditionally interpreted in a messianic context was Psalm 95. The liturgical speaker of the psalm[60] enjoins a group of worshipers to follow God's teachings: "O, if you would but heed His charge this day" (v. 7b). In the Midrash, this verse is quoted as proof that "if Israel would repent even for a single day, they would be instantly redeemed."[61] In the Talmud, the story is told of Rabbi Joshua ben Levi encountering the Messiah among the lepers assembled at the gates of Rome, where he sat binding and unbinding his wounds. Rabbi Joshua asked the Messiah, "When will you come?" but failed to understand his reply, "Today," because he did not keep in mind the verse from which that single word was taken: "Today, if you but heed God's charge" (95:7b). The Talmud states that of such a forgetful generation it is written, "They are a senseless people; they would not know My ways" (v. 10).[62]

The psalms classified as enthronement hymns were especially susceptible to a thoroughgoing messianic interpretation, because they speak of a world newly constituted in justice. Psalms 96 and 98 both begin with the phrase "Sing unto YHWH a new song," and conclude with similar phrases about God's judging the peoples of the earth. What made this song (and this judgment) new? the rabbis asked in the midrash. Elsewhere in the Bible, the feminine form of song, *širah*, is generally used. But in these instances, *šir*, the masculine form, connotes the ultimate song of messianic triumph, after which no further misfortunes would be born.[63] Another commentary, listing nine songs of supreme faithfulness to God, selects Psalm 98 as the tenth and final song to be sung in the days of the messianic deliverance.[64] This tradition was reiterated by the medieval commentator David Kimchi, who said that in the time of the Messiah, "every person will say to his neighbor 'Sing unto YHWH a new song,' because God gathered you from among the nations and from exile."[65]

The messianic interpretation of these psalms continued in the generation that suffered communal massacres at the hands of the first Crusaders in 1096. Rashi, who lived from 1040 to 1105, commented of Psalm 96, "This psalm refers to the future, and its end proves that God is coming to judge the earth." Of the phrase, "God reigns," that begins Psalm 97, Rashi claims that it speaks of a time when God will have taken away the throne from Amalek, the legendary enemy of Israel, used here as a code word for Christianity. He envisions this victory happening in the apocalyptic "wars of Gog and Magog," as prophesied by Ezekiel, in a scenario that might well have reminded him of the Crusades.[66] Gog, a general from the northern land of Magog, will invade Israel and initiate a worldwide conflagration, to which this and the accompanying psalms testify: "the earth is convulsed at the sight" (97:4b); "peoples tremble / the earth quakes" (99:1b).[67] In the midst of this battle, God will unleash against Gog all the power of the divine arsenal. The imagery of fire, lightning, and earthquakes that runs through Psalm 97 is borne out by the prophet: "I will punish him with pestilence and with bloodshed; and I will pour torrential rain, hailstones, and sulfurous fire upon him and his hordes and the many peoples with him" (Ezek. 38:22).[68] A hundred years after Rashi wrote, Kimchi explained in his commentary that God's reign on earth would begin with the war of Gog and Magog, after which "there will be no more war in the world, . . . and God will return His Shekhinah to Zion."[69]

This idea that the Shekhinah, the immanent, earth-dwelling presence of God, went into exile with the people is first attributed to Rabbi Akiba, a second-century C.E. contemporary of Bar Kochba.[70] Gershom Scholem notes that the idea gained its greatest prominence after the expulsion of over half a million Jews from the Iberian peninsula made the historical exile of the people once again "a terrible and fundamental reality of life."[71] Expulsion, of course, was not new in medieval Jewish history. The Jews had been expelled from England in 1290, from France in 1306, and from various central European cities in the wake of the Black Death of 1348, which decimated Europe's population. These expulsions, on a far smaller scale, did not have anything like the same effect as the Spanish and Portuguese expulsions, which have been credited with creating a sea change in Jewish theology, by extending the idea of exile to the very conception of the godhead.

In the first generation after the expulsion from Spain, there was a pervasive sense that the apocalyptic redemption of the Jewish people was imminent. As we have seen, medieval Jewry had kept alive the expectation of a final apocalyptic war that would bring history to an end and restore Israel to its former glory. The Midrash also had posited that the children of Israel would be redeemed "when they had gone down to the very bottom of the pit."[72] The terrible expulsions from Spain and Portugal and the travails of the refugees were thus to be seen as "the birth pangs of the Messiah," the cataclysm that was known to immediately precede the inauguration of a new era in Jewish and world history. For the exiles to make sense of their suffering, they assumed that every word of the Bible referred to the coming redemption. A commentary on Psalms produced around 1500 treated the collection as "a textbook of the millennium and the messianic catastrophe." The Psalter was envisaged "as a book of war songs and an arsenal of weapons for the 'last war.' " Before they would be used in the final apocalyptic hour, their latent transformative power would be available in the form of comfort. "But when once the absolute power of the divine words erupts from beneath the comforting guise of meditation and promise, 'all the forces will be transformed.' "[73]

With eschatological hopes nurtured by the spirit of the times and by the long-standing messianic traditions of Judaism, scattered kabbalists from all over the world converged on the land of Israel as a step toward actualizing the coming redemption. But as time went on, it became clear that the promised and long-awaited redemption did not come. As Isaac Luria (1534–72) and his disciples developed the religious significance of catastrophe and exile, they invented an elaborate mythological system, in which exile defines the nature of being in both human and divine realms. According to their theology, God, filling all time and space, could find room for a universe that would be separate from God only by an act of self-contraction (tzimtzum). Furthermore, the vessels that were to contain the light of divinity in our world (the lower seven of the ten sefirot) were too fragile; in meeting the light of divinity, they shattered, trapping the light in the husks of evil (klippot), where we encounter it in this, our corrupt and long-suffering world. In this mythology, Israel's bitter experience in exile was a painfully concrete symbol of the broken state of the cosmos. Living amid the broken vessels, subjected to evil, and cut off from the fullness of divine light, the Jewish people's present task was to focus its energies on liberating the trapped sparks of divine light from their husks by avoiding transgression and applying special mystical directions and permutations of the divine name (kavvanot) before each performance of a commanded act. The complete restitution of these sparks of divinity to the original divine essence (tikkun) would mark the end of both the exile of Israel and the cosmic exile of the Shekhinah, the Divine Presence, from the created world. Only thus could the utopian redemption promised long before by Israel's prophets come to pass.

This theology of redemption from cosmic exile was grafted onto the redemptive messianic myth in the classical Kabbalah,[74] which had already envisioned a redemptive process taking place every week in the Sabbath eve union of the feminine Shekhinah with the masculine aspect of God, the Holy One blessed be He. As one scholar has recently explained, "in its kabbalistic meaning, Shabbat refers to that state of intradivine harmony which directs and transforms the cosmos on the seventh day."[75] In this formulation of sacred marriage, the kabbalists built upon the foundation of the Talmudic rabbis, who had called the Sabbath "Bride" and "Queen," and who recommended marital intercourse on Sabbath eve.[76] It is well known that the sixteenth-century kabbalists developed a special service to effect this cosmic reunion at the time most propitious for it. The devotees, dressed in white, went out to the fields surrounding Jerusalem and Safed, where they would greet the Bride with the singing of psalms (Pss. 95–99, 29 are the six handed down by tradition), the chanting of the Song of Songs, and other mystical marriage hymns of their own composition, practices that eventually took root in the synagogue service of all Jewish communities.[77] The mystical poem "lekha dodi," written by Cordovero's teacher Shelomo Alkabetz, directly expresses the community's messianic hopes for the redemption of the Shekhinah from exile by personifying her as God's bride, with whom God is to be united at the start of Shabbat. The poem urges the Shekhinah and the Jewish people, who identify with her plight—"Long enough have you dwelt in the valley of tears, / . . . Rise up from the dust of the earth."[78] Luria himself wrote hymns to accompany each of the Sabbath meals, to facilitate the union of Shekhinah and the Holy One by exorcising the powers of evil, which prevent their union during the six days of the week.[79]

It is not surprising that in the elaboration of this ritual, the Safed kabbalists turned to the enthronement psalms as a special addition to the liturgy for welcoming the Sabbath. For they dramatize more than any other group of psalms the coming of the King, whom they envisioned as preparing to meet the Bride. Linked by several generations of commentators with Ezekiel's prophecies of the final earthly war and Israel's restoration to its homeland, these psalms would have pointed the kabbalists to the end of earthly and cosmic exile. Where Rashi and Kimchi saw the truth of these psalms as becoming manifest only in the eschatological future, to the Safed kabbalists their truth could become manifest in the present moment if the preconditions for tikkun had been met. The generation that suffered the exile from Spain had seen itself as living through the prophesied battle that would precede the final redemption. But to those cultivating a mystical rebirth in Safed, redemption no longer required new catastrophe. If the people of Israel were faithful to their messianic task, then redemption would come *"of itself,"* when "all things occupy their appropriate places in the universal scheme," resulting in "a flawless and harmonious world."[80]

The world envisioned in the six Sabbath psalms, 95–99 and 29, is one in which the fullness of Divine Being is manifest not just to Israel but to all sentient beings. We can see in their images the movement of tikkun: from the multiplicity of the life we know to the unity of a redeemed life we can only imagine. Repeatedly, God's future triumphs in these visionary psalms are witnessed by "all the earth" (96:1b, 9b), "the nations" (96:3a; 98:2b), "all peoples" (96:3b; 97:6b), "families of the peoples" (96:7a), "the many islands" (97:1b), "all the ends of the earth" (98:3b). And yet, they are all to be judged by the one God (Pss. 96:13; 98:9). The idols of the pagan nations, "all divine beings" (95:3b; 96:4b; 97:7c), are likewise reckoned among those to be judged. The sparks of divinity buried amid the greatest imaginable evil, within the husks of idolatry itself, must be part of the universal redemption, for without their inclusion, no divine victory is complete. All that is now divided will return to its source in the One.

The imagery of these psalms points to a transformation not only on the human plane but also on the plane of materiality itself. In response to this divine victory, nature is no longer inert matter, but all is animated and, as it were, humanized. Thus, the earth is to "tremble" (*ḥilw*, 96:9b), a verb generally used of women giving birth; the "fields and everything in them" are to "exult"; and "the trees of the forest" are to "shout for joy" (96:12). "Mountains melt like wax at YHWH's presence" (97:5a). "The rivers clap their hands, / and mountains sing joyously together" (98:8). With the aid of animated nature, divinity becomes again a growing thing. Thus, divine "light is sown for the righteous" (97:11a), an image with which the Lurianic mythology resonates deeply. To the circle of the Safed kabbalists, the uniquely metaphoric vision of nature in these psalms is that of a world unglimpsed since before the tzimtzum of creation, divinity's original self-contraction. As Scholem indicates, "the Last Days realize a higher, richer, and more fulfilled condition than the First Days."[81] With the Lurianic mythic framework in mind, we can see in these psalms this higher, richer life at the level of creation, as divine energy flows fully into the world for the first time.

Psalm 29, the final one of the sequence, offers a vision of the destructiveness and creativity of God, appropriate to the moment of apocalypse, just before the creation "of a new heaven and a new earth" (Isa. 65:17). YHWH is characterized as strong, powerful, majestic; the divine light that had shattered the vessels of creation is present here as a voice shattering cedars, convulsing mountains and wilderness, stripping forests, causing animals to give birth. The last verse of the psalm, a prayer for the people's "strength" and "wellbeing" (*šalom*; v. 11), expresses Israel's vulnerability. Since so much depends on the proper intentionality of the worshiper at this decisive moment, both Luria and his teacher Rabbi Moshe Cordovero give complex instructions for the recitation of this psalm. If all goes forward and YHWH consummates his long-sought reunion with the Shekhinah (kabbalistically associated with the people Israel), then Israel (and all the world) will experience "shalom," a word which gathers in its orbit the ideas of perfection, completion, payment of debt. The final "shalom" is connected by the kabbalist commentators to the sefirah of yesod, which carries associations of male sexuality. They apparently saw the psalm as dramatizing with great vividness the union of the male and female aspects of God.[82]

A number of sources mention that Luria's circle sang the Sabbath psalms with closed eyes; Scholem draws a connection between this practice and the Shekhinah, who had lost her eyes from weeping in exile.[83] To students of ritual, this is a wonderfully evocative fact, suggesting the liminal quality of this dusk service for welcoming the Bride. Ritual liminality, we recall, structures social transitions and mythic transformations. The practice shuts out the experience of the ordinary world and concentrates the worshipers' collective intention on the moment of exalted union. Like the white garments that symbolize the purity of the worshipers' intentions, closing the eyes eliminates the possibility of idle sexual glances, which would allow demonic forces to threaten the all-important union. Furthermore, through their closed eyes, male worshipers identify with the blinded state of the feminine Shekhinah. As they open their eyes and address her in the mystic poem "lekha dodi," the mythic transformation is complete if she too regains her sight, marking an end to her long exile.

The messianic anticipation that informed Lurianic Kabbalah did not belong to a small elite, but pervaded Luria's whole generation. A contemporary Portuguese Jewish historian, Samuel Usqué, explained to his fellow exiles in 1553 that their exile had preserved them by scattering them among various lands where no one enemy could succeed in destroying them all. Exile and its attendant sufferings were but a temporary stage, however, in the Jewish people's messianic career. "You have run the entire gauntlet of misfortunes," he wrote, "and have reached the end of your tribulations. And since there is no further province for you to go to, your wandering will now end; you will begin to turn your face and your heart toward the ancient lands of your yearning. . . . You can see for yourself that your children are now returning there. Not only from all corners of Europe, but also from other parts of the world, a larger number has assembled there now than ever before."[84] This is proof, he says, of Moses' prediction in Deuteronomy that only after experiencing all God's curses would the people repent enough to merit God's mercy and be gathered from among the peoples in whose midst they had been scattered.[85] Here we return to the ubiquitous typology of biblical prophecy: suffering and exile confirm Israel's sinfulness, while the return to the Holy Land, as evidenced by Luria's own holy community, marks the beginning of God's promised redemption. In contrast to a worldview rooted in notions of divine reward and punishment, the Lurianic mythology, with its story of a cosmic flaw that needed to be overcome on the cosmic level, provided many Jewish generations an alternative lens for viewing Jewish history. In Arthur Cohen's terms with which we began this chapter, Lurianic kabbalah provided a new "mythos of incorporation and consolation . . . with which to supply a nexus and continuity" to Jewish experience after catastrophic suffering.[86] While Cohen claims that no such mythos is available after the Holocaust, that no Samuel Usqué of our generation can look at the Holocaust as divine punishment, nor at the founding of the modern State of Israel as a divine blessing long deferred and finally bestowed, it cannot be denied that some Jewish theologians and groups continue to be drawn to just this biblical paradigm to explain modern Jewish history. As we examine selected Jewish accounts of the Holocaust and some of the theology created in its wake, we will see how each succeeding generation remains in dialogue with previous generations' responses to the catastrophes through which they lived, surviving to write new versions of the ancient Psalms.

The Destruction of the Jews: "As Sheep to the Slaughter"

In the discourse of Holocaust victims, survivors, and the many thinkers and writers who have responded to the impact of that genocide, verses from the Psalms have echoed and reechoed, just as they did for preceding generations of Jewish sufferers. It is difficult not to think of those in Auschwitz and Treblinka, Chelmno and Sobibor, when hearing such cries of desperation as "How long, YHWH, will You ignore me forever? / How long will You hide Your face from me?" (13:2), or "My God, my God, / why have You abandoned me; / why so far from delivering me . . . ?" (22:2), or "O God, do not be silent; / do not hold aloof; / do not be quiet, O God!" (83:2). Some of those who hid in makeshift bunkers and cellars gave them the Hebrew name *bor taḥtiot* (lit. "the pit of the depths"), taken from this psalm:

> You have put me at the bottom of the Pit,[87]
> in the darkest places, in the depths.
> Your fury lies heavy upon me;
> You afflict me with all Your breakers.   *Selah*
> You make my companions shun me;
> You make me abhorrent to them;
> I am shut in and do not go out.
> My eyes pine away from affliction;
> I call to You, YHWH, each day;
> I stretch out my hands to You. (88:7–10)

Those who lost their faith as a result of the Holocaust repeatedly invoke the very questions posed by the psalmists: Where was God during such suffering? Why did God not intervene? Why did God not speak? Why did God not answer Jewish prayer?

In the testimony of secular poets and lapsed believers, the Psalms are often used ironically to impugn the God in whom they no longer believe:

> What wilt thou do without houses of prayer
> And without Jews—no Jews anywhere?
> Who will recite the Psalm of the Day
> And who will suffer gratuitously?[88]

Less often quoted is the testimony of those Jews who kept their faith by means of the inner strength afforded them by Psalms. Thus, we hear of Hillel Zeitlin, a religious existentialist who sat in his tenement translating the Psalms into Yiddish, and went to the roundup point for the deportation dressed in prayer shawl and tefillin.[89] We hear similarly of Pinche Steier, who recited the Psalms continuously during seven days of solitary confinement,[90] and of Geza S., who dreamed in Mauthausen that his mother told him to open the Bible to Psalm 54:9, where he found the verse that sustained him till liberation; God's name, the text says, "has saved me from my foes, / and let me gaze triumphant upon my enemies."[91] Still another victim, Rabbi Mendele Alter of Pabianice, turned to the Psalms to understand how his Nazi torturers could have left off beating him when they discovered in his house a Torah that they could desecrate. The verse that he translates, "You make me wise through my enemies" (Ps. 119:28), enabled him to understand that the Nazis' ultimate purpose was to defeat the source of holiness in the world.[92] Others turned to the Psalms to couch their cries for vengeance. Rabbi Ephraim Oshry, asked soon after the war whether Jews must avoid stepping on Jewish gravestones that had been turned into paving stones, finishes his answer with the psalmic petition, "Remember, O God, what has been done to us, and avenge the blood of your servants."[93]

Among the many verses from Psalms that we find in the discourse of the Holocaust, one stands out for special notice: "It is for Your sake that we are slain all day long, / that we are regarded as sheep to be slaughtered" (44:23). Throughout the literature of the Holocaust—in memoirs, in poems, in rabbinic responsa, in public arguments over Jewish resistance or passivity—the phrase "as sheep to the slaughter" echoes its singular death knell. It offers a clear image of Israel's plight as victim: sheep are powerless to prevent their deaths, whether from wild animals or at the hands of human enemies. Pastoralism, with its images of gentle, protec-

tive care, once provided the root metaphor of ancient Israelite consciousness, but it could hardly still do so in light of the massive abandonment of
the Jews during the Holocaust. It is crucial to remember, as we pointed
out above, that the psalmist who speaks this memorable phrase cries out
in angry protest and supplication: "Rouse Yourself; why do you sleep,
YHWH? / Awaken, do not reject us forever!" (v. 24). The dire implication is that Jews become "regarded as sheep to be slaughtered" only if
God is sleeping. And if God is sleeping, then God is not what other
psalms claim: "See, the guardian of Israel / neither slumbers nor sleeps!"
(121:4). One post-Holocaust Jewish thinker draws the seemingly inevitable conclusion that "the enemy was more sleepless and slumberless
than the God of Israel."[94]

In later Jewish tradition, the idea of being slain for God's sake under-
went a decisive change. In the rabbinic period, it became grounds for kid-
dush hashem, literally, "sanctification of God's name"—through a
martyr's death. The rabbis applied the phrase to the four hundred children who committed suicide at the time of the Second Temple's destruction so as not to be taken into prostitution in Rome. Maimonides used it to
refer to the spiritual resistance of Daniel and Rabbi Akiba.[95] Throughout
the Middle Ages, especially during the Crusades, the phrase was used in
connection with persecutions, both in liturgical supplications composed
for special fast days and in historical works. We find Samuel Usqué citing it
in a petition to God that punctuates his narrative: "O merciful Lord, witness our suffering from Your habitation on high and help us. And to prove
that in the arcanum of our hearts we never wavered in our Jewish faith,
'See that out of love for You we are killed each day, and are accounted as
sheep ready to be slaughtered'" (Ps. 44:23).[96] Usqué has here embroi-
dered his prooftext; centuries of celebrated martyrdom have transformed
the psalmist's fierce anger and even skepticism about God into the historian's pious protestation of love.

How should we regard the appropriation of the phrase "as sheep to the
slaughter" in the discourse of the Holocaust? References to dying like
sheep come from the ghettos, from the extermination camps, and from
those who observed the destruction of European Jewry from afar. The
examples below show both the intensity of feeling that the biblical metaphor could evoke and the skepticism it encouraged among those who
inherited it as a way of explaining Jewish deaths.

In the diary that Chaim Kaplan kept in the Warsaw ghetto, we find an
element of incredulity in his description of Hasidim observing the holiday
of Simhat Torah. How to reconcile their dancing with what had been
endured in the ghetto, a "year of physical and mental tortures never
equalled in history"? When they were told by a heretical Jew to stop

dancing, lest they violate the positive commandment of safeguarding their lives, the Ḥasidim replied in their ecstasy: "We are not afraid of the murderer! The devil with him!" There is no question that Kaplan admires their defiance and is moved by their "inner . . . heartfelt joy," but he is also to some degree horrified at their motivation, as we hear in his bitterly ironic quotations from the Psalms and the atonement liturgy of the Days of Awe: "This is not a secular joy," he explains, "but a 'rejoicing of the Torah,' the same Torah for which we are murdered all day, for which we have become like lambs to be slaughtered, for which we have gone through fire and water. . . ."[97] We hear underneath his allusions a willingness to deny that any religious value—whether the Torah or God—could be worth all the blood shed for its sake.

"Whole groups," he writes, "are taken to slaughter only because they are Jews. Whole towns have been wiped out by killing and slaughter in a fashion barbaric beyond all murders and slaughters that have taken place in world history. We have become like sheep to be slaughtered."[98] The psalm verse is the keynote of this lament, consciously or unconsciously reminding the writer, even as he claims to be describing an unprecedented barbarousness, that the Jews have long been targeted "only because they are Jews." Having come to this conclusion, he is all the more incredulous at the silence of his brethren in the face of the Nazi onslaught. But rather than railing against God, as the psalmist had done, he uses passages from the Psalms to train his bitter invective against his fellow ghetto dwellers. So scathing is his anger that he adopts a fictional persona in order to deliver it:

> My Hirsch is screaming: "Cowards! A whole community of millions of people stands on the brink of destruction, and you keep silent! You delude yourselves out of hope that the evil will not reach you; you have eyes and see not.[99] Are you any better than the people of Lublin? The people of Cracow? The people of Lodz? If not today, then tomorrow or the next day you will be taken out like lambs to the slaughter. Protest! Alarm the world! Don't be afraid! In any case you will end by falling before the sword of the Nazis. Chicken-hearted ones! Is there any meaning to your deaths?"[100]

Better the death-defying ecstasy of the Ḥasidim than the passivity of the chicken-hearted! If they were all to be "taken out like lambs to the slaughter," then they could at least be like the psalmist and scream out in protest to "alarm the world."

The world at war, as we know, was not sufficiently alarmed about the destruction of the Jews to bomb the rail lines to Auschwitz. Yet the world at peace was willing to blame the victims for not sufficiently resisting the Nazi

oppressors. This was so especially in the early postwar years, before scholarship began to focus on Jewish resistance rather than victimization. In
Zionist ideology, disparaging the Jews of the Diaspora was a rhetorical
counterweight to celebrating the new Jews being created in the free State
of Israel. Thus, we hear David Ben-Gurion, prime minister of Israel,
claiming during the Eichmann trial that the Jews had so degenerated in
the Diaspora that they went to their deaths like sheep.[101] Combating this
demeaning point of view, an American survivor of the concentration
camps, Gerda Weissman Klein, uses the same metaphor to an utterly opposite end. The victims' passivity marked not their degeneracy but their
humanity. "Why?" she wonders. "Why did we walk like meek sheep to the
slaughter-house? Why did we not fight back? . . . I know why. Because we
had faith in humanity. Because we did not really think that human beings
were capable of committing such crimes."[102]

All these uses of the metaphor focus on Jewish powerlessness, whereas
in its original context, the image of the slaughtered sheep also reflects an
abuse of divine power. These twin concerns come together in "A Song of
the Chelm Ghetto."[103] Most of the original is in Yiddish, with lines quoted
or adapted from the Bible or the prayer book (italicized below) in
Hebrew. It is structured as a running ironic commentary on the medieval
prayers of supplication that continue to form the daily Taḥanun liturgy,
which are themselves a pastiche of psalmic and other biblical quotations.[104] Like the psalms of complaint that they adapt, the medieval litanies
state the Jewish people's urgent claims upon God to be saved from the
oppressor, because of its loyalty to God, and its conviction that God indeed
can save them. Its Holocaust counterpart is steeped in the atmosphere of
early twentieth-century Jewish protest literature, which, in the wake of the
Kishinev Pogrom of 1903, began to use the words of the Bible against
itself.[105] The ghetto song reflects this tension between ancient promise and
contemporary suffering in its bilingualism. It begins with an almost
straight transposition of psalmic quotations from the medieval litany,
before finding its own more acerbic idiom:

> *O look from heaven and behold*[106]
> Look down from the skies and see!
> *For we have become a derision,*
> *A derision among the nations,*[107]
> We are surely a laughingstock to them.
> *We are accounted as sheep to the slaughter.*[108]
> O Creator, how can You look upon this?
> Indeed, we never were at ease,
> We were always to the slaughter.

Refrain:

Therefore we plead with You ever:
Help us now, *Guardian of Israel,*[109]
Take notice now of our tears,
For still do we proclaim, *"Hear O Israel!"*[110]
O, take notice, *Guardian of this nation.*
Show all the peoples that You are our God,
We have indeed none other, just You alone,
Whose name is One.

Strangers say there is no salvation.[111]
The nations say that for us
There is no hope.
We may be driven.
We may be tormented,
We have no one to whom
We can complain.
But we surely know
That You are in heaven!
Of You the Bible says:
He doth neither slumber nor sleep.[112]
You must surely protect
Your children.
Therefore we know
That You are in heaven—
With miracles and wonders.

There is nothing in the song that could overtly prevent the pious from singing; in fact, the many quotations from liturgy seem at first glance to attest to the piety of its anonymous author. But the more the focus turns to God in heaven, where "miracles and wonders" abide, the more pronounced the irony of the biblical references becomes. It would seem that the speaker no longer believes in God's power to save, but only in the people's power to save themselves—through emigration to Palestine. The speaker is incredulous that the Jews remain in Europe: "O my Jews, my Jews, what are you doing here? / Gather your packs and take ye to Zion!"

A poet who succeeded in leaving Europe to spend the war years in Palestine takes the irony directed against God several steps further. In his poem "To My God in Europe," Uri Zvi Greenberg explodes the psalms' root metaphor of sheep and shepherd by turning the tables on God. Greenberg's bold premise is that if God insists on being Israel's Shepherd, then God must come to terms with the true state of his flock: the heavenly Shepherd no longer has any sheep to care for. I quote from Part II:

Go wander about Europe, God of Israel, Shepherd-Seer,[113] and count Your
    sheep. . . .
You will count the few forsaken ones, those who have survived, fugitive,
    whispering.
And they who light the smallest candle of hope in their darkness will be
    heartened.
You will not cry aloud in lamentation—
God has no throat of flesh and blood, nor Jewish eyes for weeping.

And so You will return to heaven, a dumb Shepherd-Seer, after the shepherding
    and the seeing,
a shepherd staff in Your hand,
leaving not even the shadow of a slender staff on the death distances of Your
    Jews
where Your dead flock lie hidden. . . . [114]

The evisceration of the heavenly shepherd and of his flock is so complete
that, even though God still carries a shepherd's staff, as in Psalm 23, it
casts no shadow on the Jews, so completely are they hidden by the shadow
of death. Europe, we discover, is that famous "valley of the shadow of
death" (RSV, 23:4), where God's people learned to fear evil, with none to
protect them. For Greenberg, the old covenant by which Israel was elected
cannot be resumed. The sign of the new, universal covenant that he offers
is the rainbow, reminiscent of God's promise to Noah never again to
destroy all humanity, but making no special promises to the Jews. God,
Greenberg insists, is the God of victors and victims alike; any version of
Judaism that persists in repeating the old metaphors without transvaluing
them is simply obsolete.

    That need to transvalue the metaphoric inheritance may explain why
Greenberg returns to the root metaphor of the poem, the slaughtered
sheep of Psalm 44:23. The third section of the poem, "No Other
Instance," begins, "We were not as dogs among the gentile: a dog is pitied
by them. . . . Not like sheep to the slaughter were we brought in train
loads," and he goes on to enumerate the abuses to Jewish bodies that
would never have been tendered to animals.

> Where are there instances of catastrophe
> like this that we have suffered at their hands?
> There are none—no other instances.
> (All words are shadows of shadows)—
> *This is the horrifying phrase:* No other instances.
>
> No matter how brutal the torture a man will suffer
> in a land of the gentiles,
> the maker of comparisons will compare it thus:

He was tortured like a Jew.
Whatever the fear, whatever the outrage,
how deep the loneliness, how harrowing the sorrow—
no matter how loud the weeping—
the maker of comparisons will say:
This is an instance of the Jewish sort.[115]

Greenberg may seem to devalue the reality-rendering powers of language ("All words are shadows of shadows"), but we should not be fooled into thinking that he makes light of artistic language. On the contrary, the makers of comparisons, if they are true to their craft, will bring a new level of penetrating realism to world literature. Imagine Psalm 44 with Greenberg's post-Holocaust substitution: "You let them devour us like Jews; / You disperse us among the nations" (v. 12). "It is for Your sake that we are slain all day long / that we are regarded as Jews to be slaughtered" (v. 23).

Greenberg means his art to do justice to the suffering of the Jewish people. He also means it to kill off the all-powerful God of Jewish history. It is therefore quite striking that he, along with other avowedly secular poets, should pursue the psalmists' liturgical mode of addressing themselves directly to God, presenting "all historical and metaphysical complaints" as if "directly to the source."[116] In Abraham Sutzkever's poem "Kol Nidre," a Jewish father similarly brings his complaint to God: "Save my child! / or else I'll stab him . . . to death." Like an automaton, he proceeds to murder the child when his prayer goes unanswered. When Zelig Kalmanovitch, a secular intellectual turned religious believer, heard this poem, with its simplistic view of prayer, read aloud, he is said to have commented, "Whoever calls God to account [*ver es hot a din-toyre mit Got*] must first of all believe in God."[117] In the poetry of the Holocaust, we have many such attempts to call God to account, but almost all by angry nonbelievers. Perhaps some of them would agree with the view of Elie Wiesel that "the very anger and controversy itself is the first stage of a new relationship, perhaps the only kind of relationship possible with God at this point in history."[118] Greenberg and Sutzkever, in bringing to light their *din toyre*, their judgment against God, remain true to their biblical original, even if, unlike the psalmist, they can no longer expect an intervention in history.

One pole of response to the Holocaust we have not yet touched on is the classic religious posture of submission to God's will. Richard Rubenstein tells the story of an encounter he had in Germany in 1961 with a Protestant clergyman who had been active in resisting the Nazis. He asked him, " 'Was it God's will that Hitler destroyed the Jews?' " In reply, the minister walked to his bookcase, removed a Bible, opened it to Psalm 44, and read, " 'For Thy sake are we slaughtered every day.' When God desires my death, I give it to Him! . . . He is the Lord, He is the Master, all is in His keeping and ordering."[119] Dean Gruber's response was in keeping with a long Christian tradition, dating back to Paul, of reading this verse as a justification for Christian martyrdom.[120] To Rubenstein, however, this encounter with orthodox Christian faith was anathema; he became convinced, he tells us, that Jews could escape from the theological constructions that Christians placed on them only by ceasing to regard themselves as chosen by God. Rubenstein, like the poet Greenberg, wants ordinariness to become the lot of the Jews.[121]

Rubenstein need not have gone to a German Christian to find a refusal to protest against the God of history. Memorial prayers recited in the contemporary synagogue have similarly cast Holocaust victims in the role of martyrs for the sanctification of God's name. Theists and atheists alike are included in such martyrologies, which provide an alternative to anger, a ceremonial way of speaking about the victims, without having at every moment to protest their victimization. We find a similar refusal to protest by Martin Buber in 1952, in the same year that Greenberg wrote his acerbic poem "To My God in Europe": "One can still 'believe' in the God who allowed those things to happen," Buber wrote, "but can one still speak to him?" How could the dialogic theologian tolerate life without dialogue? Only by positing that God was once again in hiding, and that he, Buber, would await the coming of his "cruel and merciful Lord."[122]

The Destruction of the Jews: Whither the God of History?

The enormity of the Holocaust—the deaths of one million children among its six million Jewish victims—has called into question the most basic Jewish and Enlightenment doctrines. No longer can Jews comfortably believe in the perfectibility of human beings and their societies. Even if some Jews can square a belief in God's goodness with the existence of the radical evil manifested by the Nazis, many find it difficult to believe in a God of covenantal history, who chose Israel from among the nations only to destroy the Chosen People in the gas chambers of Poland. As a result of the Holocaust, a major strain of biblical and rabbinic response to catastrophe—that God punishes the Jewish people for its sins—has become virtually untenable in our time. One encounters this position only among the most extreme elements of the Jewish community.[123] Yet Richard Rubenstein predicts that with the passing of enough time, the community of Jewish believers will once again understand the Holocaust in terms of divine retribution for Israel's waywardness, just as Usqué's generation understood the Spanish expulsion. There is no other paradigm, he claims, with which to keep the God of history alive.[124]

If Jewish theologians have not yet begun to prove Rubenstein right, they have nevertheless gone to great lengths to muster such evidence as history has provided to assert that God continues to act on behalf of the Jewish people. The counterpart of divine retribution, the promised redemption, it is widely said, is evident in the ingathering of the Jewish people to the State of Israel. Even when serious thinkers hesitate to see the hand of God in relation to the Holocaust, they nevertheless draw upon the power of the biblical associations in regard to the people's return to the land. Israel's rebirth signifies divine redemption to thinkers as different as Eliezer Berkovits, Emil Fackenheim, and Irving Greenberg.[125] We find the same significance asserted in the prayer for the welfare of the State of Israel composed by Israel's chief rabbinate, which is used in many Jewish congregations, both in Israel and in the Diaspora. In the rabbinate's liturgical phrase, the state is *rešit ṣemiḥat geʾulatenu,* "the beginning of our redemption that is to grow."[126] Israel's rabbinate mandated that the annual memorial for the victims and heroes of the Holocaust be commemorated just a few days after the end of Passover, and that it precede by just a few days Israel's Independence Day. The promises of biblical prophecy are thus made to resonate with contemporary events, which, through ritualization, acquire the effective status of a new divine revelation. Already in 1952, Buber saw how powerful was the drive to lift "purely political processes . . . into the light of superhistory,"[127] how profound Israel's yearning to be embraced once again by the God of history. How much more so has this been the case since Israel's Six Day War in 1967 achieved the reunification of Judaism's sacred city and symbolic center!

Martin Buber's post-Holocaust writing, including his writing on Psalms, provides us a useful window on the dilemma of historical theologizing in our time. Almost alone among his contemporaries, Buber was willing to acknowledge with Job that one could not claim the good as coming from God without also accepting the bad. Hence his post-Holocaust designation of God as "cruel and merciful Lord," a formula not drawn from any liturgy. Buber conceives of history as alternating between "times of great utterance, when the mark of divine direction is recognizable in the conjunction of events," and "mute times, when everything that occurs in the human world and pretends to historical significance appears to us as empty of God, with nowhere a beckoning of His finger, nowhere a sign that He is present and acts upon this our historical hour. In such times, it is difficult for the individual, and the more for the people, to understand themselves as addressed by God."[128] In the phrase "this our historical hour," Buber signals that he understood the Jewish people to be living through a time of such divine muteness. "Let us ask," he writes, "whether it may not be literally true that God formerly spoke to us and is now silent, and whether this is not to be understood as the Hebrew Bible understands it, namely, that the living God is not only a self-revealing but also a self-concealing God (Isa. 45:15)."[129]

Buber published these words in 1952. For him, the birth of the State of Israel was not the beginning of the promised redemption—that is, a world established in justice—if statehood required Israel to dispossess the other nation that inhabited the land. This outcome was not the realization of utopia, but rather an ideological deformation of prophetic values.[130] Nor would Buber assert that the Holocaust signified a rupture of the divine covenant with Israel. He is agnostic toward both events; neither shows God acting upon "this our historical hour." Despite this clear distancing from the idea that God acts in history, Buber does not revise the biblical paradigm; he simply defers its realization. It is as if he can live comfortably neither with the idea nor without it.

Buber's interpretations of five psalms in "Right and Wrong" (1952) indicate how he addressed himself to the post-Holocaust eclipse of God and paralysis of Jewish belief. Though none of the psalms he treats offers a wholly satisfactory answer to the dilemmas of theodicy, his chosen psalmists derive consolation from their presentation of one clear alternative to evil, that is, nearness to God as the only "true existence."[131] In his process of sorting out true from false existence, we see Buber distancing himself from both the reality of evil in history and the God of history, under whose mute dominion evil flourishes. Highlighting a few of Buber's interpretive emphases will enable us to see how he was pressing to go beyond the conceptual constraints of a God who intervenes in human affairs.

Buber wants desperately to show that despite the seeming victory of evil in our world, there is another scale of values, another reality, as it were, in which evil is effectively neutralized. In choosing first to interpret Psalm 12, with its clear antithesis between human lies and divine truth, Buber points us in two opposing directions. The first orientation is toward the problem itself, "the disintegration of human speech"[132] that was so evident in allowing the Nazis to perpetrate genocide as a "Final Solution" to the Jewish question. The second orientation is toward a solution to the problem of historical evil. When God says "He will 'now' arise" (v. 6), this salvation "is not just bound to come some time, but is always present and needs only to become effective."[133] Rather than seeing God's judgment day as a future historical moment, marking the end of time as we know it, Buber interprets this prophetic category as an eternal "now." "The lie," he writes, "is from time and will be swallowed up by time; the truth, the divine truth, is from eternity and is in eternity."[134] Insofar as we devote ourselves to truth, we partake of eternity. Thus, Buber might agree with the scholars who claim that resistance to the dehumanizing lie of Nazism, in whatever ways that resistance was manifest, enabled inmates to hold on to some vision of personal truth, whether or not they survived to continue affirming that truth.[135] Buber offers by way of consolation the notion that evil is defeated in eternity—not in some eternity that will one day come to the world, but rather in the perspective of eternity that believers can carry with them always.

In his interpretation of Psalm 14, Buber makes another move beyond history. He tackles the historical triumphalist posture of the Jewish people, which sees itself as good and its enemies as evil. "In our time, especially," writes Buber, "nothing is more understandable than this view, and nothing is more wrong-headed."[136] Buber resists any interpretation that would identify the wicked of the psalm with the nations of the world. He also resists identifying the phrase "my people" (v. 4) as a designation for the historical Israel. "My people" includes only the righteous and the oppressed; the oppressors who constitute the rest "are nothing but decomposed tissue, the rotting substance of a people."[137] The rift of which the psalm speaks runs "not merely through every nation, but also through every group in a nation, and even through every soul." Thus, when the psalmist asks, "O that the deliverance of Israel might come from Zion!" (v. 7), Buber understands that "the Zion of righteousness fulfilled in the land of Israel is what must be meant," not the topographical Zion.[138] In universalizing the conflicts of the psalm, Buber seeks healing for that rigidity within the post-Holocaust Jewish psyche that would mark Israel off from the nations, ensuring its permanent status as pariah and victim. National redemption, in Buber's understanding of prophetic messianism, was but the harbinger of redemption for the whole world.

Buber's third choice is Psalm 82, which he called in *At the Turning* "a picture of startling cruelty," with God depicted as a hidden ruler who allows injustice to reign on earth. The essence of the psalm, as Buber dramatically recounts it there, is the final cry of the psalmist that God judge the earth, just as God, in the psalmist's vision, judges the inferior gods. He writes, "the cry transmitted to us by Scripture becomes our own cry, which bursts forth from our hearts and rises to our lips in a time of God's hiddenness."[139] Writing a year later in "Right and Wrong," Buber expands on the terseness of the psalmist's plea, subtly changing it from a cry of the heart to a metaphysical argument: "Thine are the nations, lead them as thine own! Close the history of man which is a prey to delusion and wickedness, open his true history!" Is it a failure of perception or actual wickedness that makes the world intolerable? In distinguishing between true and false history, we see Buber hedging about the history we experience.

Strikingly, he compares the psalm to the imagined worlds created by Franz Kafka, especially in *The Trial* and *The Castle,* where rule has been given over to intermediary beings, with "no message of comfort or promise" penetrating to us from "the unknown One who gave this world into their impure hands."[140] For Kafka, God is but is not present, but for Buber, God's eternal presence is precisely what makes the ordinary world of history illusory.

This theme is most clearly stated in Buber's interpretation of Psalm 73, which asks the question posed by Jeremiah and others, "Why do the wicked prosper?" In my interpretation of the psalm in chapter 4, I suggested that the speaker's resolution of his theological doubts stemmed from his adopting the timelessness of the Temple's *axis mundi* as his own perspective. Buber takes a similar tack, but suggests that the phrase "God's sanctuary" (v. 17) refers to the orbit of God's holiness, available anywhere, not just in Jerusalem. He sets out to correct the reader who might be misled by the psalm's promise that the wicked will fall (vv. 18–19) into thinking "that the present state of affairs" is to be "replaced by a future state of affairs of a quite different kind, in which 'in the end' things go well with the good and badly with the bad." Such a mistaken view would place the conflict between good and evil in the realm of time and history. In Buber's attempt to imagine a timeless perspective on reality, "the bad do not truly exist, and their 'end' brings about only this change, that they now inescapably experience their non-existence, the suspicion of which they had again and again succeeded in dispelling." ("Their life," he says, glossing v. 20, "has been a shadow structure in a dream of God's," which dissolves when God awakes.)[141] Where the wicked exist only for the sake of bodily pleasure (vv. 4–7), the psalmist dwells in the purity of heart (v. 13) that leads one to God. The heart of the psalm is the speaker's revelation that existence consists of being "always" with God (v. 23). He or she therefore looks forward to an eternity in which there will be no separation from God.[142] "Nearness to God" (v. 28) defines the good, which is available to all human beings. The bad are simply those who are far from God, and who therefore do not share in the truth of existence.

Buber sums up the encounter between the human and the divine mystery with this aphorism: "from man's side there is no continuity, only from God's side."[143] Though we may perceive God as absent, God is not. For Buber, the human task is to adjust our perception, as the psalmist did, to find again the connection, however broken it may seem to have become. This is the essence of Buber's dialogical teaching, and central to our understanding of why he turned to exegesis of the Psalms after the Holocaust. For the psalmists who experience God's hiddenness never perceive it as a rupture or chastisement initiated by God, as the prophets do. God's hiddenness does not point to a historical fact in Psalms, but to a psychological one.[144] The psychological perception gives rise to emotional chaos, even to terror, but it is counterbalanced by an even stronger apprehension, as here in Psalm 73, that one can be "always" with God.

Writing directly about the Holocaust in *At the Turning*, Buber could characterize contemporary history only as a period of "divine muteness," but in his exegesis of Psalms, Buber avoids the painful acknowledgment that God "spoke" and redeemed the Jews in other periods, but not in ours, by focusing on the possibility of a continuous dialogue with God, an eternal "now," in which God is perceived as ever-present. Psalm 73 begins with the assertion "God is truly good to Israel, / to those whose heart is pure." Buber understands the second verset as an appositive. Thus, the statement "God is good to Israel" is true only for "those whose heart is pure." If things go ill for Israel, only those who are not pure of heart will draw the conclusion that God is not good to Israel. For one who is pure of heart or struggles to become so will understand that God has indeed been good to him or her. Even the wicked can turn from their wickedness and live again with God, Buber claims in interpreting Psalm 1. The way "is not closed from God's side," but only if we close it from ours.[145]

It is a mistake to argue, then, as one recent scholar does, that in writing these psalm interpretations, Buber was "waiting for the God of history."[146] In turning to the Psalms after the Holocaust, Buber deliberately did not choose those postcatastrophe psalms with which we began this chapter. Their angry, protesting writers were indeed waiting for the God of history, and therefore felt utterly abandoned in their moment of historical catastrophe. Instead, Buber explores psalms in which the seeming triumph of the wicked leads to moments of discontinuity in those psalmists' relationships with God. Psalm 73 provides the keystone to Buber's argument, with its revelation that ruptures in the relationship with God are merely the result of flawed human perception. Human beings can always be in relationship with God, no matter what evil or injustice they are suffering. Buber offers that psalm's contemplative path to God as an alternative to waiting for the God of history.

Among the Jewish writers who emerged from the Holocaust, one stands out especially as an inheritor of the interior spiritual path that Buber sees in Psalm 73. Etty Hillesum, a Dutch woman in her late twenties, kept a diary both in Amsterdam and at the transit camp Westerbork, where she went voluntarily in order to share in the fate of her people. From there she was transported to Auschwitz, where, like millions of her fellow Jews, she died in a crematorium.

Her diary is the record of a remarkable flowering of contemplative spirituality in the midst of an increasingly constricted life. The influences that nourished her spiritual journey were those of an assimilated university-educated Western European Jew; she read from the Bible, often at random, but especially from the Psalms and the Gospels. The authors whom she quotes most often are Rilke, Dostoevsky, and St. Augustine. Her great mentor was a charismatic palm-reader who had been analyzed by Jung. As mediated through him, Jung's theory of individuation shaped her diverse readings and gave her the guiding myth for her spiritual practice: God, she came to understand, is the "deepest and richest part" of myself, "in which I repose. . . . Truly, my life is one long hearkening unto my self and unto others, unto God. And if I say that I hearken, it is really God who hearkens inside me. The most essential and the deepest in me hearkening unto the most essential and the deepest in the other. God to God."[147] She has here translated the psalmist's "deep calls to deep" (42:8) into a new key. Choosing a relationship with the indwelling God through daily prayer and meditation made increased awareness of self and others her sacred task. Hillesum understood that being truly aware of the God within would radically change how she related to the world around her. No longer waiting for the world to serve her and fill up her inner emptiness, she would be a servant of God and the life around her.

Hillesum accords ultimate authority to the God she finds within her. "I delight in warmth and security, but I shall not rebel if I have to suffer cold, should You so decree. I shall follow wherever Your hand leads me and shall try not to be afraid. I shall try to spread some of my warmth, of my genuine love for others, wherever I go."[148] When she talks to God in this way, as if God were an agent controlling her destiny, she stresses the mutuality of their relationship. It is as if she sees God's will for her issuing in her own choices and actions: "At difficult moments like these, I wonder what You intend with me, oh God, and therefore what I intend with You."[149] For the most part, then, her God is an inner force who becomes an agent in the large historical drama of Nazis and Jews only insofar as individual human beings actualize the presence of God within them. "You cannot help us," she says to God. "We must help You to help ourselves . . . to safeguard that little piece of You, God, in ourselves"—to "defend Your dwelling place inside us to the last."[150] Because Hillesum did not grow up within the intellectual and spiritual milieu of traditional Judaism, she does not look to blame the God of history for her people's woes, as did so many of the Eastern European poets we cited above. She is adamant about not taking this way out. "God is not accountable to us for the senseless harm we cause one another. We are accountable to Him!"[151] We should note, however, that as the end closed in around her, and those she loved were daily being shipped to the east, she let out the psalmists' cry of lament to God: " 'God Almighty, what are you doing to us?' The words just escape me,"[152] she writes, as if the traditional address to a God who controls history were not really her own. Yet, a few pages later, looking unbelievingly at the mass of human beings crammed into a freight car, she again lets out that plaintive cry, "God Almighty, does all this lot have to get in as well?"[153] She knows that they do, and that even "God Almighty" can do nothing to change that fact. Hillesum's task is not to protest or to lament but to stay filled with "an infinite tenderness" for the life around her, which she records as "the thinking heart of these barracks."[154]

That is why Hillesum prays, not for specific outcomes for herself or for another, but so that she or "another have enough strength to shoulder his burden."[155] Her most emotional prayers, like those of so many psalmists, are praises to God for the gift of life. "Even if I should be locked up in a narrow cell and a cloud should drift past my small barred window, then I shall bring you that cloud, oh God, while there is still strength in me to do so."[156] Hillesum's diaries show that she knew Europe's Jews had been marked for annihilation, yet she does not despair. Like mystics of every generation, she carried even into Auschwitz that sense of being continually with God, commended by Buber as the essential revelation of the Psalms.

Hillesum's life-affirming journals, with their exalted prayers to an inner God, show what she calls her "inner preparation," the lack of which made many Jews give up, she writes, "long before they even set foot in a camp."[157] We see that traditional Judaism also could offer a similar inner preparation. The discourses of Rabbi Kalonymus Kalman Shapiro, delivered in the Warsaw ghetto during its last days, assure his parishioners that the secret of their endurance lies in their ability to empathize with God's pain:

> The weeping, the pain that a person undergoes by himself, alone—they may have the effect of breaking him, of bringing him down, so that he is incapable of doing anything. But the weeping that the person does together with God—that strengthens him. . . . It is hard to rise, time and again, above the sufferings; but when one summons the courage—stretching the mind to engage in Torah and divine service—then he enters the inner chambers where God is to be found. There he weeps and wails with Him, as it were, together. . . . [158]

Rabbi Shapiro preserves the ancient midrashic framework he inherited. Commenting on the postcatastrophe psalms and chapters of Lamentations, the second-century rabbis had reenvisioned, as we have said, their understanding of God's agency in the world. There were things that even God could not prevent from happening, as when Israel's enemies were on their path of wanton destruction. These rabbis placed God in an inner chamber of the divine palace, weeping over the sufferings of Israel. Eighteen hundred years later, Rabbi Shapiro explained to the suffering Jews of the Warsaw ghetto that God was not hiding in the divine palace out of anger, nor for some inscrutable reason, but because the sufferings of Israel were too great for God to bear in the world. "For just as God is infinite so His pain is infinite, and this, were it to touch the world, would destroy it."[159] Their task, as loyal Jews, was to break through to the divine hiddenness by sharing God's pain. Shouldering God's infinite pain together with God, Jews might return the divine image to the world by studying Torah and performing God's commandments, even amid the greatest effacement of the divine image ever perpetrated by humankind.

Etty Hillesum and Rabbi Kalonymus Shapiro, two Jews from opposite ends of the European Jewish world, both struggle to preserve the image of God in the midst of suffering by radically revising their understanding of God's power in history. To that company of strange bedfellows, I would add a third, the revisionary thinker with whom we began this chapter, Arthur Cohen, who has pushed farther than any other Jewish theologian in rethinking the categories of divine agency and speech in relation to the Holocaust. Noting that the most frequently asked theological questions by contemporary Jews are "Why did God not act during the Holocaust?" and "How could God remain silent?" Cohen sets out to provide an alternative understanding of divinity that will lead his co-religionists away from atheism. His argument, based on kabbalistic and Rosenzweigian views of creation, depends on our recognizing the independence of the created world from God. If we expect God to miraculously intervene in human history at moments of great human suffering and injustice, then "the creation we take to be real is not an emergence beyond God's being." If creation is not beyond God's being, then human life is denied "its essential freedom, returning to ethical passivity and quietism in which everything is compelled to be God's direct work."[160] The interruptive God of biblical history does not conform, he believes, to how we actually experience our own freedom, even at moments of redemption.

Cohen concedes the power of the widespread attack upon divine silence, which leads to views of God's "passivity, affectlessness, . . . indifference and ultimate malignity. Only a malign God," he writes, "would be silent when speech would terrify and stay the fall of the uplifted arm." For this critique to be valid, however, it must take God's speech in the Bible literally, that is, understand that God actually spoke in human language. This critique of God must also assume with the psalmists and other biblical authors that God's speech is action, indeed, action in the service of "the historical cause of justice and mercy," and conversely, that divine silence reverses the works of God's speech, and consequently amounts to "acquiescence in the work of murder and destruction." In Cohen's reconstruction of the biblical metaphor, "what is taken as God's speech is really always man's hearing." He urges us not to see God as "the strategist of our particularities or of our historical condition, but rather the mystery of our futurity . . . the immensity whose reality is our prefiguration." The God who interferes in human history to reward and punish is a God from whom we demand response and whose power we fear, but the God Cohen would have us worship, "whose plenitude and unfolding are the hope of our futurity," is a God, he says, to be loved and honored.[161]

Cohen's God is neither a function nor a cause of historical existence, but the inspiration for what history might become, existing in a "continuous community and nexus" with humanity. The culmination of his argument is a metaphor drawn from twentieth-century technology. "I understand divine life," he writes,

> to be a filament within the historical, but never the filament that we can identify and ignite according to our requirements, for in this and all other respects God remains God. As filament, the divine element of the historical is a precarious conductor always intimately linked to the historical . . . and always separate from it, since the historical is the domain of human freedom. . . . Man—not God—renders the filament of the divine incandescent or burns it out. There is, in the dialectic of man and God amid history, the indispensable recognition that man can obscure, eclipse, burn out the divine filament, grounding its natural movement of transcendence by a sufficient and oppository chthonic subscension. It is this which is meant by the abyss of the historical, the demonic, the *tremendum*.[162]

Cohen's metaphor can be seen as a midrash on the verse "by Your light do we see light" (Ps. 38:10b). The crematorium fires do not shed new light on the nature of God, as theologians wedded to the God of history would have us think. Rather, for Cohen, those fires are demonic inversions of the divine light that only human beings can keep lit in this world. By their demonic light, he suggests, we see what humanity truly can become when it fails to preserve the image of God in its midst.

If to save the possibility of God for our time requires, according to Cohen, that divine speech be reimagined as a description of human hearing, then the idea of divine silence, traditionally associated with God's anger and rejection of Israel, also needs to be similarly revised. Two European Jews, the French theologian André Néher and the German-language poet from Romania Paul Celan (who lived and wrote in France), have offered such revisionary accounts, each in his own genre. For both, Psalms are prominent in their post-Holocaust approaches to divine silence.

André Néher's most important work of interpretive theology is titled *The Exile of the Word: From the Silence of the Bible to the Silence of Auschwitz.*

"Silence," he says, "is the metaphysical form of the cosmos," as in Psalm 19's declaration that the heavens and the day and night speak of God's existence. Silent nature reveals and veils the infinity of "the Creator . . . whose intimate Being . . . may ultimately be identified only with Silence."[163] The best-known prooftext for this point of view is the scene on Mount Sinai in which Elijah is instructed that God is neither in the mighty wind, nor in the earthquake, nor in the fire, but in "a soft murmuring sound" (*qol demamah daqqah,* lit. "a voice of thin silence"; I Kings 19:12). As Néher explains, in this prophetic parable "the word is diminished while silence gains a positive significance. . . . Silence need no longer signify His anger or rejection but can express His Presence as well as or better than the word."[164]

Over against God's infinite silence, Néher places the finite silences of humanity that appear so often in the Bible, especially in Psalms. Néher highlights two psalmic passages in which silence is conceived as a medium for approaching the divine presence:

> Towards God with silence vibrates my soul. (Ps. 62:2a)
>
> To Thee silence alone is fitting by way of praise. (Ps. 65:2a)[165]

He notes that the medieval commentators Meir Ibn Gabbai and Maimonides concluded from these passages that silence allowed individuals to stay closely attuned to God's reality, the silent speaking of Creation; thus human beings could and indeed should praise God through silent meditation. "For the word betrays and only silence respects the organic connection which places the Ineffable before the Infinite."[166]

What silence signifies to the post-Holocaust thinker, however, is not so idealized as it was for his medieval forebears. "This silent universe is not shut in upon itself after all. A Creator dwells within it, as silent as the recesses and fastnesses of night and death, as unfathomable as the depths of hell, as ephemeral as nothingness; and this silence, this fathomlessness, this ephemerality—they are the signs of Life, of the Presence, of the Word!"[167] Néher can find God only in paradox, in a silence beyond silence, like that of Elijah's *qol demamah daqqah.* He is drawn to another psalmist, who cries out, "My God, I cry by day—You answer not / by night, and have no respite" (Ps. 22:3). The day is associated with language and verbally calling out to God (*'eqra*), but the crying out at night is associated, paradoxically, with *lo' dwmiah,* that is, literally, "non-silence," a phrase that most translations avoid with such circumlocutions as "no respite" (JPS), "but find no rest" (RSV). Though the phrase might suggest various inarticulate cries, such as the bellowings and roarings we hear about later in the psalm (v. 14), Néher insists that "nonsilence" should not be turned into just another version of the day's unceasing cry. " 'Nonsilence' is a silence more silent than silence. It is the fall of silence into a deeper stratum of nothingness; it is a shaft hollowed out beneath silence which leads to its most vertiginous depths. . . . Silence confronts us with the hidden God. Nonsilence confronts us with a God whose Being may be grasped only from the fleeting roots of Nothingness."[168] The phrase's literal negativeness must be taken into account. It is not incidental to the gravity of Néher's interpretation that he draws this evocative phrase from the best-known psalm expressing feelings of abandonment. Judaism associates Psalm 22 with Esther's utter solitude before she confronts King Ahasuerus on behalf of her people, while Christianity associates it with Jesus on the Cross.[169] In a psalm calling forth such momentous associations, the nonsilence of night, Néher is convinced, must point to some fundamental reality, a new approach to the terror of divinity, which cannot be mediated by any word. As Néher reminds us in his gloss on Psalm 139:8b, "the meeting place of God and man can be in hell."[170]

If Néher's commentary seems somewhat forced as a midrash on Psalm 22, it might well be adopted as an elaboration on the darkly brooding poetry of Paul Celan, where the meeting of human beings and God takes place in the hell of a memory and imagination shaped by the concentration camps. One scholar of Holocaust literature has described Celan's spare and intensely symbolic poetry as manifesting what Néher sees in Psalm 22, a "faith before the void . . . pure *standing* as a fundamental ontological truth." Celan, this scholar notes, is "as close as we have come to having a modern master" of the mode of writing-in-faithfulness practiced in the darkest psalms.[171] Where this reader sees "faith before the void," another describes Celan's poetry as manifesting "the spiritual emptiness and desolation experienced by the victim and the survivor in an abandoned universe."[172] Faith and desolation, the antinomies of the religious struggle in the Psalms, are the poles of Celan's poetry, each of which draws readers into its singular orbit. But rather than choosing sides between the two positions, as many have done, I would urge the reader to search for the inevitable tension between them. For this dialectical task, it is often necessary to read both what is written and what is not, for as Celan said, "poetry today . . . clearly shows a strong tendency toward silence. . . . In order to endure, it constantly calls and pulls itself back from an 'already-no-more' into a 'still-here.' " Language is thus the medium that both reveals the void of death and defends against it by conveying a living human voice, "a presence in the present."[173]

In reading Celan, it is easiest to pick up the vein of irony and satire, and therefore to see him, like Greenberg, Sutzkever, and Katznelson, as rejecting the reality of any divine presence. This is the face that he primarily shows in "Tenebrae" (Latin for "darkness"), where the "we" of the poem are the victims of genocide, perpetrated not by Germans but by God:

> Wind-awry we went there,
> went there to bend
> over hollow and ditch,
>
> To be watered we went there, Lord.
>
> It was blood, it was
> what you shed, Lord.

These creatures drank not only the blood, we are told, but also "the image that was in the blood." The poetry is brilliant in its compression. Was this their own reflection that they saw in the blood, or the image of their relatives who had perished before them? (Celan's parents were killed by the Nazis.) Or was it the reflected image of God as failed pastoral shepherd, whose divine hand shed this blood? The image refuses closure to keep all these possibilities (and others) alive. Although more subtle than the ironic invective we encountered in the Yiddish and Hebrew poems analyzed above, this poetry mines the same field. But there is another note in Celan that we sense in his focus on the victims' nearness to God. Nearness to God is that which the psalmists most adamantly seek. "We are near, Lord, / near and at hand." "Pray, Lord," he concludes, "We are near."[174] God needs to pray to, or perhaps in the presence of, the victims, because they now carry the image of the ultimate reality. A God of truth needs to learn what they have to teach, and it is the language of prayer that keeps this access to truth alive.

Celan's poetry does not reject God, but rather portrays God as God is experienced by the victims of the Holocaust. The way Celan pursues lies beyond personifications that might point to God's intimate involvement in human life. The personified, anthropomorphic Creator-God of Genesis 2, though perhaps once relevant to the story of humanity's origins, is no longer so in the poem titled "Psalm":

> No one moulds us again out of earth and clay,
> No one conjures our dust.
> No one.

Life is a one-way ticket for the dead. The God they experience is "no one," not the more abstract word, "nothing," which is reserved later in the poem for what the dead become. This "no one" points to an absent presence, the personal God who is no longer there, but whose linguistic shadow, as it were, remains. This no one's reality lies beyond personification. Whereas the psalmist protests that those who descend to the silent grave no longer can praise YHWH (Ps. 115:17), Celan's dead speakers do find an appellation for God that they can still offer in praise.

> Praised be your name, no one.
> For your sake
> we shall flower
> Towards
> you.[175]

This insistence on praising that which cannot be imaged, a "no one," is similar to the kabbalists' devotion to ein sof, literally, the "no end," limitless God, who lies beyond the emanations, beyond all the attempts of human language to encompass divine reality. In "Tenebrae," human beings were near to God, but in this poem they have gone beyond nearness; they too are "a nothing," and like the eternal God, the "no one" whose Hebrew name means "is–was–will be," they also belong to all of time:

> A Nothing
> we were, we are, we
> shall remain, blooming:
> the Nothing's rose, the
> No One's rose.
>
> With our pistil soul-bright
> with our stamen heaven-ravaged
> our corolla red
> with the crimson-word we sang
> over, o over
> the thorn.[176]

The rose, a mystical symbol of God in many religious traditions, goes back in Judaism to the Song of Songs, which depicts the rose, or "lily among thorns" (2:1–2). Rashi interprets the phrase as an allegorical image of Israel's faithfulness "despite the torments of her neighbors who try to sway her after their strange gods."[177] The Zohar reads it as an image of the Community of Israel, a rose below that parallels the thirteen-petaled rose above, whose petals signify the thirteen attributes of God's justice and mercy.[178] In identifying the "nothing" of the dead with this allegorical tradition of the rose, Celan affirms his continuity with Jewish imagining, even as he transforms that tradition through his ambivalence. The pistil and stamen, we recall, are the reproductive organs of the flower; the corolla is its outer envelope of petals. There is no question that Celan's rose is wounded, its powers of generativity bloodied through "the crimson-word" that we presume to be death. Though "heaven-ravaged," it is nevertheless "soul-bright" and eternally blooming. Like Rashi's rose, it is faithful to the face of God it has experienced, albeit a negative one. The poem may indeed be dominated by God's absence,[179] but it also sounds the plaintive note of human beings yearning, even in death, for the eternal world of spirit. Celan chooses that they remain ever-wounded, ever-blooming.

Among the many poems brought to life by the massive death of the Holocaust, Celan's are distinctive in their willingness to address the absence of divine Presence in tones of intimacy:

> O one, o none, o no one, o you:
> Where did the way lead when it led nowhere?
> O you dig and I dig, and I dig towards you,
> And on our finger the ring awakes.[180]

Celan's speaker does not give up on God, the "you" of this final stanza. He imagines a reciprocal relation between God and humanity, each digging toward the other, signifying, it would seem, the search of each for embodiment in the other. The fairytale element of the awakening ring closes the poem on an unmistakable note of promise, as if the poet truly expects some fulfillment from this new way of imagining God and humanity in terms of one another. There is another story embedded in this poem, however. Its symbolic diggers experience what we might call an inverted theophany. "There came a stillness, and there came a storm, and all the oceans came." This line both reverses the experience of Elijah on Sinai and recalls the frequent psalmic image of being overwhelmed by God's terrors, as if drowning in mighty waves.[181] These images lead us almost inevitably to consider the end of Celan's life, an apparent death by suicide in the Seine. Like many of the ancient psalmists, he had "come into the watery depths" (Ps. 69:3c), but where they keep calling out to the You who grounds their reality, Celan found no reassuring supernatural divine presence to prevent the dark flood from sweeping him away.

Though Celan's latter-day psalms often speak in the first-person plural, it is hard to imagine their idiosyncratic style and double-edged, hermetic truths in the context of public liturgy, which, as we stressed early in this study, is the context in which the Psalms were created and have continued to be used. The same can be said of the private devotions of Etty Hillesum, or the theological reflections of Martin Buber and Arthur Cohen. In finding a means of access to a God who does not control history or intervene in it miraculously to save the Jews, the poets and theologians whose work we have examined implicitly challenge what is perhaps the most distinctive element of Judaism, its collective covenant with God.

One theologian who has steadfastly refused to diminish the power of this covenant is Emil Fackenheim. For him, Zionism and the State of Israel supremely define Judaism's covenantal responsibilities. Buber pointedly asked a postwar lecture audience, "Dare we recommend to the survivors of Oswiecim [Auschwitz], to the Job of the gas chambers: 'Call to Him, for He is kind, for His mercy endures forever'?"[182] But Fackenheim, focusing not on Job but on Job's children, understands that the Hallel psalms, from which this line comes, need to be said publicly, for "hope murdered at Auschwitz, was resurrected in Jerusalem."[183] Though all significant speech, he says in another context, has been called into question for *"ever after"* by the Holocaust,[184] nevertheless he argues that collective Jewish life requires the hopefulness of Psalms:

> Can the resurrected hope, ever again, extend to a God never asleep, to a Mercy enduring forever, to an End of Days that will be all praise? . . . That Hallel will be recited . . . in a Redemption beyond history, the rabbis never doubt. But when within history? On occasions calling for praise, but just on these? . . . Hallel was ordained, we find in the Talmud, not only for festive celebrations, but also "for every disaster that threatened but did not occur."[185]

Thus, for Fackenheim, the most important time to recite Hallel is undoubtedly on Israel's Independence Day. "A wonder—not unlike that with which Jewish history begins in earnest—fills thoughtful Jews on Yom Ha-Atzmaut, about that day and all it signifies. Perhaps the more thoughtful they become, the more *sotto voce* also becomes for them [the] verse of Psalm 118, the one about a Mercy enduring forever. Yet the less *sotto voce* also becomes another from the same psalm: 'This is the day that YHWH has made— / let us exult and rejoice in it' (v. 24)."[186]

However we regard Fackenheim's nationalist theology, it is clear from the way he couches his argument how central the Psalms remain to those who come after Auschwitz and continue some form of religious practice. For the psalmists' transcendence of seeming despair with hope is their overarching lesson for those surviving catastrophe. Reminiscent of Rabbi Joshua's colloquy with the ascetics after the destruction of the Second Temple, Zelig Kalmanovitch makes a profound comment on the tension between remembering catastrophe and going on with the fullness of life:

> Eventually the Jewish people itself will forget this branch that was broken off. It will have to do without it. From the healthy trunk will come forth branches and blossoms and leaves. There is still strength and life. Dried up and decayed—this happens to every tree. There are still thousands of years ahead. Lamentation for the dead, of course, that is natural,

particularly if they are your own, close to you. But the Jewish people must
not be confused. The mourning for close ones—some people bear their
sorrow long; most find comfort. Human nature—such is the world. Whatever the earth covers up is forgotten. . . . The Jewish people will not be
hurt. It will, it is to be hoped, emerge fortified by the trial. This should fill
the heart with joyous gratitude to the sovereign of history.[187]

Kalmanovitch's "joyous gratitude" is prophetic, both in the general sense
of cogently predicting an unknown future and in the specific biblical sense
of offering Israel consolation, even in the midst of tragedy. Interned in the
Vilna ghetto, he looks ahead with utter confidence to the strength the
Jewish people will yet manifest in order to transcend the worst horror that
could be inflicted by the "sovereign of history." Though he speaks in
prose, his thoughts and cadences are the authentic tones of the Psalms: it
is not the dead but we the living who need to tender praise for the gift of
our own lives and the ongoing life of the Jewish people. In a paragraph
such as this one, we see how faith in the Jewish future was informed by the
rich corpus of the Psalms that continued to live on in his inner life and in
that of so many Holocaust poets and thinkers.

Bakhtin wrote that all utterances participate in a chain of speech communication, whose links to subsequent utterances are unknown at the
time of speaking. But the utterances are constructed from the very beginning, he claims, just for the sake of those future respondents.[188] The
psalms, it might be said, are themselves remarkable survivors in such a
chain of communication, the most prominent public remnant of Israel's
ancient Temple worship that is left to the Jewish people. In continuing a
dialogue with them, midrashic storytellers, kabbalist liturgical innovators,
and post-Holocaust poets and theologians have kept them alive for each
subsequent generation that has encountered the biblical originals and
recast them in its turn. Whether it be in Paul Celan's ironic reversal "Pray,
Lord, / pray to us, / we are near,"[189] or in Irving Feldman's affirmation
"There is no singing without God," or in his entreaty to the "vanished
bones" of the "lost people," "Do not deny your blessing, speak to us,"[190]
or in Yehuda Amichai's resolute faithfulness to life, "And I'll go on
singing / till my heart breaks, first heart and second heart. / A psalm,"[191]
we hear over and over in our time a contemporary reaccentuation of the
psalmists' words of petition and praise. From such reaccentuation of
ancient words, we discern the history and the future of our collective discourse. These contemporary poets bring us back to the words of the Bible
and to Buber's challenge that we remain open to its faith by struggling
with it on our own terms, not knowing which of its sayings or images will
enter into us and become renewed in our lives.[192]

NOTES

Preface

1. I am thinking especially of Edward Feld, *The Spirit of Renewal: Crisis and Response in Jewish Life* (Woodstock: Jewish Lights, 1991), and Arthur Green, *Seek My Face, Speak My Name: A Contemporary Jewish Theology* (Northvale: Jason Aronson, 1992).

2. As an example of their secular appeal, see Maya Angelou's Inauguration poem, *On the Pulse of the Morning* (New York: Random House, 1993), with its line "I am that Tree planted by the River," adapted from Ps. 1:3: "like a tree planted beside streams of water."

3. Martin Buber, *Israel and the World: Essays in a Time of Crisis* (1948; rpt. New York: Schocken, 1963), 93.

4. Martin Buber, *Moses: The Revelation and the Covenant* (1946; rpt. New York: Harper and Row, 1958), 53.

5. See Green, 19.

1. From Tradition to Modernity

1. For the musical history of the Psalms, see Eric Werner, *The Sacred Bridge: The Interdependence of Liturgy and Music in Synagogue and Church during the First Millennium*, 2 vols., I (New York: Columbia University Press, 1959); II (New York: Ktav, 1984).

2. Werner, II, 52.

3. Quoted in Uriel Simon, *Four Approaches to the Book of Psalms: From Saadiah to Abraham Ibn Ezra*, trans. Lenn J. Schram (Albany: State University of New York Press, 1991), 308–10.

4. See Louis Rabinowitz, "Does Midrash *Tehillim* Reflect the Triennial Cycle of Psalms?" *Jewish Quarterly Review*, n.s. 26 (1935–36), 349–68.

5. The superscript for Ps. 90 lists Moses, and for Ps. 72 Solomon; other names mentioned in superscripts (Asaph, Heman, Ethan, the sons of Korach) are presumed to be Temple musicians. The rabbis attributed Ps. 92 to Adam in collaboration with the Sabbath, for which see *The Midrash on Psalms*, trans. and ed. William G. Braude, 2 vols. (New Haven: Yale University Press, 1959), II, 112.

6. Braude, ed., I, 274.

7. Braude, ed., I, 274.

8. Braude, ed., I, 285–86.

9. See 2 Sam. 11; already in the biblical period, exegetes considered Ps. 51 a response to this sin, as can be seen by the superscript for the psalm.

10. For a list of New Testament quotations from Psalms, see Pius Drijvers, *The Psalms, Their Structure and Meaning* (New York: Herder and Herder, 1964), 261–62.

11. The classic instance of typological interpretation in the New Testament is Heb. 11; on the polemical origins of anti-Judaic midrash in the New Testament, see Rosemary R. Ruether, *Faith and Fratricide: The Theological Roots of Anti-Semitism* (New York: Seabury, 1974), 64–116; and on its consequences for Jewish-Christian relations, see Arthur A. Cohen, *The Myth of the Judeo-Christian Tradition* (New York: Harper and Row, 1970).

12. See Krister Stendhal, *Paul among Jews and Gentiles and Other Essays* (Philadelphia: Fortress Press, 1976), 1–7, 23–40; and Francis Watson, *Paul, Judaism, and the Gentiles: A Sociological Approach* (Cambridge: Cambridge University Press, 1986).

13. New Testament quotations are taken from the Revised Standard Version (RSV).

14. Augustine, *Expositions on the Book of Psalms,* 6 vols., trans. by members of the English Church (Oxford: John Henry Parker, 1847), I, 129.

15. See Jean Pépin, *Mythe et Allégorie: Les origines Grecques et les contestations judéo-chrétiènnes,* rev. ed. (Paris: Études Augustiniènnes, 1976).

16. Peter Brown, *Augustine of Hippo: A Biography* (Berkeley: University of California Press, 1969), 261.

17. Brown, 255.

18. Augustine, II, 178.

19. Augustine, I, 130.

20. Augustine, I, 126–27.

21. Edward Greenstein, "Medieval Bible Commentaries," in *Back to the Sources: Reading the Classic Jewish Texts,* ed. Barry Holtz (New York: Summit, 1984), 222–23.

22. His grandson apparently exposed him to Jerome's 4th-century Latin commentary; see Esra Shereshevsky, *Rashi: The Man and His World* (New York: Sepher Hermon Press, 1982), 119–32.

23. See Chaim Pearl, *Rashi* (New York: Grove Press, 1988), 39.

24. The translation from Rashi is my own. The JPS translation for v. 9 differs from Rashi's; it reads "restoring strength," basing itself on I Sam. 14:27–30, Pss. 13:4, 38:11, and Ezra 9:8.

25. For midrashim that cite Mal. 3:19, see Braude, ed., I, 282.

26. Ibn Ezra on Deut. 4:19, quoted in Alexander Altmann, "Astrology," *Encyclopedia Judaica* (Jerusalem: Keter, 1972), III, 792. Ibn Ezra was paraphrasing a famous Talmudic dictum, "There is no constellation for Israel," for which see *B. Shabbat* 156a.

27. Greenstein, 249.

28. See H. Jackson Forstman, *Word and Spirit: Calvin's Doctrine of Biblical Authority* (Stanford: Stanford University Press, 1962), 21–36.

29. E. William Monter, *Calvin's Geneva* (New York: John Wiley and Sons, 1961), 33.

30. John Calvin, *Commentary on the Book of Psalms,* ed. Rev. James Anderson (1845), trans. Arthur Golding (1571), 5 vols. (Grand Rapids: Eerdmans, 1949), I, 317–18.

31. Calvin, I, 328.

32. See Hans W. Frei, *The Eclipse of Biblical Narrative: A Study in Eighteenth and Nineteenth Century Hermeneutics* (New Haven: Yale University Press, 1974).

33. Hermann Gunkel, *The Psalms: A Form-Critical Introduction*, trans. Thomas M. Horner (Philadelphia: Fortress Press, 1967), 26.

34. For a view of this tradition's anti-Semitism, see Joseph Blenkinsopp, *Prophecy and Canon* (Notre Dame: University of Notre Dame Press, 1977), 17–23.

35. Sigmund Mowinckel, *The Psalms in Israel's Worship*, trans. D. R. Ap-Thomas, 2 vols. (New York: Abingdon, 1962), I, 106–92.

36. On Gunkel's and Mowinckel's domination of Psalms scholarship, see Erhard Gerstenberger, "Psalms," in *Old Testament Form Criticism*, ed. John H. Hayes (San Antonio: Trinity University Press, 1974), 179–223; for a recent work that has again shifted discussion away from the cult, see E. Gerstenberger, *Der Bittende Mensch* (Neukirchen-Vluyn: Neukirchener Verlag, 1980).

37. Gunkel (1967), 37.

38. Quoted in W. O. E. Oesterley, *The Psalms* (London: Society for the Promotion of Christian Knowledge, 1953), 169–70; for representative hymns to the sun, see James Pritchard, *Ancient Near Eastern Texts*, 2 vols. (Princeton: Princeton University Press, 1955, 1969), I, 3–12, 37–44, 60–72, 99–106, 129–42; II, 501–503, 517–18.

39. Oesterley, 170; Nahum M. Sarna, "Psalm XIX and the Near Eastern Sun-God Literature," *Proceedings of the IV World Congress of Jewish Studies*, I (1967), 171–75, notes that phrases common to ancient Near Eastern hymns to the sun are also found in this psalm's praise of Torah, suggesting to Sarna a similar conclusion—that an earlier pagan hymn has been displaced.

40. Fleming James, *Thirty Psalmists: A Study in Personalities of the Psalter as Seen against the Background of Gunkel's Type-Study of the Psalms* (New York: G. P. Putnam's Sons, 1938), 29–30.

41. James, 33.

42. James, 32, summarizes and quotes these views in his own translations; see Rudolph Kittel, *Die Psalmen*, 1st and 2nd ed. (Leipzig: A. Deichertsche Verlagsbuchhandlung, 1914), 78; Hans Schmidt, *Die Psalmen* (Tübingen: J. C. B. Mohr, 1934), 33; Hermann Gunkel, *Die Psalmen* (Göttingen: Vandenhoed and Ruprecht, 1926), 79.

43. See Lev. 1:3 and 19:5; 22:19, 29; 23:11.

44. Nahum M. Sarna, *Songs of the Heart: An Introduction to the Book of Psalms* (New York: Schocken, 1993), 95.

45. The "poetic function" of language, according to Czech linguist Roman Jakobson, is that which focuses our attention on the message; see his "Closing Statement: Linguistics and Poetics," in *Style in Language*, ed. Thomas A. Sebeok (Cambridge: MIT Press, 1960), 356–57.

46. See Michael Fishbane, *Text and Texture: Close Readings of Selected Biblical Texts* (New York: Schocken, 1979), 85.

47. Fishbane (1979), 87, 89.

48. Fishbane's suggestion that speech is the root metaphor of the psalm ([1979], 86) informs my discussion.

49. Earlier, we were told that nothing was hidden from the sun's heat, *'ein nistar meḥamato*. While the sun reached only the external objects in the world, God's knowledge and forgiveness penetrates, we are now told, even to *nistarot*, the human unconscious; see Fishbane (1979), 88.

50. Jonathan Z. Smith, *To Take Place: Toward Theory in Ritual* (Chicago: University of Chicago Press, 1987), 100.

51. Act IV, Scene 1, lines 244–47.

52. Influential work in this field by anthropologists includes Mary Douglas, *Purity and Danger: An Analysis of the Concept of Pollution and Taboo* (London: Routledge and Kegan Paul, 1966); Edmund Leach, *Genesis as Myth and Other Essays* (London: Jonathan Cape, 1969); and Julian Pitt-Rivers, *The Fate of Schechem or the Politics of Sex: Essays in the Anthropology of the Mediterranean* (Cambridge: Cambridge University Press, 1977). For recent work by biblical scholars, see Howard Eilberg-Schwartz, *The Savage in Judaism: An Anthropology of Israelite Religion and Ancient Judaism* (Bloomington: Indiana University Press, 1990); Frank H. Gorman, Jr., *Space, Time and Status in the Priestly Theology* (Sheffield: Sheffield Academic Press, 1990); J. W. Rogerson, *Anthropology and the Old Testament* (Oxford: Blackwell, 1978); and Robert R. Wilson, *Genealogies and History in the Biblical World* (New Haven: Yale University Press, 1977). For an anthology of significant essays, see Bernhard Lang, ed., *Anthropological Approaches to the Old Testament* (Philadelphia: Fortress Press, 1985).

53. Catherine Bell, *Ritual Theory, Ritual Practice* (New York: Oxford University Press, 1992), 108.

54. See Mircea Eliade, *The Sacred and the Profane: The Nature of Religion*, trans. Willard R. Trask (New York: Harper and Row, 1957), 20–68.

55. For a survey of these positions, see Bell, 171–81.

56. Susanne K. Langer, *Philosophy in a New Key*, 3rd ed. (Cambridge: Harvard University Press, 1957), 153.

57. Edmund Leach, *Culture and Communication: The Logic by Which Symbols are Connected* (Cambridge: Cambridge University Press, 1976), 84; other anthropologists drawing on a linguistic perspective for the study of ritual are Stanley J. Tambiah, *Culture, Thought, and Social Action* (Cambridge: Harvard University Press, 1985), and James Fernandez, *Persuasions and Performances: The Play of Tropes in Culture* (Bloomington: Indiana University Press, 1986).

58. On ritual as a tidying up of the messiness of ordinary life, see Jonathan Z. Smith, *Imagining Religion: From Babylon to Jonestown* (Chicago: University of Chicago Press, 1982), 63. Compare Clifford Geertz, *The Interpretation of Cultures* (New York: Basic Books, 1973), who sees in ritual not a differentiation but a fusion of "the world as lived and the world as imagined" (112).

59. John R. Searle, *Expression and Meaning: Studies in the Theory of Speech Acts* (Cambridge: Cambridge University Press, 1979), 29.

60. J. L. Austin, *How to Do Things with Words*, ed. J. O. Urmson (New York: Oxford University Press, 1962). We shall examine the speech-act theory in more detail in chapter 2.

61. John R. Searle, *Speech Acts: An Essay in the Philosophy of Language* (Cambridge: Cambridge University Press, 1969), 33–42, makes this distinction; Tambiah, 135, applies it to ritual.

62. See Erving Goffman, *Frame Analysis* (New York: Harper and Row, 1974).

63. As enumerated by Sally F. Moore and Barbara Myerhoff, eds., *Secular Ritual* (Assen/Amsterdam: Van Gorcum, 1977), 7–8.

64. In the language of information theory, it is "redundant"; see Tambiah, 143–46.

65. See Barbara Lex, "The Neurobiology of Ritual Trance," and Eugene d'Aquili and Charles D. Laughlin, "The Neurobiology of Myth and Ritual," in *The Spectrum of Ritual: A Biogenetic Structural Analysis*, ed. Eugene d'Aquili, Charles D. Laughlin, and John McManus (New York: Columbia University Press, 1979), 117–51, 152–82.

66. Colin Turnbull, "Liminality: A Synthesis of Subjective and Objective Experience," in *By Means of Performance: Intercultural Studies of Theatre and Ritual,* ed. Richard Schechner and Willa Appel (Cambridge: Cambridge University Press, 1990), 65.

67. Emil Durkheim, *The Elementary Forms of the Religious Life: A Study in Religious Sociology* (1915), trans. Joseph Ward Swain (New York: Free Press, 1965), esp. 479–96.

68. Roy A. Rappaport, *Ecology, Meaning, and Religion* (Richmond: North Atlantic Books, 1979), 209.

69. Rappaport, p. 178.

70. Ruth Finnegan, "How to Do Things with Words: Performative Utterances among the Limba of Sierra Leone," *Man* 4 (1969), 550; Rappaport, 191.

71. Tambiah, 27–29.

72. This dichotomy is the legacy of Sir James G. Frazer, *The Golden Bough: A Study in Magic and Religion*, 3rd ed., 12 vols. (London: Macmillan, 1913–15).

73. On horizontal and vertical, see Terence S. Turner, "Transformation, Hierarchy, and Transcendence: A Reformulation of Van Gennep's Model of the Structure of *Rites de Passage*," in Moore and Myerhoff, eds., 67–68.

74. Arnold Van Gennep, *The Rites of Passage* (1909), trans. M. B. Vizedom and G. L. Caffee (Chicago: University of Chicago Press, 1960), 20.

75. Victor W. Turner, *The Forest of Symbols: Aspects of Ndembu Ritual* (Ithaca: Cornell University Press, 1967), esp. 27–30.

76. Victor W. Turner, *The Ritual Process: Structure and Anti-Structure* (Chicago: Aldine, 1969), 94–97, 131–40; Turner's view of liminality as antistructural is similar to the play concept of Johann Huizinga, *Homo Ludens: A Study of the Play Element in Culture* (1938), trans. by the author (Boston: Beacon Press, 1955); and the presentation of carnival forms in literature by Mikhail Bakhtin, *Rabelais and His World,* trans. Helene Iswolsky (Cambridge: MIT Press, 1968).

77. Victor W. Turner, *Drama, Fields, and Metaphors: Symbolic Action in Human Society* (Ithaca: Cornell University Press, 1974), 23–59.

78. "Pilgrimages as Social Processes," in Turner (1974), 166–230.

2. The World of the Psalms

1. J. W. Rogerson, "Sacrifice in the Old Testament: Problems of Method and Approach," in *Sacrifice,* ed. M. F. C. Boudrillon and M. Fortes (London: Academic Press, 1980), 45.

2. Yehezkel Kaufmann, *The Religion of Israel: From Its Beginnings to the Babylonian Exile* (1937–56), trans. and abridged by Moshe Greenberg (New York: Schocken, 1960), 175–211.

3. Julius Wellhausen, *Prolegomena to the History of Ancient Israel* (1878), trans. J. S. Black and Allan Menzies (New York: Meridian, 1957).

4. Jacob Milgrom, *Leviticus 1–16,* The Anchor Bible (New York: Doubleday, 1991), 13–34, places the origin of P at the tabernacle of Shiloh, ca. 1200 B.C.E.; Menahem Haran, *Temples and Temple-Service in Ancient Israel* (Oxford: Clarendon Press, 1978), 132–48, dates P to the reign of Hezekiah. Both take the exile to be the end of the redaction process.

5. For an earlier attempt to date the Psalms, see Moses Buttenweiser, *The Psalms: Chronologically Treated with a New Translation,* Prolegomenon by Nahum M. Sarna (New York: Ktav, 1969).

6. See Avi Hurvitz, *Bein lašon le lašon: Le toldot lešon ha miqra' be yemei bayit šeni* (Jerusalem: Bialik Institute, 1972), who has found eight psalms and phrases in fifteen others whose postexilic date can be demonstrated linguistically.

7. Moshe Greenberg, "Religion: Stability and Ferment," in *The World History of the Jewish People: The Age of the Monarchy,* ed. A. Malamat (Jerusalem: Massada Press, 1979), 82.

8. John H. Hayes, *Introduction to Old Testament Study* (Nashville: Abingdon, 1979), 306.

9. Mowinckel, II, 25.

10. Kaufmann, 109.

11. See Nahum M. Sarna, "The Psalm Superscriptions and the Guilds," in *Studies in Jewish Religious and Intellectual History,* ed. S. Stein and R. Lowe (University: University of Alabama Press, 1979), 281–300.

12. Eliade (1957), cited above; and Mircea Eliade, *The Myth of the Eternal Return, or, Cosmos and History* (1949), trans. Willard R. Trask (Princeton: Princeton University Press, 1954).

13. On the legitimation of the king through ritual, see Amelie Kuhrt, "Usurpation, Conquest, and Ceremonial: From Babylon to Persia," in *Rituals of Royalty: Power and Ceremonial in Traditional Societies,* ed. David Cannadine and Simon Price (Cambridge: Cambridge University Press, 1987), 20–55.

14. The central expositor of this view is Mowinckel, I, 106–92; see also Aubrey R. Johnson, "The Role of the King in the Jerusalem Cultus," in S. H. Hooke, ed., *The Labyrinth: Further Studies in the Relation between Myth and Ritual in the Ancient World* (London: Society for Promoting Christian Knowledge, 1935), 71–111; Theodor H. Gaster, *Thespis: Ritual, Myth, and Drama in the Ancient Near East,* rev. ed. (Garden City, N.Y.: Doubleday, 1961), esp. 442–53; for a view that disputes the idea of an annual ritual reenthronement of God, see Hans Joachim Kraus, *The Theology of the Psalms,* trans. Keith Crim (Minneapolis: Augsburg, 1986), 86–91.

15. See Ps. 132:1–10; for connections between the Psalms and Israel's prose traditions of sacral kingship, see Baruch Halpern, *The Constitution of the Monarchy in Israel* (Chico: Scholars Press, 1981); Choon Leong Seow, *Myth, Drama and the Politics of David's Dance* (Atlanta: Scholars Press, 1989); and Joel Rosenberg, *King and Kin: Political Allegory in the Hebrew Bible* (Bloomington: Indiana University Press, 1986), 124.

16. On the idea of negotiated consent in ritualization, derived from Antonio Gramsci and Pierre Bourdieu, see Bell, 190–93.

17. Exod. 40:19, 20, 23, 27, 28, 32; on the septadic structure of the initial commandments to build the Tabernacle, see Peter J. Kearney, "Creation and Liturgy: The P Redaction of Exodus 25–30," *Zeitschrift für Alttestamentliche Wissenschaft* 89 (1977), 375–87.

18. Joseph Blenkinsopp, "The Structure of P," *Catholic Bible Quarterly* 38 (1976), 275–92, points out that a parallel phrase is used in Josh. 19:51 to indicate that the dividing up of the land among the Israelite tribes was the ultimate conclusion of the sacralizing process begun when the sanctuary was erected.

19. Compare Deut. 5:15 and Exod. 20:11.

20. Jon D. Levenson, *Creation and the Persistence of Evil: The Jewish Drama of Divine Omnipotence* (San Francisco: Harper and Row, 1988), 109–11.

21. See also 23:6, 26:8, 84:11.

22. Levenson (1988), 127.

23. Haran, 175–88.

24. See Leach (1976), 81–82.

25. Jon D. Levenson, *Sinai and Zion: An Entry into the Jewish Bible* (Minneapolis: Winston, 1985), 139.

26. Moses Hadas, ed., *Aristeas to Philocrates*, trans. Moses Hadas (New York: Harper, 1951), 139 (para. #99).

27. The role of sacred time and space in the consciousness of worshipers is taken up in chapter 4.

28. See Exod. 28–30, especially 30:17–21; Lev. 8–9; Num. 8.

29. These are described in I Kings 7:23–31. Note the references to prior washing in Pss. 26:6 and 73:3; Milgrom, 957–68, points out that washing preceded all sacrifices in Israel and the ancient Near East.

30. Leach (1976), 83.

31. This is the view of A. Marx, "Sacrifice Pour Les Péchés ou Rite de Passage? Quelques réflexions sur la fonction du *Hattat*," *Revue Biblique* 96 (1989), 27–48, who argues that one Israelite sacrifice in particular, the *hattat*, is a mechanism for the transitions that society needs: to reintegrate the sinner and the unclean, to mark a transition between sacred and secular states, or to rejuvenate the territory.

32. For comments on the symbolism of the Temple in antiquity, see Raphael Patai, *Man and Temple in Ancient Jewish Myth and Ritual* (London: Thomas Nelson, 1947), 105–32.

33. On the narrative dimension of the priestly writings, see David Damrosch, *The Narrative Covenant: Transformations of Genre in the Growth of Biblical Literature* (San Francisco: Harper and Row, 1987), 261–97.

34. Typically in religious ceremonies, only the right hand is considered fit to act on behalf of God; see Robert Hertz, "The Pre-eminence of the Right Hand: A Study in Religious Polarity" (1909), trans. Rodney Needham, in *Right and Left: Essays on Dual Symbolic Classification*, ed. Rodney Needham (Chicago: University of Chicago Press, 1973), 11–15.

35. Leach (1976), 91; on the idea of human beings as sacrifice, see Num. 8:10, where the people lay their hands on the Levites as they are being consecrated, just as they would on animals being offered to God.

36. On the decoration, see I Kings 6:35; Damrosch, 268–78, offers interesting (but different) commentary on the names and their relevance to episodes in patriarchal, Sinaitic, and monarchical history.

37. Max Weber, *The Sociology of Religion* (1922), trans. Ephraim Fischoff (Boston: Beacon, 1964).

38. For a view of these rites in the context of ancient Israelite magical beliefs, see Baruch A. Levine, *In the Presence of the Lord: A Study of Cult and Some Cultic Terms in Ancient Israel* (Leiden: Brill, 1974), 80–82.

39. *M. Yoma* 6:5.

40. Douglas Davies, "An Interpretation of Sacrifice in Leviticus," in Lang, ed., 157.

41. The noun *hattat*, usually translated as "sin offering," is derived from the *pi'el* form (intensifying conjugation) of the verb *hatta*, meaning "to cleanse" (Lev. 8:15); taking this into account, more recent translations call it a purification offering. See Baruch A. Levine, *Leviticus: The Traditional Hebrew Text with the New JPS Translation*, commentary by Baruch A. Levine (Philadelphia: Jewish Publication

Society, 1989), 18–19; and Milgrom, 253–54. Levine argues that the *ḥaṭṭat* blood purifies individuals of guilt and impurity, but Milgrom, 302, argues that individuals already had to be purified through confession and ablution before they could enter the sanctuary to bring sacrifice.

42. Davies, 158.

43. Henri Hubert and Marcel Mauss, *Sacrifice: Its Nature and Function* (1898), trans. W. D. Halls (Chicago: University of Chicago Press, 1964), 98–100.

44. For the general line of argument in this paragraph, see Hubert and Mauss, 102–103.

45. Rappaport, 231–34.

46. Arthur Waskow, *Seasons of Our Joy: A Handbook of Jewish Festivals* (New York: Bantam, 1982), xvii–xxiv, argues that there is also a solar pattern implicit in Israel's seasonal festivals.

47. See Marcel Mauss, *The Gift: Forms and Functions of Exchange in Archaic Societies*, trans. Ian Cunnison (New York: Norton, 1967); and Lewis Hyde, *The Gift: Imagination and the Erotic Life of Property* (New York: Random House, 1983), Part I.

48. Turner (1967), 52, notes that "the same symbol may be reckoned to have different senses at different phases in a ritual performance"; often these are organized around what he calls "sensory" and "ideational" poles (28).

49. Jack Goody, *The Logic of Writing and the Organization of Society* (Cambridge: Cambridge University Press, 1986), 13; Lev. 1:5 is ambiguous about exactly who does the slaughtering, offerer or priest.

50. 2 Kings 6:17; Jer. 37:3, 42:1–5.

51. See Aubrey R. Johnson, *The Cultic Prophet and Israel's Psalmody* (Cardiff: University of Wales Press, 1979). Wellhausen had tried to drive a wedge between priestly and prophetic religion in ancient Israel; the institution of cultic prophecy shows how closely the two could be aligned.

52. For an overview, see Greenberg (1977), 92–94.

53. See Exod. 28:6–30; I Sam. 23:9, 30:7.

54. See Lev. 10:10; Deut. 33:10; Jer. 2:8.

55. See Ezek. 44:24; II Chron. 19:8.

56. See Deut. 14:29, 16:14; I Chron. 23:5; Ezra 2:40–42.

57. Mowinckel, II, 58.

58. *M. Middot* 2:5; *M. Sukkah* 5:4 specifies that the Levites played there during the Rejoicing for the Water Libations, a dusk-to-dawn, torchlit celebration during the week-long autumn pilgrimage festival, Sukkot.

59. Hadas, ed., 137 (paras. #92–95).

60. Isa. 30:29; Pss. 150, 122:1, 118:27, 42:5, 68:26, 22:26, 35:18, 40:10; see Greenberg (1977), 89.

61. For more on this distinction, see chapter 3.

62. Blood and expiation are explicitly linked in these contexts: Lev. 1:4–5; 4:18–20, 25–26, 30–31, 34–35; 5:9–10; 6:23; 8:15; 9:7–8; 16:14, 17; 17:11. Blood serves to purge or decontaminate (*kapper*) an object in Lev. 8:15; 16:16, 18, 19, 27. Stephen A. Geller, "Blood Cult: Toward a Literary Theology of the Priestly Work in the Pentateuch," *Prooftexts: A Journal of Jewish Literary History* 12 (1992), 113, argues that P's substitution focuses a contrast between blood in the " 'old dispensation' of Noah," where it is a symbol of human sinfulness, and in the " 'new dispensation' of Sinai," where it is the means of atonement for sin.

63. Gorman, 123.

64. Mowinckel, II, 25.

65. Analyzed in chapter 1.

66. The Wisdom of Sirach 50:14–19; this same ritual order—sacrifice, libation, trumpet blasts, and song—is followed in the description of the daily rite in *M. Tamid* 7:3.

67. "Two Aspects of Language and Two Types of Aphasic Disturbances," in Roman Jakobson, *Selected Writings,* II (The Hague: Mouton, 1971), 239–59: by the first mode of arrangement, constituent linguistic signs are combined into longer utterances; by the second mode, we select within a given set of signs to give a message its internal coherence.

68. Metaphor is a figure of speech in which a name or descriptive term is transferred to some object to which it is not properly applicable. Jakobson (254) describes it as a mental operation based on selection and similarity. To compare one term to another, one selects from a set of possible alternatives. The compared term is both like and unlike the new term selected, but metaphor (including simile and analogy) emphasizes the similarity. To think about the abstraction, God, we need to think about God *as* something, a shepherd, or a mighty fortress. Metonymy is a figure of speech that substitutes for the name of a thing the name of an attribute of it; synecdoche, a related figure, substitutes a part for the whole. Jakobson ([1971], 254) describes metonymy as an operation of contexture. "The pen," we say, "is mightier than the sword," because pens are associated with the act of writing, swords with the act of warfare. "Pentagon" and "White House" are metonyms, substituting the name of the building for those who exercise authority in that building.

69. See Langer, 161.

70. Tambiah, 36–37, 53, distinguishes between the efficacy of the technical actions and the symbolic, self-communicative functions of the language; this position has been criticized as failing to take into account the performers' perception of the spells as efficacious by Benjamin Ray, " 'Performative Utterances' in African RItuals," *History of Religions* 13 (1973), 16–35.

71. Fernandez, 8.

72. For this distinction, see J. H. M. Beattie, "On Understanding Sacrifice," in *Sacrifice,* ed. M. F. C. Boudrillon and M. Fortes (London: Academic Press, 1980), 38. These general categories may be applied to the specific sacrifices enumerated in Leviticus: the communion type includes those offered for thanksgiving (*todah*), to fulfill vows (*neder*), out of free will (*nedabah*), and as a gift of greeting or well-being (*šelamim*); the separation type includes those offered for purification (*ḥattat*) and for guilt (*ašam*). Two of Israel's sacrifices, the burnt or ascent offering (*ʿolah*) and the gift of grain (*minḥah*), include aspects of both, depending on the circumstances in which they are offered.

73. See Kraus (1986), 93–95, for a different binary scheme that distinguishes two basic types, the shared offering (*zevah*), eaten by the worshipers and priests, and the gift (*minḥah*), wholly given over to God.

74. On postbiblical efforts at such reconciliation, see chapter 5.

75. Claude Lévi-Strauss, *Totemism,* trans. Rodney Needham (Boston: Beacon Press, 1966).

76. See Eilberg-Schwartz, 115–40.

77. Rappaport, 195.

78. On performance in the ritual, confessional, and ethical modes, see Tom F. Driver, *The Magic of Ritual: Our Need for Liberating Rites That Transform Our Lives and Our Communities* (San Francisco: Harper Collins, 1991), 79–127.

79. Driver, 113.

80. Moshe Greenberg, "On the Refinement of the Conception of Prayer in Hebrew Scriptures," *Association for Jewish Studies Review* 1 (1976), 77, notes that vv. 14 and 15 are reversed, in terms of the order of events in the process.

81. Other psalms commemorating celebratory offerings are 27:6, 54:8, 107:22, and 116:17–18.

82. Greenberg (1976), 77.

83. For an elaboration of this idea, see Susan Sontag, *AIDS and Its Metaphors* (New York: Farrar, Straus, Giroux, 1989).

84. Douglas (1966), and Mary Douglas, *Natural Symbols: Explorations in Cosmology* (New York: Pantheon, 1970).

85. Mary Douglas, *Implicit Meanings: Essays in Anthropology* (London: Routledge and Kegan Paul, 1975), 269.

86. Following Douglas, Eilberg-Schwartz, 141–94, shows the many homologies that exist between these sets of rules.

87. Haran, 9–12, hypothesizes that though composed during the time of Hezekiah, P was not disseminated until nearly three hundred years later, in the time of Ezra and Nehemiah, to a much wider audience than was originally intended.

88. Douglas (1966), 53.

89. Douglas (1975), 263–66, expands upon the version in (1966), 54–57; for a critique, see Michael P. Carroll, "One More Time: Leviticus Revisited," in Lang, ed., 117–26. See also Jean Soler, "The Dietary Prohibitions of the Hebrews," *The New York Review of Books* 26 (June 14, 1979), 24–30; and Robert Alter, "A New Theory of Kashrut," *Commentary* 68 (August 1979), 46–51, for a review of both Soler and Douglas.

90. Eilberg-Schwartz, 186–89, argues in addition that the uncontrollability of seminal and menstrual fluids makes them dangerous to the priestly mind and therefore contaminating, as opposed to the controllability of the body's waste products.

91. Lev. 22:18–25 and 21:17–23.

92. For an overview of the biblical concept, see Jacob Neusner, *The Idea of Purity in Ancient Judaism* (Leiden: Brill, 1973), 7–31, with critique and commentary by M. Douglas, 137–42.

93. The rabbis infer from the case of Miriam that ordinary leprosy can likewise be construed as punishment for sin; see, for example, *B. 'Arakin* 16b, cited by Rashi on Lev. 14:46.

94. Gorman, 162–63, 168–69, treats leprosy as a passage into the realm of death, and the ritual as a return; on the symbolism of boundaries in the ritual, see 175.

95. Gorman, 168.

96. It is a metaphor for God (Jer. 2:13, 17:13) and for the beloved (Song of Songs 4:15), and a metonym for the messianic days (Zech. 14:8).

97. Levine (1989), 87, suggests that the *ašam* is not offered to expiate guilt, but simply because it is the only one of the three sacrifices whose blood could be used in the anointing ritual; Milgrom, 856, justifies the *ašam* on the grounds of an Israelite association with scale disease as a punishment for *ma'al*, trespassing against the sanctuary, as is reported of Hezekiah in 2 Chron. 26:16–19.

98. Levine (1974), 83–84.

99. Turner (1969), 95.

100. E. R. Dodds, *The Greeks and the Irrational* (Berkeley: University of California Press, 1968), 28–63, argues for a transition in ancient Greece from "shame-culture to guilt-culture," that is, from socially dominated to internally motivated emotions; a similar development seems to be evident in the literature of the Bible.

101. Milgrom, 776, points out that P uses *nega'* exclusively for *sara'at;* in Psalms, it is used in a more general sense, for which see 38:12; 39:11; 73:5, 14; 89:33; and 91:10.

102. Other translations give this line to the worshiper, but to do so they must amend v. 9, where the Levitical speaker, clearly in his own voice, says to the worshiper, "because you took YHWH, my refuge, as your haven." Other translations emend this line to remove the speaker's first-person references: "Because you have made the Lord your refuge / the Most High your habitation" (RSV, v. 9).

103. The verb *yitlonan* may suggest an overnight stay.

104. Psalmic images of *seter* will be a major focus of chapter 4.

105. Fernandez, 50.

106. Bell, 141, 208.

107. Rashi on v. 6; André Caquot, "Sur quelques démons de l'Ancien Testament: Reshep, Qeteb, Deber," *Semitica* 6 (1956), 53–68.

108. Fernandez, 62.

109. Kraus (1986), 103.

110. Epilogue to *The Tempest,* lines 9–10, 18–20.

111. Since boundaries are central to its identity as a people set apart by and for God, Judaism has never abandoned all such rules, though the general tendency of the liberal branches of Judaism has been in that direction.

112. I am indebted to the description of Israelite pilgrimage in Hans-Joachim Kraus, *Worship in Israel: A Cultic History of the Old Testament,* trans. Geoffrey Buswell (Richmond: John Knox Press, 1965), 208–18.

113. Turner (1974), 207.

114. Turner (1974), 203.

115. Turner (1974), 197.

116. *M. Middot* 2:5 indicates that the fifteen songs of ascent correspond to the fifteen steps between the courts of the Women and of the Levites; this suggests that they might have been sung as a literal ascent up steps, though an exterior setting seems equally plausible.

117. Turner (1969), 165.

118. *b-k-'* and *b-k-h;* see Rashi on v. 7.

119. On the elaboration of this ritual utterance as part of the "sacred myth" of the Passover Seder, see Lawrence A. Hoffman, *Beyond the Text: A Holistic Approach to Liturgy* (Bloomington: Indiana University Press, 1987), 79–102.

120. Mitchell Dahood, *Psalms: A New Translation with Introduction and Commentary,* Anchor Bible, 3 vols. (Garden City, N.Y.: Doubleday, 1965–70), III, 217, places even this imperative in the past tense.

121. On imperatives, see chapter 3.

3. An Audience with the King

1. Nina Perlina, "Mikhail Bakhtin and Martin Buber: Problems of Dialogic Imagination," *Studies in Twentieth Century Literature* 9 (1984), 13–28.

2. Mikhail Bakhtin, *Estetika slovesnogo tvorchestva* [The Aesthetics of Verbal Art] (Moscow: Iskusstvo, 1979), 326, translated in Perlina, p. 25.

3. Martin Buber, *The Knowledge of Man: A Philosophy of the Interhuman*, ed. Maurice Friedman, trans. Maurice Friedman and Ronald Gregor Smith (New York: Harper and Row, 1965), 112.

4. Bakhtin, *Problems of Dostoevsky's Poetics*, ed. and trans. Caryl Emerson (Minneapolis: University of Minnesota Press, 1984), 40.

5. Buber, *I and Thou* (1923), 2nd ed., trans. Ronald Gregor Smith (New York: Scribner's, 1958), 18.

6. Buber (1958), 15.

7. Buber (1958), 11.

8. Buber (1965), 115.

9. Anthony Ugolnik, "Tradition as Freedom from the Past: Contemporary Eastern Orthodoxy and Ecumenism," Institute for Ecumenical and Cultural Research, Occasional Papers, no. 17 (November 1982), 6. Because of the period of Soviet history through which he lived, Bakhtin's writings do not address Christianity directly; our knowledge of his religious convictions rests on the testimony of those who knew him.

10. Michael Holquist, *Dialogism: Bakhtin and His World* (London: Routledge, 1990), 30.

11. Buber (1965), 112.

12. Bakhtin (1979), 293, trans. by and quoted in Gary Saul Morson and Caryl Emerson, *Mikhail Bakhtin: Creation of a Prosaics* (Stanford: Stanford University Press, 1990), 59–60.

13. Katerina Clark and Michael Holquist, *Mikhail Bakhtin* (Cambridge: Harvard University Press, 1984), 12.

14. See the useful summaries in Holquist, 27–29, and Morson and Emerson, 49–50.

15. Holquist, 38.

16. See his "Crossing Brooklyn Ferry."

17. Buber (1958), 4.

18. Buber (1958), 6.

19. Franz Rosenzweig, *The Star of Redemption*, trans. William W. Hallo (Notre Dame: University of Notre Dame Press, 1971), 175.

20. See Fishbane (1979), 88, and my discussion above in chapter 1.

21. Rosenzweig, 174–75.

22. Buber (1958), 83.

23. André Néher, *The Exile of the Word: From the Silence of the Bible to the Silence of Auschwitz*, trans. David Maisel (Philadelphia: Jewish Publication Society, 1981), 48.

24. Walter J. Ong, *Orality and Literacy: The Technologizing of the Word* (London: Methuen, 1982), 73.

25. Walter J. Ong, *The Presence of the Word: Some Prolegomena for Cultural and Religious History* (New Haven: Yale University Press, 1967), 114.

26. Ong (1967), 130.

27. Compare Ong (1967), 189, with Goody, 39–41.

28. On interpretive elites, see Goody, 11–12, 15–16, 27.

29. Ong (1967), 189.

30. This paragraph draws on Ong (1982), 36–77.

31. On this last point, see Roland Barthes, *The Pleasure of the Text*, trans. Richard Miller (New York: Hill and Wang, 1975).

32. Albert B. Lord, *The Singer of Tales* (New York: Atheneum, 1973).

33. On the fixed-pair hypothesis and orality, see Robert C. Culley, *Oral Formulaic Language in the Biblical Psalms* (Toronto: University of Toronto Press, 1967); the hypothesis has been challenged by Adele Berlin, *The Dynamics of Biblical Parallelism* (Bloomington: Indiana University Press, 1985), 67–80, who cites psycholinguistic studies to show that fixed pairs are normally recurring word associations in everyday speech, not necessarily part of a special guild's vocabulary; on the deliberate manipulation of such formulae, see E. Z. Melamed, "Breakup of Stereotype Phrases as an Artistic Device in Biblical Poetry," *Scripta Hierosolymitana* 8 (1961), 115–53.

34. Ps. 102:18–22 asks that the spoken psalm be written as testimony for future generations; see similarly Jer. 36:1–8 on the writing and reading of a prophecy already delivered orally. An exception to this pattern may be noted in the royal marriage hymn recorded as Ps. 45, in which the courtly speaker says, "my tongue is the pen of an expert scribe" (v. 2).

35. As cited by Ziony Zevit, "A Psycholinguistic Experiment and Its Implications for Understanding the Structure of Biblical Poetry," paper delivered at Association for Jewish Studies, Boston, December 1991.

36. James L. Kugel, *The Idea of Biblical Poetry: Parallelism and Its History* (New Haven: Yale University Press, 1981), 23. Kugel's work is a polemic against the traditional taxonomy developed by Bishop Robert Lowth in *Lectures on the Sacred Poetry of the Hebrews* (1787; Lat. 1753), who argued for three distinct types of parallelism: synonymous, antithetic, and synthetic.

37. Robert Alter, *The Art of Biblical Poetry* (New York: Basic Books, 1985), 19.

38. For an overview, see James J. Fox, "Roman Jakobson and the Comparative Study of Parallelism," in *Roman Jakobson: Echoes of His Scholarship*, ed. D. Armstrong and C. Van Schooneveld (Lisse: Peter de Redder, 1977), 59–90; for use of all these categories in the analysis of biblical parallelism, see Berlin.

39. It has been a hallmark of twentieth-century literary criticism that there is no such thing as true synonymy; see Victor Shklovsky, "Art as Technique," in *Russian Formalist Criticism*, ed. L. T. Lemon and M. J. Reis (Lincoln: University of Nebraska Press, 1965): "the purpose of parallelism is . . . to make a unique semantic modification" (21).

40. The tent may also have been factual; for the view that the wilderness Tabernacle was re-erected in the Temple, see chapter 4.

41. See Pss. 100:5; 106:1; 107:1, 8, 15, 21, 31; 135:3; 136:1, and as a refrain for each half-line; see its use as a communal refrain in Ezra 3:11.

42. Used as a refrain between lines of Ps. 145; see James A. Sanders, ed., *The Dead Sea Psalms Scroll* (Ithaca: Cornell University Press, 1967), 16.

43. Kugel (1981), 85.

44. Gary H. Gossen, "To Speak with a Heated Heart: Chanula Canons of Style and Good Performance," in Richard Bauman and Joel Sherzer, eds., *Explorations in the Ethnography of Speaking* (Cambridge: Cambridge University Press, 1974), 389–413.

45. Everett Fox, *Genesis and Exodus: A New English Rendition* (New York: Schocken, 1990), 106.

46. Moshe Greenberg, *Biblical Prose Prayer Viewed as a Window on the Popular Religion of Ancient Israel* (Berkeley: University of California Press, 1983), 45.

47. Mikhail M. Bakhtin, *Speech Genres and Other Late Essays,* ed. Caryl Emerson and Michael Holquist, trans. Vern W. McGee (Austin: University of Texas Press, 1986), 94.

48. See Claus Westermann, *Praise and Lament in the Psalms,* trans. Keith R. Crim and Richard N. Soulen (Atlanta: John Knox Press, 1981), 64.

49. Greenberg (1983), 10–11.

50. Greenberg (1976), 88.

51. Bakhtin (1986), 97.

52. Buber (1958), 75.

53. See Jeffrey H. Tigay, "On Some Aspects of Prayer in the Bible," *Association for Jewish Studies Review* 1 (1976), 365.

54. See Searle (1979), 1–29; for an excellent summary, see Mary Louise Pratt, *Toward a Speech Act Theory of Literary Discourse* (Bloomington: Indiana University Press, 1977), 79–87.

55. On this aspect of performatives, see Pierre Bourdieu, *Language and Symbolic Power,* ed. John B. Thompson, trans. Gino Raymond and Matthew Adamson (Cambridge: Harvard University Press, 1991), 107–16.

56. Searle (1979), 29.

57. Austin, 108.

58. My choice is influenced by the discussion of Emily M. Ahern, "The Problem of Efficacy: Strong and Weak Illocutionary Acts," *Man* n.s. 14 (1979), 1–18.

59. See Michael Hancher, "Performative Utterance, the Word of God, and the Death of the Author," *Semeia* 41 (1988), 27–40; and Anthony C. Thistleton, "The Supposed Power of Words in the Biblical Writings," *Journal of Theological Studies* n.s. 25 (1974), 283–99.

60. This translation would accord with the view of Milgrom that "confession in P must be verbalized because it is the act that counts, not just its intention. Confession in thought (*balleb*) would therefore be inadequate" (301).

61. Austin, 57.

62. Rosenzweig, 180–81.

63. See, for instance, Pss. 42:8; 69:2–3, 15; 88:18.

64. On psalmic spatializing of emotional images, see chapter 4.

65. Gabriel Josipovici, *The Book of God: A Response to the Bible* (New Haven: Yale University Press, 1988), 162.

66. Searle (1979), 3–4, distinguishes between performatives whose words attempt to match the world (assertives) and those which ask the world (here, the self) to match the words spoken (promises and requests).

67. Sheldon Blank, "Some Observations concerning Biblical Prayer," *Hebrew Union College Annual* 32 (1961), 90; see also Greenberg (1983), 34–36.

68. On the imperative of love, see Rosenzweig, 177–78.

69. Richard Bauman, "Verbal Art as Performance," *American Anthropologist* 77 (1975), 293, cites this self-referentiality as a distinctive feature of performed language.

70. Barbara Herrnstein Smith, *On the Margins of Discourse: The Relation of Literature to Language* (Chicago: University of Chicago Press, 1978), 15.

71. Emile Benveniste, *Problems in General Linguistics,* trans. Mary Elizabeth Meek (Coral Gables: University of Miami Press, 1971), 218.

72. Smith (1978), 116.

73. Harold Fisch, *Poetry with a Purpose: Biblical Poetics and Interpretation* (Bloomington: Indiana University Press, 1988), 118.

74. See Brevard S. Childs, "Psalm Titles and Midrashic Exegesis," *Journal of Semitic Studies* 16 (1971), 137–50.

75. James Kugel, "Topics in the History of the Spirituality of the Psalms," in *Jewish Spirituality: From the Bible through the Middle Ages,* ed. Arthur Green (New York: Crossroad, 1988), 136, argues that the Psalms attained these Davidic headings at a point when Israelites felt the need to write new prayers and consign the psalms to the realm of Scripture, which, like other books of the Bible, had known historical authors.

76. Terence Collins, "Decoding the Psalms: A Structural Approach to the Psalter," *Journal for the Study of the Old Testament* 37 (1987), 56.

77. Collins, 43–44.

78. My argument follows Collins, 47–49; see also Craig C. Broyles, *The Conflict of Faith and Experience in the Psalms* (Sheffield: JSOT Press, 1989).

79. Rappaport, 209.

80. On the Aristotelian view, see Stephen Halliwell, *Aristotle's Poetics* (Chapel Hill: University of North Carolina Press, 1986), 168–202.

81. On the incommensurability of Job and Greek tragedy, see Baruch Kurzweil, "Job and the Possibility of Biblical Tragedy," in *Arguments and Doctrines: A Reader of Jewish Thinking in the Aftermath of the Holocaust,* ed. Arthur A. Cohen (New York: Harper and Row, 1970), 325–44; and Fisch (1988), 26–42.

82. See chapter 2.

83. See Maurice Bloch, "Symbols, Song, Dance and Features of Articulation: Is Religion an Extreme Form of Traditional Authority?" *Archives Européènes de Sociologie* 15 (1974), 55–81.

84. Bell, 191.

85. Bell, 190. Bell draws on the views of Pierre Bourdieu, "Symbolic Power," trans. Colin Wringe, in *Identity and Structure: Issues in the Sociology of Education,* ed. Denis Gleeson (Driffield: Nafferton Books, 1977), 112–19; Antonio Gramsci, *The Modern Prince and Other Writings,* trans. Louis Marks (New York: International Publishers, 1957); and Fredric Jameson, *The Political Unconscious* (Ithaca: Cornell University Press, 1981), 83–84.

86. Rappaport, 194.

87. Driver, 156.

88. Mikhail M. Bakhtin, *The Dialogic Imagination: Four Essays,* ed. Michael Holquist, trans. Caryl Emerson and Michael Holquist (Austin: University of Texas Press, 1981), 342–45.

89. Bakhtin (1981), 342–43.

90. Bakhtin (1981), 341.

91. Robert Gordis, "Quotations as a Literary Usage in Biblical, Rabbinic, and Oriental Literature," *Hebrew Union College Annual* 22 (1949), 157–220, cites numerous examples of quoted indirect discourse not marked by quotations in the JPS translation.

92. Bakhtin (1981), 285.

93. Bakhtin (1986), 96.

94. See Johnson (1979), and the discussion in chapter 2.

95. Bakhtin (1981), 343.

96. An alternative interpretation is possible; we could be hearing here a duet, one voice describing God, and the other echoing in God's own words.

97. Bakhtin (1981), 343.

98. Bakhtin (1981), 342. This comment bears a striking resemblance to Harold Bloom's theory of strong poetry originating in Oedipal struggle; see his *The Anxiety of Influence* (New York: Oxford University Press, 1973).

99. Pss. 50, 75, 81, 91, 95, 132.

100. On a similar blurring of boundaries where Moses dialogizes and internalizes the monologic, authoritative word of God, see Robert Polzin, "Dialogic Imagination in the Book of Deuteronomy," *Studies in Twentieth-Century Literature* 9 (1984), 135–43.

101. The imperative "return" is a fundamental prophetic word, found in the major prophets, Isaiah, Jeremiah, and Ezekiel, as well as in the minor prophets, Hosea, Joel, Zechariah, and Malachi.

102. For Alter (1985), 127, this human echoing of the divine reflects "the chastened self-knowledge of the poetic discourse."

103. See E. T. Mullen, Jr., *The Assembly of the Gods: The Divine Council in Canaanite and Early Hebrew Literature* (Chico: Scholars Press, 1980).

104. Matitiahu Tsevat, "God and the Gods in Assembly: An Interpretation of Psalm 82," in *The Meaning of the Book of Job and Other Biblical Studies* (New York: Ktav, 1980), 137, argues convincingly that v. 5 should be regarded as an aside by God, spoken *in camera* before pronouncing final judgment; if this verse were taken as an interruption by the narrator, it would greatly diminish the ironic force of the apostrophic conclusion.

105. For a wide range of examples, including many from Psalms, see Berend Gemser, "The *rib-* or Controversy Pattern in Hebrew Mentality," in *Wisdom in Israel and the Ancient Near East,* ed. Martin Noth and D. Winton Thomas, *Vetus Testamentum* Supplement 3 (Leiden: Brill, 1955), 120–37.

106. Bakhtin (1981), 345.

107. Quoted in Néher, 48.

108. Bakhtin (1986), 150.

109. The wicked speak as enemies of the psalmist in Pss. 3, 11, 13, 22, 35, 40, 41, 42, 70, 71, and as enemies of God in 10, 12, 14 = 53, 64, 73, 94; allied to these is the self-reliant individual quoted in 49. As enemies of Israel and Israel's God, they are quoted in 59, 74, 79, 83, 115, and 137.

110. Jean Starobinski, "The Inside and the Outside," *Hudson Review* 28 (1975), 336.

111. Pss. 10:6, 11:13, 14:1 = 53:2, 35:25, 74:8.

112. Hans Walter Wolf, "Das Zität im Prophetenspruch," in *Gesammelte Studien zum Alten Testament* (Munich: Kaiser, 1964), 73.

113. Othmar Keel, *Feinde und Gottesleugner: Studien zum Image der Widersacher in den Individualpsalmen* (Stuttgart: Katholisches Bibelwerk, 1969), 179–90.

114. Bakhtin (1981), 347.

115. Bakhtin (1981), 345–46.

116. See the parallel in Ps. 35, where the language of the wicked's "Aha, aha, we have seen it!" (v. 21) becomes part of the psalmist's language challenging God, "You have seen it, YHWH; / do not hold aloof!" (v. 22).

117. Bakhtin (1981), 347.

118. Artur Weiser, *The Psalms: A Commentary,* Old Testament Library (Philadelphia: Westminster Press, 1962), 148.

119. Dahood, I, 61.

120. Bell, 208.

121. Bakhtin (1981), 348.

122. Michel Foucault, "The Subject and the Power," in *Michel Foucault: Beyond Structuralism and Hermeneutics,* 2nd ed., ed. Hubert L. Dreyfus and Paul Rabinow (Chicago: University of Chicago Press, 1983), 225.

123. Bakhtin (1981), 345.

124. For more on this interpretation of v. 27, see my discussion of Buber's reading in chapter 5.

125. Bakhtin (1981), 341.

126. My translation.

127. Other psalms of this type include 31, 40, and 41.

128. The phrase is bivalent, depending on who speaks it and in what conditions of faith or faithlessness; see the opposite sense in Psalms 16:8 and 62:3.

129. On this point, see the discussion of Ps. 139 in chapter 4.

130. Buber (1965), 112.

131. Buber (1958), 115.

132. Buber (1958), 45.

133. Martin Buber, *Between Man and Man,* trans. Ronald Gregor Smith (London: Routledge and Kegan Paul, 1947), 31.

134. Buber (1947), 176.

135. Rosenzweig, 250–53.

136. Rosenzweig, 252.

137. Rosenzweig, 252.

138. Rosenzweig, 253.

139. Rosenzweig, 253.

140. Rosenzweig, 251.

4. From Here to Eternity

1. Fragment #20–21 in *The Presocratics,* ed. Philip Wheelwright (New York: Odyssey, 1966), 70–71.

2. Kraus (1986), 77.

3. Eliade (1957), 68–69.

4. Eliade (1957), 21.

5. Eliade (1954), 34–35.

6. Eliade (1954), 91.

7. Cf. Isa. 11:1–10, 51:3; on the Edenic waters of life, Ezek. 47:1–12; Joel 4:18; Zech. 14:8. The most explicit connection between Zion and creation is found in *Midrash Tanḥuma* on *Qodošim* (10): "Just as the navel is found at the center of a human being, so the Land of Israel is found at the center of the world . . . and it is the foundation of the world. Jerusalem is at the center of the Land of Israel. The Temple is at the center of Jerusalem, the Holy of Holies is at the center of the Temple. The ark is at the center of the Holy of Holies, and the Foundation Stone is in front of the ark, which spot is the foundation of the world." In Arthur Hertzberg, ed., *Judaism* (New York: Braziller, 1962), 150.

8. See, for instance, Jer. 4:23; Ezek. 38–39; and see below my discussion of Isa. 65:17–25.

9. Eliade (1954), 86.

10. Eliade (1954), 118.

11. See, on the new exodus, Isa. 10:26, 43:16; Zech. 10:10; on the wilderness miracles revisited, Mic. 7:15, Isa. 43:19; on the new covenant, Jer. 31:31–35; and on the renewed Davidic kingdom, Hos. 3:5, Jer. 30:9, and Ezek. 34:23.

12. On changing conceptions of Sheol, see R. H. Charles, *Eschatology, the Doctrine of a Future Life in Israel, Judaism and Christianity: A Critical History* (1899; rpt. New York: Schocken, 1963); and Colleen McDannell and Bernhard Lang, *Heaven: A History* (New Haven: Yale University Press, 1988).

13. Martin Buber, *Good and Evil: Two Interpretations* (New York: Scribner's, 1953), 46.

14. Metaphoric uses of this root will be treated in detail below.

15. Out of eighteen uses of this word in Psalms, only two are absolutely positive (16:11; 68:17), while two others are used in the context of double negatives (9:19; 103:9); Ps. 74, a bleak communal lament, has the most instances.

16. James Barr, *Biblical Words for Time* (London: SCM Press, 1962), 86, discounts the view of Conrad von Orelli, in *Die Hebraischen Synonyma der Zeit und Ewigkeit Genetisch und Sprachvegleichend dargestellt* (Leipzig, 1871), 98, that 'olam is "the time, the limits of which are not perceptible or not existent" (i.e., hidden), 'ad is "the time which carries on to the uttermost thinkable limits," and neṣah is "the time which transcends all limits."

17. See, for each category listed, one among many possible psalms: 104:31, 117:2, 119:142, 33:11, 119:89, 146:10, 105:10, 110:4, 106:31, 125:1.

18. See Pss. 52:10, 115:18, 30:13, 52:11, 79:13, 86:12, 5:12, 75:10, 119:44.

19. This is the view of Henri Bergson, *Time and Free Will* (New York: Macmillan, 1910).

20. See the superscript in the Septuagint and the designation in *M. Tamid* 7:4.

21. Pss. 89:10–11 and 104:6–8.

22. Pss. 77:20 and 114:3, 5.

23. My reading of the dialogue between temporal perspectives in this psalm is indebted to Alter (1985), 127–29.

24. Alter (1985), 128.

25. Holquist, 20.

26. Brevard S. Childs, *The Book of Exodus: A Critical, Theological Commentary,* Old Testament Library (Philadelphia: Westminster, 1974), 207–14, describes the exegesis of Passover in early Judaism and Christianity as a dialectic between memory and hope, a tension which pertains equally to the circumstances of Israel in its Babylonian exile.

27. See, for example, Pss. 78, 105, and 106.

28. For the miraculous crossings, see Exod. 14 and Josh. 3; on water from the rock, see Exod. 17:1–7 and Num. 20:2–11.

29. See Exod. 19:18: "and the whole mountain trembled violently."

30. For a summary of these and other readings of the psalm, see Brevard S. Childs, *Memory and Tradition in Israel* (London: SCM Press, 1962), 61–63.

31. For raised hands as a gesture of prayer, see Ps. 134:2.

32. My translation; JPS emends the text of v. 7 to read "I recall . . . their jibes at me," presumably based on the plural *neginatam* in Job 30:9 and Lam. 3:14. I find no contextual justification for this reading.

33. Weiser (529) translates as "The illness from which I suffer is this / that the right hand . . ."; RSV translates as "It is my grief that . . ."

34. Childs (1962), 63.

35. Compare the pastoral imagery in Pss. 23, 95, and 100.

36. See the parallel imagery in Exod. 15:6, 16.

37. See Rashi on v. 3.

38. See Psalms 66, 78, 105, 106, 135, 136, and the parallel pattern in Exod. 15. Psalm 81, like 77, is an exception to this rule.

39. *M. Pesahim* 10:4; on the Haggadah as a postdestruction rabbinic innovation, see Baruch M. Bokser, *The Origins of the Seder: The Passover Rite and Early Rabbinic Judaism* (Berkeley: University of California Press, 1984).

40. On this topic, see Mowinckel, I, 225–46, though he is dealing with a different group of psalms.

41. None of the five has Ezra's phrase "for Israel" in the refrain.

42. Alternatively, Childs (1971), 137–51, suggests that psalm headings reflect the midrashic activity of late postexilic exegetes, who sought to relate the words and events of Scripture to the spiritual life of the community; the heading might therefore reflect the rededication of the Temple after the Maccabean revolt in 164 B.C.E. This would be in keeping with the tradition of reciting Ps. 30 on Hannukah, for which see *Masseket Soferim* 18:3 in A. Cohen, ed., *The Talmud: Minor Tractates*, trans. A. Cohen (London: Soncino, 1984). Sarna (1993), 150, cites the mishnaic testimony (*M. Bikkurim* 3:4) that associated the psalm with Shavuot, another occasion of communal thanksgiving.

43. James Barr, *The Semantics of Biblical Language* (Glasgow: Oxford University Press, 1961), 80, claims that the aspect system of Hebrew verbs clarifies "orientation in past, present, or future time; continuous or repeated action; commencement of action, or attempted action; action momentary or durative; action complete or incomplete."

44. At least one reader of the psalm sees the whole psalm happening in the present of this imperative, with neither memory nor thanksgiving indicated; in this view, the perfect forms of the verb are "precative," for the purposes of entreaty; see Buttenwieser, 574–78.

45. Gunkel (1967), 18.

46. For use of the Hallel psalms in Temple worship, see *M. Pesahim* 5:7, 9:3, 10:6, 7; *M. Sukkah* 3:9, 4:1, 8; *M. Rosh Hashanah* 4:7; *M. Ta'anit* 4:4, 5; *M. Megillah* 2:5.

47. Rosenzweig, 186.

48. J. Hillis Miller, *The Linguistic Moment from Wordsworth to Stevens* (Princeton: Princeton University Press, 1985), xvi.

49. Friedrich Kummel, "Time as Succession and the Problem of Duration," in J. T. Fraser, ed., *The Voices of Time* (New York: Braziller, 1966), 53.

50. Driver, 190.

51. Buber (1958), 113–15.

52. See Bell, 125.

53. In addition to the already cited work by Levenson (1985), see Michael A. Fishbane, "The Sacred Center: The Symbolic Structure of the Bible," in *Texts and Responses: Studies Presented to Nahum N. Glatzer on the Occasion of His Seventieth Birthday by His Students,* ed. Michael A. Fishbane and Paul R. Flohr (Leiden: Brill, 1975), 6–27; and Robert L. Cohn, *The Shape of Sacred Space: Four Biblical Studies* (Chico: Scholars Press, 1981), 62–79.

54. See chapter 2.

55. See Ps. 119:45, 96.

56. On the liminality of the desert period in Israelite history and myth, see Cohn, 6–23.

57. Culley, 103, takes this psalm to be 40% formulaic; the estimate should be even higher when taking into account several more formulaic elements that I discuss below.

58. The JPS translation of v. 2 , "may I never be disappointed," could just as appropriately be translated as "let me not be ashamed forever"; cf. also v. 18.

59. See Ernst Jenni and Claus Westermann, eds., *Theologisches Handwörterbuch zum Alten Testament* (Munich: Kaiser, 1971), 174.

60. See I Kings 20:12, 16, and Jon. 4:5.

61. See Num. 9:15–17.

62. Samuel E. Balentine, *The Hidden God: The Hiding of God's Face in the Old Testament* (New York: Oxford University Press, 1983).

63. Balentine, 165.

64. See Walter Brueggemann, *The Message of the Psalms: A Theological Commentary* (Minneapolis: Augsburg, 1984).

65. Richard E. Friedman, *The Exile and Biblical Narrative: The Formation of the Deuteronomistic and Priestly Works* (Chico: Scholars Press, 1981), 52–53; Othmar Keel, *The Symbolism of the Biblical World: Ancient Near Eastern Iconography and the Book of Psalms*, trans. Timothy J. Hallett (New York: Seabury, 1978), 162–63.

66. Culley, 11–14, distinguishes in oral composition between *formulae,* which repeat the same roots and syntax without variation, and *formulaic systems,* which use the same roots but with slight variations among the syntactic patterns, affording more freedom to the poet. Formulae and formulaic systems establish repeated connections between words and concepts, so that they come to seem as inevitable to the listeners as they are to the poet. Their repetitive nature helps establish such associations as traditional ways of viewing their subject. For a full discussion of a formulaic system among the roots *s-t-r, s-p-n,* and *s-k-k* in Pss. 27, 31, and 10, see my article "The Symbolic *Sukkah* in Psalms," *Prooftexts: A Journal of Jewish Literary History* 7 (1987), 259–67.

67. Rashi claims the Temple, and Ibn Ezra Jerusalem to be the place implied by the *sukkah/'ohel* of 27:5; see Keel (1978), 179–83, for *sur* as an epithet for God in the Temple.

68. See, for instance, Weiser, 244–55, who treats them totally independently.

69. See also Pss. 13:2, 22:25, 30:8, 44:25, 69:18, 88:15, 102:3, 104:29, and 143:7.

70. For a view of the unity of the psalm that overlooks the pivotal role of *s-t-r,* see Hans-Joachim Kraus, *Psalms 1–59: A Commentary,* trans. Hilton C. Oswald (Minneapolis: Augsburg, 1988), 330–37.

71. The contrasting paths are evoked in Pss. 1, 5:9–10, 35:6, 107:17, 146:9.

72. For this usage, see Pss. 45:7 and 67:5.

73. See Gaston Bachelard, *The Poetics of Space,* trans. Maria Jolas (Boston: Beacon, 1969), 29–32, for comments on the symbolism of the primitive hut.

74. Harold Fisch, *A Remembered Future: A Study in Literary Mythology* (Bloomington: Indiana University Press, 1984), 134, claims the same duality for the *sukkah* in Jon. 4:5, where it "symbolizes extreme vulnerability but also miraculous protection."

75. My argument at this point suggests a dependence of Ps. 10 on already formulated material; Balentine, 54–55, argues similarly in showing that Ps. 10 may be a point-by-point inversion of the themes of praise in Ps. 9, which scholars often combine with Ps. 10 in a single acrostic scheme.

76. For an analysis of how quoting another's word functions in this passage, see chapter 3.

77. See the discussion of Ps. 73 in chapter 3.
78. See Levenson (1985), 121.
79. See Levenson (1985), 138–39.
80. See Bell, 207.
81. On liminality as such a breakthrough, see Turnbull, 80.
82. Bakhtin (1986), 7.

5. Through the Valley of the Shadow of Death and Beyond

1. Arthur A. Cohen, *The Tremendum: A Theological Interpretation of the Holocaust* (New York: Crossroad, 1981), 54.
2. Readers interested in Christian theological responses to the Holocaust should consult A. Roy Eckardt, *Elder and Younger Brothers: The Encounter of Jews and Christians* (New York: Scribner's, 1967); Franklin H. Littell, *The Crucifixion of the Jews* (New York: Harper and Row, 1975); Michael B. McGarry, *Christology after Auschwitz* (New York: Paulist Press, 1977); and the essays by G. Baum and J. Pawlikowski in *Auschwitz—Beginning of a New Era? Reflections on the Holocaust,* ed. Eva Fleischner (New York: Ktav, 1977).
3. Arthur A. Cohen (1981), 24.
4. Richard Rubenstein, *After Auschwitz: Radical Theology and Contemporary Judaism* (Indianapolis: Bobbs Merrill, 1966), 152.
5. Eliezer Berkovits, *Faith after the Holocaust* (New York: Ktav, 1973), 99.
6. See Elisabeth Kübler-Ross, *On Death and Dying* (New York: Macmillan, 1969).
7. See also Lam. 4:14–15.
8. See also vv. 18, 22, where this emphasis is repeated.
9. Gen. 28:20–22.
10. Ps. 74 offers a similar contrast in v. 19: "Do not deliver Your dove to the wild beast"; Northrop Frye, *The Great Code: The Bible and Literature* (New York: Harcourt, Brace, Jovanovich, 1982), 166–67, characterizes such pairs of images as apocalyptic and demonic.
11. See the discussions of Pss. 27 and 30 in chapter 4.
12. See the discussions of Ps. 91 in chapter 2, Ps. 32 in chapter 3, and Pss. 27 and 31 in chapter 4.
13. See Isa. 54:8, Jer. 33:5–6, Ezek. 39:29.
14. Néher, 52–53, contrasts prophetic and psalmic approaches to the hidden God.
15. See Yosef Haim Yerushalmi, *Zakhor: Jewish History and Jewish Memory* (Seattle: University of Washington Press, 1982), 15.
16. Though it is not much observed, the psalm is designated for daily recitation before the grace after meals.
17. See, for instance, C. S. Lewis, *Reflections on the Psalms* (London: Geoffrey Bles, 1958), 20–21, and 136, where he attempts to "save" the psalm by allegorizing its curse.
18. In postbiblical Jewish literature, Edom signified first Rome, and later Christianity; with these mental substitutions, the psalm could continue to be an outlet for Jewish rage.

19. Though this psalm exemplifies a typical function of psalmody, I do not mean to imply that it necessarily dates from the First Temple period.

20. See also Exod. 17:8–15 and I Sam. 15.

21. See Martin Buber, *On the Bible: Eighteen Studies* (New York: Schocken, 1968), 195–96.

22. The Septuagint adds that he lived 240 years in all, 70 before the tragedy and 170 after; Marvin H. Pope, *Job,* The Anchor Bible (New York: Doubleday, 1973), 353, hypothesizes that the 140 of the Masoretic Text represents two life spans, one before and one after the death of his children; whether we count the 140 as the span of his whole life or just the postcatastrophe portion, it is clear that he is represented as living into a new era.

23. From "Gerontion."

24. Martin Buber, *At the Turning: Three Addresses on Judaism* (New York: Farrar, Straus and Young, 1952), 61.

25. *M. Tamid* 7:4 cites Pss. 24, 48, 82, 94, 81, 93, and 92.

26. See *B. Rosh Hashanah* 31a.

27. See Rashi on *B. Sukkah* 55a; on the similar commentaries of H. Graetz and I. Maarsen, see Yehuda Aryeh Liebreich, "Mizmorei ha lewiim le yemei ha šabu ʿa," *Eretz-Israel* 3 (1954), 170, nn. 5–6.

28. Liebreich, 170–73, noting the many verbal parallels, makes an argument very similar to mine, though with far less emphasis on the dimension of ideological struggle in the sequence.

29. I am indebted to Sarna (1993), 131, for his noting that the gates open upward.

30. On the historicity of these images, see Sarna (1993), 158–63.

31. See the discussion in chapter 3.

32. See Ps. 92:7.

33. See Exod. 20:2.

34. On hearing God's revelatory voice, see Exod. 19:7 and Deut. 5:20–24.

35. For the incident, see Exod. 17:1–7 and Num. 20:2–13; as an emblematic name, see Deut. 33:8 and Pss. 95:8 and 106:32.

36. These images echo Deut. 33:13.

37. In the Septuagint, five of the seven mention the day on which they were recited; Pss. 81 and 82 are missing this superscript.

38. On the relation between psalmody and Sabbath themes in Second Temple Judaism, see Moshe Weinfeld, "Sabbath, Temple, and the Enthronement of the Lord—The Problem of the *Sitz im Leben* of Genesis 1:1–2:3," in *Mélanges Bibliques et orientaux en l'honneur de M. Henri Cazelles, Alter Orient und Altes Testament* 212 (1981), ed. A. Caquot and M. Delcor (Neukirchen-Vluyn: Neukirchener, 1981), 509–10; see also my discussion of Ps. 92 in chapter 2.

39. See I Kings 6:18, 31; on the psalm's complex nature imagery, see Fisch (1988), 128–34.

40. *M. Tamid* 7:4 (my translation).

41. On the origin of the current form of this blessing, see Yehuda Liebes, "Masmiah keren yešu ʿa," *Mehqerei Yerušalayim be mahšebet Yisra'el* 3 (1984), 313–48.

42. *The Authorized Daily Prayerbook,* rev. ed., ed. Joseph H. Hertz (New York: Bloch, 1975), 821; on its history, see Ismar Elbogen, *Jewish Liturgy: A Comprehensive History,* rev. ed., trans. Raymond P. Scheindlein (Philadelphia and New York: Jewish Publication Society and Jewish Theological Seminary, 1993), 111–13.

43. On the range of responses, see Robert Goldenberg, "Early Rabbinic Explanations of the Destruction of Jerusalem," *Journal of Jewish Studies* 33 (1982), 517–25.

44. Jer. 1:15.

45. Isa. 60:17ff.

46. Braude, ed., II, 45–46.

47. Jer. 5:8.

48. Braude, ed., II, 46. The JPS translation "faithful" is rendered by Braude as "saints."

49. The exposure of their bones is punishment for idolatry.

50. See the comments on this genre in connection with Ps. 82, analyzed in chapter 3.

51. See David Stern, *Parables in Midrash: Narrative and Exegesis in Rabbinic Literature* (Cambridge: Harvard University Press, 1991), 131.

52. Braude, ed., II, 334.

53. *Midrash Rabbah,* ed. H. Freedman and Maurice Simon, 10 vols. Vol. 7: *Lamentations,* trans. A. Cohen (London: Soncino), proem XXIV, p. 43; see also proem II, pp. 4–6; proem XVI, p. 22; proem XX, p. 25; proem XXIV, pp. 37–38, 40–49; proem XXV, pp. 50–51; proem XXXIV, pp. 63–64.

54. On the trope of divine pathos, see Peter Kuhn, *Gottes Trauer und Klage in der Rabbinischen Überlieferung* (Leiden: Brill, 1978), 240–87; and Alan Mintz, *Ḥurban: Responses to Catastrophe in Hebrew Literature* (New York: Columbia University Press, 1984), 58–62.

55. Braude, ed., II, 335–36.

56. The midrash mentions some less well known examples: something is to be left out of a feast, out of a woman's repertoire of self-adornment, and in building a house, a space is to be left unplastered; see Braude, ed., II, 335–36.

57. For this custom, see *Masseket Soferim* 18:3.

58. On the tension between restorative and utopian messianism, see Gershom G. Scholem, *The Messianic Idea in Judaism and Other Essays in Jewish Spirituality,* trans. Michael A. Meyer (New York: Schocken, 1971), 1–36.

59. Karl Mannheim, *Ideology and Utopia: An Introduction to the Sociology of Knowledge,* trans. Louis Wirth and Edward Shils (New York: Harcourt, Brace and World, 1936), 192.

60. God also speaks in the psalm in vv. 8–11; see the discussion in chapter 3.

61. *Midrash Rabbah,* vol. 3: *Exodus,* trans. S. M. Lehrman, XXV, 12 (315).

62. *B. Sanhedrin,* 98a.

63. For the view that the masculine is stronger and more enduring than the feminine, see *Midrash Rabbah,* vol. 3: *Exodus,* XXIII, 11 (289–90); for other uses of *šir,* see Pss. 33:3, 40:4, 149:1 and Isa. 42:10.

64. *Mekilta de Rabbi Ishmael,* ed. Jacob Z. Lauterbach (Philadelphia: Jewish Publication Society, 1933), II, 6.

65. My translation of Kimchi on Ps. 96:1.

66. The war between two mighty opponents would have naturally suggested to Rashi the conflict between Christian Europe and the Muslim Near East; see Pearl, 14, for other linkages between Rashi's Psalm commentaries and Jewish suffering during the Crusades.

67. Rashi, *ad locum,* connects both verses to the wars of Gog and Magog.

68. Cited by Rashi on Ps. 97:3; he cites Ezek. 21:3 on Ps. 97:4.

69. My translation of Radak on Ps. 99:1.

70. Lauterbach, ed., I, 113–15; on the tension between the Akiban view and the idea of the Shekhinah remaining in the Temple, see Ephraim E. Urbach, *The Sages: Their Concepts and Beliefs,* trans. Israel Abrahams (Cambridge: Harvard University Press, 1979), 54–63.

71. Gershom G. Scholem, *Major Trends in Jewish Mysticism,* 3rd rev. ed. (New York: Schocken, 1954), 275.

72. On Ps. 45:3, see Braude, ed., I, 450.

73. Scholem (1954), 248, summarizes the views of the *Kaf ha qetoret,* with special reference to Ps. 29.

74. On messianic redemption in the classical Kabbalah, see Yehuda Liebes, *Studies in the Zohar,* trans. Arnold Schwartz, Stephanie Nakache, and Penina Peli (Albany: State University of New York Press, 1993).

75. Elliot K. Ginsburg, *The Sabbath in the Classical Kabbalah* (Albany: State University of New York Press, 1989), 69.

76. *B. Shabbat* 119a; *B. Ketubot* 62b.

77. The prayer books of Luria and his teacher Moshe Cordovero (*Siddur ha arizal* and *Siddur tefilah le moshe*) include special *kawwanot* only for Ps. 29, which has been connected to the Sabbath at least since Talmudic times (see *Y. Taanit* 2:2); but Moshe ben Machir in *Seder hayom* (1599), a generation after Luria's death, cites all six psalms; Y. Yosef Cohen, "Seder qabbalat šabbat u pizmon 'leka dodi' be minhagei yisra'el," in *Sefer 'Adam Noah: Zikaron le 'Adam Noah Braun* (Jerusalem: Harry Fischel, 1970), 322–24, claims that Cordovero initiated the recitation of Pss. 95–99, based on testimony in the Siddur of R. Yaakov Emden, *Palatin beit 'el,* but that Luria and his circle recited only Ps. 29. Cohen concludes that Cordovero's custom was picked up by the Ashkenazic and Yemenite rites, and Luria's by the Sephardic and other Eastern rites.

78. My translation, adapted from Hertz, ed., 357.

79. Gershom G. Scholem, *On the Kabbalah and Its Symbolism* (New York: Schocken, 1965), 145.

80. Scholem (1971), 47.

81. Scholem (1971), 13.

82. Cordovero focuses on the sevenfold repetition of *qol YHWH,* the voice of God, to envision a kind of intra-sefirotic dance, in which the various sefirot unite with one another in order to quell the forces of judgment and release the merciful forces within the godhead; at the moment this is accomplished, female and male, Shekhinah (*malkhut*) and YHWH (*tiferet*), unite. Luria unfolds a more complicated version of intra-sefirotic union, adding a cosmology of four worlds, and seven palaces within each world, and cross-referencing each line of the psalm to a verse of *ana be qoah,* the theurgic prayer that followed the recitation of this psalm and preceded "lekha dodi." I am indebted to Arthur Green for his help in deciphering their *kawwanot* to Ps. 29.

83. Scholem (1965), 141.

84. Samuel Usqué, *Consolation for the Tribulations of Israel,* trans. Martin A. Cohen (Philadelphia: Jewish Publication Society, 1965), 227, 236.

85. Usqué, 235; Deut. 30:1–3.

86. A. Cohen (1981), 54.

87. The phrase is also found in Lam. 3:55; see Robert Kirschner, trans. and ed., *Rabbinic Responsa of the Holocaust Era* (New York: Schocken, 1985), 82.

88. Yitzhak Katznelson, "Song about the Radziner," trans. David Roskies, in David Roskies, ed., *The Literature of Destruction: Jewish Responses to Catastrophe* (Philadelphia: Jewish Publication Society, 1989), 219.

89. Roskies, ed., 212.

90. Eliezer Berkovits, *With God in Hell: Judaism in the Ghettoes and Deathcamps* (New York: Sanhedrin, 1979), 17.

91. Yaffa Eliach, *Hasidic Tales of the Holocaust* (New York: Oxford University Press, 1982), 169.

92. Berkovitz (1979), 91.

93. Based on Ps. 79:4; see Ephraim Oshry, *Responsa from the Holocaust,* trans. Y. Leiman (New York: Judaica Press, 1983), 163.

94. Emil L. Fackenheim, *The Jewish Bible after the Holocaust: A Re-reading* (Bloomington: Indiana University Press, 1990), 47.

95. *B. Gittin* 57b; *Mišneh torah: Hilkhot yesodei ha torah* (chap. 5, para. 4); cited in Hirsch Jakob Zimmels, *The Echo of the Nazi Holocaust in Rabbinic Literature* (New York: Ktav, 1977), 356–57; the phrase, quoted in an 11th-century penitential hymn, is recited in the daily Taḥanun service, followed by the remonstrance "Yet, despite, all this, we have not forgotten Your name" (Hertz, ed., 183).

96. Usqué, 205.

97. *The Warsaw Diary of Chaim A. Kaplan,* rev. ed., ed. Abraham I. Katsh (New York: Collier, 1973), 214 (October 25, 1940); see "avinu malkenu" for reference to those "who went through fire and water for the sanctification of Thy name" (Hertz, ed., 167).

98. Chaim A. Kaplan, "Pages from the Diary" (February 2, 1942), trans. Jeffrey M. Green, in Roskies, ed., 441.

99. Pss. 115:5 and 135:16.

100. June 16, 1942; Kaplan, 352.

101. See Hannah Arendt, *Eichmann in Jerusalem: A Report on the Banality of Evil,* 2nd ed. (New York: Viking, 1964), 10; as an answer to Ben Gurion et al., see K. Shabbetai, *As Sheep to the Slaughter? The Myth of Cowardice,* introduction by Gideon Hausner (New York and Tel Aviv: World Federation of the Bergen-Belsen Survivors Associations, 1963).

102. Gerda Weissman Klein, *All but My Life* (New York: Hill and Wang, 1957), 89.

103. In Lucy S. Davidowicz, ed., *A Holocaust Reader* (New York: Behrman House, 1976), 177–78.

104. The models are *YHWH 'elohei yisra'el,* an 11th-century prayer, and *somer yisra'el,* originally a fast-day hymn; see Elbogen, 68, 70, 404 n. 18.

105. See, for instance, Hayim Naḥman Bialik's mock-prophetic poem "Beʿir ha haregah" [In the City of Slaughter].

106. Isa. 63:15; Hertz, ed., 182.

107. Hertz, ed., 182, adapted from Pss. 79:4 and 44:15.

108. Ps. 44:23; Hertz, ed., 182.

109. Ps. 121:4; Hertz, ed., 184; here the poem shifts to quoting from the next Taḥanun hymn.

110. Deut. 6:4; Hertz, ed., 184.

111. Hertz, ed., 182; the poem shifts back to quoting from *YHWH 'elohei yisra'el.*

112. Ps. 121:4; for this, the most ironic quotation, the poet goes outside the context of Taḥanun.

113. Roskies, ed., 573, notes that in Hebrew these words are punning homonyms: *ha ro'eh ha ro'eh.*

114. Trans. Robert Friend, in Roskies, ed., 573; the title is incorrectly given as "To God in Europe."

115. Roskies, ed., 574–75.

116. Roskies, ed., 566.

117. Quoted in David Roskies, *Against the Apocalypse: Responses to Catastrophe in Modern Jewish Culture* (Cambridge: Harvard University Press, 1984), 241.

118. As paraphrased by Irving Greenberg, "Cloud of Smoke, Pillar of Fire: Judaism, Christianity, and Modernity after the Holocaust," in Fleischner, ed., 40.

119. Rubenstein, 53–54.

120. See Romans 8:36; and, among many others, see Augustine, II, 209: "Let us then hear in this psalm the voice of the Martyrs; and see how good is the cause which the voice of the martyrs pleads"; and Calvin, IX, 171: "We are adopted in Christ, we are appointed to the slaughter . . . it behooves us to drink the cup which God puts into our hands."

121. In this vein, see also Kadia Molodowsky's "God of Mercy," in Roskies, ed., 570–71.

122. Buber (1952), 61.

123. The leader of the Satmar Ḥasidim, Rabbi Joel Teitelbaum, has blamed the Holocaust on the sins of Zionism in his work *'Al ha ge'ulah ve'al ha temurah* (Brooklyn: Jerusalem Publications, 1967).

124. Richard L. Rubenstein, "Naming the Unnameable, Thinking the Unthinkable (A Review Essay of Arthur Cohen's *The Tremendum*), *Journal of Reform Judaism* 31 (Spring 1984), 46.

125. See Berkovits (1973), 144–58; Fackenheim (1990), 49–53, 97–98; Greenberg (1977), 31–35.

126. See *Ha siddur ha shalem,* ed. Philip Birnbaum (New York: Hebrew Publishing Co., 1949), 789.

127. Buber (1952), 24.

128. Buber (1952), 58.

129. Martin Buber, *Eclipse of God: Studies in the Relation between Religion and Philosophy* (1952), ed. Robert M. Seltzer (Atlantic Highlands: Humanities Press International, 1988), 66.

130. See Buber (1963), 253–63.

131. Buber (1953), 6.

132. Buber (1953), 9.

133. Buber (1953), 11.

134. Buber (1953), 13–14.

135. On this point, see Terrence Des Pres, *The Survivor: An Anatomy of Life in the Death Camps* (New York: Oxford University Press, 1976).

136. Buber (1953), 16.

137. Buber (1953), 18.

138. Buber (1953), 19.

139. Buber (1952), 60–61.

140. Buber (1953), 30.

141. Buber (1953), 39–40.

142. Buber (1953), 46, interprets *kabod* in v. 24 as "the fulfillment of . . . existence" that comes with death.

143. Buber (1953), 41.

144. See Néher, 52.

145. Buber (1953), 60; this point is amplified by Emil L. Fackenheim, *Quest for Past and Future* (Bloomington: Indiana University Press, 1968), 231: "A full heart within indicates the Divine Presence; an empty heart bespeaks not the non-existence or unconcern of God, but merely His temporary absence."

146. Steven Kepnes, *The Text as Thou: Martin Buber's Dialogical Hermeneutics and Narrative Theology* (Bloomington: Indiana University Press, 1992), 140–43, uses this phrase as the title for his discussion of Buber's psalm interpretations in the context of his post-Holocaust thought.

147. *An Interrupted Life: The Diaries of Etty Hillesum, 1941–43*, ed. J. G. Gaarlandt, trans. Arno Pomerans (New York: Pantheon, 1983), 173.

148. Hillesum, 52.

149. Hillesum, 182.

150. Hillesum, 151.

151. Hillesum, 127.

152. Hillesum, 211.

153. Hillesum, 217.

154. Hillesum, 191.

155. Hillesum, 155.

156. Hillesum, 152.

157. Hillesum, 155.

158. Sermon of March 14, 1942, in Roskies, ed., 508.

159. Emil L. Fackenheim, *What Is Judaism? An Interpretation for the Present Age* (New York: Summit, 1987), 291, paraphrases the discourse.

160. Arthur A. Cohen (1981), 96.

161. Arthur A. Cohen (1981), 97.

162. Arthur A. Cohen (1981), 97–98.

163. Néher, 9–10.

164. Néher, 85.

165. Néher's translations insist on the root *d-w-m* (closely related to *d-m-m*, the root of *demamah* in the Elijah passage, cited above), while the JPS translators pick the root *d-m-h*, connoting resemblance, to arrive at "Praise befits You . . . O God."

166. Néher, 11–12.

167. Néher, 85.

168. Néher, 68–69.

169. See Braude, ed., I, 298–326, for repeated connections between the Purim story and the psalm; and see Matt. 27:46, Mark 15:34, and references to 22:19 in Matt. 27:35, Mark 15:24, Luke 23:34, and John 19:24.

170. Néher, 86.

171. Alvin H. Rosenfeld, *A Double Dying: Reflections on Holocaust Literature* (Bloomington: Indiana University Press, 1980), 106.

172. Sidra DeKoven Ezrahi, *By Words Alone: The Holocaust in Literature* (Chicago: University of Chicago Press, 1980), 144.

173. Paul Celan, *Collected Prose*, trans. Rosmarie Waldrop (Manchester: Carcanet, 1986), 48–49.

174. Paul Celan, *Poems*, ed. and trans. Michael Hamburger (New York: Persea, 1980), 97.

175. Celan (1980), 142; in the German original, *Dir* ("To You") is capitalized.

176. Celan (1980), 143.

177. Rashi, *ad locum*.

178. *The Zohar,* ed. Maurice Simon, trans. Harry Sperling and Maurice Simon (1934; rpt. London: Soncino, 1970), I, 3.

179. See Rosenfeld, 88; and Ezrahi, 144, who calls it "perhaps the most anguished of the blasphemies to be encountered in the literature."

180. "There Was Earth inside Them," Celan (1980), 131.

181. See, for instance, Pss. 32:6; 42:8; 69:2, 16; 88:18.

182. Buber (1952), 61, could be referring to Pss. 106:1, 107:1, 118:1, or 136:1.

183. Fackenheim (1990), 99.

184. Emil L. Fackenheim, *To Mend the World: Foundations of Future Jewish Thought* (New York: Schocken, 1982), 197.

185. Fackenheim (1990), 99, citing *B. Pesaḥim* 117a.

186. Fackenheim (1990), 98 (JPS translation inserted).

187. Roskies, ed., 511.

188. Bakhtin (1986), 94.

189. "Tenebrae," Celan (1980), 97.

190. Irving Feldman, *New and Selected Poems* (New York: Viking, 1979), 69.

191. *Selected Poetry of Yehuda Amichai,* ed. and trans. Chana Bloch and Stephen Mitchell (New York: Harper and Row, 1986), 91.

192. Buber (1963), 93.

WORKS CITED

Ahern, Emily M.

   1979. "The Problem of Efficacy: Strong and Weak Illocutionary Acts." *Man* n.s. 14.

Alter, Robert

   1979. "A New Theory of Kashrut." *Commentary* 68 (August).

   1985. *The Art of Biblical Poetry.* New York: Basic Books.

Altmann, Alexander

   1972. "Astrology." *Encyclopedia Judaica.* Jerusalem: Keter.

Amichai, Yehuda

   1986. *Selected Poetry of Yehuda Amichai.* Edited and translated by Chana Bloch and Stephen Mitchell. New York: Harper and Row.

Angelou, Maya

   1993. *On the Pulse of the Morning.* New York: Random House.

Arendt, Hannah

   1964. *Eichmann in Jerusalem: A Report on the Banality of Evil.* 2nd ed. New York: Viking.

Augustine, Saint

   1847. *Expositions on the Book of Psalms.* 6 vols. Translated by members of the English Church. Oxford: John Henry Parker.

Austin, J. L.

   1962. *How to Do Things with Words.* Edited by J. O. Urmson. New York: Oxford University Press.

Bachelard, Gaston

   1969. *The Poetics of Space.* Translated by Maria Jolas. Boston: Beacon.

Bakhtin, Mikhail M.

   1968. *Rabelais and His World.* Translated by Helene Iswolsky. Cambridge: MIT Press.

   1979. *Estetika slovesnogo tvorchestva* [The Aesthetics of Verbal Art]. Moscow: Iskusstvo.

   1981. *The Dialogic Imagination: Four Essays.* Edited by Michael Holquist. Translated by Caryl Emerson and Michael Holquist. Austin: University of Texas Press.

   1984. *Problems of Dostoevsky's Poetics.* Edited and translated by Caryl Emerson. Minneapolis: University of Minnesota Press.

   1986. *Speech Genres and Other Late Essays.* Edited by Caryl Emerson and Michael Holquist. Translated by Vern W. McGee. Austin: University of Texas Press.

Balentine, Samuel E.
1983. *The Hidden God: The Hiding of God's Face in the Old Testament.* New York: Oxford University Press.

Barr, James
1961. *The Semantics of Biblical Language.* Glasgow: Oxford University Press.
1962. *Biblical Words for Time.* London: SCM Press.

Barthes, Roland
1975. *The Pleasure of the Text.* Translated by Richard Miller. New York: Hill and Wang.

Bauman, Richard
1975. "Verbal Art as Performance." *American Anthropologist* 77.

Beattie, J. H. M.
1980. "On Understanding Sacrifice." In *Sacrifice,* ed. M. F. C. Boudrillon and M. Fortes. London: Academic Press.

Bell, Catherine
1992. *Ritual Theory, Ritual Practice.* New York: Oxford University Press.

Benveniste, Emile
1971. *Problems in General Linguistics.* Translated by Mary Elizabeth Meek. Coral Gables: University of Miami Press.

Bergson, Henri
1910. *Time and Free Will.* New York: Macmillan.

Berkovits, Eliezer
1973. *Faith after the Holocaust.* New York: Ktav.
1979. *With God in Hell: Judaism in the Ghettoes and Deathcamps.* New York: Sanhedrin.

Berlin, Adele
1985. *The Dynamics of Biblical Parallelism.* Bloomington: Indiana University Press.

Birnbaum, Philip, ed.
1949. *Ha siddur ha shalem.* New York: Hebrew Publishing.

Blank, Sheldon
1961. "Some Observations concerning Biblical Prayer." *Hebrew Union College Annual* 32.

Blenkinsopp, Joseph
1976. "The Structure of P." *Catholic Bible Quarterly* 38.
1977. *Prophecy and Canon.* Notre Dame: University of Notre Dame Press.

Bloch, Maurice
1974. "Symbols, Song, Dance and Features of Articulation: Is Religion an Extreme Form of Traditional Authority?" *Archives Européènes de Sociologie* 15.

Bloom, Harold
1973. *The Anxiety of Influence.* New York: Oxford University Press.

Bokser, Baruch
1984. *The Origins of the Seder: The Passover Rite and Early Rabbinic Judaism.* Berkeley: University of California Press.

Bourdieu, Pierre
1977. "Symbolic Power." In *Identity and Structure: Issues in the Sociology of Education,* ed. Denis Gleeson, trans. Colin Wringe. Driffield: Nafferton Books.
1991. *Language and Symbolic Power.* Edited by John B. Thompson. Translated by Gino Raymond and Matthew Adamson. Cambridge: Harvard University Press.

Braude, William G., ed.

1959. *The Midrash on Psalms.* 2 vols. Translated by William G. Braude. New Haven: Yale University Press.

Brown, Peter

1969. *Augustine of Hippo: A Biography.* Berkeley: University of California Press.

Broyles, Craig C.

1989. *The Conflict of Faith and Experience in the Psalms.* Sheffield: JSOT Press.

Brueggemann, Walter

1984. *The Message of the Psalms: A Theological Commentary.* Minneapolis: Augsburg.

Buber, Martin

1947 [1936]. *Between Man and Man.* Translated by Ronald Gregor Smith. London: Routledge and Kegan Paul.

1952. *At the Turning: Three Addresses on Judaism.* New York: Farrar, Straus and Young.

1953. *Good and Evil: Two Interpretations.* New York: Scribner's.

1958 [1923]. *I and Thou.* 2nd ed. Translated by Ronald Gregor Smith. New York: Scribner's.

1958 [1946]. *Moses: The Revelation and the Covenant.* New York: Harper and Row.

1963 [1948]. *Israel and the World: Essays in a Time of Crisis.* New York: Schocken.

1965. *The Knowledge of Man: A Philosophy of the Interhuman.* Edited by Maurice Friedman. Translated by Maurice Friedman and Ronald Gregor Smith. New York: Harper and Row.

1968. *On the Bible: Eighteen Studies.* New York: Schocken.

1988 [1952]. *Eclipse of God: Studies in the Relation between Religion and Philosophy.* Edited by Robert M. Seltzer. Atlantic Highlands: Humanities Press International.

Buttenweiser, Moses

1969 [1938]. *The Psalms: Chronologically Treated with a New Translation.* Prolegomenon by Nahum M. Sarna. New York: Ktav.

Calvin, John

1949 [1571, 1845]. *Commentary on the Book of Psalms.* 5 vols. Edited by James Anderson. Translated by Arthur Golding. Grand Rapids: Eerdmans.

Caquot, André

1956. "Sur quelques démons de l'Ancien Testament: Reshep, Qeteb, Deber." *Semitica* 6.

Carroll, Michael P.

1985. "One More Time: Leviticus Revisited." In *Anthropological Approaches to the Old Testament,* ed. Bernhard Lang. Philadelphia: Fortress.

Celan, Paul

1980. *Poems.* Edited and translated by Michael Hamburger. New York: Persea.

1986. *Collected Prose.* Translated by Rosmarie Waldrop. Manchester: Carcanet.

Charles, R. H.

1963 [1899]. *Eschatology, the Doctrine of a Future Life in Israel, Judaism and Christianity: A Critical History.* New York: Schocken.

Childs, Brevard S.

1962. *Memory and Tradition in Israel.* London: SCM Press.

1971. "Psalm Titles and Midrashic Exegesis." *Journal of Semitic Studies* 16.

1974. *The Book of Exodus: A Critical, Theological Commentary.* The Old Testament Library. Philadelphia: Westminster.

Clark, Katerina, and Holquist, Michael
1984. *Mikhail Bakhtin.* Cambridge: Harvard University Press.
Cohen, A., ed.
1984. *The Talmud: Minor Tractates.* Translated by A. Cohen. London: Soncino.
Cohen, Arthur A.
1970. *The Myth of the Judeo-Christian Tradition.* New York: Harper and Row.
1981. *The Tremendum: A Theological Interpretation of the Holocaust.* New York: Crossroad.
Cohen, Y. Yosef
1970. "Seder qabbalat šabbat u pizmon 'leka dodi' be minhagei yisra'el." In *Sefer 'Adam Noah: Zikaron le 'Adam Noah Braun.* Jerusalem: Harry Fischel.
Cohn, Robert L.
1981. *The Shape of Sacred Space: Four Biblical Studies.* Chico: Scholars Press.
Collins, Terence
1987. "Decoding the Psalms: A Structural Approach to the Psalter." *Journal for the Study of the Old Testament* 37.
Culley, Robert C.
1967. *Oral Formulaic Language in the Biblical Psalms.* Toronto: University of Toronto Press.
d'Aquili, Eugene, and Laughlin, Charles D.
1979. "The Neurobiology of Myth and Ritual." In *The Spectrum of Ritual: A Biogenetic Structural Analysis,* ed. Eugene d'Aquili, Charles Laughlin, and John McManus. New York: Columbia University Press.
Dahood, Mitchell
1965–70. *Psalms: A New Translation with Introduction and Commentary.* The Anchor Bible. 3 vols. Garden City: Doubleday.
Damrosch, David
1987. *The Narrative Covenant: Transformations of Genre in the Growth of Biblical Literature.* San Francisco: Harper and Row.
Davidowicz, Lucy S., ed.
1976. *A Holocaust Reader.* New York: Behrman House.
Davies, Douglas
1985. "An Interpretation of Sacrifice in Leviticus." In *Anthropological Approaches to the Old Testament,* ed. Bernhard Lang. Philadelphia: Fortress Press.
Des Pres, Terrence
1976. *The Survivor: An Anatomy of Life in the Death Camps.* New York: Oxford University Press.
Dodds, E. R.
1968. *The Greeks and the Irrational.* Berkeley: University of California Press.
Douglas, Mary
1966. *Purity and Danger: An Analysis of the Concept of Pollution and Taboo.* London: Routledge and Kegan Paul.
1970. *Natural Symbols: Explorations in Cosmology.* New York: Pantheon.
1975. *Implicit Meanings: Essays in Anthropology.* London: Routledge and Kegan Paul.
Drijvers, Pius
1964. *The Psalms, Their Structure and Meaning.* New York: Herder and Herder.
Driver, Tom F.
1991. *The Magic of Ritual: Our Need for Liberating Rites That Transform Our Lives and Our Communities.* San Francisco: Harper Collins.

Durkheim, Emil

1965 [1915]. *The Elementary Forms of the Religious Life: A Study in Religious Sociology.* Translated by Joseph Ward Swain. New York: Free Press.

Eckardt, A. Roy

1967. *Elder and Younger Brothers: The Encounter of Jews and Christians.* New York: Scribner's.

Eilberg-Schwartz, Howard

1990. *The Savage in Judaism: An Anthropology of Israelite Religion and Ancient Judaism.* Bloomington: Indiana University Press.

Elbogen, Ismar

1993 [1913, 1972]. *Jewish Liturgy: A Comprehensive History.* Translated by Raymond P. Scheindlein. Philadelphia and New York: Jewish Publication Society and Jewish Theological Seminary.

Eliach, Yaffa

1982. *Hasidic Tales of the Holocaust.* New York: Oxford University Press.

Eliade, Mircea

1954 [1949]. *The Myth of the Eternal Return, or, Cosmos and History.* Translated by Willard R. Trask. Princeton: Princeton University Press.

1957. *The Sacred and the Profane: The Nature of Religion.* Translated by Willard R. Trask. New York: Harper and Row.

Ezrahi, Sidra DeKoven

1980. *By Words Alone: The Holocaust in Literature.* Chicago: University of Chicago Press.

Fackenheim, Emil L.

1968. *Quest for Past and Future.* Bloomington: Indiana University Press.

1982. *To Mend the World: Foundations of Future Jewish Thought.* New York: Schocken.

1987. *What Is Judaism? An Interpretation for the Present Age.* New York: Summit.

1990. *The Jewish Bible after the Holocaust: A Re-reading.* Bloomington: Indiana University Press.

Feld, Edward

1991. *The Spirit of Renewal: Crisis and Response in Jewish Life.* Woodstock: Jewish Lights.

Feldman, Irving

1979. *New and Selected Poems.* New York: Viking.

Fernandez, James

1986. *Persuasions and Performances: The Play of Tropes in Culture.* Bloomington: Indiana University Press.

Finnegan, Ruth

1969. "How to Do Things with Words: Performative Utterances among the Limba of Sierra Leone." *Man* 4.

Fisch, Harold

1984. *A Remembered Future: A Study in Literary Mythology.* Bloomington: Indiana University Press.

1988. *Poetry with a Purpose: Biblical Poetics and Interpretation.* Bloomington: Indiana University Press.

Fishbane, Michael

1975. "The Sacred Center: The Symbolic Structure of the Bible." In *Texts and Responses: Studies Presented to Nahum N. Glatzer on the Occasion of His Seventieth*

Birthday by His Students, ed. Michael A. Fishbane and Paul R. Flohr. Leiden: Brill.

1979. *Text and Texture: Close Readings of Selected Biblical Texts.* New York: Schocken.

Fleischner, Eva, ed.

1977. *Auschwitz—Beginning of a New Era? Reflections on the Holocaust.* New York: Ktav.

Forstman, H. Jackson

1962. *Word and Spirit: Calvin's Doctrine of Biblical Authority.* Stanford: Stanford University Press.

Foucault, Michel

1983. "The Subject and the Power." In *Michel Foucault: Beyond Structuralism and Hermeneutics,* 2nd ed., ed. Hubert L. Dreyfus and Paul Rabinow. Chicago: University of Chicago Press.

Fox, Everett

1990. *Genesis and Exodus: A New English Rendition.* New York: Schocken.

Fox, James J.

1977. "Roman Jakobson and the Comparative Study of Parallelism." In *Roman Jakobson: Echoes of His Scholarship,* ed. D. Armstrong and C. Van Schooneveld. Lisse: Peter de Redder.

Frazer, James G.

1913–15. *The Golden Bough: A Study in Magic and Religion.* 3rd ed. 12 vols. London: Macmillan.

Freedman, H., and Simon, Maurice, eds.

1939. *Midrash Rabbah.* Vol. 3: *Exodus,* trans. S. M. Lehrman. Vol. 7: *Lamentations,* trans. A. Cohen. London: Soncino.

Frei, Hans W.

1974. *The Eclipse of Biblical Narrative: A Study in Eighteenth and Nineteenth Century Hermeneutics.* New Haven: Yale University Press.

Friedman, Richard E.

1981. *The Exile and Biblical Narrative: The Formation of the Deuteronomistic and Priestly Works.* Chico: Scholars Press.

Frye, Northrop

1982. *The Great Code: The Bible and Literature.* New York: Harcourt, Brace, Jovanovich.

Gaster, Theodor H.

1961. *Thespis: Ritual, Myth, and Drama in the Ancient Near East.* Rev. ed. Garden City: Doubleday.

Geertz, Clifford

1973. *The Interpretation of Cultures.* New York: Basic Books.

Geller, Stephen A.

1992. "Blood Cult: Toward a Literary Theology of the Priestly Work in the Pentateuch." *Prooftexts: A Journal of Jewish Literary History* 12.

Gemser, Berend

1955. "The *rib*- or Controversy Pattern in Hebrew Mentality." In *Wisdom in Israel and the Ancient Near East,* ed. Martin Noth and D. Winton Thomas. *Vetus Testamentum* Supplement 3. Leiden: Brill.

Gerstenberger, Erhard

1974. "Psalms." In *Old Testament Form Criticism,* ed. John H. Hayes. San Antonio: Trinity University Press.

1980. *Der Bittende Mensch.* Neukirchen-Vluyn: Neukirchener Verlag.

Ginsburg, Elliot K.
1989. *The Sabbath in the Classical Kabbalah.* Albany: State University of New York Press.

Goffman, Erving
1974. *Frame Analysis.* New York: Harper and Row.

Goldenberg, Robert
1982. "Early Rabbinic Explanations of the Destruction of Jerusalem." *Journal of Jewish Studies* 33.

Goody, Jack
1986. *The Logic of Writing and the Organization of Society.* Cambridge: Cambridge University Press.

Gordis, Robert
1949. "Quotations as a Literary Usage in Biblical, Rabbinic, and Oriental Literature." *Hebrew Union College Annual* 22.

Gorman, Frank H., Jr.
1990. *Space, Time and Status in the Priestly Theology.* Sheffield: Sheffield Academic Press.

Gossen, Gary H.
1974. "To Speak with a Heated Heart: Chanula Canons of Style and Good Performance." In *Explorations in the Ethnography of Speaking,* ed. Richard Bauman and Joel Sherzer. Cambridge: Cambridge University Press.

Gramsci, Antonio
1957. *The Modern Prince and Other Writings.* Translated by Louis Marks. New York: International Publishers.

Green, Arthur
1992. *Seek My Face, Speak My Name: A Contemporary Jewish Theology.* Northvale: Jason Aronson.

Greenberg, Irving
1977. "Cloud of Smoke, Pillar of Fire: Judaism, Christianity, and Modernity after the Holocaust." In *Auschwitz—Beginning of a New Era? Reflections on the Holocaust,* ed. Eva Fleischner. New York: Ktav.

Greenberg, Moshe
1976. "On the Refinement of the Conception of Prayer in Hebrew Scriptures." *Association for Jewish Studies Review* 1.
1979. "Religion: Stability and Ferment." In *The World History of the Jewish People: The Age of the Monarchy,* ed. A. Malamat. Jerusalem: Massada Press.
1983. *Biblical Prose Prayer Viewed as a Window on the Popular Religion of Ancient Israel.* Berkeley: University of California Press.

Greenstein, Edward
1984. "Medieval Bible Commentaries." In *Back to the Sources: Reading the Classic Jewish Texts,* ed. Barry Holtz. New York: Summit.

Gunkel, Hermann
1926. *Die Psalmen.* Göttingen: Vandenhoed and Ruprecht.
1967. *The Psalms: A Form-Critical Introduction.* Translated by Thomas M. Horner. Philadelphia: Fortress Press.

Hadas, Moses, ed.
1951. *Aristeas to Philocrates.* Translated by Moses Hadas. New York: Harper.

Halliwell, Stephen
1986. *Aristotle's Poetics.* Chapel Hill: University of North Carolina Press.

Halpern, Baruch
 1981. *The Constitution of the Monarchy in Israel.* Chico: Scholars Press.
Hancher, Michael
 1988. "Performative Utterance, the Word of God, and the Death of the Author."
 Semeia 41.
Haran, Menahem
 1978. *Temples and Temple-Service in Ancient Israel.* Oxford: Clarendon Press.
Hayes, John H.
 1979. *Introduction to Old Testament Study.* Nashville: Abingdon.
Hertz, Joseph H., ed.
 1975. *The Authorized Daily Prayerbook.* Rev. ed. New York: Bloch.
Hertz, Robert
 1973 [1909]. "The Pre-eminence of the Right Hand: A Study in Religious
 Polarity." In *Right and Left: Essays on Dual Symbolic Classification,* trans. and ed.
 Rodney Needham. Chicago: University of Chicago Press.
Hertzberg, Arthur, ed.
 1962. *Judaism.* New York: Braziller.
Hillesum, Etty
 1983. *An Interrupted Life: The Diaries of Etty Hillesum, 1941–43.* Edited by J. G.
 Gaarlandt. Translated by Arno Pomerans. New York: Pantheon.
Hoffman, Lawrence A.
 1987. *Beyond the Text: A Holistic Approach to Liturgy.* Bloomington: Indiana University Press.
Holquist, Michael
 1990. *Dialogism: Bakhtin and His World.* London: Routledge.
Hubert, Henri, and Mauss, Marcel
 1964 [1898]. *Sacrifice: Its Nature and Function.* Translated by W. D. Halls. Chicago:
 University of Chicago Press.
Huizinga, Johann
 1955 [1938]. *Homo Ludens: A Study of the Play Element in Culture.* Translated by the
 author. Boston: Beacon Press.
Hurvitz, Avi
 1972. *Bein lašon le lašon: Le toldot lešon ha miqra' be yemei bayit šeni.* Jerusalem: Bialik
 Institute.
Hyde, Lewis
 1983. *The Gift: Imagination and the Erotic Life of Property.* New York: Random
 House.
Jakobson, Roman
 1960. "Closing Statement: Linguistics and Poetics." In *Style and Language,* ed.
 Thomas A. Sebeok. Cambridge: MIT Press.
 1971. "Two Aspects of Language and Two Types of Aphasic Disturbances." In
 Selected Writings, vol. II. The Hague: Mouton.
James, Fleming
 1938. *Thirty Psalmists: A Study in Personalities of the Psalter as Seen against the Background of Gunkel's Type-Study of the Psalms.* New York: G. P. Putnam's Sons.
Jameson, Fredric
 1981. *The Political Unconscious.* Ithaca: Cornell University Press.
Jenni, Ernst, and Westermann, Claus, eds.
 1971. *Theologisches Handwörterbuch zum Alten Testament.* Munich: Kaiser Verlag.

Johnson, Aubrey R.
1935. "The Role of the King in the Jerusalem Cultus." In *The Labyrinth: Further Studies in the Relation between Myth and Ritual in the Ancient World*, ed. S. H. Hooke. London: Society for Promoting Christian Knowledge.
1979. *The Cultic Prophet and Israel's Psalmody*. Cardiff: University of Wales Press.
Josipovici, Gabriel
1988. *The Book of God: A Response to the Bible*. New Haven: Yale University Press.
Kaplan, Chaim A.
1973. *The Warsaw Diary of Chaim A. Kaplan*. Revised ed. Edited by Abraham I. Katsh. New York: Collier.
Kaufmann, Yehezkel.
1960 [1937–56]. *The Religion of Israel: From Its Beginnings to the Babylonian Exile*. Translated and abridged by Moshe Greenberg. New York: Schocken.
Kearney, Peter J.
1977. "Creation and Liturgy: The P Redaction of Exodus 25–30." *Zeitschrift für Alttestamentliche Wissenschaft* 89.
Keel, Othmar
1969. *Feinde und Gottesleugner: Studien zum Image der Widersacher in den Individualpsalmen*. Stuttgart: Katholisches Bibelwerk.
1978. *The Symbolism of the Biblical World: Ancient Near Eastern Iconography and the Book of Psalms*. Translated by Timothy J. Hallett. New York: Seabury.
Kepnes, Steven
1992. *The Text as Thou: Martin Buber's Dialogical Hermeneutics and Narrative Theology*. Bloomington: Indiana University Press.
Kirschner, Robert, ed.
1985. *Rabbinic Responsa of the Holocaust Era*. New York: Schocken.
Kittel, Rudolph
1914. *Die Psalmen*. Leipzig: A. Deichertsche Verlagsbuchhandlung.
Klein, Gerda Weissman
1957. *All but My Life*. New York: Hill and Wang.
Kraus, Hans-Joachim
1965. *Worship in Israel: A Cultic History of the Old Testament*. Translated by Geoffrey Buswell. Richmond: John Knox Press.
1986. *The Theology of the Psalms*. Translated by Keith Crim. Minneapolis: Augsburg.
1988. *Psalms 1–59: A Commentary*. Translated by Hilton C. Oswald. Minneapolis: Augsburg.
Kübler-Ross, Elisabeth
1969. *On Death and Dying*. New York: Macmillan.
Kugel, James L.
1981. *The Idea of Biblical Poetry: Parallelism and Its History*. New Haven: Yale University Press.
1988. "Topics in the History of the Spirituality of the Psalms." In *Jewish Spirituality: From the Bible through the Middle Ages*, ed. Arthur Green. New York: Crossroad.
Kuhn, Peter
1978. *Gottes Trauer und Klage in der Rabbinischen Überlieferung*. Leiden: Brill.
Kuhrt, Amelie
1987. "Usurpation, Conquest, and Ceremonial: From Babylon to Persia." In

Rituals of Royalty: Power and Ceremonial in Traditional Societies, ed. David Cannadine and Simon Price. Cambridge: Cambridge University Press.

Kummel, Friedrich

1966. "Time as Succession and the Problem of Duration." In *The Voices of Time,* ed. J. T. Fraser. New York: Braziller.

Kurzweil, Baruch

1970. "Job and the Possibility of Biblical Tragedy." In *Arguments and Doctrines: A Reader of Jewish Thinking in the Aftermath of the Holocaust,* ed. Arthur A. Cohen. New York: Harper and Row.

Lang, Bernhard, ed.

1985. *Anthropological Approaches to the Old Testament.* Philadelphia: Fortress Press.

Langer, Susanne K.

1957. *Philosophy in a New Key.* 3rd ed. Cambridge: Harvard University Press.

Lauterbach, Jacob Z., ed.

1933. *Mekilta de Rabbi Ishmael.* 3 vols. Translated by Jacob Z. Lauterbach. Philadelphia: Jewish Publication Society.

Leach, Edmund

1969. *Genesis as Myth and Other Essays.* London: Jonathan Cape.

1976. *Culture and Communication: The Logic by Which Symbols Are Connected.* Cambridge: Cambridge University Press.

Levenson, Jon D.

1985. *Sinai and Zion: An Entry into the Jewish Bible.* Minneapolis: Winston.

1988. *Creation and the Persistence of Evil: The Jewish Drama of Divine Omnipotence.* San Francisco: Harper and Row.

Levine, Baruch A.

1974. *In the Presence of the Lord: A Study of Cult and Some Cultic Terms in Ancient Israel.* Leiden: Brill.

1989. *Leviticus: The Traditional Hebrew Text with the New JPS Translation.* Commentary by Baruch A. Levine. Philadelphia: Jewish Publication Society.

Levine, Herbert

1987. "The Symbolic *Sukkah* in Psalms." *Prooftexts: A Journal of Jewish Literary History* 7.

1990. "The Dialogic Discourse of Psalms." In *Mappings of the Biblical Terrain: The Bible as Text,* ed. Vincent L. Tollers and John Maier. *Bucknell Review* 33.

1993. "Divine Timespace and Religious Experience." In *Worlds of Jewish Prayer: A Festschrift in Honor of Rabbi Zalman M. Schachter-Shalomi,* ed. Shohama Harris Wiener and Jonathan Omer-Man. Northvale: Jason Aronson.

Levi-Strauss, Claude

1966. *Totemism.* Translated by Rodney Needham. Boston: Beacon Press.

Lewis, C. S.

1958. *Reflections on the Psalms.* London: Geoffrey Bles.

Lex, Barbara

1979. "The Neurobiology of Ritual Trance." In *The Spectrum of Ritual: A Biogenetic Structural Analysis,* ed. Eugene d'Aquili, Charles D. Laughlin, and John McManus. New York: Columbia University Press.

Liebes, Yehuda

1984. "Maṣmiaḥ keren yešuʿah." *Meḥqerei yerušalayim be maḥšebet yisraʾel* 3.

1993. *Studies in the Zohar.* Translated by Arnold Schwartz, Stephanie Nakache, Penina Peli. Albany: State University of New York Press.

Liebreich, Yehuda Aryeh
  1954. "Mizmorei ha lewiim le yemei ha šabu'a." *Eretz-Israel* 3.
Littell, Franklin H.
  1975. *The Crucifixion of the Jews.* New York: Harper and Row.
Lord, Albert B.
  1973. *The Singer of Tales.* New York: Atheneum.
Lowth, Robert
  1969 [1787]. *Lectures on the Sacred Poetry of the Hebrews.* Hildesheim: Georg Olms
    Verlag.
Mannheim, Karl
  1936. *Ideology and Utopia: An Introduction to the Sociology of Knowledge.* Translated
    by Louis Wirth and Eward Shils. New York: Harcourt, Brace and World.
Marx, A.
  1989. "Sacrifice Pour Les Péchés ou Rite de Passage? Quelques réflexions sur la
    fonction du Hattat." *Revue Biblique* 96.
Mauss, Marcel
  1967 [1923]. *The Gift: Forms and Functions of Exchange in Archaic Societies.* Trans-
    lated by Ian Cunnison. New York: Norton.
McDannell, Colleen, and Lang, Bernhard
  1988. *Heaven: A History.* New Haven: Yale University Press.
McGarry, Michael B.
  1977. *Christology after Auschwitz.* New York: Paulist Press.
Melamed, E. Z.
  1961. "Breakup of Stereotype Phrases as an Artistic Device in Biblical Poetry."
    Scripta Hierosolymitana 8.
Milgrom, Jacob
  1991. *Leviticus 1–16.* The Anchor Bible. New York: Doubleday.
Miller, J. Hillis
  1985. *The Linguistic Moment from Wordsworth to Stevens.* Princeton: Princeton Uni-
    versity Press.
Mintz, Alan
  1984. *Hurban: Responses to Catastrophe in Hebrew Literature.* New York: Columbia
    University Press.
Monter, E. William
  1961. *Calvin's Geneva.* New York: John Wiley and Sons.
Moore, Sally F., and Myerhoff, Barbara, eds.
  1977. *Secular Ritual.* Assen/Amsterdam: Van Gorcum.
Morson, Gary Saul, and Emerson, Caryl
  1990. *Mikhail Bakhtin: Creation of a Prosaics.* Stanford: Stanford University Press.
Mowinckel, Sigmund
  1962. *The Psalms in Israel's Worship.* Translated by D. R. Ap-Thomas. 2 vols. New
    York: Abingdon.
Mullen, E. T., Jr.
  1980. *The Assembly of the Gods: The Divine Council in Canaanite and Early Hebrew
    Literature.* Chico: Scholars Press.
Néher, André
  1981. *The Exile of the Word: From the Silence of the Bible to the Silence of Auschwitz.*
    Translated by David Maisel. Philadelphia: Jewish Publication Society.
Neusner, Jacob
  1973. *The Idea of Purity in Ancient Judaism.* Leiden: Brill.

Oesterley, W. O. E.
  1953. *The Psalms.* London: Society for the Promotion of Christian Knowledge.
Ong, Walter J.
  1967. *The Presence of the Word: Some Prolegomena for Cultural and Religious History.* New Haven: Yale University Press.
  1982. *Orality and Literacy: The Technologizing of the Word.* London: Methuen.
Orelli, Conrad von
  1871. *Die Hebraischen Synonyma der Zeit und Ewigkeit Genetisch und Sprachvegleichend dargestellt.* Leipzig.
Oshry, Ephraim
  1983. *Responsa from the Holocaust.* Translated by Y. Leiman. New York: Judaica Press.
Patai, Raphael
  1947. *Man and Temple in Ancient Jewish Myth and Ritual.* London: Thomas Nelson.
Pearl, Chaim
  1988. *Rashi.* New York: Grove Press.
Pépin, Jean
  1976. *Mythe et allégorie: Les origines Grecques et les contestations judéo-chrétiènnes.* Rev. ed. Paris: Études Augustiniènnes.
Perlina, Nina
  1984. "Mikhail Bakhtin and Martin Buber: Problems of Dialogic Imagination." *Studies in Twentieth Century Literature* 9.
Pitt-Rivers, Julian
  1977. *The Fate of Schechem or the Politics of Sex: Essays in the Anthropology of the Mediterranean.* Cambridge: Cambridge University Press.
Polzin, Robert
  1984. "Dialogic Imagination in the Book of Deuteronomy." *Studies in Twentieth-Century Literature* 9.
Pope, Marvin H.
  1973. *Job.* Anchor Bible. New York: Doubleday.
Pratt, Mary Louise
  1977. *Toward a Speech Act Theory of Literary Discourse.* Bloomington: Indiana University Press.
Pritchard, James
  1955. *Ancient Near Eastern Texts.* 2 vols. Princeton: Princeton University Press.
Rabinowitz, Louis
  1935–36. "Does Midrash *Tehillim* Reflect the Triennial Cycle of Psalms?" *Jewish Quarterly Review* n.s. 26.
Rappaport, Roy A.
  1979. *Ecology, Meaning, and Religion.* Richmond: North Atlantic Books.
Ray, Benjamin
  1973. "'Performative Utterances' in African Rituals." *History of Religions* 13.
Rogerson, J. W.
  1978. *Anthropology and the Old Testament.* Oxford: Blackwell.
  1980. "Sacrifice in the Old Testament: Problems of Method and Approach." In *Sacrifice,* ed. M. F. C. Boudrillon and M. Fortes. London: Academic Press.
Rosenberg, Joel
  1986. *King and Kin: Political Allegory in the Hebrew Bible.* Bloomington: Indiana University Press.

Rosenfeld, Alvin H.
    1980. *A Double Dying: Reflections on Holocaust Literature.* Bloomington: Indiana University Press.
Rosenzweig, Franz
    1971 [1930]. *The Star of Redemption.* 2nd ed. Translated by William W. Hallo. Notre Dame: University of Notre Dame Press.
Roskies, David
    1984. *Against the Apocalypse: Responses to Catastrophe in Modern Jewish Culture.* Cambridge: Harvard University Press.
Roskies, David, ed.
    1989. *The Literature of Destruction: Jewish Responses to Catastrophe.* Philadelphia: Jewish Publication Society.
Rubenstein, Richard L.
    1966. *After Auschwitz: Radical Theology and Contemporary Judaism.* Indianapolis: Bobbs Merrill.
    1984. "Naming the Unnameable, Thinking the Unthinkable: A Review Essay of Arthur Cohen's *The Tremendum.*" *Journal of Reform Judaism* 31, no. 2.
Ruether, Rosemary R.
    1974. *Faith and Fratricide: The Theological Roots of Anti-Semitism.* New York: Seabury.
Sanders, James A., ed.
    1967. *The Dead Sea Psalms Scroll.* Ithaca: Cornell University Press.
Sarna, Nahum M.
    1967. "Psalm XIX and the Near Eastern Sun-God Literature." *Proceedings of the IV World Congress of Jewish Studies* I.
    1979. "The Psalm Superscriptions and the Guilds." In *Studies in Jewish Religious and Intellectual History,* ed. S. Stein and R. Lowe. University: University of Alabama Press.
    1993. *Songs of the Heart: An Introduction to the Book of Psalms.* New York: Schocken.
Schmidt, Hans
    1934. *Die Psalmen.* Tübingen: J. C. B. Mohr.
Scholem, Gershom G.
    1954. *Major Trends in Jewish Mysticism.* 3rd rev. ed. New York: Schocken.
    1965. *On the Kabbalah and Its Symbolism.* New York: Schocken.
    1971. *The Messianic Idea in Judaism and Other Essays in Jewish Spirituality.* Translated by Michael A. Meyer. New York: Schocken.
Searle, John R.
    1969. *Speech Acts: An Essay in the Philosophy of Language.* Cambridge: Cambridge University Press.
    1979. *Expression and Meaning: Studies in the Theory of Speech Acts.* Cambridge: Cambridge University Press.
Seow, Choon Leong
    1989. *Myth, Drama and the Politics of David's Dance.* Atlanta: Scholars Press.
Shabbetai, K.
    1963. *As Sheep to the Slaughter? The Myth of Cowardice.* New York and Tel Aviv: World Federation of the Bergen-Belsen Survivors Associations.
Shereshevsky, Esra
    1982. *Rashi: The Man and His World.* New York: Sepher Hermon Press.
Shklovsky, Victor
    1965. "Art as Technique." In *Russian Formalist Criticism,* ed. L. T. Lemon and M. J. Reis. Lincoln: University of Nebraska Press.

Simon, Maurice, ed.

  1970 [1934]. *The Zohar.* Translated by Harry Sperling and Maurice Simon. London: Soncino.

Simon, Uriel

  1991. *Four Approaches to the Book of Psalms: From Saadiah to Abraham Ibn Ezra.* Translated by Lenn J. Schram. Albany: State University of New York Press.

Smith, Barbara Herrnstein

  1978. *On the Margins of Discourse: The Relation of Literature to Language.* Chicago: University of Chicago Press.

Smith, Jonathan Z.

  1982. *Imagining Religion: From Babylon to Jonestown.* Chicago: University of Chicago Press.

  1987. *To Take Place: Toward Theory in Ritual.* Chicago: University of Chicago Press.

Soler, Jean

  1979. "The Dietary Prohibitions of the Hebrews." *The New York Review of Books* 26 (June 14).

Sontag, Susan

  1989. *AIDS and Its Metaphors.* New York: Farrar, Straus, Giroux.

Starobinski, Jean

  1975. "The Inside and the Outside." *Hudson Review* 28.

Stendhal, Krister

  1976. *Paul among Jews and Gentiles and Other Essays.* Philadelphia: Fortress Press.

Stern, David

  1991. *Parables in Midrash: Narrative and Exegesis in Rabbinic Literature.* Cambridge: Harvard University Press.

Tambiah, Stanley J.

  1985. *Culture, Thought, and Social Action.* Cambridge: Harvard University Press.

Teitelbaum, Joel

  1967. *'Al ha ge'ulah ve'al ha temurah.* Brooklyn: Jerusalem Publications.

Terrien, Samuel

  1978. *The Elusive Presence: Toward a New Biblical Theology.* New York: Harper and Row.

Thistleton, Anthony C.

  1974. "The Supposed Power of Words in the Biblical Writings." *Journal of Theological Studies* n.s. 25.

Tigay, Jeffrey H.

  1976. "On Some Aspects of Prayer in the Bible." *Association for Jewish Studies Review* 1.

Tsevat, Matitiahu

  1980. *The Meaning of the Book of Job and Other Biblical Studies.* New York: Ktav.

Turnbull, Colin

  1990. "Liminality: A Synthesis of Subjective and Objective Experience." In *By Means of Performance: Intercultural Studies of Theatre and Ritual,* ed. Richard Schechner and Willa Appel. Cambridge: Cambridge University Press.

Turner, Terence S.

  1977. "Transformation, Hierarchy, and Transcendence: A Reformulation of Van Gennep's Model of the Structure of *Rites de Passage.*" In *Secular Ritual,* ed. Sally F. Moore and Barbara Myerhoff. Assen/Amsterdam: Van Gorcum.

Turner, Victor W.

1967. *The Forest of Symbols: Aspects of Ndembu Ritual.* Ithaca: Cornell University Press.

1969. *The Ritual Process: Structure and Anti-Structure.* Chicago: Aldine.

1974. *Drama, Fields, and Metaphors: Symbolic Action in Human Society.* Ithaca: Cornell University Press.

Ugolnik, Anthony

1982. "Tradition as Freedom from the Past: Contemporary Eastern Orthodoxy and Ecumenism." Institute for Ecumenical and Cultural Research, Occasional Papers, no. 17.

Urbach, Ephraim E.

1979. *The Sages: Their Concepts and Beliefs.* Translated by Israel Abrahams. Cambridge: Harvard University Press.

Usqué, Samuel

1965. *Consolation for the Tribulations of Israel.* Translated by Martin A. Cohen. Philadelphia: Jewish Publication Society.

Van Gennep, Arnold

1960 [1909]. *The Rites of Passage.* Translated by M. B. Vizedom and G. L. Caffee. Chicago: University of Chicago Press.

Waskow, Arthur

1982. *Seasons of Our Joy: A Handbook of Jewish Festivals.* New York: Bantam.

Watson, Francis

1986. *Paul, Judaism, and the Gentiles: A Sociological Approach.* Cambridge: Cambridge University Press.

Weber, Max

1964 [1922]. *The Sociology of Religion.* Translated by Ephraim Fischoff. Boston: Beacon.

Weinfeld, Moshe

1981. "Sabbath, Temple, and the Enthronement of the Lord—The Problem of the *Sitz im Leben* of Genesis 1:1–2:3." In *Mélanges Bibliques et orientaux en l'honneur de M. Henri Cazelles, Alter Orient und Altes Testament* 212, ed. A. Caquot and M. Delcor. Neukirchen-Vluyn: Neukirchener.

Weiser, Artur

1962. *The Psalms: A Commentary.* The Old Testament Library. Philadelphia: Westminster Press.

Weiss, Meir

1984. *The Bible from Within: The Method of Total Interpretation.* Jerusalem: Magnes Press.

Wellhausen, Julius

1957 [1878]. *Prolegomena to the History of Ancient Israel.* Translated by J. S. Black and Allan Menzies. New York: Meridian.

Werner, Eric

1959. *The Sacred Bridge: The Interdependence of Liturgy and Music in Synagogue and Church during the First Millennium.* Vol. 1. New York: Columbia University Press.

1984. *The Sacred Bridge: The Interdependence of Liturgy and Music in Synagogue and Church during the First Millennium.* Vol. 2. New York: Ktav.

Westermann, Claus

1981. *Praise and Lament in the Psalms.* Translated by Keith R. Crim and Richard N. Soulen. Atlanta: John Knox Press.

Wheelwright, Philip, ed.
　1966. *The Presocratics*. New York: Odyssey.
Wilson, Robert R.
　1977. *Genealogies and History in the Biblical World*. New Haven: Yale University Press.
Wolf, Hans Walter
　1964. *Gesammelte Studien zum Alten Testament*. Munich: Kaiser Verlag.
Yerushalmi, Yosef Haim
　1982. *Zakhor: Jewish History and Jewish Memory*. Seattle: University of Washington Press.
Zevit, Ziony
　1991. "A Psycholinguistic Experiment and Its Implications for Understanding the Structure of Biblical Poetry." Paper delivered at Association for Jewish Studies, Boston.
Zimmels, Hirsch Jakob
　1977. *The Echo of the Nazi Holocaust in Rabbinic Literature*. New York: Ktav.

INDEX TO SCRIPTURAL AND RABBINIC PASSAGES

GENERAL INDEX

Aaron, 45–47, 65
Adam, 229n5
Akiba, 188, 199
Alkabetz, Shelomo, 201
Allegory, 9
Ambrose, 1
Amichai, Yehuda, 228
Amos, 163–64
Aristotle, 107
Augustine, 1, 9–10, 13
Austin, J. L., 24, 54–55, 95, 98

Babylonian exile, 34, 63, 76–78, 127, 144, 149, 179–86; and Job, 187
Bakhtin, Mikhail, 79, 118, 119, 121, 123–24, 173, 228, 240n9; on dialogue with God, 80–82; on the discourse of the novel, 108–109, 110, 112–14; on intimate speech, 92
Balentine, Samuel E., 248n75
Barr, James, 246n16, 247n43
Bathsheba, 7, 105
Bell, Catherine, 243n85
Ben-Gurion, David, 208
Benveniste, Emile, 103
Berkovits, Eliezer, 213
Berlin, Adele, 241n33
Bloom, Harold, 244n98
Bourdieu, Pierre, 234n16
Buber, Martin, 79, 89, 212, 228; on community, 126–27; on dialogue with God, 80–85; on God in time and space, 156–57; on God's presence in history, 213–17, 226; and *I-Thou* relations, 83–85; on Job, 187; Psalms commentary, 213–17

Calvin, John, 13–14
Carpentier, Raymond, 119
Celan, Paul, 221, 223–26, 228
Chanula tribe, 88–89, 90
Childs, Brevard S., 246n26, 247n42
Christ, 7, 9, 81
Christianity, 9–10, 12–14; Gentiles in, 7–8; and ritual, 22
Chrysostom, John, 1
Cohen, Arthur, 178, 204, 220–21, 226
Cohen, Y. Yosef, 252n77

Collins, Terence, 105
Community, 126–29
Confession, 21, 98–100
Cordovero, Moshe, 201, 202, 252n77, 252n82
Cosmogony, 35–37, 40
Crusades, 198–99, 206, 251n66
Culley, Robert C., 241n33, 248n57, 248n66
Cultic interpretation, 15–16, 21

Damrosch, David, 235n36
David (King): and Bathsheba, 7, 105; Calvin on, 14; Psalms authorship, 1–2, 4, 9, 12, 15, 105, 243n75
Day of Atonement, 48, 51, 52
Death, 134–35
Deliverance: in space, 156–63; in time, 143–56
Derash, 10–11
Dialogue, 80–82; with God, 81, 82, 83–85, 91–93, 95–102, 108
Divine warrior, 35–37, 40
Dodds, E. R., 239n100
Douglas, Mary, 62, 64
Dramatism, psalmic, 103–108, 109–12
Durkheim, Emil, 26–27, 62

Eden, 134
Eilberg-Schwartz, Howard, 238n86, 238n90
Eliade, Mircea, 35, 131–32, 143, 157
Elijah, 222
Elisha, 52
Esau, 89–90
Expulsion from Spain, 199–200, 203
Ezra, 34, 63

Fackenheim, Emil, 213, 227, 255n145
Feldman, Irving, 228
Fisch, Harold, 105, 248n74
Fishbane, Michael, 20, 231n48
Form-criticism, 15–19, 21
Foucault, Michel, 123
Frye, Northrop, 249n10

Gaon, Saadiah, 12
Geertz, Clifford, 232n58
Geller, Stephen A., 236n62

277

HERBERT LEVINE is a Wexner Graduate Fellow at the Reconstructionist Rabbinical College, where he is editor of *The Reconstructionist* and of a new Passover Haggadah for the Reconstructionist movement. He is author of *Yeats's Daimonic Renewal* and articles on the poetry of Walt Whitman.